MISSOURI PACIFIC
DIESEL POWER

FOR NADEAN - EVER MY ONE AND ONLY

WHITERIVER
PRODUCTIONS

6545 Scenic Drive, Kansas City, MO   64133

MISSOURI PACIFIC DIESEL POWER

Published by White River Productions, 6545 Scenic Drive, Kansas City, Missouri 64133.

Printed and bound in the United States of America.

Library of Congress Catalog Card Number:

ISBN: 0-89745-99-1

Edited by Lon EuDaly
Layout & Artwork by Kevin EuDaly

Contents

Acknowledgments

Any historical published effort is never the work of one person. Such is the case with this effort, which could not have been done without the help and support of many, many people. From the relatively unknown photographer who sent in three MoPac slides to the large collections of the well-known photohistorians, the MoPac's diesels could not have been covered in significant pictorial detail without the combined efforts of the photographers who shot the MoPac, T&P, C&EI and the many subsidiaries of this Midwestern road.

In this writer's humble opinion, every submitted photograph was important in completing the entire story of the MoPac's dieseldom. Though there is only room for a small percentage of the tens of thousands of photographs that were viewed for this project, there were many times that the files of submitted photos were used for reference. As would be expected, the folks who sent in large quantities of photographs make up the bulk of the photography in this book, yet many are represented who only sent in a few. Those who submitted photographs or supporting materials are offered a sincere thanks and are as follows:

Rick Acton	Bill Haines	Bruce Petty
Ken Albrecht	Mark Hall	Jack Pfeifer
Jerry Alexander	George Hamlin	George Pitarys
Glenn Anderson	Ed Hawkins	Jerry Pitts
Ralph Back	James Holder	Vic Pickle
Dave Beach	Tom Hughes	Bill Phillips
Steve Beleck	Gene Hull	John Phillips, Jr.
Lee Berglund	Lloyd Hurst	Ronald Plazzotta
Ken Borg	Lavergne Isaac	Jeff Pletcher
Don Bowen	Paul Jansson	Dan Pope
Thomas Bowers	Barton Jennings	Gary Rich
Alan Bradley	Brian Jenneson	R. E. Robertson
Dave Burton	David Johnston	Ervin Sanders
Larry Byers	Randy Keller	John Sanders
Tom Byrnas	Robert Kinerk	Dennis Schmidt
Barry Carlson	David King	C. R. Scholes
John Carr	Tom Kline	Dan Shroeder
Terry Chickwak	Virgil Knopp	Robert Seale
Ken Church	Charles Kodesh	Andy Smith
Joe Collias	J. Parker Lamb	J. W. Swanberg
Chuck Conway	Mike Leach	Robin Thomas
Lon Coone	John Leopard	Dan Tracy
Ray Curl	Peter Limas	J. W. Traylor
Paul DeLuca	Bob Malinoski	Mike Vana
Dale DeVene, Jr.	Louis Marre	Melvin Vineyard
T. J. Donahue	Joe McMillan	Harold K. Vollrath
Charlie Duckworth	George Melvin	Curtis Wagner
James EuDaly	Paul Meyer	Dick Wallin
Lon EuDaly	Jerry Michels	Don Wallworth
David Fasules	Keel Middleton	Paul Walters
Tony Fey	Rick Morgan	John Wegner
J. R. Fisk	William T. Morgan	Douglas Weitzman
Steve Forrest	Dan Munson	Darrell Wendt
Charles Geletzke, Jr.	Scott Muskopf	Steve Wilch
Steve Glischinski	Eric Nabe	Keith Wilhite
Phil Gosney	William J. Neill	J. Harlen Wilson
Bob Gottier	Mark Nelson	Richard Yremko
Britt Graber	Mike Nelson	Charles Zeiler
Carl Graves	Steve Patterson	Gary Zuters

Front dust jacket and page 1 top: A cool spring day in April, 1962 finds GP9 4345 leading four 4800-seires GP18's at Van Buren, Arkansas. *Louis Marre*

Front dust jacket and page 1 bottom: MoPac's flying eagle buzz-saw graces a sign at Neff Yard in Kansas City, Missouri on September 15, 1984. *Kevin EuDaly*

Above: A trio of B-30-7A's crest the summit of Kirkwood Hill at the hill's namesake city, Kirkwood, Missouri. The lashup includes 4809, 4814, and the last B30-7A, 4854. The confetti scattered about is a result of the "I-70" World Series, which proved to be a disaster for the St. Louis Cardinals, who lost to the Kansas City Royals in seven games. The series spawned several passenger runs between the two cities. The B-Boats roll westbound on October 24, 1985 past one of the MoPac's best-known landmarks. *Kevin EuDaly*

Several of the listed photographers either sent in or allowed viewing their entire collection or significant portions of their MoPac material, and a special thanks goes to these folks: Ken Albrecht, Glenn Anderson, Ken Church, Lon Coone, Ray Curl, Paul DeLuca, Charlie Duckworth, James EuDaly, Lon EuDaly, Tony Fey, Steve Forrest, Mark Hall, Ed Hawkins, David Johnston, J. Parker Lamb, Randy Keller, Louis Marre, Joe McMillan, Paul Meyer, Jerry Michels, Steve Patterson, Jerry Pitts, Dan Schroeder, Harold K. Vollrath, Keith Wilhite, J. Harlen Wilson, and probably a few others I've missed.

Many hours of research were required to complete the roster. This task couldn't have been completed without help from some significant sources whose work contributed to the roster. Roster information was gathered from numerous sources, and assimilated into as complete a representation as could be accomplished without working for more than one lifetime.

Roster sources include first and foremost *Extra 2200 South*. The job that *Extra 2200's* staff did throughout its first 20 years can only be called phenomenal, and a significant portion of the MoPac story is a direct result of the efforts of the *Extra 2200* staff. In the big picture, much is owed the Dovers, Dick Will, and the many contributors of Extra 2200 South.

Another major contributor of roster information was Bruce Murray and the Missouri Pacific Historical Society. Bruce's data base and its subsequent confirmation of roster data was an invaluable tool in the compilation of roster data. His data base filled many, many holes.

Additional sources of information included Joe Collias, Ray Curl, Charlie Duckworth, John Eagan, Peter Limas, Jerry Michels, and Don Strack. A thanks to all for the data that made this effort possible.

Something also must be said concerning the Diesel Spotter's Guides and the efforts of Jerry Pinkepank and Louis Marre to document the broader scope of dieseldom, which added significantly to this work.

A thanks also for the first hand help that was provided by Chris Gus, who painstakingly went through piles of magazines and flagged information on the MoPac. And thanks also to Dale Sanders of Hyrail Productions, who continually answered questions throughout this project.

Also a heartfelt thanks to my brother Lon EuDaly, who proofread and edited the text, the photo captions, and the roster, and offered substantial encouragement along the way.

The C&EI coverage has been supplied by Ray Curl, a long-time employee of the C&EI, and later the MoPac and the UP. The C&EI chapters were written by Ray, and as can be seen, many of the photographs are from his collection. His expertise, knowledge, and collection were paramount to this entire effort, not only for the C&EI coverage but for the MoPac as well. His help and enthusiasm are tremendously appreciated.

And finally, a hearty thanks to Dan Kane, Henry Corona, Mike Corona, Larry Cabrera, Santos Rocha, Jack Hammes, and the rest of the folks at Corona Litho who showed endless patience while doing the color separations and halftones for this book.

It is hoped that those who read this book will send any corrections to the text or roster to the publisher.

The Beginning of the Diesel

The first apparent mention of compression ignition was by a French physicist, Sadi Carnot, in 1824. Typical gasoline engines moderately compress the fuel and provide a spark to ignite the fuel, whereas the Diesel engine uses only compression to ignite the fuel. Rudolph Diesel was born in 1858 in Germany, and is generally credited with inventing the machine that carries his name today. He grew up in Paris, but was deported to England when war broke out between Germany and France in 1870. He quickly established a brilliant scholastic record, and later imposed upon himself the task of developing an internal combustion engine. He moved to Berlin in 1890, and in 1892 he obtained a development patent from Germany for his engine.

He first tried burning powderized coal, but abandoned that after tests failed to achieve what he had hoped. His experimental engines culminated in 1897, when he demonstrated a 25 horsepower, 4-stroke engine with a single vertical cylinder. The high efficiency of Diesel's engine brought immediate commercial success and great wealth to the inventor in royalties from his patents.

On a ride across the English Channel in 1913, Diesel apparently fell from the deck of the *Dresden*, a mail-carrying steamer, and drowned. Sadly he was gone by the time his machine was significantly applied to the railroad industry. This was in part because he insisted that all engines manufactured under his licenses operate at constant pressure, which restricted the engines to very slow speeds. This resulted in engines that were very large and heavy in proportion to their power output, which had little application to the rail industry. His untimely death undoubtedly sped up the application of his invention to operating climates where higher speed was a necessity.

By the mid-1940's the Diesel engine had become the dominant source of industrial power world-wide for units up to 5,000 horsepower, mainly because of the efficiency achieved and the relatively low cost of the low grade Diesel fuels. Sometime around 1947 the general rail enthusiast press dropped the capitalization of Diesel, converting it in print into the noun it had become.

For the railroads the diesel was generally used as a power plant to drive electric traction motors, hence the term diesel-electric. For the rail enthusiast, practicality results in the generic term "diesel" applied to nearly any internal combustion engine on rails. The earliest internal combustion locomotives on the Missouri Pacific were not diesels, however, but were little gasoline electrics of not much more power than today's lawn tractor.

The Missouri Pacific had a small subsidiary in the New Orleans area called the New Orleans and Lower Coast which bought one of

Below: The Texas & Pacific was an important part of the MoPac system from long before dieseldom. The T&P dieselized heavily with EMD's F7, buying well over one hundred of the handsome carbody units. The 916 was one from their last F-unit order, an order that totaled 25 units. On January 24, 1970, the F7 leads SD40's 735 and 711 and F7A 882 eastbound through Roscoe, Texas. The F's days are numbered. *Glenn Anderson*

Above: The MoPac relied heavily on EMD's GP7 but bought relatively few GP9's. Two of the 40 GP9's purchased for the MoPac proper pull tonnage past Tower 55 in Fort Worth, Texas in late summer, 1974, with some help from GP18 446. The two GP9's, 359 and 350, would continue pulling freight for the MoPac until they were both retired in 1981, and traded in on newer power from EMD. The trailing GP18 would only last three years longer than the GP9's. *K B King photo, Kevin EuDaly collection*

Right: The C&EI was an interesting addition to the MoPac fold when it was acquired in 1967. The C&EI had a relatively small roster, and relied heavily on EMD's GP35 for second generation road freight power. Within a short time of the merger, the C&EI units were scattered amongst the MoPac fleet. Here C&EI GP35 658 leads MoPac sister GP35 624 through Meeker, Louisiana on April 14, 1973 with a T&P eastbound freight. *Glenn Anderson*

these little gas-electrics. Built by Plymouth in October, 1926, this gas-electric was sold to the Fair River Gravel Company of Belle Chase, Louisiana. From there it was sold to Overseas Railways, Inc., of New Orleans, and was subsequently bought by the NO&LC. It has the earliest build-date of any internal combustion driven locomotive on the Missouri Pacific system, with the exception of several motorcars, which the Missouri Pacific apparently never considered as locomotives. EMC had begun building motorcars in February, 1924.

Plymouth had been building internal combustion locomotives for rail use since 1914, and by the early 1970's had built nearly 7,000 locomotives. Most of these were small mining and industrial type engines. Their first diesel was built in 1927, making the NO&LC engine a gasoline engine built just prior to the beginning of the diesel for Plymouth. Plymouth also built propane and butane burning locomotives in these early years.

The Missouri Pacific roster is not a simple one, and as with any roster of a Class I, there are numerous wyes where one must decide which is the best or most logical way to organize the effort. For the Missouri Pacific, there were numerous other railroads that were subsidiaries. Most of these were eventually merged into the parent, but many held out as separate companies well into the diesel era.

The Missouri Pacific, or the MoPac to its followers, and its subsidiaries including the Chicago and Eastern Illinois and the Texas and Pacific, rostered a total of 3,062 diesel units over the life of the railroad before its assimilation into the Union Pacific. This is a chronicle of the lives

Below: As the geep fleet began to age, the MoPac looked for a way to replace them at a reasonable cost. EMD offered the GP15-1, which utilized some components from geeps, and also offered a substantial tax advantage over buying new locomotives. On the day before Christmas, 1977, one-year-old GP15-1 1589 rolls the McPherson local through Newton, Kansas. *Gary A Rich*

of the diesels that moved tonnage on this Midwestern road.

The MoPac and its Predecessors

To get some idea of how all the pieces fit together, one must first take a look at the subsidiaries and merger partners before deciding what was and what wasn't the MoPac. For the most part, the roster and locomotive history presented in this book is as complete as is reasonable for the subsidiaries. Most had small quantities of locomotives, and while some were forced to buy engines compatible with the MoPac's own purchases, others were left on their own to decide for themselves. These small other rosters add a significant number of odd units, and units that were not built to MoPac specifications.

For the MoPac it is obvious that the Texas subsidiary, the Texas and Pacific, or T&P, should be included within the MoPac because it was nearly always under MoPac control, though not completely merged in the formal sense until 1976. By the early 1880's, the famous Jay Gould assimilated an empire of rails that laced the midwest, southwest and western portions of this country. He bought controlling interest in the Missouri Pacific on November 17, 1879, and in a short period he also bought control of the Texas and Pacific. The MoPac and the T&P have long been associates.

In 1881, Gould bought a controlling interest in the St. Louis Iron Mountain and Southern. These three railroads, the MoPac, the T&P, and the SLIM&S, along with the western half of the C&EI, form the backbone of the latter day MoPac system. On the last day of 1881, the MoPac officially took control of the SLIM&S. In 1901 the MoPac acquired the Union Terminal Railway (URM) of Memphis by purchasing 55% of its stock. By 1915 many of the smaller roads that comprised the now growing MoPac system were consolidated completely into the system.

In 1915 the MoPac and the Iron Mountain went bankrupt, and came out of receivership in 1917. On January 1, 1925, the MoPac pur-

chased three-fourths of the outstanding stock of the New Orleans, Texas and Mexico Railway (NOT&M), which was the parent company of the "Gulf Coast Lines." All the Gulf Coast Lines, which included the Kansas, Oklahoma and Gulf (KO&G), the Midland Valley (MV), and the International Great Northern (IGN), were now under MoPac control, adding 2,087 miles to the MoPac system.

On March 31, 1933 the MoPac failed financially again and went into bankruptcy. The trusteeship for the MoPac lasted until March, 1956, and when the MoPac came out of receivership the Gulf Coast Lines, the IGN, and their subsidiaries were merged into the Missouri Pacific Railroad Company that is the subject of this book, and which lasted until the MoPac in turn became a subsidiary of the Union Pacific.

By 1956 it was late enough that many of these subsidiaries had purchased diesel locomotives, and these were essentially part of the Missouri Pacific's fleet. After the 23-year trusteeship ended in 1956, Paul J. Neff was selected as the president of the road. One year later he was elected Chairman of the Board, but died three weeks after this appointment. On January 16, 1961 Downing B. Jenks was elected as president of the railroad, and became the president of the T&P on December 3, 1963. The MoPac's later solid blue paint scheme was inaugurated under his rule, thus the terminology of "Jenks Blue" for the later MoPac scheme.

The MoPac system officially acquired the KO&G and the MV on September 25, 1964, officially adding these subsidiaries' fleets into the MoPac's diesel fold. After this date their independence was gone and their paint schemes vanished into the list of fallen flags.

The Chicago & Eastern Illinois had not formerly seen any MoPac control, but on May 12, 1967 the MoPac assumed control of the C&EI through stock ownership. Mr. Jenks then became the president of the C&EI as well. The Chicago-based C&EI was an 862-mile road with lines from Chicago to St. Louis and Thebes, Illinois, and a line in eastern Illinois from Chicago to Evansville, Indiana. The C&EI also had a subsidiary, the Chicago Heights Terminal Transfer (CHTT), and several units were owned by this subsidiary. Some of the CHTT units wore CHTT sublettering, but several didn't, being painted as any other C&EI unit would have been.

The acquisition of the C&EI by the MoPac remained in limbo from an outsider's viewpoint as the respective parties hammered out the final merger details. An agreement was reached a year later for the sale of the eastern Illinois line to the Louisville and Nashville Railroad, which complied with the ICC order and allowed the MoPac complete control of the remaining portion of the C&EI. The C&EI's Evansville line and about half of the C&EI's equipment were sold to the L&N on June 6, 1969, completing that aspect of the merger agreement. The C&EI's diesel fleet was split between its two new own-

ers. The MoPac took over operation of the C&EI on February 7, 1968.

The decision of what to include in the MoPac roster is not so clear cut with the C&EI. In the interest of presenting as complete a picture as possible, the C&EI has been included, and because the C&EI was a later addition to the MoPac, the C&EI coverage has been assimilated into five chapters by itself. The first four cover a pre-MoPac C&EI, and the last covers the assimilation of the C&EI into the MoPac, and the engines that came to the C&EI after the MoPac had complete control.

On March 5, 1968 the ICC authorized the purchase of the Alton and Southern Railway Company, which then became 50% owned by the MoPac and 50% by the Chicago and North Western on May 9, 1968. The A&S operations were taken over on August 1, 1968. The A&S's diesel fleet has likewise been added as a separate chapter.

On April 1, 1970, the KO&G was merged into the T&P, putting it under the official control of the T&P. The KO&G units that were around at the time were renumbered into T&P numbers.

This included one NW2, four F7A's and two F7B's, nine GP7's, and two GP28's. Two of the GP7's and the two GP28's would later receive MoPac numbers.

On October 15, 1976 the T&P and the C&EI were officially merged into the MoPac in a move initiated in 1974, losing their independent identities. The last railroad to fall under the MoPac flag was surprisingly the little Missouri-Illinois, which was officially merged on October 25, 1978. A number of other subsidiaries fell into the MoPac at about the same time, including the Abilene & Southern, the Fort Worth Belt, the NO&LC, the St. Joseph Belt, the Union Terminal Railway (of St. Joseph, Missouri), the Union Railway (of Memphis) and the TNM.

The beginning of the end for the MoPac occurred on this writer's 20th birthday, when the stockholders of the MoPac and the UP approved on April 18, 1980 a merger plan which would make the MoPac a wholly owned subsidiary of the Union Pacific. Not my idea of happy birthday!

Multiple renumberings, a lot of odds and ends, and a relatively large diesel fleet make the

Above: In October, 1939, two new E3 passenger units rolled out of EMC's plant at La Grange for the MoPac's new flagship train *The Eagle*. The two new units, 7000 and 7001, began rolling off multi-million mile careers. The 7001 is near Jefferson City, Missouri with the *Missouri River Eagle* in November, 1940. *Harold K Vollrath collection*

MoPac's all-time roster a complicated one. In presenting a complete roster, it is difficult to organize it in a perfect manner. Organizing by number has difficulties as it fouls up any kind of chronological look, and chronological jumbles the numbers, so no method is ideal for every reader.

The methodology for the presentation of the roster is as chronological as practical and is generally organized by locomotive model. Though it may be somewhat difficult to find certain numbers where the locomotive model is not known, in general the student or modeler of a particular era should find everything pertaining to their particular interest in one area of the book.

The MoPac's Diesel Fleet

There has not been a complete attempt to present the entire history of the MoPac's many renumberings. In general, the first large-scale renumbering occurred in early 1961, but was modified because Baldwin S-12's and Alco FA's were retained on the roster longer than anticipated. SW1200 and GP18 orders pushed number series higher than what was originally intended. Renumbering and repainting dates are part of the overall information that has not been assimilated into this effort, in part to keep this book at a reasonable page count, and also due to the incompleteness and inconsistency of many of these records. Photographs tell far more than this data could show.

The merger of the C&EI, KO&G, and MV also threw hitches in the roster, and this was followed by another thorough renumbering in 1974 based on horsepower. Throughout the 1970's renumberings of particular classes were commonplace, and when the UP exercised its control in the mid-1980's, many numbers again changed. The MoPac's roster was deemed "the ultimate challenge" in the late 1960's, and in a lot of ways little has changed regarding the difficulty of assimilating the MoPac's complete roster. Partial renumberings were the result of only having part of a particular class retired when another class invaded the number series, making the MoPac's many renumberings particularly difficult to follow.

The MoPac's paint schemes represent a relatively simple tale when compared to some other Class I railroads, who seem to change paint schemes on an almost annual basis. The early days saw switchers in a simple black scheme, with road and passenger power in the attractive blue and gray. This standard had a number of variations, and lasted until the early 1960's, when a less expensive and more practical solid blue scheme replaced the blue and gray.

The solid blue came with 3-inch frame stripes, 3-inch chevrons on both ends, small numbers on the upper portion of the long hood, and the familiar red and white buzz-saw under the cab windows. Units that were turbocharged, which for second generation power began with GP35's, received the large white "screaming eagle" on their long hoods. The T&P, C&EI, and M-I units wore sublettering to indicate their ownership. In the earlier blue and white dress both T&P and M-I had their railroad names spelled out on the units.

The T&P's early passenger paint scheme was nearly identical to the MoPac's, and its switchers started out in black paint like the MoPac's. Later the T&P adopted a paint scheme consisting of Swamp Holly Orange and black. Switchers, geeps, and their single RS-2 all received the orange and black scheme.

Kansas Oklahoma & Gulf's early scheme, and sister road Midland Valley's, was an odd black scheme with a red band and white pinstripes, yet the one KO&G NW2 switcher came

without the white pinstripes. The F-units came in the MoPac's blue and gray, with a large rectangle name plate. Later, the KO&G and the MV units wore the MoPac's standard blue scheme of the 1960's.

On the C&EI side of things a MoPac style buzz-saw was applied to many units that were acquired with that road on February 7, 1968, with "C&EI" across the middle of the buzz-saw. Units delivered after that date for the C&EI received the standard MoPac paint scheme with the C&EI buzz-saw. A variation was seen when C&EI "GP7u" 84 was repainted for an official train with C&EI replacing MoPac above the small screaming eagle over the buzz-saw, referred to as the "flying eagle buzz-saw," which brings up the 1974 re-styling of the standard MoPac dress.

In 1974 the standard blue scheme was revised. The "new" scheme put a small red and white screaming eagle over a red buzz-saw on the cab sides beneath the engineer's and fireman's

Below: For heavy-haul road freight power in the second generation, the MoPac somewhat standardized on EMD's SD40-2, buying 231 without dynamic brakes and 74 with dynamic brakes for coal service. In December, 1975, SD40-2 3151 leads two more SD40-2's and a U23B up Boyd Hill east of Hoisington, Kansas on an eastbound freight. The 3151 was one of 14 SD40-2's (3150-3163) bought for the C&EI in March, 1974. *Lee Berglund*

windows, hence the terminology "flying eagle buzz-saw." The flying eagle buzz-saw had first appeared in 1969 in the employee newsletter. The large screaming eagle on the engine's flank was eradicated and the number was enlarged from small 8-inch numbers to much larger 20-inch numbers. The frame stripes and nose chevrons were changed from the previous 3-inch width to a 5-inch width. In both schemes this striping was "Scotchlite," a reflective material intended to make the units more visible at night. Units delivered to the T&P or C&EI received small sublettering initials on the cab sides. The flying eagle buzz-saw found its way onto highway vehicles and piggyback trailers in 1976, and finally made it onto freight car sides in 1978.

As repainting progressed there were numerous units that received combinations of these two schemes. Many units got the new small eagle and buzz-saw on their cab sides while retaining the 3-inch striping. A few units received the new screaming eagle on the cab side while retaining the original large white screaming eagle on their long hoods. These were quickly dubbed "double-eagles," and became a highly desired target for the shooter's lens. The eradication of the C&EI name was responsible for many of the double-eagles, as small screaming eagle decals were placed over existing C&EI buzz-saws. Other units that wore the double-eagles were apparently only chosen at random. Though it may have had something to do with the buzz-saws becoming worn under the cab sides, and hence the replacement with the small flying eagle buzz-saw, this is only conjecture. At the risk of missing a few, a list of known double-eagles has been compiled. The units known to have worn the double-eagle variation included GP35's 2518, 2554, 2556, 2558, 2559, and 2564, U30C's 2981 and 2999, SD40's 3010, 3011, 3023, 3044, 3051 and 3064, SD40-2's 3092, 3099, 3110, 3129, 3132, 3146, 3150, 3151, 3152, 3154, 3155, 3156, 3158, and 3161, and U23B's 2256 and 4503.

At least two units that were not turbocharged are known to have received the large screaming eagle on their long-hood sides. Ex-KO&G GP28 2001 (sublettered T&P) got the large herald, as did GP38 MP-857, presumably a result of lack of attention in the paint shop. There are no records that turbochargers were added to these two units, and no reason to believe that the MoPac would have added them when the general pattern at that time was to remove turbochargers, as with the GP35's. In late 1974 orders began arriving without chevrons on the rear of the units. The first of these were GP38-2's beginning with MP-2111 and U23B's beginning with MP-2257. As units were repainted, there was some inconsistency in whether or not units wore chevrons on the long-hood end.

There were several units with strange adaptations. Number placement occasionally varied, and SD40-2 MP-3093 even got the large num-

bers placed right on top of the long-hood side on top of the screaming eagle, while retaining the small numbers above the eagle as well, though the small numbers were faded and essentially indiscernible. This was apparently only on the right side of the unit. Pages and pages could be taken up with strange variations; a unit from a Mexican wreck coming back with the screaming eagle backwards, a geep with mighty mouse on the long hood, numbers in all kinds of strange places, and other general oddities. SD40-2 MP-3278 wore a large "2378" on its left flank, representing what could happen on a bad day in the paint shop.

For the MoPac enthusiast, however, this effort is aimed at interpreting the MoPac's diesel fleet, its standard paint schemes, and most importantly at yielding a balanced look at the motive power that made up the fleet. If the photographic documentation stressed all the oddities, the reader would be deceived as to the increasing standardization of the MoPac's fleet throughout its history as a diesel purchaser, therefore this book will generally show photographs of the rules rather than the exceptions.

In January, 1976, the MoPac added another paint scheme in the form of two bicentennial units. C&EI "GP7u" 84 was renumbered MP-1776 and with "GP18u" MP-1976 was repainted in the red, white, and blue scheme. The two units wore a modified eagle with wings composed on an American flag with "76" on the field and carrying a banner that proclaimed "Happy Birthday America." The renumbering of C&EI-84 to MP-1776:2 forced the renumbering of "GP7u" MP-1776:1 to MP-1639. July 4, 1976 also marked the 125th anniversary of the original ground-breaking ceremony for the Pacific Railroad, the MoPac's predecessor. A year and a half later, the MP-1776 bicentennial geep was wrecked and retired.

The final paint scheme was a relatively short-lived interim Union Pacific yellow and gray scheme with Missouri Pacific lettering on the side. The first repaint was SD40-2 MP-3291, which rolled out of the Kansas City paint shop in Armour Yellow and Harbor Mist Gray on May 14, 1984. Even the standards for this varied, as North Little Rock applied lettering and numbering with a distinctively square appearance compared to UP's standard scheme. In the roster this is referred to as NLR "block" style lettering, and yellow MoPac units are also denoted. The SD50's and C36-7's were delivered in the UP livery with MoPac lettering, the last diesels lettered for the MoPac. The screaming eagle was indeed gone. In the interim period between the UP's purchase of the MoPac and the eradication of the MoPac name, a number of units were repainted into yellow and gray with MoPac lettering.

The MoPac's roster of diesel locomotives is, or was, an interesting fleet by anyone's standard. It evolved as many rosters did in the early years. With a couple of these and a few of those, it slowly grew into a fleet of modern power

designed to move massive tonnage. In the troubling late 1970's the MoPac continued to be a steady purchaser of motive power while many other roads stood by and tried to make do with what they had.

In the early years few models were bought in any significant quantity. The first diesels in the U.S. were produced by General Electric in 1918. Within four decades of that first switcher, mainline steam power would be nearly obliterated. Prior to World War II, the diesel was just beginning to be developed for long distance railroad applications, and as development progressed in the late 1930's, railroads slowly began to look at the diesel locomotive as having the potential to add efficiency to operations where steam power simply couldn't compete.

Perhaps the foremost pioneer of the long-distance run were Santa Fe's boxcabs, built in August, 1935. They were only slightly preceded by EMD demonstrators 511 and 512, two boxcabs built in May, 1935, whose remains ironically would wind up on the MoPac. They were also preceded by EMD streamliner power cars, which were built with a trailing truck that was shared by the first passenger car of their respective trains. These included the famous Burlington Zephyrs, UP's M-10000, and Boston and Maine's Flying Yankee, number 6000. UP's M-10001 of October, 1934 was the first application of the 16-cylinder Winton 201-A engine, though it was still a power car type design rather than a true locomotive.

The boxcabs then came along with two 12-cylinder 201-A engines in a locomotive strictly designed to pull conventional equipment, unlike the power cars which were semi-permanently coupled to their respective trains. And so it began, a handful of switchers shuffling cars around the yards, making short transfer runs, and never stopping for coal or water. When the boxcabs ran across the nation, those who were alert in the industry would forecast that steam's end was near. Fortunately for the steam fan most were not alert and World War II intervened.

After some switchers from a variety of builders, the MoPac placed an order with EMD for two E3A's. This was actually before EMD existed as an entity, but rather was the Electro-Motive Corporation, which had been purchased by General Motors in 1930. Electro-Motive's main supplier of diesel engines was the Winton Engine Company, which was also purchased by GM when EMC was added to their fold. The Winton Engine Company was purchased by EMC on the last day of the year, 1930.

GM diesel switchers and passenger engines were first marketed in 1935, and by 1939 mass production for freight diesels was in place as the FT was offered. By 1937, EMD had the EA on the market, all of which went to the B&O, and by the time the MoPac made a purchase the E1's, E2's, and E4's were passed by and E3's were chosen (though they overlap, E3 production began after E4 production had started, and E4 production ended before E3 production was finished). The MoPac's first significant road power was purchased in 1939, when two E3A's arrived in October for *The Eagle*. They were officially outshopped at EMC on October 20, 1939.

From that humble beginning, the MoPac grew into a company that embraced power from several builders, eventually sampling a smattering of road units from GE in the later stages of MoPac diesels. In the last few years of the MoPac, in fact, GE and EMD orders were nearly equal. Throughout its existence, the MoPac rarely went for any great length of time between locomotive purchases, and usually didn't purchase large quantities of any particular model. For early dieseldom only the GP7 model exceeded 200 units on MoPac's roster.

Later, the GP38-2 and the SD40-2 would also top the 200 mark, and those three models would stand at the top of MoPac's popularity poll, not only in quantity, but also in appeal to the crews. The early dieselization was also completed with almost 200 F7's and nearly 150 Alco FA's.

On the MoPac, steam's fires were falling into the ash pits by the early 1950's, and by the end of 1955 the mighty diesel had crushed steam's empire on the MoPac forever. The second generation ushered in a higher level of technology, and though it lacked the media-drawing monsters of the UP and SP such as EMD DDA40X's, ALCO C855's, and GE U50's, the MoPac's fleet was comprised of a host of more utilitarian units that out-performed and outlasted the big twin-engine diesel era.

With the notable exception of its passenger trains; *The Eagles*, the MoPac always seemed to revel in somewhat of an obscure existence, quietly carrying on while UP, Santa Fe and Midwest granger roads grabbed the spotlight. The attractive early blue and gray paint scheme slowly gave way to the practical Jenks blue, the two nose chevrons and the screaming eagle being the MoPac's trademarks for its final three decades. As the end of the MoPac drew near, and UP's influence began to take over, the blue fell under a coat of yellow and gray, and as occasionally happens, the MoPac name was retained for a short time.

On merger day the MoPac had more units and route-miles than the UP, but it was the UP who purchased the MoPac, not vice versa. The UP shield slowly obliterated the eagle, and in a scant few years "Missouri" fell to "Union." As this is being written, only a handful of units in tattered blue paint remain of the legacy of diesel power that comprised the Missouri Pacific fleet. These last few are no longer owned by UP, as the last blue unit was repainted yellow in December, 1993, but rather are part of latter day lease fleets who work for anyone who will pay the short-term bill for their horses.

The earliest build-date on a MoPac diesel was July 9, 1937, when four EMC SC's were purchased from the fledgling builder and numbered MP-9000 through MP-9003. Two NC2's were bought the same month, numbered MP-4100-4101, with builder's dates of July 31, 1937. Both of the NC2's were gone by May, 1962, and the last SC, working for subsidiary St. Joseph Belt, was sold to Precision in 1965. The last MoPac unit purchased was GE C36-7 number MP-9059, built in November, 1985, and still running off the miles for its owner, UP. Between these two units, a fascinating array of MoPac power has wheeled freight and passengers across MoPac iron. The following pages chronicle their entrance and passage into history.

Interpreting the Roster

The process of tabulating a numerical roster encompassing over 3,000 engines and numerous statistics on those engines would be difficult to publish in its entirety without the extensive use of abbreviations. To claim that

Below: As first generation freight units began to ply the rails, EMD had an advantage over the other builders due to war time restrictions on other builders that kept them from being able to produce freight units. Alco, however, tried to overcome the opposition with their FA series of freight units. The MoPac bought a respectable number of the handsome Alco FA's. FA-2 352 is ready for service in St. Louis, Missouri having just been delivered in December, 1951. *MoPac photo, Kevin EuDaly collection*

there are virtually no mistakes in a roster the size of the MoPac's would not only be foolish, but extremely naive. There are mistakes. Hopefully, they are few and minor in nature.

There is no perfect way to organize a roster. The roster has been broken out into pieces in each of the chapters that covers the story of each class of MoPac motive power. Each chapter provides a condensed list at the beginning to help the reader find particular classes quickly. This general approach makes the effort essentially chronological, but there are significant deviations. Some attempt has been made at keeping all members of each locomotive model together, which results in a significant deviation of the chronological presentation, as some models were acquired over a number of years and may span more than one chapter. An index is supplied so the reader can quickly find a particular class of units of interest.

The C&EI presented another difficult fork in the road. While many of the C&EI diesels either became part of the MoPac or were purchased while under MoPac control, a number of them were off the roster by the time the MoPac acquired the C&EI. These are covered in the chapters that deal exclusively with the C&EI diesel story. It should be noted that the C&EI always figured locomotive weights based on one-half supplies (i.e., fuel tank half full, sand at one-half capacity, etc..) while the MoPac normally chose to calculate weights based on full supplies. All C&EI unit's weights are presented

from the C&EI records, at one-half supplies, except for the GP15-1's and the SD40-2's, which were purchased under MoPac control.

In compiling the roster, there were numerous times when conflicting information was located. As a general rule, taking information from three out of four sources does not necessarily mean that the right information is presented. The case may be that two of those three sources got their information from the third, and all three are therefore wrong. It is safe to say that the attempt was made to retain the information from the most reliable source. In the world of science this is called "best professional judgement," but in the case of the MoPac, it was sometimes a shot in the dark.

Model types in the roster are the builder's, with the exception that notes refer to railroad rebuilds with the accepted nomenclature developed by the staff of *Extra 2200 South*. This uses a "u" to represent an upgraded unit, such as first generation geeps rebuilt and upgraded by the MoPac. The RS-2's and RS-3's were remanufactured with EMD prime movers installed in place of Alco's 244 engine. The MoPac referred to these as "GP12's," which does not follow typical nomenclature but was utilized by the railroad. They also are called "RS-2m's" or "RS-3m's." The same goes for the remanufactured RS-11's, which became known as "GP16's." A remanufactured unit involves a more complete change of engine components, such as with the application of 645 power assem-

blies to the 567-powered GP35's, resulting in the "GP35m's." The "F5" was a hybrid freight model in between the F3 and F7, and is discussed later. C&EI called the E7A an "EA7," but this was later revised on the drawings to read E7A. Model designations that are strictly the railroad's are put in quotes to identify them as a non-standard application as far as the builder's model numbers are concerned. Some of these designations are likely the invention of rail enthusiasts, rather than railroad personnel.

In the roster (not in the text), any number in parentheses indicates that it was assigned that number but was never actually renumbered. An example of this is the I-GN and St. Louis Brownsville & Mexico (STLB&M) VO1000's. Occasionally, this was difficult to ascertain from reliable records, and again judgement was applied.

Retirement dates and dispositions represent a condensation of available data, but are by no means the complete picture to date. Second-hand engine sales are now so commonplace that it is virtually impossible to keep track of every engine sale for a given road's ex-motive power, since this would require keeping track of second, third and higher tier sales through numerous owners across the country.

For many units a trade-in notation is the last notation, such as "T-I to EMD." This typically means one of two things, either the unit was scrapped or it was later resold. For the majority of older MoPac units the former was the case. "Scrapped" has not been added to a unit's disposition unless there are records at the scrapper that this was the case. Many early units are known to be scrapped, but records of their scrapping have not come to light. In a nutshell, no information was fabricated, regardless of an engine's apparent fate.

It is also important to realize that sometimes even the best of records winds up reversed. An engine can be retired by the railroad and later called back to service. It appears that this situation was a rarity for the MoPac. Switcher SC MP-9000 is an example of this. It was sold to Big Rock Stone and Material Company of Little Rock, and later returned to the MoPac in trade for an NW2.

In both the text and the roster railroad engine numbers are preceded by their ownership. This is intended to eliminate confusion in the ownership due to the many subsidiaries that lasted late into dieseldom. Many of the subsidiary owners were identified by sublettering

beneath the herald on the cab side, but occasionally this was not the case, as with the previously mentioned CHTT.

The data on each locomotive type is the as-built data, as is standard with any roster. Railroad modifications are included with additional information directly beneath the as-built section. Notes that apply to an entire group are included above each roster section. Most of the information is self-explanatory, but it should be noted that the minimum continuous speed is the minimum continuous speed for the tractive effort indicated.

In the roster many engine numbers are used more than once. If a number is used twice with the same reporting marks, :1 and :2 are added to the engine number to indicate first and second engine to carry this number and railroad initials.

For medium-horsepower road freight service in the second generation, nothing came close to the GP38-2 on the MoPac. They first began arriving in January, 1972, and the final unit was built nearly 10 years later, in August, 1981. In between, well over 300 of the B-B EMD's were bought by the MoPac.

Opposite page top: The 2197 awaits duty at Odem, Texas on January 19, 1985. The scarred plow is indicative of several years of service. *Curtis Wagner*

Opposite page bottom: The 2166 leads a GP35m and another GP38-2 through Malvern, Arkansas on the Hot Springs turn on October 2, 1981. *Mike Leach*

Below: 2078 leads GP15-1 1689 on the Lee's Summit local flying westbound at Colburn Road on the west side of Lee's Summit, Missouri on May 26, 1983. *Lon EuDaly*

For example, MP-3000:1 was the first time 3000 was used on a MoPac locomotive, and was an ex-NO&LC Plymouth switcher. MP-3000:2 was their first SD40. The : designations are chronological, so :1 wore that number before :2 did. Sometimes a later built unit may carry a number first, and then later an earlier built unit is renumbered into the series. An example of this is GP35 MP-626:2 was built much later than GP7 MP-626:3, but the GP35 wore the number before the GP7 did.

Though some abbreviation is used, it is generally kept at a minimum. The following is a list of the abbreviations that are used in the text and in the roster:

Alco = American Locomotive Company
ALCO = ALCO Products (Alco became ALCO on April 19, 1955)
Alco-GE = Alco and GE joint marketing from 1940-1953
A&S = Alton & Southern
BLW = Baldwin Locomotive Works
BSL&W = Beaumont Sour Lake & Western
Build# = Builder's Number
C&EI = Chicago & Eastern Illinois
CHTT = Chicago Heights Terminal Transfer
CRI&P = Chicago, Rock Island & Pacific
EMC = Electro-Motive Corporation
EMD = Electro-Motive Division of General Motors
FWB = Fort Worth Belt
Fuel = Fuel tank capacity in gallons
GATX = General American Transportation
GE = General Electric
ICC = Interstate Commerce Commission
IGN = International Great Northern
KO&G = Kansas Oklahoma & Gulf
L&N = Louisville and Nashville
MI or M-I = Missouri-Illinois Railroad
MP = Missouri Pacific (MoPac)

mph = miles per hour
m-u = multiple-unit
MV = Midland Valley
NO&LC = New Orleans & Lower Coast
NRE = National Railway Equipment (dealer)
PC&N = Point Comfort & Northern
PNC = Precision National Corporation (locomotive dealer)
r# = Renumbered
SAU&G = San Antonio, Uvalde & Gulf
SJB = St. Joseph Belt (MO)
STLB&M = St. Louis Brownsville & Mexico
TE = Tractive Effort in pounds
T-I = Traded In
T-L = To Lessor
T&P = Texas & Pacific
TPMPT = Texas Pacific Missouri Pacific Terminal (New Orleans)
UP = Union Pacific
URM = Union Railway of Memphis
USS = US Steel
UT = Union Terminal Railway (St. Joseph, MO)
Wheels = Wheel diameter in inches
WT = Weight in pounds

And finally, something should be said about dates. Don Dover of *Extra 2200 South* perhaps said it best when he wrote in that magazine (Issue 87): "And, we have discovered 'official records' from railroads, builders, AAR, ICC, or authorities cannot be taken for granted; all need to be verified and interpreted. It is of no use to merely pronounce any record as accurate or just to believe in any source as always accurate. All records are kept by humans, enough said. Official dates are a special problem, if given at all. Interpretation is always needed to decide if date given is a: build date, ship date, arrival date, transaction date, in-service date, plate date, etc., or just a convenient clerical date put down on paper to meet a target date."

January 1, 1941 when EMC and Winton were merged into GM, becoming EMD. A final subsidiary, the SJB, also acquired one more of the SW1's (SJB-12), a post-war version built in April, 1947.

Even as the first of the MoPac's SW1's were coming off the floor at La Grange, the MoPac also had a single NW2 (MP-9104) in production. The NW2 was even a more popular model than the SW1, with a production total of 1,143 units. The MoPac's first NW2 came off the shop floor in September, 1939, and was powered with a 12-cylinder 12-567 prime mover that generated 1,000 horsepower, a little more punch than the SW1. Like the SW1, the NW2 came with an FT-type control stand and a notchless throttle. It also had no transition, the traction motors being wired in permanent series. The MoPac went back for two more NW2's in 1940 and 1941, and later the T&P bought 20 of the model between November, 1946 and May, 1949. Additionally, the FWB, Missouri - Illinois (M-I), and Kansas Oklahoma & Gulf (KO&G) each bought a single NW2, all post-war era units.

Straying from EMC

In the late 1939 group of switchers there were two units from other builders, one from Alco and one from Baldwin, both of whom had long been major producers of steam power. Alco had been producing steam locomotives since the 1850's, and ventured slowly into the gasoline and diesel market in the mid 1920's.

They originally worked closely with Ingersoll-Rand, and later relied almost exclusively on GE for electrical components. From 1940 to 1953 they marketed their locomotives under the designation of "Alco-GE," a joint marketing agreement that is a mirror of their corporate relationship during this period.

For the MoPac, the Alco unit came before the Baldwin, a 1,000 horsepower HH1000 built in September (MP-9102). The HH1000 was a turbocharged unit, a concept which was first introduced for Alcos in 1937. Though there would be other Alcos, the lone HH1000 was never accompanied by any more of this model. It was a one-of-a-kind on the MoPac. The HH1000 was powered by the 539 turbocharged engine. Alco's engines were numbered according to their month and year of beginning production (the 539 engine dates from May, 1939). Only 34 HH1000's were built, with production running only from 1939-1940.

Turbocharging on these early units, as well as all later GEs and Alcos, was via an exhaust-driven propeller blade. Since it was exhaust driven, it would tend to build up carbon during idle periods, which would be blown skyward the first time the unit was revved up. EMD's turbocharger came along much later, and was both propeller and gear driven, which kept the turbocharger in operation even when the unit was at idle.

The other odd unit delivered in late 1939 was a Baldwin VO1000 (MP-9103). This first VO1000 would be joined by an additional 13

units on the MoPac roster, but the rest would be produced near the end of World War II. Baldwin had been in the locomotive business since the 1830's, and produced small gas-mechanical locomotives for industrial use between 1910 and 1928. Baldwin was associated with Westinghouse early on, with Westinghouse supplying the electrical components much as GE did for Alco. Switchers were introduced in 1939, the year that MoPac's first VO1000 was produced, while road diesels followed in 1945.

The VO1000 was a 1,000 horsepower unit built around the 8-cylinder VO power plant, which was based on the De La Vergne marine engine. In fact, the first VO's produced by Baldwin in 1937 and 1938 had used the De La Vergne engine, but early tests indicated that it was too rigid for rail applications, and suffered cracking of the rigid A-frame under the normal stresses of the railroad environment. The De La Vergne engine was redesigned with a more durable fabricated A-frame, and all of the

MoPac's Baldwins came with the later engines, produced at Baldwin's Eddystone, Pennsylvania plant. All of the Baldwin engines were based on the same De La Vergne design, and all operated at 625 rpm.

The MoPac laid claim to the first VO1000 produced, but the Santa Fe had VO1000's in production at the same time. According to trade publications, the MoPac ordered the first VO1000 in April, 1939, while Santa Fe's order for five VO1000's was actually dated June, 1939. The Santa Fe had been an early supporter of Baldwin dieseldom, and had been involved in the design of the Baldwin switcher truck. Santa Fe orders were expected, and the Santa Fe order had an earlier order number. The MoPac unit (MP-9103) was shipped on November 3, 1939, and was placed in service at St. Louis on November 17. The Santa Fe units were placed in service at Chicago on November 23, 1939. MP-9103 would be the only MoPac Baldwin to ride on the Baldwin switcher truck.

The VO1000 was a rather successful early switcher model, with a production total of 548 units. Baldwin actually began producing switchers before orders were in, and since there were few options available, they would simply match up orders with units that were nearly finished. It would be almost five years before the MoPac would go back to Baldwin for more VO1000's, but they would first sample the VO660.

The Final Pre-War Surge

As America's involvement in Europe drew ever closer, few forecasted the change that would effect the domestic locomotive market. As the depression heightened, railroads were strapped with what they had, and few could afford large-scale locomotive replacement programs. It was still a few at a time. In the last two years before the bombing of Pearl Harbor and full-scale war for the U.S., the MoPac ordered an odd assortment of switchers in the attempt to replace smoky steamers from the large cities they served.

Three basic switcher models were purchased; Baldwin's VO660, Alco-GE's S-1, and 44-Tonners from a variety of builders, including GE. After the breaking in of the VO1000, the railroad was sufficiently impressed to endow Baldwin with another switcher order.

In August, 1940, two VO660's (MP-9009-9010) arrived on the MoPac property to begin their toilsome career shuffling cars to and fro in the yards. These were 660 horsepower 6-cylinder machines designed for yard and transfer use. The MoPac would place subsequent orders for another unit for the MoPac proper (MP-9012), and would ultimately purchase three more for subsidiaries, two for the Union Railway of Memphis (URM-9090-9091), and one for the SAU&G (SAU&G-9206). The VO660 total for the MoPac would stay at six units.

Below: The first SC switcher from EMD for the MoPac was 9000, working at Dupo, Illinois on March 17, 1956. A classic early EMC switcher, the SC designation indicates that the unit has a cast frame, as opposed to a

The MoPac ordered two S-1's from Alco-GE (MP-9007-9008), delivered in October, 1940. A month later the Texas Pacific-Missouri Pacific Terminal received its first diesel, S-1 TPMPT-3. Almost a year later, the TPMPT got another S-1 (TPMPT-4). Alco's S-1 was a 660 horsepower switcher based on the 539 engine. It was in production for just over 10 years, from April, 1940 to June, 1950, and was fairly popular with a production total of 540 units. No more S-1's would arrive for the MoPac until the NO&LC would get three in 1947 (NO&LC-9013-9015).

88,000 pounds

Then came the 44-Tonner. The MoPac seemed to buy 44-Tonners from everyone for everywhere, and in fact bought 44-Tonners from four builders; GE, Porter, Bessler and Whitcomb. All the 44-Ton units on the MoPac's roster were built between October, 1940 and February, 1942, even though 44-Ton production, at least for GE, lasted into 1956. Though covered elsewhere, the Alton and Southern did acquire a 44-Tonner second-hand from the PC&N which had a builder's date of November, 1948.

The 44-Ton design was specifically adopted for common-carrier service so that the unit to slide in just under the 90,000 pound limit, which was the cutoff for the 1937 diesel agreement that

welded frame on the SW. This is one of a group of four delivered in July, 1937, and was later rebuilt by EMD with a 12-567B engine and designated "SCm." *R R Wallin photo, Louis Marre collection*

44-Tonners on the MoPac

It is interesting to take a step back in time and see how the MoPac's employee magazine was attempting to deal with the gradual dieselization of the system. In 1940, only the very beginning phases of the transition had started, and few in regular engine service could imagine what would occur over the next few years. They were already thinking about it, though.

The *Missouri Pacific Lines Magazine* ran the following report in November, 1940, which illustrates how the early diesels were viewed. It is humorous in hindsight, an obvious attempt to get the crews ready for the inevitable dieseldom that was on the horizon.

"First 360-Horse Power Diesel Now in Service"

"Weighing but 44 tons and delivering only 360 horsepower, a diesel-electric switch engine of so-called 'vest-pocket' size went to work early this month on Missouri Pacific rails at Springfield, Missouri. Jokes reminiscent of those told in Model T days very shortly began going the rounds, and railroaders schooled in the tradition of huge steam locomotives were inclined to raise skeptical eyebrows. But nevertheless, the

Below: GE 44-Tonner 3502 rests at Kansas City, Missouri on October 10, 1964, awaiting its next assignment. It was originally MoPac 811, and is now near the end of its days; it will go to Precision as scrap in April, 1965. *Joe McMillan*

midget-sized locomotive immediately began doing a man-sized daily stint, performing with utmost satisfaction.

"On the day after it arrived in Springfield, the 44-Ton diesel was called on to move a cut of 18 cars. It moved them with the greatest of ease. Next day a cut of 22 cars was handled without any trouble; members of the train crew, however, expressed the view that the movement with the 22 cars was somewhat slower than with a steam switcher. Further, the little fellow experienced no difficulty in moving eight cars up and over a one percent grade. Later it moved seven cars over the same grade with wet rails, this apparently being the maximum possible without wheel slippage.

"Representing Missouri Pacific's initial venture into the field of lightweight diesel-electric switch locomotives, the unit now working Springfield is the first of five such engines to be produced under specifications furnished by our Engineering Department, and ordered for delivery later this year. It carries the number 804, and is being used to break up or build freight trains, for industrial switching, and for connecting line switching.

"Like all diesel-electric locomotives, the switcher commands its top tractive effort as it first gets under way, a fact which makes it unnecessary to back up and take slack and which, incidentally, eliminates rough handling to a considerable extent.

"It is impossible to overload the traction motors at starting, for the wheels will spin like a top before the motors bog down under a too-heavy load. Tractive effort of the 44-Ton new-

comer compares favorably with that of a 9400 series steam switcher (0-6-0's).

"The first locomotive of this kind to be received was built by the Whitcomb Locomotive Works, Rochelle, Illinois, and has much in common with four similar-sized engines now being completed for our railroad, for delivery later in the year. One is being built by the H. K. Porter Company, Pittsburgh; another by the Davenport-Bessler Company, Davenport, Iowa, and two by the General Electric Company, Erie, Pennsylvania.

"Each will have two 193 horsepower, 4-cycle diesel motors, which, after deducting a total of 26 horsepower for auxiliary service, will leave 360 horsepower available to feed the four traction motors with which each unit is equipped. All five frames will be of similar pattern, being made of fabricated and welded steel construction and will have electrical equipment made by Westinghouse.

"Cab and controls will be about the same on all five jobs, the cabs being centrally located with respect to the frames and the two diesel motors, and offering full visibility on both forward and back-up movements. Oil heaters are provided to warm the cabs during winter months. The fuel tanks are to hold 300 gallons of fuel oil, or roughly enough for 100 hours of operation.

"It has been tentatively planned to place the second light switcher to be delivered in service at Sedalia, working both as a switcher in the yards and as a road engine on the Warsaw branch; the third at Concordia, Kansas; the fourth in road service on the LeRoy-Mason district; and the fifth at Independence, Kansas."

Left: In August, 1962, SC 9000 was rebuilt by EMD with a 12-567B engine and a raised hood. It was redesignated "SCm," and spent five more years in MoPac service. The oddball unit was in Little Rock, Arkansas on the last day of the year, 1962, shortly after repowering. It was the only SC that was rebuilt, and it outlasted its three litter-mates by several years. *Louis Marre*

Right: The Union Terminal Railway rostered two SW's, originally numbered 5 and 10. The 5 was renumbered 6005, and remained in service for the MoPac until August, 1965. The EMC switcher is at Kansas City, Missouri on March 13, 1965, with only three months of MoPac service left. The unit later went to Precision, and then to the Pickens Railroad. *Joe McMillan*

Below: An odd pair, 2400 is a little gasoline electric model ML6-2, Type 6 built by Plymouth in June, 1931. The 4-wheel Plymouth is at Kansas City, Missouri on October 10, 1964, the same month it was retired from the MoPac. Its companion, GE 44-Tonner 3500 had been retired for three years when this photo was taken, but was not disposed of until April, 1965. *Joe McMillan*

protected firemen's jobs. At 88,000 pounds, the 44-Tonner could be operated without firemen, which was a cost-savings for the common-carriers who ordered them. By contrast, the 70-Tonner was designed for light branch lines where restricted axle loadings required the lighter locomotive. This was not necessarily the case for the 44-Tonner, though it would follow that the 44-Tonners would also work well on light rail on decrepit branch lines.

The majority of 44-Tonners on the MoPac were acquired in a group purchased for the MoPac proper and numbered sequentially from MP-800-811. Four more were bought for subsidiaries, one for IGN (IGN-812), two for STLB&M (STLB&M-813-814), and one for the Beaumont, Sour Lake & Western (BSL&W-815). These units were typically assigned to terminal areas where light rail prevailed and smaller crews could be employed. Springfield, Missouri, at the end of a branch line where substantial switching duties existed, was a favorite home of the 44-Tonners, and is typical of their assignments.

The typical GE 44-Ton design was comprised of two 8-cylinder Caterpillar D17000 engines, but all of the MoPac's (and their subsid-

iaries) had Hercules DFXD engines. Only 23 units out of the 348 GE 44-Tonners produced had non-Caterpillar engines, and the MoPac's account for seven of these. Only two other units were built with the DFXD engines, and these were purchased by Chattanooga Traction.

As with the GE 44-Tonners, the MoPac's Porter unit (MP-802) was also unusual, but even more so than apparent at first. Porter had been in the gasoline-powered locomotive business since 1911, and in September, 1930 built its first diesel-electric. Porter went on to produce some 197 diesel-electrics and 47 diesel-mechanicals before selling their designs to Davenport and exiting the locomotive business in 1950. They only built one four-motor 44-Ton locomotive, and naturally it wound up on the MoPac. It performed its duties on the MoPac until the mid-1960's, when it was unceremoniously scrapped. It was Porter's only 44-Tonner.

Four of the 44-Ton locomotives were built by Bessler, one unit built in October, 1940 (MP-803), and the other three (MP-808-810) part of an order delivered between November, 1941 and January, 1942.

The other four MoPac 44-Tonners were Whitcomb engines with Westinghouse equip-

ment. Whitcomb began gasoline powered locomotive production in 1906, and by the time they were fully merged into Baldwin-Lima-Hamilton in December, 1952 had produced 2,054 diesel units. Only 41 of these units were railroad-style 44-Tonners

Whitcomb 44-Ton production lasted from June, 1940 through January, 1945, but all of the MoPac's were pre-war units. The first Whitcomb 44-Ton unit for the MoPac was purchased in October, 1940 (MP-804), and the other three (MP-805-807) were acquired as a batch between October and December, 1941.

On December 7, 1941, the dawn over Pearl Harbor was lit up with the Japanese attack, and the U.S. was hurled into World War II. The War Production Board consequently suspended locomotive production from 1942 to 1945, and the resultant competitive advantage that EMD gained from pre-war and wartime research and experimentation lasted long into dieseldom. After the war, locomotive production took on a whole new direction, and units for long haul service arrived in substantial quantities. Gone would be the many-builder phase that was present during the early dieselization of America's railroad switching industry.

Plymouth Switchers
Various Models 4 units
Gasoline Electrics

1st No	2nd No	3rd No	Model	WT	hp	Built	Build#	Notes & Dispositions
FRGC-2917	ORI-2917	NO&LC-2917	DLC, Type 6		63	10/26	2352	Originally Fair River Gravel Company of Belle Chase, LA, then Overseas Railways, Inc., New Orleans, LA. Sold 1935 to Equitable Equipment Co., New Orleans, LA
NO&LC-3000	MP-3000:1	MP-2400	ML6-2, Type 6	30T	225	06/31	3643	Retired 10/64
NO&LC-3001			WLD-2, Type 2	30T	170	07/32	3685	Retired 10/61, to Kansas & Missouri Elevator Co., 10/25/61, to Jones Coal
NO&LC-3002			JLA, Type 2	12T	100	05/35	3802	Retired 8/57, sold 4/3/59 to T.P. Thompson Co., Kenner, LA. Resold to New Orleans Sewage Water Board as L/4

EMC NC2 900 hp 2 units
TE = 64,475   WT = 257,900
Wheels = 40"   Fuel = 600
Engine: Winton 12-201A V-type 12-cylinder 2-cycle
Min Speed for TE = N/A
59:16 Gearing   65 mph Max

1st No	Built	Build#	Notes & Dispositions
MP-4100	07/37	714	Retired 5/61, scrapped
MP-4101	07/37	715	Retired 12/60, to Braswell S&G

EMC SC 600 hp 3 units
TE = 50,930   WT = 203,720
Wheels = 40"   Fuel = 600
Engine: Winton 8-201A 8-cylinder 2-cycle
Min Speed for TE = N/A
68:16 Gearing   40 mph Max

1st No	2nd No	Built	Build#	Notes & Dispositions
MP-9000:1	MP-1023	07/37	710	Repowered 8/62 with 12-567B by EMD (raised hood), designated "SCm." Retired 02/67, to Big Rock Stone & Material Co., Little Rock, AR, r# BRSM-1023, returned to MoPac 12/69 in trade for NW2 1028. Retired
MP-9001:1		07/37	711	Retired 11/59, sold 12/59 to Dardanelle & Russellville, r# D&R-14
MP-9003:1	MP-6009:1	07/37	713	Scrapped 8/64

Above: Dimunitive four-wheeler 3002, a Plymouth model JLA, Type 2, rests at Algiers, Louisiana on July 25, 1948. *E M Kahn photo, Louis Marre collection*

EMC SC   600 hp   1 unit
TE = 50,400   WT = 201,610
Wheels = 40"   Fuel = 600
Engine: Winton 8-201A 8-cylinder 2-cycle
Min Speed for TE = N/A
68:16 Gearing   40 mph Max
Retired and sold 10/44 to SJB, to PNC 1965, to Pickens r# PIRR-4

1st No	2nd No	3rd No	4th No	5th No	Built	Build#
MP-9002:1	SJB-2	SJB-11	SJB-6007	MP-6007:1	07/37	712

EMC-GE SW   600 hp   2 units
TE = 50,400   WT = 201,610
Wheels = 40"   Fuel = 600
Engine: Winton 8-201A 8-cylinder 2-cycle
Min Speed for TE = N/A
68:16 Gearing   40 mph Max

1st No	2nd No	3rd No	Built	Build#	Notes & Dispositions
UT-5	SJB-5	MP-6005:1	05/38	718	Retired 8/65, to PNC, to Pickens r# PIRR-3
UT 10	SJB-10	MP-6006:1	12/38	751	Retired 9/63, scrapped

EMC NW4   900 hp   2 units
TE = 64,475   WT = 257,900
Wheels = 38"   Fuel = 600
Engine: Winton 12-201A V-type 12-cylinder 2-cycle
Min Speed for TE = N/A
Equipped with steam generators
59:18 Gearing for 4102 77 mph Max
59:17 Gearing for 4103 77 mph Max
Equipped with steam generators

1st No	2nd No	Built	Build#	Notes & Dispositions
EMC-823	MP-4102	08/38	823	Retired 2/61, scrapped
EMC-824	MP-4103	08/38	824	Retired 3/61, scrapped

Above: Only two NW4's were built for the MoPac. The 4102 is sparkling new in this builder's photo taken before the new switcher had turned a wheel. The shroud over the air tanks on the front porch was a short-lived inconvenience for the mechanical department. *Ed Hawkins collection*

EMC SW1   600 hp   1 unit
TE = 50,025   WT = 199,600
Wheels = 40"   Fuel = 600
Engine: EMC 6-567 V-type 6-cylinder 2-cycle
Min Speed for TE = 5.0 mph
62:15 Gearing   45 mph Max

1st No	2nd No	Built	Build#	Notes & Disposition
FWB-1	FWB-6018	01/39	803	Retired 1966, T-I to EMD

EMC SW1   600 hp   2 units
TE = 50,410   WT = 201,635
Wheels = 40"   Fuel = 600
Engine: EMC 6-567 V-type 6-cylinder 2-cycle
Min Speed for TE = 5.0 mph
62:15 Gearing   45 mph Max
Retired 1966, T-I to EMD

1st No	2nd No	Built	Build#
MP-9004:1	MP-6010:1	09/39	895
MP-9005:1	MP-6011:1	09/39	896

Above: SW1 9005 was one of two SW1's that rolled off the EMC shop floor in September, 1939. Its career spanned nearly three decades, lasting until 1966. The classy little switcher is at St. Louis, Missouri as the shutter is tripped in 1942. *Joe Collias collection*

EMC SW1   600 hp   4 units
TE = 50,410   WT = 201,635
Wheels = 40"   Fuel = 600
Engine: EMC 6-567 V-type 6-cylinder 2-cycle
Min Speed for TE = 6.5 mph
62:15 Gearing   45 mph Max

1st No	2nd No	3rd No	Built	Build#	Notes & Dispositions
IGN-9200	IGN-9016:1	MP-6014:1	01/40	990	Retired 1966, T-I to EMD
IGN-9201	IGN-9017:1		12/39	991	Retired 2/59, to Clyde Gary
IGN-9202	IGN-9018:1	MP-6015:1	12/39	992	Retired 1966, T-I to EMD
IGN-9203	IGN-9019:1	MP-6016:1	12/39	993	Retired 1966, T-I to EMD

Below: SW1 9018 wears the standard black MoPac paint scheme typical of switchers in the early diesel years. The unit is shuffling cars at San Antonio, Texas on September 2, 1952. *RH Carlson photo, Louis Marre collection*

Below: VO660 9091, sublettered for the Union Railroad of Memphis, works the yard at Memphis on April 13, 1962. *Louis Marre collection*

EMC SW1   600 hp   2 units
TE = 49,655   WT = 198,630
Wheels = 40"   Fuel = 600
Engine: EMC 6-567 V-type 6-cylinder 2-cycle
Min Speed for TE = 5.0 mph
62:15 Gearing   45 mph Max
Retired 1966, T-I to EMD

1st No	2nd No	Built	Build#
MP-9006:1	MP-6012:1	08/40	1083
MP-9011:1	MP-6013:1	08/41	1314

EMD SW1   600 hp   2 units
TE = 49,565   WT = 198,260
Wheels = 40"   Fuel = 600
Engine: EMD 6-567 V-type 6-cylinder 2-cycle
Min Speed for TE = 6.5 mph
62:15 Gearing   45 mph Max
Retired 1966, T-I to EMD

1st No	2nd No	3rd No	Built	Build#
IGN-9204	IGN-9020:1	MP-6017:1	06/41	1338
IGN-9205	IGN-9021:1		06/41	1339

EMD SW1   600 hp   1 unit
TE = 50,410   WT = 201,635
Wheels = 40"   Fuel = 600
Engine: EMD 6-567 V-type 6-cylinder 2-cycle
Min Speed for TE = 5.0 mph
62:15 Gearing   45 mph Max

1st No	2nd No	Built	Build#	Notes & Disposition
SJB-12	MP-6008:1	04/47	4793	Retired 2/66, T-I to EMD

Alco HH1000   1,000 hp   1 unit
TE = 57,600   WT = 230,400
Wheels = 40"   Fuel = 625
Engine: Alco V-type 6-cylinder 4-cycle Turbocharged
Min Speed for TE = 5.0 mph
59:16 Gearing   60 mph Max

1st No	2nd No	Built	Build#	Disposition
MP-9102	MP-1035	09/39	69146	Scrapped

Baldwin VO660   660 hp   2 units
TE = 50,800   WT = 203,200
Wheels = 40"   Fuel = 600
Engine: Baldwin VO 6-cylinder 4-cycle
Min Speed for TE = 5.0 mph
76:16 Gearing   45 mph Max

1st No	2nd No	Built	Build#	Notes & Dispositions
MP-9009:1	MP-6612	08/40	62397	Retired 1966, T-I to EMD, scrapped
MP-9010:1		08/40	62398	Retired 6/59, to Witt Gravel, to Parish Line

Baldwin VO660   660 hp   4 units
TE = 49,165   WT = 196,660
Wheels = 40"   Fuel = 600
Engine: Baldwin VO 6-cylinder 4-cycle
Min Speed for TE = 6.5 mph
76:16 Gearing   60 mph Max

1st No	2nd No	Built	Build#	Notes & Dispositions
SAU&G-9206	SAU&G-9022	06/41	62498	Retired 3/59, to Texas Crushed Stone, r# GRR-1000
MP-9012:1	MP-6613	07/41	62500	Retired 1966, T-I to EMD
URM-9090	URM-6610	03/42	64248	Retired 1966, to EMD
URM-9091	URM-6611	03/42	64249	Retired 1966, to EMD

Alco-GE S-1   660 hp   2 units
TE = 50,540   WT = 202,150
Wheels = 40"   Fuel = 635
Engine: Alco 539 6-cylinder 4-cycle
Min Speed for TE = 6.5 mph
75:16 Gearing   60 mph Max

1st No	2nd No	Built	Build#	Notes
TPMPT-3	MP-6602	11/40	69381	Note 1
TPMPT-4	MP-6603	08/41	69500	Note 2

Note 1: Retired 11/66, to Standard Gravel Co., Clifton, LA 12/66
Note 2: Retired 2/67, to Silcott Railway Equipment 2/67, to PNC, to REL, to Morrell & Co., Ottumwa, IA

Above: Alco S-1 switcher still wears the NO&LC sublettering, having been renumbered 6606. It is resting on the Brooklyn Eastern District Terminal at Kent Avenue and North 7th Street in New York. It will soon be renumbered BEDT-24, and was retired by the MoPac about a month before this photo was taken in April, 1963. *Matthew Herson, Jr photo, Kevin EuDaly collection*

Alco-GE S-1   660 hp   2 units
TE = 49,075   WT = 196,300
Wheels = 40"   Fuel = 635
Engine: Alco 539 6-cylinder 4-cycle
Min Speed for TE = 6.5 mph
75:16 Gearing   60 mph Max

1st No	2nd No	Built	Build#	Notes & Dispositions
MP-9007:1	MP-6600	10/40	69197	Scrapped
MP-9008:1	MP-6601	10/40	69198	To Brooklyn Eastern District Terminal

Alco-GE S-1   660 hp   3 units
TE = 49,500   WT = 198,000
Wheels = 40"   Fuel = 635
Engine: Alco 539 6-cylinder 4-cycle
Min Speed for TE = 6.5 mph
75:16 Gearing   60 mph Max
To Silcott Railway Equipment 3/63, to Brooklyn Eastern District Terminal

1st No	2nd No	Built	Build#	Notes & Dispositions
NOL&C-9013	MP-6604	10/47	75525	Retired 3/63, r# BEDT-22
NOL&C-9014	MP-6605	10/47	75526	Retired 4/63, r# BEDT-23
NOL&C-9015	MP-6606	11/47	75527	Retired 3/63, r# BEDT-24

GE 44-Ton   350 hp   2 units
TE = 21,955   WT = 87,830
Wheels = 35"   Fuel = 250
Engine: Two Hercules DFXD 6-cylinder 4-cycle
Min Speed for TE = N/A
74:15 Gearing   35 mph Max

1st No	2nd No	Built	Build#	Notes & Dispositions
MP-800:1	MP-3500:1	02/41	12974	Retired 4/62, to Silcott 4/65, to PNC, scrapped
MP-801:1	MP-3501:1	02/41	12975	Retired 2/62, to PNC, scrapped

Porter (no model) 44-Ton   350 hp   1 unit
TE = 21,955   WT = 87,830
Wheels = 34"   Fuel = 350
Engine: Two Hercules DFXD 6-cylinder 4-cycle
Min Speed for TE = 8.5 mph
75:13 Gearing   30 mph Max
Listed by builder at 386 hp

1st No	2nd No	Built	Build#	Notes & Disposition
MP-802:1	MP-3504:1	02/41	7286	R# 4/62. Retired 11/63, scrapped

Davenport-Bessler DE44 (44-Ton)   350 hp   1 unit
TE = 21,955   WT = 87,830
Wheels = 34"   Fuel = 300
Engine: Two Hercules DFXD 6-cylinder 4-cycle
Min Speed for TE = 6.6 mph
75:13 Gearing   30 mph Max

1st No	Built	Bui#	Notes & Disposition
MP-803:1	10/40	2306	Retired 9/57, scrapped

Whitcomb 44DE6 (44-Ton) 350 hp 1 unit
TE = 21,955   WT = 87,830
Wheels = 34"   Fuel = 300
Engine: Two Hercules DFXD 6-cylinder 4-cycle
Min Speed for TE = 8.5 mph
75:13 Gearing   30 mph Max

1st No	2nd No	Built	Buil#	Notes & Dispositions
MP-804:1	MP-3505:1	11/40	60049	Retired mid 1960's, scrapped

Whitcomb 44DE22 (44-Ton) 350 hp 3 units
TE = 21,955   WT = 87,830
Wheels = 34"   Fuel = 300
Engine: Two Hercules DFXD 6-cylinder 4-cycle
Min Speed for TE = 8.5 mph
75:13 Gearing   30 mph Max

1st No	Built	Buil#	Notes & Dispositions
MP-805:1	10/41	60080	Retired 4/58, to Pan Am Engineering
MP-806:1	11/41	60081	Retired 9/57, to Whisler, to Dominion, r# DOM-15
MP-807:1	12/41	60082	Retired 4/58, to Pan Am Engineering

Davenport-Bessler DE44 (44-Ton) 350 hp 3 units
TE = 21,955   WT = 87,830
Wheels = 34"   Fuel = 300
Engine: Two Hercules DFXD 6-cylinder 4-cycle
Min Speed for TE = 6.6 mph
75:13 Gearing   30 mph Max

1st No	Built	Buil#	Notes & Dispositions
MP-808:1	12/41	2349	Retired 9/57, to Whisler Equipment
MP-809:1	12/41	2350	Retired 9/57, to Whisler Equipment
MP-810:1	01/42	2351	Retired 12/56, to Okmulgee Northern

GE 44-Ton 350 hp 5 units
TE = 21,955   WT = 87,830
Wheels = 34"   Fuel = 250
Engine: Two Hercules DFXD 6-cylinder 4-cycle
Min Speed for TE = N/A
72:15 Gearing   35 mph Max

1st No	2nd No	3rd No	Built	Buil#	Notes
MP-811:1	MP-3502:1		01/42	13177	Note 1
IGN-812	STLB&M-812	MP-812:1	01/42	13178	Note 2
STLB&M-813	MP-813:1		01/42	13179	Note 3
STLB&M-814	MP-3503:1		01/42	13180	Note 4
BSL&W-815	MP-815:1		01/42	13181	Note 5

Note 1: Retired 4/62, to PNC 4/65, scrapped
Note 2: Transferred to MP 3/56, retired 4/56, to Pan Am Engineering 4/58, to Canton & Carthage Ry 100, to Whisler Equipment 11/59, to Craig Co. 3/60, r# CRC-100
Note 3: Retired 4/56, to Fort Worth Sand and Gravel, to Structural Metals, Inc., r# SMI-76
Note 4: Retired 4/62, to PNC, scrapped
Note 5: Retired 4/58, to Pan Am Engineering, to Chicago Gravel Co., r# CGC-510

Plymouth JDT 2 units

1st No	2nd No	WT	Hp	Built	Build#	Notes
NO&LC-3003	NO&LC-1650	18T	165	08/57	6037	Note 1
NO&LC-3004	MP-2401	25T	240	04/61	6261	Note 2

Note1: Retired and sold 5/74 to Bartlett Grain, KC, KS, r# BGC-1650
Note 2: Leased to Continental Grain, KC, KS as 2401

Below: Little four-wheel Plymouth model JDT sits under a crystal clear blue sky in Kansas City, Missouri in October, 1975. The 18-ton unit wound up spending much of its later life shuffling cars for Bartlett Grain in Kansas City, Kansas. *Mac Owen photo, Kevin EuDaly collection*

EMC/EMD
E3
AA6
E6

The now long-ago year of 1939 marked the true beginning of diesels on the MoPac that were recognized as a direct threat to steam road power. In October two E3A's (MP-7000-7001) rolled off the shop floor at fledgling EMC, and within a short time it was obvious that these were something entirely different than anything the MoPac had owned before. They were nothing short of magnificent, with long sleek bodies and slant noses. Their image was one of speed and power, but above all they represented the beginning of the diesel era for long-haul passenger service.

The young of the time quickly fell in love with these shiny new beasts in such attractive paint schemes. The old black steamers that were still plugging away on tonnage trains couldn't compete with these newcomers for the attention of the youth. The slightly older, however, began to slowly recognize the threat these invaders posed on their beloved iron horses. Amazingly, within 16 years of the arrival of the first E3 on the MoPac, steam's fires would be out forever over MoPac rails, an incredibly short transition period considering the scope of the transition.

The later versions in the E-series (E3's through E7's) from EMC, and later EMD, were built around two 567 engines of various designations that generated 1,000 horsepower each. Each engine supplied the power for two traction motors, and the three-axle trucks employed an idler axle to reduce axle-loadings and improve tracking at high speeds. The earliest E's, from EA's to E2's employed two 201-A engines at 900 horsepower each, but by the time the MoPac ordered, production was entirely 567 power plants.

Early E-unit production at EMC included EA's, E1's and E2's, not counting the boxcabs, and by mid-1938 29 of these three E-series units had been produced. In October, 1938 E4's were in production, and the E3's first rolled off the floor at La Grange in March, 1939. By November, 1939 E6's were in production and by June, 1940 E3 production was over. Only 16 E3A's were pro-

duced, and typical for the pre-war era no single railroad bought more than four.

E-series production was suspended during the war, and when it resumed all E-unit production was in the form of the graceful E7's. Getting back to the MoPac, the two E3's arrived on the property on October 20, 1939, and *The Eagle* launched itself onto MoPac rails and into MoPac diesel and passenger train history. *The Eagle* was significant in many ways for the MoPac, it was not only the premier service for the MoPac's many Midwestern routes, but it became the corporate symbol of a growing system. The eagle emblem itself could be found on the MoPac

locomotives from the time those first two E3's hit the rails until the MoPac fell under UP's yellow and gray image some 50 years later.

MP-7000 and 7001 cranked out multi-million mile careers, hauling who knows how many passengers across the system. EMC indeed had something with these pre-war prede-

Below: E3's 7000 and 7001 pull out of Little Rock bound for Memphis with train 220 on June 15, 1960. In less than two years they were both scrapped, falling to the torch in May, 1962. They were MoPac's first two E-units, delivered in October, 1939. By the time this photo was taken they were the dinosaurs of passenger power. *J Parker Lamb*

cessors of first generation diesel power. A growing number of roads were becoming interested in the potential of the new diesels to reduce the operating costs associated with steam.

In June, 1940 the MoPac announced plans for a new *Eagle*. It would be a three unit streamlined train, an engine and two cars, that would operate a fast schedule twice daily between Tallulah, Louisiana and Memphis, Tennessee. The train was named the *Dixie Eagle* in an employees contest for the name, but this was changed to the *Delta Eagle* by January, 1941. In August, 1940, the MoPac took delivery of a truly unique passenger unit from EMC for this train. The E-unit, delivered with essentially the carbody of an E6, was actually half an E6, with only one 567 engine powering only the front truck. In the area where the second engine

Right: E6A 7003 is ready to depart with the *Texas Eagle* at San Antonio, Texas in September, 1950. The E6 was the most popular pre-war E-unit, with sales totaling 92 A-units and 26 B-units. *Harold K Vollrath collection*

Below: The *Missouri River Eagle* streaks westward at milepost 104 just west of Chamois, Missouri with E3A 7000 in command in July, 1940. Only 16 E3A's were built in a production period from March, 1939 to June, 1940. MoPac had two of the sleek units, and no single road bought more than four. *Harold K Vollrath collection*

Opposite page top: One of the strangest pieces of MoPac passenger power was the 7100, built in August, 1940. The locomotive had one 1,000 horsepower prime mover instead of two, making it half of an E6. Where the second prime mover would have been was instead a baggage compartment. The portholes were a custom MoPac feature, as well. The bizarre E-unit is on the *Delta Eagle* at Marianna, Arkansas in 1941. *Joe Collias*

Opposite page bottom: The semaphore has yet to begin falling as the 7003 races by with the *Colorado Eagle*. The E3, E4 and E6's all came in identical carbodies, and the MoPac's were the only ones with portholes. The two E6A's were the only E-units with the Rio Grande lettering on the nose. *Otto Perry photo, Charlie Duckworth collection*

Below: Still new E3A 7000 sparkles at St. Louis, Missouri on March 10, 1940 getting ready for another run out of Union Station. The stainless steel eagle catches a glint of sunshine. *Joe Collias*

Bottom: Millions of miles have gone by under her wheels as E6A 11 pulls at St. Louis, Missouri on January 3, 1965. Now decked in solid blue, the eagle on her nose reminds one of her heritage. *Louis Marre*

should have been was a baggage compartment, and the resulting odd porthole variation was a custom feature for the MoPac. The unit was ideal for small passenger runs, where the additional power from the second engine was unnecessary.

The MoPac and EMC referred to this unit as an "AA," while the official MoPac records term it an "AA6," and it was numbered MP-7100. EMC classed it as a "1000 hp motorcar," making it the last motorcar built by EMC. The MoPac never considered it a motorcar, but rather classed it as a locomotive. It was built for service on the MoPac's *Delta Eagle*, and served much of its career in this service.

The final pre-war passenger power for the MoPac came in the form of the graceful E6. Two E6 cabs (MP-7002-7003) and two boosters (MP-7002B-7003B) were added to the roster in October, 1941. Unlike the first odd-ball E6 MP-7100 these were true E6's. Total E6 production resulted in 92 A-units (not counting the MP-7100) and 26 B-units. During E6 production, EMC was folded into General Motors and consequently became the Electro-Motive Division of GM, or EMD. The MoPac's E6's were the first EMD passenger units for the railroad, though they were externally identical to the E3's.

As with the switchers, World War II interfered with diesel production, as America directed its metal resources to armaments and shell casings. After the war, the predictable post-war boom led to a tremendous upsurge in traffic levels, which was only complicated by the wartime surge in troop-train movements. America's railroad equipment was strained during the war, and the pressure only increased as the economy surged upward after the conflict in Europe and the Pacific came to an end.

Railroads found themselves power hungry after having been called upon to move soldiers in tremendous numbers during the war. The builders had been forced to shelve production, and now that the war was over had to make up for lost time at their drawing boards. Though production of passenger units essentially ceased during World War II, EMD was allowed to continue some freight production. This freight production during the war put EMD in a position that would result in their domination of the domestic freight market for decades. Only when fuel consumption would become a major factor nearly 50 years later would the more efficient 4-cycle GEs really begin to take hold of a significant share of the market, and by this late date all the other builders had already given up.

EMC-GE E3A 2,000 hp 2 units
TE = 54,100   WT = 321,000 (216,400 on powered wheels)
Wheels = 36"   Fuel = 1,200
Engine: Two EMC 567 V-type 12-cylinder 2-cycle
Min Speed for TE = 34.0 mph
55:22 Gearing   98 mph Max
Equipped with steam generators
Retired 5/62, scrapped

1st No	Built	Build#
MP-7000	10/39	936
MP-7001	10/39	937

EMC AA6 (1/2 of an E6)   1,000 hp   1 unit
TE = 24,425   WT = 247,340 (97,700 on powered wheels)
Wheels = 36"   Fuel = 1,200
Engine: EMC 567 V-type 12-cylinder 2-cycle
Min Speed for TE = 34.0 mph
55:22 Gearing   98 mph Max
Equipped with steam generator
Last Motorcar built by EMC

1st No	Built	Build#	Notes & Disposition
MP-7100	08/40	1082	Retired 2/62, scrapped

EMD E6 series   2,000 hp   4 units
TE = 54,850 (A-units) 52,925 (B-units)
WT = 325,800 (A-units) (219,400 on powered wheels)
314,300 (B-units) (211,700 on powered wheels)
Wheels = 36"   Fuel = 1,200
Engine: Two EMD 12-567 V-type 12-cylinder 2-cycle
Min Speed for TE = 34.0 mph
55:22 Gearing   98 mph Max
Equipped with steam generators

1st No	2nd No	Built	Build#	Dispositions
MP-7002	MP-11	10/41	1389	Scrapped
MP-7002B	MP-11B	10/41	1391	Scrapped
MP-7003	MP-12	10/41	1390	Scrapped
MP-7003B	MP-12B	10/41	1392	Scrapped

Though locomotive production was suspended for the most part during the war, the War Production Board did allow several builders to continue to build units necessary for the continued success of the American rail industry. For most builders this was comprised primarily of switchers, but a number of units that were certainly not switchers managed to come out of EMD.

Baldwin
VO1000

Alco-GE
S-2

EMD
FT

EMC had pioneered a freight version of its heavy-haul locomotive series in the form of the 1,350 horsepower 16-cylinder FT, which used the 567 power plant that had found its way into the E-series locomotives. The FT demo set was outshopped at EMC in October, 1939. The set was numbered 103, and represents the first road freight diesel. For road freight diesels in active service, EMC was ahead of the pack, and would never give up their first place position. FT production was essentially in parallel with the E3 through E6 production, with the exception that EMD was allowed to produce FT's throughout the war. And produce them they did. By war's end and prior to the evolution of the F2, EMD had rolled 555 FT A-units out of the plant and 541 FT B-unit boosters to go with them.

GE only managed to produce industrial switchers during the war, but really hadn't pursued the domestic large-size locomotive market anyway. Alco produced S-1's, S-2's and RS-1's during the war, but also had not really ventured into significant road power.

Baldwin produced VO660's and VO1000's during the war, but had only just begun to develop larger power with through-freight capabilities. Their one really significant unit produced during the war was the 6,000 horsepower experimental locomotive number 6000 that was to be powered with an incredible eight 8-cylinder engines, though only four were ever installed. It rode on a centipede-style undercarriage. It was produced in 1943, and its running gear was later used under the centipede demonstrator. Neither of these demonstrators were ever sold.

Fairbanks-Morse got into the locomotive business, outshopping their first diesel locomotive at Beloit, Wisconsin on August 21, 1944.

They built a number of H10-44's near the end of the war, but the MoPac never went for FM and its opposed-piston design. They were never really in the running for the forefront position. Too little, too late.

The FT stands out as the lone heavy-haul unit produced in any quantity during the war, and the MoPac bought its share. The MoPac found itself increasingly in demand and significantly underpowered in the motive power department during the war. Wartime demands brought traffic levels on the MoPac system to an all-time high. The railroad begged the War Production Board for more power, and in addition to switchers they managed to get the go ahead for some FT's from EMD.

Below: An FT A-B-B set led by the 502 pauses momentarily at Russellville, Arkansas on February 13, 1949. FT production began just before World War II broke out, and this gave EMC a substantial advantage during the war. They were the only major builder allowed to build freight units during the war, and they turned out 1,096 of the FT's before production ended in November, 1945. The 502 is one of a truly mass-produced locomotive. *Charles Winters, Louis Marre collection*

The first order was for eight permanently coupled A-B pairs of FT's, which were produced in two batches. The first four pairs (MP-501-504 and MP-501B-504B) were delivered in November and December, 1943, and with the FT in production EMD was racing ahead of the other diesel manufacturers, gaining valuable experience while others were forced to stand idly by. The second batch of A-B sets from this order (MP-505-508 and MP-505B-508B) were delivered in September and October, 1944.

In the meantime, Alco-GE produced ten S-2's for the MoPac (MP-9107-9116) between August, 1941 and May, 1945. These were delivered in five batches in groups of one, two, three, two and then two, respectively. An additional three S-2's (IGN-9156-9158) were purchased for the IGN, and were built in September and October, 1945. No more S-2's would be purchased until long after the war, when the TPMPT ordered two pairs (TPMPT-11-14) which came in March and May, 1948. The MoPac itself bought three in May and June, 1949 (MP-9128-9130), and another pair in October, 1949 (MP-9131-9132). A pair also came for the IGN in July, 1949 (IGN-9168-9169).

The S-2 was easily Alco's most popular model, with a production total of 1,502 units. The RS-3 was a close second at 1,370, but no other Alco product came even close to these two models. The S-2 was built in Alco's general

Above: FT 502 has some miles under her belt by the time the company photographer tripped the shutter in mid-1944. The handsome FT is working a freight south at Dupo, Illinois. *Missouri Pacific photo, Joe Collias collection*

Below: S-2 production began in April, 1940, over a year before America's direct involvement in WWII. The S-2 was Alco's most popular locomotive of all time, with 1,502 produced by the time production ceased in **June, 1950. For Alco, only the RS-3 came close, with 1,370 units. IGN-9158 is one of five built for that road.** *R S Plummer, Sr photo, Joe Collias collection*

switcher configuration of the time and was similar to the S-1, S-3 and S-4. The S-2 came with a 1,000 horsepower 539 6-cylinder engine. The S-1's and S-2's rode on Blunt trucks, which is one characteristic that distinguishes them from S-3's and S-4's. The MoPac had both S-1's and S-2's, but never bought any of the later Alco S-3 or S-4 switchers. From a production viewpoint, the S-1 and S-2 were in production at the same time (the S-1 being the 660 horsepower version), and then both were replaced with the new line of S-3's and S-4's.

The MoPac had purchased one VO1000 before the war (MP-9103), and late in the war Baldwin finally got into the act for the MoPac, and built 11 more VO1000's for the MoPac and its subsidiaries. Only three of these were for the MoPac (MP-9117-9119), and there were also three for the IGN (IGN-9150-9152), three for the STLB&M (STLB&M-9153-9155), and two for the URM (URM-9198-9199). MoPac later added two more VO1000's after the war, for the STLB&M (STLB&M-9160-9161). These units came on the property in April, 1946, and brought the VO1000 total to 14.

As the war drew to a close, an EMD order was placed and the up and coming builder delivered four more A-B pairs of FT's (MP-509-512 and MP-509B-512B) in July, 1945. A final order with EMD added two E7's, an A-unit and a B-unit (MP-7004 and 7004B). The E7 was the only passenger model offered with the 567A engine, and was rated at 2,000 horsepower just like all the E's since the E3. A significant number of E7's would be added to the MoPac's fleet before EMD's transition to the E8 in 1949.

The FT had helped EMD to continue its growth into the dominant locomotive builder, and the War Production Board's decision to allow them to continue production during the war turned out to be a blessing to the folks at EMD.

The 12 pairs of FT freight units brought the economy of diesel power to the MoPac's freight operations. The drawbar between the A-B pairs kept the units running in sets, and the A-B-B-A lashup became quite commonplace on MoPac rails. Each unit brought 1,350 horsepower to the front-end of the MoPac's freights, and were built with the 567 engine, which was ever growing in popularity with early diesel mechanics.

Once the war was over, domestic locomotive production was returned to the control of the builders, and the horsepower race was on, a race that has not ended to this day.

Baldwin VO1000   1,000 hp   1 unit
TE = 60,500   WT = 242,015
Wheels = 40"   Fuel = 700
Engine: Baldwin VO 8-cylinder 4-cycle
Min Speed for TE = 8.3 mph
59:16 Gearing   65 mph Max
T-I to EMD, scrapped

1st No	2nd No	Built	Build#
MP-9103	MP-1062:1	10/39	62301

Baldwin VO1000   1,000 hp   6 units
TE = 60,300   WT = 241,200
Wheels = 40"   Fuel = 700
Engine: Baldwin VO 8-cylinder 4-cycle
Min Speed for TE = 5.0 mph
68:14 Gearing   60 mph Max
T-I to EMD, scrapped

1st No	2nd No	Built	Build#
IGN-9150	(MP-1084)	03/44	70167
IGN-9151	(MP-1085)	03/44	70168
IGN-9152	(MP-1086)	03/44	70169
STLB&M-9153	(MP-1087)	02/44	70160
STLB&M-9154	(MP-1088)	02/44	70161
STLB&M-9155	MP-1089:1	03/44	70170

Baldwin VO1000   1,000 hp   3 units
TE = 60,500   WT = 242,015
Wheels = 40"   Fuel = 700
Engine: Baldwin VO 8-cylinder 4-cycle
Min Speed for TE = 8.3 mph
68:14 Gearing   60 mph Max
T-I to EMD, scrapped

1st No	2nd No	Built	Build#
MP-9117	MP-1063:1	03/45	71750
MP-9118	MP-1064	04/45	72012
MP-9119	MP-1065	07/45	72026

Baldwin VO1000   1,000 hp   2 units
TE = 60,300   WT = 241,200
Wheels = 40"   Fuel = 700
Engine: Baldwin VO 8-cylinder 4-cycle
Min Speed for TE = 8.3 mph
68:14 Gearing   60 mph Max
Retired 2/66, T-I to EMD, scrapped

1st No	2nd No	Built	Build#
URM-9198	URM-1098	09/45	71526
URM-9199	URM-1099	09/45	71527

Above: The VO1000 was a rather successful switcher model for Baldwin, with the final tally indicating 548 were built, all for U. S. roads. The first four VO1000's bought by the MoPac proper were acquired piecemeal, and the 9119 was the last of these four. All subsequent VO1000 orders would be for subsidiaries, as were two previous orders. The unit is at the builder, awaiting delivery to the MoPac in July, 1945. *Baldwin photo, Charlie Duckworth collection*

Baldwin VO1000   1,000 hp   2 units
TE = 60,300   WT = 241,200
Wheels = 40"   Fuel = 700
Engine: Baldwin VO 8-cylinder 4-cycle
Min Speed for TE = 8.3 mph
68:14 Gearing   60 mph Max
T-I to EMD, scrapped

1st No	2nd No	Built	Build#
STLB&M-9160	MP-1090:1	04/46	71565
STLB&M-9161	MP-1091:1	04/46	71566

Right: The MoPac bought 12 FT A-units, and an equal number of B-units. The 24 FT's began the invasion of the diesel into the ranks of freight steam power. FT 506 is at Van Buren, Arkansas in July, 1957. *Louis Marre*

Lower right: The S-2 was fairly popular with the MoPac and its subsidiaries. They bought 25, but never more than three at a time. The 9110 is in Brownsville, Texas on June 18, 1956. *R H Carlson photo, Louis Marre collection*

Alco-GE S-2   1,000 hp   10 units
TE = 57,600   WT = 230,400
Wheels = 40"   Fuel = 635
Engine: Alco V-type 6-cylinder 4-cycle Turbocharged
Min Speed for TE = 9.0 mph
75:16 Gearing   60 mph Max

1st No	2nd No	Built	Build#	Dispositions
MP-9107	MP-1036	08/41	69522	Scrapped
MP-9108	MP-1037	11/43	70954	Scrapped
MP-9109	MP-1038	11/43	70955	Scrapped
MP-9110	MP-1039	12/43	71291	Scrapped
MP-9111	MP-1040	12/43	71292	Scrapped
MP-9112	MP-1041	12/43	71293	Scrapped
MP-9113	MP-1042	02/44	72008	Scrapped
MP-9114	MP-1043	02/44	72009	Scrapped
MP-9115	MP-1044	05/45	73367	Scrapped
MP-9116	MP-1045	05/45	73368	Scrapped

Alco-GE S-2   1,000 hp   4 units
TE = 57,600   WT = 230,400
Wheels = 40"   Fuel = 635
Engine: Alco 539 6-cylinder 4-cycle
Min Speed for TE = 9.0 mph
75:16 Gearing   60 mph Max

1st No	2nd No	Built	Build#	Notes & Dispositions
IGN-9156	MP-1051	09/45	73639	Retired
IGN-9157	MP-1052	09/45	73640	Scrapped
IGN-9158	MP-1053	10/45	74343	Sold to Sacramento Northern
STLB&M-9159	MP-1054	05/46	74464	Retired 7/66, to Gifford Hill Sand

Alco-GE S-2   1,000 hp   4 units
TE = 57,500   WT = 230,000
Wheels = 40"   Fuel = 635
Engine: Alco V-type 6-cylinder 4-cycle Turbocharged
Min Speed for TE = 9.0 mph
75:16 Gearing   60 mph Max

1st No	2nd No	Built	Build#	Notes & Dispositions
TPMPT-11	MP-1057	03/48	75658	Retired 2/67, to Silcott Railway Equipment 2/67, to Washington Western, to Standard Gravel Co.
TPMPT-12	MP-1058	03/48	75659	Retired 1/67, to Duffy & Son 1/67, to Tidewater Southern r# TS-744
TPMPT-13	MP-1059	05/48	75677	To Agrico Chemical 9/66 r# ACC-10
TPMPT-14	MP-1060	05/48	75678	To Agrico Chemical 9/66 r# ACC-11

Alco-GE S-2   1,000 hp   5 units
TE = 57,600   WT = 230,400
Wheels = 40"   Fuel = 635
Engine: Alco 539 6-cylinder 4-cycle Turbocharged
Min Speed for TE = 9.0 mph
68:14 Gearing   60 mph Max

1st No	2nd No	Built	Build#	Notes & Dispositions
MP-9128	MP-1046	05/49	76773	Scrapped
MP-9129	MP-1047	06/49	76774	Sold to Tidewater Southern, r# TS-744
MP-9130	MP-1048	06/49	76775	Sold to Sacramento Northern
MP-9131	MP-1049	10/49	77159	Scrapped
MP-9132	MP-1050	10/49	77160	Scrapped

Alco-GE S-2   1,000 hp   2 units
TE = 57,600   WT = 230,400
Wheels = 40"   Fuel = 635
Engine: Alco 539 6-cylinder 4-cycle
Min Speed for TE = 9.0 mph
75:16 Gearing   60 mph Max

1st No	2nd No	Built	Build#	Dispositions
IGN-9168	MP-1055	07/49	76929	Scrapped
IGN-9169	MP-1056	07/49	76930	Scrapped

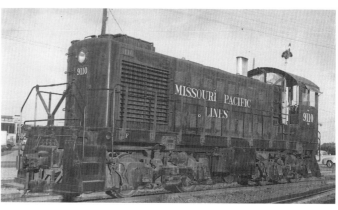

EMD FT   1,350 hp   24 units
TE = 57,035 (A-units) 55,665 (B-units)
WT = 228,140 (A-units) 222,660 (B-units)
Wheels = 40"   Fuel = 1,200
Engine: EMD 16-567A V-type 16-cylinder 2-cycle
Min Speed for TE = 14.5 mph
62:15 Gearing   65 mph Max
T-I to EMD

1st No	Built	Build#
MP-501:1	11/43	2072
MP-501B	11/43	2080
MP-502:1	11/43	2073
MP-502B	11/43	2081
MP-503:1	12/43	2074
MP-503B	12/43	2082
MP-504:1	12/43	2075
MP-504B	12/43	2083
MP-505:1	09/44	2076
MP-505B	09/44	2084
MP-506:1	09/44	2077
MP-506B	09/44	2085
MP-507:1	10/44	2078
MP-507B	10/44	2086
MP-508:1	10/44	2079
MP-508B	10/44	2087
MP-509:1	07/45	3358
MP-509B	07/45	3362
MP-510:1	07/45	3359
MP-510B	07/45	3363
MP-511:1	07/45	3360
MP-511B	07/45	3364
MP-512:1	07/45	3361
MP-512B	07/45	3365

EMC/EMD
NW2

Alco-GE
RS-2

Baldwin
DS-4-4-1000
DRS-4-4-1500

After the war, the MoPac found itself with an aging fleet of steamers that were, in the minds of the motive power folks, outdated and unable to accomplish railroad tasks with the efficiency that was being demanded. Just before and during the war, the Sedalia shops had rebuilt the 1901-class 2-8-4 Berkshires into 2101-class 4-8-4 Northerns. Baldwin had delivered 15 2201-class Northerns in 1943, and the acquisition of steam power was over for the MoPac. Diesels were here to stay and the sentence of doom fell upon the steam-powered machine.

The late 1940's was a time of overall expansion in the post-war economy, and the railroad turned to the diesel manufacturers for a variety of engines to cover their motive power needs. The MoPac went back for many of the same models they had purchased before the war, but in ever-increasing quantities.

The need for more and more switchers to handle terminal chores sent the MoPac looking for additional small locomotives, and they went to their favorite three builders; EMD, Baldwin, and Alco. The Baldwins came first, as the MoPac's final two VO1000's (STLB&M-9160-9161) arrived in April, 1946. These two rounded out the VO1000 total at 14 for the MoPac and its subsidiaries.

In May, 1946 another single switcher arrived in the MoPac family, as the STLB&M acquired an Alco S-2 (STLB&M-9159).

The next switcher order was for another subsidiary, the FWB, which purchased a single NW2 (FWB-2) in October, 1946. The first NW2's had come for the MoPac before the war when two single-unit purchases added MP-9104 and MP-9105 to the roster in September, 1939 and August, 1940, respectively. One more came during the war (MP-9106). Another NW2 order was placed for the T&P, and added 9 NW2's (T&P-1000-1008) to the Texas subsidiary's roster. These were built between November, 1946 and February, 1947, and most lived a long life, operating on the MoPac system for nearly 25 years.

The final switcher group for 1947 was three more S-1's for the NO&LC (NO&LC-9013-9015). The MoPac's S-1 total would stay at seven units, all

but two of which were for subsidiaries. Though the C&EI would wind up with four S-1's, these would not make it to the day the C&EI flag fell to the MoPac.

As the new decade approached, diversity among the switcher fleet continued to be the rule. In February, 1948 the MoPac received three Baldwin DS-4-4-1000 1,000 horsepower switchers (MP-9120-9122), a new model for the MoPac. These used the 6-cylinder 606SC engine, which Baldwin had recently developed to replace the VO-series power plants in their switcher line. The DS-4-4-1000 is essentially indistinguishable from the S-12, and the MoPac wound up with both on their roster.

In March and April, 1948, the TPMPT received four S-2's (TPMPT-11-14) in two orders to go with their two S-1's. The MoPac went back for more S-2's in mid-1949, which were delivered in three groups, one of which was for the IGN. The first group was for the MoPac (MP-9128-9130), delivered in May and June, 1949. The second group was the IGN pair (IGN-9168-9169), and those were followed closely by the final MoPac pair (MP-9131-9132), delivered in October, 1949, for a grand total of 25 S-2's on the MoPac's roster.

Also in April, 1948 the TPMPT got two RS-2's (TPMPT-21-22), their first roadswitchers. These 1,500 horsepower handsome roadswitchers featured the 12-cylinder 244 engine, and were the first roadswitchers on any piece of MoPac iron, though the C&EI had already purchased four RS-1's. The C&EI units would be long gone by the time C&EI came under MoPac control. Alco in fact was responsible for the creation of what has been termed the ultimate unit - the roadswitcher.

The roadswitcher was born out of the desire of the President of the Rock Island to see the

diesel play a larger role in cost cutting and increased operating efficiency. His intrigue with the diesel locomotive led to the conclusion that there could be a diesel unit with the flexibility of a switcher and yet with the capability to handle mainline road freight assignments. Since the Rock Island had been a good customer in the days of steam, Alco came up with a design to incorporate these ideas into a diesel locomotive.

Alco modified its 1,000 horsepower yard engine by lengthening it by 8 and one half feet, lengthening the wheel base of the trucks and adding a short hood. At the same time the Atlanta and St. Andrews Bay approached Alco with an interest in these roadswitchers. Just as production began it was stalled by the War Production Board, which restricted Alco units to 1,000 horsepower or less and granted General Motors road unit production.

The T&P also got one RS-2 (T&P-1100), which later went to the TPMPT and eventually went to the A&S. It was the T&P's only non-EMD motive power. The Missouri-Illinois also bought one RS-2 (MI-61), which was delivered in November, 1949. The remaining group of RS-2's that fell under MoPac control were those of the A&S, which are covered in detail later.

Meanwhile over at EMD, the shop forces were hard at work on more NW2's for the T&P. An order was placed for eleven units for the T&P

Below: Missouri-Illinois had exactly one RS-2, but it led the way for considerable purchases of RS-3's. In June, 1951, the handsome Alco roadswitcher is working the northbound local 90 at BB Siding, Illinois, while MoPac 2-8-0 72 and motorcar 625 are in the siding running as No. 1 south. *Ray Tobey photo, Joe Collias collection*

(T&P-1009-1019), and two extras, one each for the KO&G (KO&G-1001) and the M-I (MI-51). These rounded out the MoPac NW2 total at 26 units, not counting C&EI's six (C&EI-119-124), three of which went to the L&N after the MoPac-C&EI deal, and three of which stayed on the C&EI.

During this same acquisition period, the folks at Baldwin were cranking out units on a series of orders for more DS-4-4-1000's, the most successful Baldwin switcher with the MoPac. In March, 1949, Baldwin built 11 of this model for the MoPac (MP-9123-9127) and the STLB&M (STLB&M-9162-9167). Another order delivered in March and April, 1950, yielded an additional 11 DS-4-4-1000 switchers (STLB&M-9148-9149 and MP-9133-9141). These 22 units, with the previous three for the MoPac, brought the total to 25 units, a respectable quantity for the old steam builder.

In February, 1949, Baldwin got into the roadswitcher act with the MoPac with four DRS-4-4-1500's for the STLB&M subsidiary (STLB&M-4112-4115). The DRS-4-4-1500 employed the 8-cylinder 608SC engine, and was rated at 1,500 horsepower. Only 32 DRS-4-4-1500's were built in a production run from 1947 to 1950.

The DRS-4-4-1500 was replaced in Baldwin's catalog with the AS-16, which utilized the 608A engine which increased the

Above: T&P bought more NW2's than any other faction of the MoPac, buying 20 over a 2 1/2 year period. The MoPac proper bought only three, and the KO&G, M-I, and FWB each bought a single unit. T&P 1017 is at work in Dallas on July 25, 1963, painted in MoPac's standard blue with the T&P herald. *Louis Marre*

Below: The MoPac took a unique approach to extending the life of their early Alco roadswitcher fleet. RS-2's and RS-3's were rebuilt with EMD prime movers and redesignated "GP12's." At least three of the four RS-2's received the new engines, one of which is the 1062, at Yard Center in Dolton, Illinois in July, 1971. *Paul Hunnell photo, James Holder collection*

horsepower figure by 100, for a total of 1,600 horsepower.

By early 1950, the MoPac began leaning towards EMD power, though Baldwin would deliver four groups of S-12's totaling 40 units. The S-12's would be the last non-EMD switcher power for the MoPac with the exception of two Plymouth switchers for the NO&LC in 1957 and 1961. The MoPac's 40 unit S-12 fleet was the third largest, right behind Pennsylvania Railroad's 87 units and Southern Pacific's 59.

Monongahela's fleet of S-12's was the next largest with 27 units. The S-12's were typically operated well beyond their twentieth birthdays, but on the MoPac a wholesale purge of four-cycle power began in 1962, and the MoPac's S-12's were soon found only in dead lines. The transition to standardization on EMD 2-cycle power had begun.

Between the end of 1945 and early 1950, the MoPac had acquired 2 VO1000's, 22 DS-4-4-1000's and 4 DRS-4-4-1500's from Baldwin for a total of 28 units from the builder at Eddystone, Pennsylvania. EMD had supplied the MoPac's rails with 23 NW2's, while Alco provided three S-1's, nine S-2's and four RS-2's, for a total of 16 units from Schenectady, New York. By late 1950 the orders would nearly all go to EMD, and the other builders would slowly drift into obscurity under piles of SW-series switchers from EMD.

Above: The NW2 was by all accounts a very successful switcher model for EMC and later EMD. There were 1,119 of the model produced for U. S. roads, and another 24 sold in Canada. The MoPac's three along with subsidiaries' 23 add only a paltry sum to the total. They were, however, the predecessor to later switchers that the MoPac would buy in abundance. T&P 1003 is at Dallas in 1950. *R S Plummer photo, Gordon Bassett collection*

EMC NW2   1,000 hp   2 units
TE = 62,655   WT = 250,620
Wheels = 40"   Fuel = 600
Engine: EMD 12-567 V-type 12-cylinder 2-cycle
Min Speed for TE = 5.0 mph
62:15 Gearing   60 mph Max

1st No	2nd No	Built	Build#	Notes & Dispositions
MP-9104	MP-1021	09/39	848	Retired 1968, T-I to EMD
MP-9105		08/40	1084	Retired 1/60, scrapped

EMD NW2   1,000 hp   1 unit
TE = 61,400   WT = 245,600
Wheels = 40"   Fuel = 600
Engine: Two EMD 12-567 V-type 12-cylinder 2-cycle
Min Speed for TE = 5.0 mph
62:15 Gearing   60 mph Max

1st No	2nd No	Built	Build#	Notes & Disposition
MP-9106	MP-1022	08/41	1315	Retired 1968, T-I to EMD

EMD NW2   1,000 hp   3 units
TE = 61,400   WT = 245,600
Wheels = 40"   Fuel = 600
Engine: EMD 12-567 V-type 12-cylinder 2-cycle
Min Speed for TE = 5.0 mph
62:15 Gearing   60 mph Max

1st No	2nd No	3rd No	Built	Build#	Notes & Dispositions
FWB-2	FWB-1020		10/46	3962	Retired 1/73, T-I to EMD on SW1500's
MI-51	MI-1028	MP-1028	07/49	7376	To Big Rock Stone 12/69, r# BRSM-400
KO&G-1001	KO&G-1027		05/49	6672	Retired 11/74, to DuPont, Deepwater, NJ, r# DUP-109

EMD NW2   1,000 hp   20 units
TE = 61,400   WT = 245,600
Wheels = 40"   Fuel = 600
Engine: EMD 12-567 V-type 12-cylinder 2-cycle
Min Speed for TE = 5.0 mph
62:15 Gearing   60 mph Max

1st No	Built	Build#	Notes & Dispositions
T&P-1000	11/46	3963	Retired 1/70, to PNC 1974, to Granite City Steel, r# GCS-1001
T&P-1001	11/46	3964	Retired 1/70, to PNC 1974, to Sahara Coal, r# SC-10
T&P-1002	12/46	4588	Retired 11/71, to Hyman-Michaels, to Upper Merion & Plymouth 1972
T&P-1003	12/46	4589	Retired 4/70, to Birmingham R&L, to Pullman Standard, Bessemer, AL, r# PS-410
T&P-1004	02/47	4590	Retired 11/74, to PNC, scrapped
T&P-1005	02/47	4591	Retired 4/70, to Birmingham R&L to Patapsco & Black River RR, r# P&BR-118
T&P-1006	02/47	4592	Retired 4/70, to Birmingham R&L to Patapsco & Black River RR, r# P&BR-119
T&P-1007	02/47	4593	Retired 9/71, to US Steel Texas Works, r# USS-LM1
T&P-1008	02/47	4594	Retired 9/71, to US Steel Texas Works, r# USS-LM2
T&P-1009	09/48	6581	Retired 11/71, to Hyman-Michaels, to Upper Merion & Plymouth 1972, to Wisconsin Southern
T&P-1010	09/48	6582	Retired 11/74, to PNC 11/74, to Swift, Des Moines, IA, r# SWIF-185, plant taken over by A E Staley
T&P-1011	10/48	6583	Retired 11/74, to PNC 11/74, leased to AMT as PNC-1011
T&P-1012	10/48	6584	Retired 1972, to US Steel Texas Works 6/72, r# USS-LM3
T&P-1013	10/48	6585	Retired 11/74, to McGeorge Construction 11/74, used at Granite Mountain Quarries, Sweet Home, AR, r# GMQ-4743
T&P-1014	05/49	6586	Retired 5/74, to US Steel 5/74, Fairfield, AL, r# USS-18
T&P-1015	05/49	6587	Retired 5/74, to US Steel 5/74, Fairfield, AL, r# USS-19
T&P-1016	05/49	6588	Retired 11/74, to PNC, leased to Illinois Power as PNC-1016
T&P-1017	05/49	6589	Retired 11/74, to Arkansas Louisiana & Missouri, to Olin Kraft, West Monroe, LA
T&P-1018	05/49	6590	Retired 5/74, to US Steel Texas Works, r# USS-LM6
T&P-1019	05/49	6591	Retired 5/74, to US Steel Texas Works, r# USS-LM5

Alco-GE RS-2   1,500 hp   4 units
TE = 61,000   WT = 244,000
Wheels = 40"   Fuel = 1,200
Engine: Alco 244-H V-type 12-cylinder 4-cycle Turbocharged
Min Speed for TE = 9.0 mph
74:18 Gearing   65 mph Max
Rebuilt with EMD 12/567 1,200 hp engine, designated "RS-2m" or "GP12."
After rebuilding (T&P-1061, 1062, and MI-1064):
TE = 60,460   WT = 241,840
Engine: EMD 12-567B V-type 12-cylinder 2-cycle
Min Speed for TE = 12.0
74:18 Gearing   65 mph Max

1st No	2nd No	3rd No	4th No	Built	Build#	Notes
TPMPT-21	TPMPT-956:1	T&P-1061		04/48	75704	Note 1
TPMPT-22	TPMPT-957:1	T&P-1062	MP-1062	04/48	75934	Note 2
T&P-1100	TPMPT-23	TPMPT-958:1	(T&P-1063)	01/49	76633	Note 3
MI-61	MI-960	MI-1064		11/49	77566	Note 4

Note 1: Rebuilt 8/65. Retired 2/73, T-I to GE 1/73
Note 2: Retired 8/67, traded to PNC for F7A DRGW-5684, to Peabody Coal
Note 3: Not rebuilt. Retired 8/67, traded to PNC for F7A DRGW-5694, to
   A&S as A&S-33:2 (replaced wrecked A&S-33:1), r# A&S-1053
Note 4: Rebuilt 1965. Retired 1/73, T-I to GE 1/73

Baldwin DS-4-4-1000   1,000 hp   8 units
TE = 57,450   WT = 229,815
Wheels = 40"   Fuel = 650
Engine: Baldwin 606SC 6-cylinder 4-cycle Turbocharged
Min Speed for TE = 9.0 mph
68:14 Gearing   60 mph Max

1st No	2nd No	Built	Build#	Dispositions
MP-9120	MP-1066	02/48	73582	Scrapped
MP-9121	MP-1067	02/48	73583	Scrapped
MP-9122	MP-1068:1	02/48	73584	Scrapped
MP-9123	MP-1069	03/49	73963	Scrapped
MP-9124	MP-1070	03/49	74090	Scrapped
MP-9125	MP-1071	03/49	74091	Scrapped
MP-9126	MP-1072	03/49	74092	Scrapped
MP-9127	MP-1073	03/49	74093	Scrapped

Baldwin DS-4-4-1000   1,000 hp   6 units
TE = 57,450   WT = 229,815
Wheels = 40"   Fuel = 650
Engine: Baldwin 606SC 6-cylinder 4-cycle Turbocharged
Min Speed for TE = 9.0 mph
68:14 Gearing   60 mph Max

1st No	2nd No	Built	Build#	Dispositions
MP-9133	MP-1074:1	03/50	74765	Scrapped
MP-9134	MP-1075:1	03/50	74766	Scrapped
MP-9135	MP-1076:1	03/50	74767	Scrapped
MP-9136	MP-1077:1	03/50	74768	Scrapped
MP-9137	MP-1078:1	03/50	74769	Scrapped
MP-9138	MP-1079	03/50	74770	Scrapped

Baldwin DS-4-4-1000   1,000 hp   3 units
TE = 59,505   WT = 238,020
Wheels = 40"   Fuel = 650
Engine: Baldwin 606SC 6-cylinder 4-cycle Turbocharged
Min Speed for TE = 9.0 mph
68:14 Gearing   60 mph Max

1st No	2nd No	Built	Build#	Dispositions
MP-9139	MP-1080:1	04/50	74771	Scrapped
MP-9140	MP-1081	04/50	74772	Scrapped
MP-9141	MP-1082:1	04/50	74773	Scrapped

Baldwin DS-4-4-1000   1,000 hp   2 units
TE = 57,450   WT = 229,815
Wheels = 40"   Fuel = 650
Engine: Baldwin 606SC 6-cylinder 4-cycle Turbocharged
Min Speed for TE = 9.0 mph
68:14 Gearing   60 mph Max

1st No	2nd No	Built	Build#	Notes & Dispositions
STLB&M-9148	MP-1083:1	03/50	74763	Scrapped
STLB&M-9149		03/50	74764	Retired 1/62, scrapped

Baldwin DS-4-4-1000   1,000 hp   6 units
TE = 57,450   WT = 229,815
Wheels = 40"   Fuel = 650
Engine: Baldwin 606SC 6-cylinder 4-cycle Turbocharged
Min Speed for TE = 9.0 mph
68:14 Gearing   60 mph Max

1st No	2nd No	Built	Build#	Dispositions
STLB&M-9162	MP-1092:1	03/49	74094	Scrapped
STLB&M-9163	MP-1093:1	03/49	74095	Scrapped
STLB&M-9164	MP-1094:1	03/49	74096	Scrapped
STLB&M-9165	MP-1095:1	03/49	74097	Scrapped
STLB&M-9166	MP-1096:1	03/49	74098	Scrapped
STLB&M-9167	MP-1097:1	03/49	74099	Scrapped

Below: The STLB&M bought two groups of DS-4-4-1000's from Baldwin. The 9165 was part of the first order, which was for six units. Though the DS-4-4-1000 came in both 6-cylinder and 8-cylinder versions, the MoPac's were all the later 6-cylinder version. The blocky Baldwin was idling at Brownsville, Texas in November, 1949. *Harold K Vollrath collection*

Baldwin DRS-4-4-1500   1,500 hp   4 units
TE = 60,550   WT = 242,200
Wheels = 42"   Fuel = 900
Engine: Baldwin 608SC 8-cylinder 4-cycle Turbocharged
Min Speed for TE = 10.5 mph
63:15 Gearing   65 mph Max
T-I to EMD, scrapped

1st No	Built	Build#
STLB&M-4112	02/49	73647
STLB&M-4113	02/49	73648
STLB&M-4114	02/49	73649
STLB&M-4115	02/49	73650

Below: In the MoPac fold only the STLB&M bought Baldwin DRS-4-4-1500's, and only a total of four were purchased in February, 1949. The 4115 is at Brownsville, Texas on May 28, 1956. The DRS-4-4-1500 (which in Baldwin parlence stands for Diesel Roadswitcher-4 axle-4 axle 1500 horsepower) was a fairly rare model, with only 32 produced from 1947 to 1950. *R H Carlson photo, Louis Marre collection*

EMD
E7
E8

Baldwin
DR-4-4-1500

Alco-GE
PA-1
PA-2
PA-3

The war effort had already set the stage for diesel acquisitions, and the MoPac picked up right where they had left off before the war, with the E7. Though EMD was slowly emerging as the dominant builder, the postwar period when the MoPac was ordering units for high-speed cross-country travel yielded an atypical trend. Though the MoPac was ordering substantial quantities of E7's, Baldwin and Alco would share a major slice of the MoPac's motive power pie.

MoPac's first A-B pair (MP-7004 and 7004B) were purchased shortly before the end of the war. MP-7004 and its companion B-unit had ticked off many miles by the time the MoPac went back for more passenger power. The MoPac's motive power people were sufficiently impressed to go back to EMD for more of the graceful E-units. The E7 acquisition was piecemeal, but by the end the MoPac had 32 of the sleek-bodied bulldog-nosed E7's, 24 A-units and eight B-units. The E7 proved to be the most popular E-series model produced by EMD,

with 428 A-units and 82 B-units produced.

The first MoPac order was for 11 units, eight A-units and three B-units, all delivered in February and March, 1947. Four A-units (MP-7005-7006 and MP-7010-7011) and two B-units (MP-7010B-7011B) came for the MoPac. These were very closely followed by a two A-units for the IGN (IGN-7007 and IGN-7012) and a B-unit for the IGN (IGN-7012B). The final two units were a pair of E7A's for the T&P (T&P-2000-2001).

A little later in March, 1947 two more E7A's came for the STLB&M (STLB&M-7008-7009), another six A-units arrived on the T&P (T&P-2002-2007), and in September a final E7A came for the IGN (IGN-7013). No more would arrive until June, 1948, when the MoPac would receive eight A-B pairs (MP-7014-7017 and MP-7014B-7017B). Though the T&P acquired two more in April, 1949 (T&P-2008-2009), there was a surprise in the air in motive power land.

The MoPac tried another builder for passenger power. In January, 1945, Baldwin sent out a 2,000 horsepower A1A-A1A passenger diesel unit. The graceful unit was designed during the war, but wartime restrictions prevented its production. It was the first 2,000 horsepower passenger unit produced after the

war, slightly beating EMD's first E7 of February, 1945. It demonstrated all over North America, and found its way onto MoPac rails in April, 1945. It had performed well over most trackage, but the MoPac trip was plagued with minor electrical problems. Even more disastrous for Baldwin, the unit fell short in comparisons with EMD E-units, running 5 to 10 mph slower in head-to-head competition, and burning more fuel as well. After the MoPac trips, the unit went back to Eddystone for modification. The unit (numbered BLW-2000) and a redesigned sister (BLW-2001) toured over the Texas and Pacific between Dallas and El Paso.

Even with the poor comparisons with E-units, the MoPac went back to Baldwin, this time for a real oddity on the MoPac, the DR-4-4-1500 "babyface" units. From 1947 through 1948, the DR-4-4-1500's came in the babyface car body, a unique and interesting version of the cab unit. Baldwin joined in the fray of competition for streamlined freight units with the DR-4-4-1500, first produced for the Central of New Jersey in 1947 (though on order since 1945). The MoPac bought eight A-units (MP-201-208) and four boosters (MP-201B-204B) during this production period, and put them to work in A-B-A sets. These were the third order for the freight carbody units, behind a New York Central

Opposite page: Graceful T&P E7A 2009 is on the lead of the *Texas Eagle* at Big Spring, Texas in January, 1962. The unit was the last of a 10-unit order for E7A's for the T&P. They later went back for E8's in 1951. The E7 was EMD's most popular E-unit, outselling the E8 by fifty units. There were 428 E7A's and 82 E7B's built between February, 1945 and April, 1949. *Paul Meyer*

Left: E8A 42 was bought second-hand from the Boston & Maine in 1962, and is making a station stop at Lee's Summit, Missouri. The date is May 19, 1969, and the E has the eastbound *Missouri River Eagle*, train 16, well in hand. *James EuDaly*

Above: The usefulness of the E's comes to an end for the MoPac on May 1, 1971, "Amtrak Day," as E8A 40 makes its first station stop at Sedalia, Missouri pulling Amtrak passengers. Yesterday, the ticket read MoPac, and for some, life will never be the same. The *National Limited* will soon be in St. Louis, and already is a shadow of its former self. *Alan Bradley*

Below: E8A 39 was one of four E8A's bought by the MoPac in June, 1950. It is now working for Amtrak, at the headend of number 15 at Jefferson City, Missouri on July 31, 1971. *James Holder photo, J Harlen Wilson collection*

order. The MoPac and NYC units were redesigned from the CNJ units to cure air intake and electrical problems. All were built in November and December, 1948, and began their short and spotty careers on the MoPac.

Interestingly, because the MoPac ordered their DR-4-4-1500's with steam generators, they were three feet longer than CNJ's or NYC's babyface units. There were 32 "babyface" DR-4-4-1500's built, and the remainder of the DR-4-4-1500's were "sharknose" units, very similar to the RF-16 sharks. The MoPac's were the last babyface units, and another order for the freight carbody units from Baldwin was not received until the Pennsylvania Railroad ordered their sharks in the fall of 1948.

The DR-4-4-1500's came with 63:15 gearing, making them good for 65 mph. These units would not m-u with any other power, and so were destined to be the odd-men-out. They were in service for less than 10 years, and then were traded in on RS-11's and scrapped. They didn't even make it to the 1962 4-cycle purge. The DR-4-4-1500's were quite simply unreliable locomotives. They were plagued with poor and haphazard wiring and plumbing, and had chronic air intake problems. They also experienced a high percentage of piston and turbocharger failures, as was typical of early 608SC powered units. Their Westinghouse trucks and traction motors would continue to roll off the miles under the RS-11's, but their carbodies would become another pile of scrap metal.

The next move was to go to Alco, which had introduced the PA design in September, 1946. The PA design was one of the most impressive passenger locomotives in dieseldom, and has been claimed by many to represent the zenith of cab-unit appearance. Personal preferences aside, it can be said that the PA-series was at the very least a successful model for Alco, with a total of 247 A-units and 47 B-units produced over a seven-year period. The PA utilized the 16-cylinder 244 engine, with the PA-1 generating 2,000 horsepower, while the PA-2's and PA-3's produced 2,250 horsepower.

The MoPac started with an order for eight PA-1's (MP-8001-8008), delivered in October and November, 1949. One month earlier, in September, 1949, Baldwin built their last steam locomotive, a C&O 2-6-6-2 mallet numbered 1309, an engine essentially from a 1910 design. After this first group of PA's, the MoPac almost immediately went back for four more, but this time it was PA-2's, as the new model had supplanted the previous PA-1. The first four PA-2's came in May and June, 1950, with two for the MoPac (MP-8009-8010) and two for subsidiary IGN (IGN-8011-8012). The IGN units were the only PA's for any of the subsidiaries.

At the same time, an order was placed with EMD for four E8's (MP-7018-7021), which by now had replaced the E7 in EMD's catalog. The E8 utilized two 567B engines, for a total horsepower rating of 2,250. A total of 421 A-units were built between August, 1949 and December, 1953, a production run of just over four years. A fifth E8 was added to the MoPac roster later, an ex Boston and Main unit.

The E8 was a significantly different locomotive than the previous members of the E-series, such as the immediate predecessor, the E7. The most noticeable difference between the E7 and the E8 was the repositioning and placement of the engine and generators. In the E7, both engines or prime movers faced the rear of the locomotive, with the main generator end facing forward. This is similar to Alco's DL-series cab units. In the E8, the front of each prime mover faced each other in the middle of the carbody, and both were farther forward, leaving significant space for steam generator equipment. A separating bulkhead allowed the steam generator compartment to utilize its own air and maintain its own temperature control.

An accessory rack in the E8 made this possible, with the oil cooler, coolant expansion tank, oil filter tank, strainer housing, load regulator, and air compressor all located together at the front of the engine room. On the E7's, these items were scattered around the perimeter of the engine compartment, filling up any extra space.

Also in the E8, the main generator blower and the auxiliary generator and traction motor blower were located atop the main generator at the rear of the engine compartment, whereas they were in front of and behind the prime movers in the E7's. The carbody air systems were also significantly different.

The trucks under all the E-units are essentially identical Blomberg A-1-A passenger trucks. Due to the design of the cooling system through the hollow bolster of the A-1-A truck, the center axle could not be powered. The riding qualities of the Blomberg passenger truck are excellent, and only get better at high speeds. The 52:25 gearing was the fastest for the E's, resulting in a top speed of 117 mph. The MoPac's E7's 7004 and 7004B were originally geared with the 52:25 gears, the rest of the E's were geared at a higher ratio (the higher the gear reduction the lower the top speed).

By the middle of 1951, the MoPac was again in need of passenger power, as steam was slowly being relegated to secondary trains and branch lines. It was back to Alco again for more PA's, though the E-unit cumulative total would always stay ahead of the PA total. Again it was PA-2's that were in the catalog, as the PA-3 would not be introduced until April, 1952. This time the order added six to the roster (MP-8013-8018), built in May and June, 1951. All the PA's were geared for 100 mph, but in the late 1950's the MoPac redesignated their maximum speed as 98 mph, putting them in line with the EMD passenger power.

Below: One of MoPac's most bizarre purchases was the acquisition of four A-B-A sets of Baldwin DR-4-4-1500 in the babyface style carbody in late 1948. The units would not m-u with other power, and were destined for a short lifetime. In January, 1953, a typical A-B-A lashup of the Baldwins leads a freight eastbound along the Missouri River at Jefferson City, Missouri. *George Drake, Sr photo, Kevin EuDaly collection*

Within two months the T&P was getting E8's, all A-units. Built in two groups of four units (T&P-2010-2017), all were delivered in August, 1951. The MoPac also picked up a used E8 in 1962 from the Boston & Maine (MP-42). Though the E8's would last over twenty years, the competition's PA's would barely last a dozen years. Competition being what it was, the MoPac consistently ordered from a variety of builders during this era.

By early 1952, the motive power department ordered more of the handsome Alcos. By this time PA-3 production was in place, and the MoPac went for three orders of four units and a final order of six units, for a total of 18 more of the attractive passenger units from Alco (MP-8019-8036). They came between May and September, 1952 and brought the PA total to 36 for the MoPac.

If the length of time a class of motive power is in service is an indicator of that model's worth, the E-units have to be the best passenger locomotives ever built. A high percentage of the MoPac's twin-engine E-units maintained careers well over 20 years. By the time they were retired they had racked up over five million miles. EMD's competition came nowhere close, most lasting only 12 or 15 years. A few of the MoPac's PA's ran for about 17 years.

It is undeniable that through the 1940's there was a revolution occurring on America's railroads as long-haul passenger operations and schedules were being drastically altered with the economy of diesel-powered trains. The diesel was first used to supplant yard switchers. Slowly, however, motive power departments began to visualize the economy that could be attained as steam was replaced. Passenger power was the first to switch over, as the public relations people could quickly capitalize on the "modern" aspect of the diesel-electric. Once the ball started rolling, the freight departments woke up to dieseldom, and a little time and money later steam was gone.

Above: The Missouri Pacific bought two batches of PA-2's, the first for four units and the second for six units. Two of the first group went to the IGN, while two were for the MoPac itself. One of the MoPac pair leads the *Southerner* out of Little Rock for its overnight run to St. Louis in mid-1960. *J Parker Lamb* **Below: A trio of glamour girls, two E7's and a PA, lead a westbound out of Union Station, St. Louis in 1959. The 7016 was part of an order for four A-B pairs delivered in June, 1948 for the MoPac.** *J Parker Lamb*

Right: PA 8012 was one of two PA-2's bought for the IGN in June, 1950. Though the PA's had a distinctive character, they lacked the more graceful curves of the E-units. They also lacked in the sales department; only 247 A-units (PA-1, PA-2, and PA-3) were built over a production run that lasted just over seven years. Only 28 were PA2's. The 8012 peeks out of the garage at Pueblo, Colorado on June 12, 1960. *Bob Malinoski*

Opposite page top: E8A 37 is running past Sheffield Tower in Kansas City, Missouri in February, 1971 with train 16. Amtrak operations will begin soon. *John Wegner*

Opposite page bottom: E8A 41 is ready to polish the rail at Houston, Texas in April, 1968. The 41 was the last E-unit purchased new by the MoPac. A final E8 was added when the MoPac purchased an A-unit from the Boston & Maine and numbered it 42. *Ralph Back*

Below: In a scene that defies all principles of the usual luck at trackside, a freight led by F7A 899 pulls by T&P E8A 36 on train 22. Wings overhead complete the scene at Dallas, Texas on May 11, 1969. The graceful E has but eight months left until retirement, when her shining hulk will become another ledger entry at a scrap dealer. *Steve Patterson*

EMD E7A 2,000 hp 10 units
TE = 53,750   WT = 322,670 (215,100 on powered wheels)
Wheels = 36"   Fuel = 1,200
Engine: Two EMD 12-567A V-type 12-cylinder 2-cycle
Min Speed for TE = 30.0 mph
55:22 Gearing   98 mph Max
Later regeared to 57:20   85 mph Max
Equipped with steam generators

1st No	2nd No	Built	Build#	Notes & Dispositions
T&P-2000:1	T&P-1	03/47	3767	Scrapped, 03/67
T&P-2001:1	T&P-2	03/47	3768	Scrapped, 03/67
T&P-2002	T&P-3	03/47	3936	Scrapped, 01/68
T&P-2003	T&P-4	03/47	3937	Scrapped, 11/68
T&P-2004	T&P-5	03/47	3938	Scrapped, 08/68
T&P-2005	T&P-6	03/47	3939	Scrapped, 08/68
T&P-2006	T&P-7	03/47	3940	T-I to EMD 01/69
T&P-2007	T&P-8	03/47	3941	Scrapped, 08/69
T&P-2008	T&P-9	04/49	8464	Scrapped, 08/68
T&P-2009	T&P-10	04/49	8465	Scrapped, 08/67

EMD E7 2,000 hp 22 units
TE = 55,500 (A-units) 54,020 (B-units)
WT = 329,560 (A-units) (222,000 on powered wheels)
320,820 (B-units) (216,080 on powered wheels)
Wheels = 36"   Fuel = 1,200
Engine: Two EMD 12-567A V-type 12-cylinder 2-cycle
Min Speed for TE = 30.0 mph
55:22 Gearing   98 mph Max
Equipped with steam generators
MP-7004 A & B geared 52:25 with 117 mph max, regeared 55:22, 98 mph Max

1st No	2nd No	Built	Build#	Notes & Dispositions
MP-7004	MP-13	09/45	2895	Scrapped
MP-7004B	MP-13B	09/45	2896	Scrapped
MP-7005	MP-14	02/47	3762	Scrapped
MP-7006	MP-15:1	03/47	3763	Scrapped
IGN-7007	MP-16:1	03/47	3766	Scrapped
STLB&M-7008	MP-17:1	03/47	3887	Scrapped
STLB&M-7009	MP-18:1	03/47	3888	Scrapped
MP-7010	MP-19:1	02/47	3758	Scrapped
MP-7010B	MP-14B	02/47	3760	Scrapped
MP-7011	MP-20:1	02/47	3759	Retired 8/67, to PNC, to L&N-754
MP-7011B	MP-15B	02/47	3761	Scrapped
IGN-7012	MP-21:1	03/47	3764	Retired 8/67, to PNC, to L&N (parts)
IGN-7012B	MP-16B	03/47	3765	Scrapped
IGN-7013	MP-22:1	09/47	4795	T-I to EMD
MP-7014	MP-23:1	06/48	5443	Retired 5/70, T-I to EMD
MP-7014B	MP-17B	06/48	5447	Scrapped
MP-7015	MP-24:1	06/48	5444	Retired 1968-1970, T-I to EMD
MP-7015B	MP-18B	06/48	5448	Scrapped
MP-7016	MP-25:1	06/48	5445	Scrapped
MP-7016B	MP-19B	06/48	5449	Scrapped
MP-7017	MP-26:1	06/48	5446	Retired 1968-1970, T-I to EMD
MP-7017B	MP-20B	06/48	5450	Scrapped

Baldwin DR-4-4-1500 1,500 hp 12 units
TE = 63,100 (A-units) 61,965 (B-units)
WT = 252,400 (A-units) 247,860 (B-units)
Wheels = 42"   Fuel = 1,200
Engine: Baldwin 608SC 8-cylinder 4-cycle Turbocharged
Min Speed for TE = 10.5 mph
63:15 Gearing   65 mph Max, equipped with steam generators
Retired 9/57, scrapped 9/59, trucks and traction motors to RS-11's 4601-4612

1st No	Built	Build#
MP-201:1	11/48	73734
MP-201B	11/48	73742
MP-202:1	11/48	73736
MP-202B	11/48	73743
MP-203:1	12/48	73738
MP-203B	12/48	73744
MP-204:1	12/48	73740
MP-204B	12/48	73745
MP-205:1	11/48	73735
MP-206:1	11/48	73737
MP-207:1	12/48	73739
MP-208:1	12/48	73741

Alco-GE PA-1 2,000 hp 8 units
TE = 52,620   WT = 315,730 (210,490 on powered wheels)
Wheels = 40"   Fuel = 1,200
Engine: Alco 244-C V-type 16-cylinder 4-cycle Turbocharged
Min Speed for TE = 23.0 mph
60:23 Gearing   100 mph Max
Equipped with steam generators

1st No	2nd No	Built	Build#	Notes & Dispositions
MP-8001:1	MP-44	10/49	77503	Retired 1966, T-I to EMD
MP-8002:1	MP-45	10/49	77504	Retired 1966, T-I to EMD
MP-8003:1	MP-46	10/49	77505	Retired 1966, T-I to EMD
MP-8004:1	MP-47	10/49	77506	Retired 1966, T-I to EMD
MP-8005:1	MP-48	11/49	77507	Retired 1966, T-I to EMD
MP-8006:1	MP-49	11/49	77508	Retired 1964-1965, to PNC
MP-8007:1	MP-50	11/49	77509	Retired 1964-1965, to PNC
MP-8008	MP-51	11/49	77510	Retired 1964-1965, to PNC

Alco-GE PA-2 2,250 hp 4 units
TE = 52,600   WT = 315,570 (210,380 on powered wheels)
Wheels = 40"   Fuel = 1,200
Engine: Alco 244-C V-type 16-cylinder 4-cycle Turbocharged
Min Speed for TE = 21.0 mph
60:23 Gearing   100 mph Max
Equipped with steam generators

1st No	2nd No	Built	Build#	Notes & Dispositions
MP-8009	MP-52	05/50	78135	Retired 1964-1965, to Chandeysson Electric
MP-8010	MP-53	05/50	78136	Retired 4/65, to PNC
IGN-8011	MP-54	06/50	78137	Retired 1966, T-I to EMD
IGN-8012	MP-55	06/50	78138	Retired 4/65, to Chandeysson Electric

Alco-GE PA-2 2,250 hp 6 units
TE = 52,800   WT = 316,800 (211,200 on powered wheels)
Wheels = 40"   Fuel = 1,200
Engine: Alco 244-C V-type 16-cylinder 4-cycle Turbocharged
Min Speed for TE = 21.0 mph
60:23 Gearing   100 mph Max
Equipped with steam generators

1st No	2nd No	Built	Build#	Notes & Dispositions
MP-8013	MP-56	05/51	78734	Retired 1966, T-I to EMD
MP-8014	MP-57	05/51	78735	Retired 5/64, to Chandeysson Electric
MP-8015	MP-58	06/51	78736	Retired 1966, T-I to EMD
MP-8016	MP-59	06/51	78737	Retired 4/65, to PNC
MP-8017	MP-60	06/51	78738	Retired 5/64, to Chandeysson Electric
MP-8018	MP-61	06/51	78739	Retired 1966, to EMD

Alco-GE PA-3 2,250 hp 18 units
TE = 53,180   WT = 319,050 (212,700 on powered wheels)
Wheels = 40"   Fuel = 1,200
Engine: Alco 244-D V-type 16-cylinder 4-cycle Turbocharged
Min Speed for TE = 21.0 mph
60:23 Gearing   100 mph Max
Equipped with steam generators

1st No	2nd No	Built	Build#	Notes & Dispositions
MP-8019	MP-62	05/52	79042	Retired 5/64, to Chandeysson Electric
MP-8020	MP-63	05/52	79043	Retired 5/64, to Chandeysson Electric
MP-8021	MP-64	06/52	79044	Retired 4/65, to PNC
MP-8022	MP-65	06/52	79045	Retired 5/64, to Chandeysson Electric
MP-8023	MP-66	06/52	78208	Retired 5/64, to Chandeysson Electric
MP-8024	MP-67	06/52	78209	Retired 5/64, to Chandeysson Electric
MP-8025	MP-68:1	06/52	78210	Retired 5/64, to Chandeysson Electric
MP-8026	MP-69:1	06/52	78211	Wore Jenks blue as MP-8026. Retired 5/64, to Chandeysson Electric
MP-8027	MP-70:1	07/52	78957	Retired 5/64, to Chandeysson Electric
MP-8028	MP-71:1	07/52	78958	Retired 4/65, to PNC
MP-8029	MP-72:1	07/52	78959	Retired 5/64, to Chandeysson Electric
MP-8030	MP-73:1	08/52	78960	Retired 4/65, to PNC
MP-8031	MP-74:1	08/52	80045	Retired 5/64, to Chandeysson Electric
MP-8032	MP-75:1	08/52	80046	Wore Jenks blue as MP-8032. Retired 4/65, to PNC
MP-8033	MP-76:1	08/52	80047	Retired 5/64, to Chandeysson Electric
MP-8034	MP-77:1	08/52	80048	Retired 5/64, to Chandeysson Electric
MP-8035	MP-78:1	08/52	80049	Retired 1966, T-I to EMD
MP-8036	MP-79:1	09/52	80050	Retired 1966, T-I to EMD

EMD E8A   2,250 hp   4 units
TE = 55,950   WT = 332,220 (223,810 on powered wheels)
Wheels = 36"   Fuel = 1,200
Engine: Two EMD 12-567B V-type 12-cylinder 2-cycle
Min Speed for TE = 30.0 mph
55:22 Gearing   98 mph Max
Equipped with steam generators
T-I to EMD on GP38-2's

1st No	2nd No	Built	Build#	Notes & Dispositions
MP-7018	MP-38	06/50	8635	Retired 1/72, scrapped
MP-7019	MP-39	06/50	8636	Retired 5/72, scrapped
MP-7020	MP-40	06/50	8637	Retired 5/72, to Pielet, scrapped
MP-7021	MP-41	06/50	8638	Retired 5/72, scrapped

EMD E8A   2,250 hp   9 units
TE = 55,870   WT = 335,270 (223,510 on powered wheels)
Wheels = 36"   Fuel = 1,200
Engine: Two EMD 12-567B V-type 12-cylinder 2-cycle
Min Speed for TE = 21.5 mph
57:20 Gearing   85 mph Max
Equipped with steam generators
"Straight" passenger style pilot
B&M-3821 had   WT = 332,220 and TE of 55,360
Scrapped

1st No	2nd No	Built	Build#	Notes & Dispositions
B&M-3821	MP-42	01/50	9088	Bought from Boston & Maine 06/62. Retired 1972, T-I to EMD on GP38-2's
T&P-2010	T&P-30	08/51	14548	Retired 3/70, T-I to EMD on SD40's
T&P-2011	T&P-31	08/51	14549	Retired 4/69, T-I to GE on U30C's
T&P-2012	T&P-32	08/51	14557	Retired 4/69, T-I to GE on U30C's
T&P-2013	T&P-33	08/51	14558	Retired 3/70, T-I to EMD on SD40's
T&P-2014	T&P-34	08/51	11584	Retired 4/69, T-I to GE on U30C's
T&P-2015	T&P-35	08/51	11585	Retired 3/70, T-I to EMD on SD40's
T&P-2016	T&P-36	08/51	11586	Retired 1/70, T-I to EMD on SD40's
T&P-2017	T&P-37	08/51	11587	Retired 1/70, T-I to EMD on GP38-2's

Top : For E8A 36, the only remnant of the T&P name resides in the heralds on the locomotive's flank and nose which read "Texas Pacific lines." She's covered some miles by the time this photograph was taken on march 13, 1965 at Kansas City, Missouri. *Joe McMillan*

Above: PA-1 8001 has just come off Alco's shop floor in October, 1949, the first of 36 PA's for the MoPac. The MoPac only bought A-units. *Charlie Duckworth collection*

Below: Forty-five hundred horsepower of new Baldwin muscle poses for the Baldwin company photographer outside the shops in December, 1948. After a short and spotty career, they'll all be cut up, a relief to the crews that had to operate them. Their trucks and traction motors would run off more miles under RS-11's. *Charlie Duckworth collection*

EMD
F3
"F5"
F7
BL2

Alco-GE
FA-1
FA-2
FPA-2

Opposite page top: T&P F7A 882 leads three more F-units and a GP18 through San Marcos, Texas on March 13, 1971. The only outward indication that this is a T&P unit is small sublettering beneath the buzz saw on the locomotive side. *Ralph Back*

Opposite page bottom: MoPac F7A 813 swings around a curve at Van Buren, Arkan-sas leading an A-B-B-A lashup of F-units in November, 1963. *Louis Marre*

Above: The T&P bought more F7's than any other first generation diesel, and T&P-1913 is the third number the lead unit has worn. She leads 1921 and 1869, all T&P units, through Alexandria, Louisiana on March 17, 1973. *Glenn Anderson*

Below: The "F5" was the rarest carbody freight unit on the MoPac, though it was externally identical to later F7's. The "F5" was simply an F3 with F7 electrical gear and traction motors; "F5" was only a nickname. The first IGN "F5" sweeps around the curve at North Little Rock on September 10, 1961 trailed by an F7 and three FA's. *Louis Marre*

One can quickly get an idea of the progressiveness of a particular railroad's motive power department by looking at the initial large orders of diesels. If those first orders were early E's, FT's and the first F-units, it can be conjectured that the railroad replaced steam rather early, if it was later F's and "geeps," they probably were on the later side of dieselization. The MoPac falls partly in between, as they ordered quite a few early units, but really got in gear when they went looking for freight units in the late 1940's.

The motive power purchases in the early diesel years were dependent on three main factors; the age of the steam fleet, the desire of the management staff to begin the transition, and the financial posture making diesel purchases possible. The MoPac had a relatively old fleet of steamers, having come through financial difficulties during the depression and the war. Eastern roads in Appalachia hung on to steam much longer than the Midwestern roads, mainly because of the cheap and abundant sources of coal for their steam power.

While the Chesapeake and Ohio had Lima working on their massive H-8 Class Allegheny 2-6-6-6's, the MoPac was quietly ordering F3's. Over the course of only nine months, the F3 became the MoPac's most abundant diesel power, easily outnumbering every model ordered over the previous ten years.

The acquisition of the F3's began the replacement of steam for freight service at a previously unparalleled pace. The MoPac purchased four groups of F3's, two for the MoPac

Above: Brand new Alco's pose outside the shop at Schenectady, New York before delivery in May, 1950. FA-1 324 poses with FB-1 322B and another FA-1 in overcast spring light. The MoPac bought a surprising number of the FA series engines, buying FA-1's, FA-2's, and FPA-2's, as well as FB-1 and FB-2 B-units. The 324 was part of their second order for the freight Alco's. *Alco photo, Charlie Duckworth collection*

Below: MoPac F7A 800 swings through Pollock, Louisiana with a northbound freight in mid-summer, 1969. The tenacious F-unit has little time left. *Glenn Anderson*

proper and two for subsidiaries IGN and STLB&M. The first group delivered arrived in November, 1947, and was composed of 18 units, 12 A-units (MP-513-524) and six B-units (MP-513B-518B). Designed to operate as A-B-A sets, the units immediately began their duties of hauling freight across the MoPac. And haul it they did.

The F3 was a popular model for EMD, generating sales of 1,111 A-units and 696 B-units for a total of 1,807 units. They used the familiar 16-cylinder 567B engine, and generated 1,500 horsepower. An A-B-A set like the MoPac was using resulted in a 4,500 horsepower total, which was excellent for the early diesel years.

The second group of F3's were acquired for the IGN and the STLB&M. The IGN got two A-B-A sets (IGN-525-528 and 525B-526B), and the STLB&M got 12 A-units (STLB&M-529-540). But before more F3's arrived the motive power people turned to Alco again, this time for FA-1's.

As EMD began selling the socks off their new line of freight engines, other builders were trying to keep pace from a development viewpoint. The FA was Alco's answer to EMD's F-units, and was powered with a 12-cylinder 1,500 horsepower 244 engine. Though they were obviously playing catch-up with regards to EMD's FT of nearly a decade before, the FA came out only six months after the F3. The two builders were nearly on a par, and competition at this point was stiff.

By 1939 Alco had realized the need for a freight locomotive that would provide competition to the FT. The 539 engine that was in use at the time was expanded into an 8-cylinder turbocharged engine, but still could only deliver 1,350 horsepower. A design program resulted in the 241 prime mover, however, this was not until the war was over, in about late 1945.

Meanwhile, the 244 engine was being developed, and was put in the FA's, essentially resulting in the 241 and 244 programs overlapping significantly. By the time the 241 was put

in the three "Black Maria" units, it was simply an "experimental" program; yet another war orphan.

The FA-1 purchase of early 1948 was a significant one, totaling 20 A-units (MP-301-320) and 10 B-units (MP-310B-310B), which like the F3 were designed to be lashed up in A-B-A fashion. The FA's were delivered in March and April, and had only just begun revenue service when the MoPac went to EMD for a truly bizarre beast; the BL2. It has been said that there are many forms of beauty, but ugly is homogenous. For most enthusiasts, the BL2 would fall into the latter category.

In a lot of ways the BL-series, which was comprised of the BL1 demonstrator (later bought by the C&EI) and the BL2 production model, was a tangible predecessor to the GP7. The BL2 is almost a roadswitcher, but still more like an F-unit. In fact, in appearance it is similar to both, a strange hybrid between the cab units of the mid-1940's and the true roadswitcher of the late 1940's and early 1950's. It was not a cross between F-units and geeps, however, as it retained its F-unit carbody structural principles where the carbody carried the structural load, rather than the frame, as on a geep.

There is not a real or identifiable external difference between the BL1 and the BL2's. The BL terminology in the model designation stood for "Branch Line," indicating the purpose for which they were intended. EMD's demonstrator for the BL-series was the BL1, numbered EMD-499 because the EMD project number for the BL-series was 89499.

EMD hesitated to build a roadswitcher until 1949, but produced these altered F3's to yield better rear visibility and decent end platforms for freight switching work. The design was an attempt to make it attractive for suburban and local passenger train service, but attractive is certainly an overstatement for these engines. The MoPac BL2's were not steam generator equipped, and thus were not intended for passenger service at all. Like the F3, it was powered with the 1,500 horsepower 567B engine. Unlike

the F3, its production run was only a 13-month period from April, 1948 through May, 1949. The BL2 was never offered with dynamic brakes, a fact that had little bearing on the MoPac. The MoPac received eight of the BL2's (MP-4104-4111), the first arriving in May, 1948. They lasted 14 years and then were traded in on GP18's. The C&EI got the only BL1, which was supposedly distinguishable by the fact that the carbody intakes on the long hood were open and covered only with chicken wire, whereas on BL2's only the radiator intakes were covered with chicken wire, the carbody intakes being covered with louvers.

In actuality, chicken wire screens were used on production BL2's through May, 1948. Ten-louver sets were utilized on all subsequent production versions, and the earlier MoPac units were retrofitted with the louvers. The BL1 was originally built with an air throttle, never intended to be used in m-u operation with other units. No railroad ordered the air throttle, however, recognizing the limitation of a unit that would not m-u with the rest of the fleet. The air throttle in the demo BL1 left it as a unit that would not m-u with F3's, the road unit of choice at the time. To alleviate this problem, EMD

rebuilt their demo BL1 (EMD-499) to BL2 specifications by exchanging its air throttle to a standard throttle exactly like that of an F3.

The third order for F3's, 12 A-units, all went to the STLB&M (STLB&M-541-552), and brought the F3 total to 48 units in all (40 A-units and 8 B-units). The F3's ushered in EMD dominance in the MoPac's motive power fleet, a dominance that would rule throughout MoPac dieseldom. Prior to the F's, the MoPac had ordered a variety of models from several builders, but the reliability and ease of maintenance on the F-units resulted in EMD's competition slowly being left behind.

Still more F3's came in 1948, the last batch for the MoPac being delivered in August, adding an additional 12 A-units (MP-561-566 and 571-576) and six B-units (MP-561B-566B). These units brought the MoPac F3 total to 66 units, 52 A-units and 14 B-units.

Within months, more units were coming from EMD, but by this time EMD was beginning to further develop their F-series units. By official records the next group of four A-B pairs were F3's. However, they were built between August, 1948 and February, 1949, and came with F7 traction motors, and thus were nicknamed "F5's." Two orders were delivered in September, eight MoPac A-B pairs (MP-567-570 and 567B-570B), as well as a group of eight A-units (IGN-553-560) and four B-units (IGN-553B-556B) for the IGN. Many of the F3's

would later be rebuilt and upgraded to the equivalent of an F7.

In February, 1949, EMD's F7 replaced F3 production, and orders poured in from all over the country. The F7 became EMD's most popular model produced up to that time. In four years and 10 months EMD produced 2,366 A-units and 1,483 B-units. The MoPac was one of the many roads that went for the F7's in quantity, especially for the T&P. By the time F7 production ended, the MoPac had 190 F7's hauling

Above: F7A 580 pauses between runs at North Little Rock on July 10, 1961. The F7A was one of EMD's most popular models ever, with a total of 2,261 sold in the U.S. F7A's and B's combine for a total production figure of 3,849 engines. *Louis Marre*

Below: A T&P eastbound freight rolls through Texmo Junction in Alexandria, Louisiana in March, 1970. The GP35 behind the lead unit represents the next chapter in dieseldom: The second generation. *Glenn Anderson*

freight all over the system. Their F7's were built between September, 1949 and July, 1952.

Nearly every subsidiary wound up with F7's, but it was the T&P who went for the latest carbody units from EMD in quantity. The T&P bought a total of 118 F7's, 83 A-units (T&P-1500-1582) and 35 B-units (T&P-1500B-1534B). Two of the T&P F7A's were equipped with steam generators for passenger service (T&P-1500-1501) and the last four of the B-units were as well (T&P-1531B-1534B). Interestingly, T&P's last F-unit, F7A T&P-1582, would later have the distinction of being the final F-unit on the MoPac's roster in the early 1970's. It served over 23 years, and was finally retired on September 4, 1974. Before its retirement, there was a number game being played out as the MoPac was in the process of renumbering the diesel fleet. To keep from duplicating numbers, GP38-2's MP-859 and MP-932 were among the first of that group to be renumbered, becoming MP-2010 and MP-2083, respectively. This allowed the last two F-units on the roster, MP-1859 and MP-1932, to be renumbered back to their previous numbers again, becoming MP-859 and MP-932. Both units account for their :1 numbers and their :2 numbers, certainly a rare happenstance.

The MoPac also bought 14 F7A's and two F7B's for IGN (IGN-595-606, 617-618 and 595B-596B), 10 F7A's for STLB&M (STLB&M-607-616), and four A's and two B's for the KO&G (KO&G-751-754 and 755B-756B). For the MoPac proper, 26 F7A's and 10

F7B's (MP-577-594, 619-626, 587B-594B and 619B-620B) were purchased, bringing the total to 186 F7's bought new by the MoPac. The other four were two A-B pairs picked up second-hand for the TPMPT in August, 1967, and were originally D&RGW units built in June, 1950. They had been sold by the Rio Grande to Precision, and subsequently were sold to the TPMPT (TPMPT-848-849 and 848B-849B).

As the F7's were arriving from EMD, additional Alco cab units were also being added to the roster. An order for FA-1's was delivered in May and June, 1950, adding 10 A-units and five B-units (MP-321-330 and 321B-325B). These were late FA-1's, and were rated at 1,600 horsepower rather than the 1,500 rating of the previous FA-1's. They lasted 12 years and then were traded in on GP18's.

A year later, in April, 1951, more cab units came from Alco in the form of FA-2's, which had replaced the FA-1 in Alco's line of cab locomotives. The main difference between FA-1's and FA-2's was available space at the rear of the FA-2's for a steam generator. Units that were steam generator equipped were called FPA-2's, the added "P" denoting "passenger." Like late FPA-1's the FPA-2's were 12-cylinder 1,600 horsepower 244 power plants. The FA-2 was two feet longer than the FA-1, which in combination with a general rearrangement in the location of the main air reservoirs and batteries left enough room for a steam generator in the A-units. Those

so equipped were FPA-2's, and though this gave the FA-2 dual service capabilities, few railroads chose steam generator units. The MoPac was one of the few.

The MoPac bought FA-2's through April, 1954, winding up with 102 FA-2-series units before cab unit acquisitions came to a close. The FA-2's came in four main orders all for the MoPac proper, the first being 14 FA-2 A-units (MP-331-344) and five FB-2 B-units (MP-331B-

Above: Alco FA-1 303 and three sister units rest at North Little Rock, awaiting their next assignment on September 10, 1961. The torch is not far off. *Louis Marre*

Below: A pair of T&P F7A's on a caboose hop idle their time away at Monahans, Texas in the warm sun of a cool winter's day in January, 1962. The T&P bought 118 F7's, pushing steam from the rails. *Paul Meyer*

335B) delivered in April, 1951. The second order was for 16 FA-2's (MP-345-360), 12 FB-2's (MP-345B-356B), and 12 FPA-2's (MP-361-372) equipped with steam generators. These came to the MoPac in December, 1951 and January, 1952.

The third batch was for one more FPA-2 (MP-373), seven FA-2's (MP-374-380, and 11 FB-2's (MP-370B-380B). These were delivered between June and August, 1953. The final group of Alco cab units was again a mixture of the three types, six FA-2's (MP-381-386), six FPA-2's (MP-387-392), and 12 FB-2's (MP-381B-392B) delivered between January and April, 1954. This brought the totals to 43 FA-2's, 40 FB-2's and 19 FPA-2's.

The FA-2's were the last cab units for the MoPac, after which the roadswitcher would take over sales and become the dominant type of unit on not only the MoPac but on America's railroads in general in a few short years.

EMD F3 1,500 hp 36 units
TE = 57,555 (A-units) 55,935 (B-units)
WT = 230,230 (A-units) 223,740 (B-units)
Wheels = 40" Fuel = 1,200
Engine: EMD 16-567B V-type 16-cylinder 2-cycle
Min Speed for TE = 15.5 mph
62:15 Gearing 65 mph Max

1st No	2nd No	Built	Build#	Notes & Dispositions
MP-513:1	MP-700:1	11/47	4234	Retired 1966, T-I to EMD
MP-513B	MP-790B	11/47	4246	Retired 3/70, T-I to EMD
MP-514:1	MP-701:1	11/47	4236	Retired 1966, T-I to EMD
MP-514B	MP-791B	11/47	4247	Retired 1968-1970, T-I to EMD
MP-515:1	MP-702:1	11/47	4238	Retired 1966, T-I to EMD
MP-515B	MP-792B	11/47	4248	Retired 1968-1970, T-I to EMD
MP-516:1	MP-703:1	11/47	4240	Retired 1966, T-I to EMD
MP-516B	MP-793B	11/47	4249	Retired 1968-1970, T-I to EMD
MP-517:1	MP-704:1	11/47	4242	Retired 1966, T-I to EMD
MP-517B	MP-794B	11/47	4250	Retired 1968-1970, T-I to EMD
MP-518:1	MP-705:1	11/47	4244	Retired 1966, T-I to EMD
MP-518B	MP-795B	11/47	4251	Retired 1968-1970, T-I to EMD
MP-519:1	MP-706:1	11/47	4235	Retired 1966, T-I to EMD
MP-520:1	MP-707:1	11/47	4237	Retired 1966, T-I to EMD
MP-521:1	MP-708:1	11/47	4239	Retired 1966, T-I to EMD
MP-522:1	MP-709:1	11/47	4241	Wore Jenks blue as MP-522. Retired 1966, T-I to EMD
MP-523:1	MP-710:1	11/47	4243	Retired 1966, T-I to EMD
MP-524:1	MP-711:1	11/47	4245	Retired 1966, T-I to EMD
IGN-525	MP-712:1	11/47	4371	Retired 1966, T-I to EMD
IGN-525B	MP-796B	11/47	4375	Retired 1968-1970, T-I to EMD
IGN-526	MP-713:1	11/47	4373	Retired 1966, T-I to EMD
IGN-526B		11/47	4376	T-I to EMD
IGN-527	MP-714:1	11/47	4372	Retired 1966, T-I to EMD
IGN-528		11/47	4374	T-I to EMD
STLB&M-529	MP-715:1	11/47	4359	Retired 1966, T-I to EMD
STLB&M-530	MP-716:1	11/47	4360	Retired 1966, T-I to EMD
STLB&M-531	MP-717:1	11/47	4361	Retired 1966, T-I to EMD
STLB&M-532	MP-718:1	11/47	4362	Retired 1966, T-I to EMD
STLB&M-533	MP-719:1	11/47	4363	Retired 1966, T-I to EMD
STLB&M-534	MP-720:1	11/47	4364	Retired 1966, T-I to EMD
STLB&M-535	MP-721:1	11/47	4365	Retired 1966, T-I to EMD
STLB&M-536	MP-722:1	11/47	4366	Retired 1966, T-I to EMD
STLB&M-537	MP-723:1	11/47	4367	Retired 1966, T-I to EMD
STLB&M-538	MP-724:1	11/47	4368	Retired 1966, T-I to EMD
STLB&M-539	MP-725:1	11/47	4369	Retired 1966, T-I to EMD
STLB&M-540	MP-726:1	11/47	4370	Retired 1966, T-I to EMD

EMD F3A 1,500 hp 12 units
TE = 57,155 WT = 228,620
Wheels = 40" Fuel = 1,200
Engine: EMD 16-567B V-type 16-cylinder 2-cycle
Min Speed for TE = 15.5 mph
62:15 Gearing 65 mph Max
Retired 1966, T-I to EMD, scrapped

1st No	2nd No	Built	Build#
STLB&M-541	MP-727:1	06/48	5459
STLB&M-542	MP-728:1	06/48	5460
STLB&M-543	MP-729:1	06/48	5461
STLB&M-544	MP-730:1	06/48	5462
STLB&M-545	MP-731:1	06/48	5463
STLB&M-546	MP-732:1	06/48	5464
STLB&M-547	MP-733:1	06/48	5465
STLB&M-548	MP-734:1	06/48	5466
STLB&M-549	MP-735:1	06/48	5467
STLB&M-550	MP-736:1	06/48	5468
STLB&M-551	MP-737:1	06/48	5469
STLB&M-552	MP-738:1	06/48	5470

Above: STLB&M 549 is ready to pull at Kingsville, Texas on November 9, 1949. The unit is not yet two years old, and as yet has no dents in the plow.
W C Whittaker collection

EMD F3 series 1,500 hp 12 units
TE = 59,780 (A-units) 61,200 (B-units)
WT = 239,130 (A-units) 244,800 (B-units)
Wheels = 40" Fuel = 1,200
Engine: EMD 16-567B V-type 16-cylinder 2-cycle
Min Speed for TE = 15.5 mph
62:15 Gearing 65 mph Max
Equipped with steam generators

1st No	2nd No	Built	Build#	Notes & Dispositions
MP-561:1	MP-765:1	08/48	5417	Retired 1968, scrapped
MP-561B	MP-801B	08/48	5429	Retired 1970-1971, T-I to EMD
MP-562:1	MP-766:1	08/48	5419	Retired 1968, scrapped
MP-562B	MP-802B	08/48	5430	Retired 1968-1970, T-I to EMD
MP-563:1	MP-767:1	08/48	5421	Retired 1968, T-I to GE
MP-563B	MP-803B	08/48	5431	Retired 1968-1970, T-I to EMD
MP-564:1	MP-768:1	08/48	5423	Retired 1968, T-I to GE
MP-564B	MP-804B	08/48	5432	Retired 1970-1971, T-I to EMD
MP-565	MP-769:1	08/48	5425	Retired 1966, T-I to EMD
MP-565B	MP-805B	08/48	5433	Retired 1970-1971, T-I to EMD
MP-566	MP-770:1	08/48	5427	Retired 1966, T-I to EMD
MP-566B	MP-806B	08/48	5434	Retired 1970-1971, T-I to EMD

EMD F3A 1,500 hp 6 units
TE = 57,155 WT = 228,620
Wheels = 40" Fuel = 1,200
Engine: EMD 16-567B V-type 16-cylinder 2-cycle
Min Speed for TE = 15.5 mph
62:15 Gearing 65 mph Max

1st No	2nd No	Built	Build#	Notes & Dispositions
MP-571	MP-790:1	08/48	5418	Retired 2/71, T-I to EMD, scrapped
MP-572:1	MP-791:1	08/48	5420	Retired 1968-1970, T-I to EMD
MP-573:1	MP-792:1	08/48	5422	Retired 1968-1970, T-I to EMD
MP-574:1	MP-793:1	08/48	5424	Retired 1968-1970, T-I to EMD
MP-575:1	MP-794:1	08/48	5426	Retired 1968-1970, T-I to EMD
MP-576:1	MP-795:1	08/48	5428	Retired 1968-1970, T-I to EMD

Alco-GE FA-1 series (FA-1 and FB-1)
1,500 hp   30 units
TE = 58,650 (A-units) 56,250 (B-units)
WT = 234,600 (A-units) 225,000 (B-units)
Wheels = 40"   Fuel = 1,200
Engine: Alco 244 V-type 12-cylinder
4-cycle Turbocharged
Min Speed for TE = 10.5 mph
74:18 Gearing   65 mph Max
T-I to EMD on GP18's MP-400-499, scrapped

1st No	Built	Build#	Notes
MP-301:1	03/48	75719	Retired 1961
MP-301B	03/48	75762	Retired 1961
MP-302:1	03/48	75721	Retired 1961
MP-302B	03/48	75763	Retired 1961
MP-303:1	04/48	75723	Retired 1961
MP-303B	04/48	75764	Retired 1961
MP-304:1	04/48	75725	Retired 1961
MP-304B	04/48	75765	Retired 1961
MP-305:1	04/48	75727	Retired 1961
MP-305B	04/48	75766	Retired 1962
MP-306:1	04/48	75729	Retired 1961
MP-306B	04/48	75767	Retired 1962
MP-307:1	04/48	75731	Retired 1961
MP-307B	04/48	75768	Retired 1961
MP-308:1	04/48	75733	Retired 1961
MP-308B	04/48	75769	Retired 1962
MP-309:1	04/48	75735	Retired 1961
MP-309B	04/48	75770	Retired 1961
MP-310:1	04/48	75737	Retired 1961
MP-310B	04/48	75771	Retired 1962
MP-311:1	04/48	75720	Retired 1961
MP-312:1	04/48	75722	Retired 1961
MP-313:1	04/48	75724	Retired 1961
MP-314:1	04/48	75726	Retired 1961
MP-315:1	04/48	75728	Retired 1961
MP-316:1	04/48	75730	Retired 1961
MP-317:1	04/48	75732	Retired 1961
MP-318:1	04/48	75734	Retired 1962
MP-319:1	04/48	75736	Retired 1962
MP-320:1	04/48	75738	Retired 1961

Alco-GE FA-1 series (continued)

1st No	Built	Build#	Notes & Dispositions
MP-321B	05/50	78130	Retired 1962
MP-322:1	05/50	78120	Retired 1962
MP-322B	05/50	78131	Retired 1962
MP-323:1	05/50	78121	Retired 1962
MP-323B	06/50	78132	Retired 1962
MP-324:1	05/50	78122	Retired 1962
MP-324B	06/50	78133	Retired 1962
MP-325:1	06/50	78123	Retired 1962
MP-325B	06/50	78134	Retired 1962
MP-326:1	06/50	78124	Retired 1962
MP-327:1	06/50	78125	Retired 1962
MP-328:1	06/50	78126	Retired 1962
MP-329:1	06/50	78127	Retired 1961
MP-330:1	06/50	78128	Retired 1962

Alco-GE FA-2 series (FA-2 and FB-2)
1,600 hp   19 units
TE = 60,740 (A-units) 60,200 (B-units)
WT = 242,970 (A-units) 240,600 (B-units)
Wheels = 40"   Fuel = 1,200
Engine: Alco 244-D V-type 12-cylinder
4-cycle Turbocharged
Min Speed for TE = 9.0 mph
74:18 Gearing   65 mph Max
T-I to EMD on GP18's MP-400-499, scrapped

1st No	Built	Build#	Notes & Dispositions
MP-331:1	04/51	78626	Retired 1962
MP-331B	04/51	78659	Retired 1962
MP-332:1	04/51	78627	Retired 1962
MP-332B	04/51	78660	Retired 1962
MP-333:1	04/51	78628	Retired 1961
MP-333B	04/51	78661	Retired 1962
MP-334:1	04/51	78629	Retired 1962
MP-334B	04/51	78662	Retired 1962
MP-335:1	04/51	78630	Wore Jenks blue as MP-335. Retired 1962
MP-335B	04/51	78663	Retired 1962
MP-336:1	04/51	78631	Retired 1962
MP-337	04/51	78632	Retired 1962

Alco-GE FA-2 series (FA-2 and FB-2)
1,600 hp   28 units
TE = 60,390 (A-units) 59,930 (B-units)
WT = 241,540 (A-units) 239,720 (B-units)
Wheels = 40"   Fuel = 1,200
Engine: Alco 244-D V-type 12-cylinder
4-cycle Turbocharged
Min Speed for TE = 9.0 mph
74:18 Gearing   65 mph Max
T-I to EMD on GP18's MP-400-499, scrapped

1st No	Built	Build#	Notes & Dispositions
MP-345	12/51	79447	Retired 1961
MP-345B	12/51	79748	Retired 1961
MP-346:1	12/51	79448	Retired 1961
MP-346B	12/51	79749	Retired 1961
MP-347:1	12/51	79449	Retired 1961
MP-347B	12/51	79750	Retired 1962
MP-348:1	12/51	79450	Retired 1961
MP-348B	12/51	79751	Retired 1961
MP-349:1	12/51	79451	Retired 1962
MP-349B	12/51	79752	Retired 1961
MP-350:1	12/51	79452	Retired 1961
MP-350B	01/52	79753	Retired 1961
MP-351:1	12/51	79453	Retired 1962
MP-351B	01/52	79754	Retired 1961
MP-352:1	12/51	79454	Retired 1961
MP-352B	01/52	79755	Retired 1961
MP-353:1	12/51	79455	Retired 1961
MP-353B	01/52	79756	Retired 1961
MP-354:1	12/51	79456	Retired 1961
MP-354B	01/52	79757	Retired 1962
MP-355:1	12/51	79457	Retired 1962
MP-355B	01/52	79758	Retired 1961
MP-356:1	12/51	79458	Retired 1961
MP-356B	01/52	79759	Retired 1961
MP-357:1	12/51	79459	Retired 1961
MP-358:1	12/51	79460	Retired 1961
MP-359:1	01/52	79461	Retired 1961
MP-360:1	01/52	79462	Retired 1961

Above: FPA-2 388 is barely broken in at St. Louis, Missouri in 1954. The 388 was one of six FPA-2's delivered in March and April, 1954, with steam generators for passenger service. *Joe Collias*

Above: FA-1 318 is ready for service at Van Buren, Arkansas on September 3, 1959. *Louis Marre*

Alco-GE FA-1 series (FA-1 and FB-1)
1,600 hp   15 units
TE = 60,130 (A-units) 60,015 (B-units)
WT = 240,520 (A-units) 240,060 (B-units)
Wheels = 40"   Fuel = 1,200
Engine: Alco 244-C V-type 12-cylinder
4-cycle Turbocharged
Min Speed for TE = 9.0 mph
74:18 Gearing   65 mph Max
T-I to EMD on GP18's MP-400-499, scrapped

1st No	Built	Build#	Notes
MP-321:1	05/50	78119	Retired 1962

Alco-GE FA-2 series (continued)

1st No	Built	Build#	Notes & Dispositions
MP-338	04/51	78633	Retired 1961
MP-339	04/51	78634	Retired 1962
MP-340	04/51	78635	Retired 1962
MP-341	04/51	78636	Retired 1962
MP-342	04/51	78637	Retired 1961
MP-343	04/51	78638	Retired 1962
MP-344	04/51	78639	Retired 1962

Left: F3A 724 leads two more covered wagons on a through freight at Lancaster Yard in Fort Worth, Texas in November, 1963. The tenacious F3 is a bit worn by this late date but still has three more years left in her. *Dan Munson collection*

Below: Well worn F7A 1919 leads a freight through Houston, Texas on February 4, 1973, with only six months left until the scrapper's torch will cut her up. The F-unit is racking up her last miles for the T&P, whose F7A's saw lengthy careers. *Ralph Back*

Opposite page top: A pair of F7A's led by 1856 roll through Pearland, Texas on Santa Fe rails on November 27, 1971. *Ralph Back*

Opposite page bottom: A perfectly symmetrical A-B-A lashup of F7's roll a southbound through Antonia, Louisiana on August 21, 1970. *Glenn Anderson*

Below: The end of the F-unit on the MoPac is near as U30C 17 poses next to T&P F7A 1921 at Alexandria, Louisiana on May 4, 1973. Exactly four months later the last active F-unit, T&P 1932, will be stricken from the roster. An era passes. *Glenn Anderson*

Alco-GE FA-2 series (FA-2 and FB-2)
1,600 hp 31 units
TE = 63,490 (A-units 361-372) 63,530 (A-unit 373)
60,030 (A-units 374-380) 59,790 (B-units)
WT = 253,960 (A-units 361-372) 254,110 (A-unit 373)
240,120 (A-units 374-380) 239,150 (B-units)
Wheels = 40" Fuel = 1,200
Engine: Alco 244-D V-type 12-cylinder 4-cycle Turbocharged
Min Speed for TE = 9.0 mph
74:18 Gearing 65 mph Max
373-380A and 370-380B were equipped with a 244-G engine
361-373 A-units equipped with steam generators (FPA-2's)
Traded in to EMD on GP18's MP-400-499 and scrapped

1st No	2nd No	Built	Build#	Notes
MP-361:1		01/52	79463	Retired 1961
MP-362:1		01/52	79464	Retired 1961
MP-363:1		01/52	79465	Retired 1961
MP-364:1		01/52	79466	Retired 1961
MP-365:1		01/52	79467	Retired 1961
MP-366:1		01/52	79468	Retired 1961
MP-367:1		01/52	79469	Retired 1961
MP-368:1		01/52	79470	Retired 1961
MP-369:1		01/52	79471	Retired 1961
MP-370:1	MP-1370:1	01/52	79707	Retired 1961
MP-370B		06/53	80034	Retired 1962
MP-371:1		01/52	79708	Retired 1961
MP-371B		06/53	80035	Retired 1962
MP-372:1		01/52	79709	Retired 1961
MP-372B		06/53	80036	Retired 1962
MP-373:1		08/53	80008	Retired 1962
MP-373B	MP-1373:1	06/53	80037	Retired 1962
MP-374:1	MP-1374:1	06/53	80001	Retired 1962
MP-374B		06/53	80038	Retired 1962
MP-375:1	MP-1375:1	06/53	80002	Retired 1962
MP-375B		07/53	80039	Retired 1962
MP-376:1	MP-1376:1	07/53	80003	Retired 1962
MP-376B		08/53	80040	Retired 1962
MP-377:1	MP-1377:1	08/53	80004	Retired 1962
MP-377B		08/53	80041	Retired 1962
MP-378:1	MP-1378:1	08/53	80005	Retired 1962
MP-378B		08/53	80042	Retired 1962
MP-379:1	MP-1379:1	08/53	80006	Retired 1962
MP-379B		08/53	80043	Retired 1962
MP-380:1	MP-1380:1	08/53	80007	Retired 1962
MP-380B		08/53	80044	Retired 1962

Above: FA-2 373 is ready to go to work at Van Buren on September 17, 1958. It was part of an order for 20 FA-2's and 10 FB-2's, making ten A-B-A sets. This was standard for the early FA MoPac orders, though later orders were generally split evenly between A-units and B-units. *Louis Marre*

Alco-GE FA-2 series (FA-2 and FB-2)
1,600 hp 24 units
TE = 59,865 (A-units 381-386) 63,480 (A-units 387-392) 59,680 (B-units)
WT = 239,460 (A-units 381-386) 253,930 (A-units 387-392) 238,720 (B-units)
Wheels = 40" Fuel = 1,200
Engine: Alco 244-G V-type 12-cylinder 4-cycle Turbocharged
Min Speed for TE = 9.0 mph
74:18 Gearing 65 mph Max
387-392 A-units equipped with steam generators (FPA-2's)
Retired 1962, T-I to EMD on GP18's MP-400-499, scrapped

1st No	2nd No	Built	Build#	Notes
MP-381:1	MP-1381:1	01/54	80825	
MP-381B		01/54	80913	
MP-382:1	MP-1382:1	02/54	80826	Wore Jenks blue as MP-382
MP-382B		02/54	80914	
MP-383:1	MP-1383:1	02/54	80827	
MP-383B		02/54	81111	
MP-384:1	MP-1384:1	03/54	80828	
MP-384B		03/54	81112	
MP-385:1	MP-1385:1	03/54	80829	
MP-385B		03/54	81113	
MP-386	MP-1386:1	03/54	80830	
MP-386B		03/54	81114	
MP-387	MP-1387:1	03/54	80831	
MP-387B		03/54	81115	
MP-388	MP-1388:1	03/54	80832	
MP-388B		03/54	81116	
MP-389	MP-1389:1	04/54	80833	
MP-389B		04/54	81117	
MP-390	MP-1390:1	04/54	80834	
MP-390B	MP-1390B	04/54	81118	
MP-391	MP-1391:1	04/54	80895	
MP-391B	MP-1391B	04/54	81119	
MP-392	MP-1392:1	04/54	80896	
MP-392B		04/54	81120	

Above: The final FA order was for 12 each FA-2's and FB-2's, delivered between January and April, 1954. The 392 has just arrived on the property at St. Louis in April, the final FPA-2. *MoPac photo, Joe Collias collection*

EMD BL2 1,500 hp 8 units
TE = 55,300 WT = 221,210
Wheels = 40" Fuel = 1,000
Engine: EMD 16-567B V-type 16-cylinder 2-cycle
Min Speed for TE = 15.5 mph
62:15 Gearing 65 mph Max
4104-4107 originally listed as WT = 230,000
Retired 1962, T-I to EMD on GP18's MP-534-549, scrapped

1st No	Built	Build#
MP-4104	05/48	5451
MP-4105	05/48	5452
MP-4106	05/48	5453
MP-4107	05/48	5454
MP-4108	09/48	5455
MP-4109	09/48	5456
MP-4110	09/48	5457
MP-4111	09/48	5458

Above: EMD's first stab at the roadswitcher concept was the BL2, a unique hybrid in appearance. In actuality, they were more like F-units, employing carbody structural principles for their support rather than a frame. The 4109 is brand new at Sedalia, Missouri in September, 1948. *Harold K Vollrath collection*

EMD "F5" 1,500 hp 12 units
TE = 56,560 (A-units) 54,930 (B-units)
WT = 226,250 (A-units) 219,720 (B-units)
Wheels = 40" Fuel = 1,200
Engine: EMD 16-567B V-type 16-cylinder 2-cycle
Min Speed for TE = 15.5 mph
62:15 Gearing 65 mph Max
Retired 1966, T-I to EMD, scrapped

1st No	2nd No	Built	Build#
IGN-553	MP-739:1	09/48	5471
IGN-553B	MP-797B	09/48	5479
IGN-554	MP-740:1	09/48	5473
IGN-554B	MP-798B	09/48	5480
IGN-555	MP-741:1	09/48	5475
IGN-555B	MP-799B	09/48	5481
IGN-556	MP-742:1	09/48	5477
IGN-556B	MP-800B	09/48	5482
IGN-557	MP-743:1	09/48	5472
IGN-558	MP-744:1	09/48	5474
IGN-559	MP-745:1	09/48	5476
IGN-560	MP-746:1	09/48	5478

EMD "F5" 1,500 hp 8 units
TE = 59,780 (A-units) 61,200 (B-units)
WT = 239,130 (A-units) 244,800 (B-units)
Wheels = 40" Fuel = 1,200
Engine: EMD 16-567B V-type 16-cylinder 2-cycle
Min Speed for TE = 15.5 mph
62:15 Gearing 65 mph Max
Equipped with steam generators. Scrapped

1st No	2nd No	Built	Build#	Notes & Dispositions
MP-567	MP-771:1	09/48	5435	Retired 1968, T-I to GE
MP-567B	MP-807B	09/48	5439	Retired 3/71, T-I to EMD on SD40's
MP-568	MP-772:1	09/48	5436	Retired 1968, T-I to GE
MP-568B	MP-808B	09/48	5440	Retired 4/71
MP-569	MP-773:1	09/48	5437	Retired 1968, T-I to GE
MP-569B	MP-809B	09/48	5441	Retired 1968-1970, T-I to GE
MP-570	MP-774:1	09/48	5438	Retired 1966, T-I to EMD
MP-570B	MP-810B	09/48	5442	Retired 1970-1971, T-I to EMD

EMD F7 1,500 hp 36 units
TE = 58,150 (A-units) 58,545 (B-units)
WT = 232,720 (A-units) 234,190 (B-units)
Wheels = 40" Fuel = 1,200
Engine: EMD 16-567B V-type 16-cylinder 2-cycle
Min Speed for TE = 11.0 mph
62:15 Gearing 65 mph Max
Scrapped

1st No	2nd No	Built	Build#	Notes & Dispositions
MP-577:1	MP-796:1	09/49	7996	Retired 1968-1970, T-I to EMD
MP-578	MP-797:1	09/49	7997	Retired 2/69, T-I to EMD
MP-579	MP-798:1	09/49	7972	Retired 1968-1970, T-I to EMD
MP-580	MP-799:1	09/49	7973	Retired 1968-1970, T-I to EMD

EMD F7 (continued)

1st No	2nd No	3rd No	Built	Build#	Notes & Dispositions
MP-581	MP-800:2		09/49	7974	Retired 1968-1970, T-I to EMD
MP-582	MP-801:2		09/49	7975	Retired 1970-1971, T-I to EMD
MP-583	MP-802:2		09/49	7976	Retired 1967-1972
MP-584	MP-803:2		09/49	7977	Retired 1970-1971, T-I to EMD
MP-585	MP-804:2		10/49	7978	Retired 1967-1972
MP-586	MP-805:2		10/49	7979	Retired 3/70, T-I to EMD
MP-587	MP-806:2		10/49	7980	Retired 1968-1970, T-I to EMD
MP-587B	MP-811B		09/49	7988	Retired 1968-1970, T-I to EMD
MP-588	MP-807:2		10/49	7981	Retired 1972
MP-588B	MP-812B		09/49	7989	Retired 1966, T-I to EMD
MP-589	MP-808:2	MP-1808:1	10/49	7982	Retired 5/73, to Pielet
MP-589B	MP-813B		09/49	7990	Retired 2/70, T-I to EMD on SD40's
MP-590	MP-809:2		10/49	7983	Retired 1966, T-I to EMD
MP-590B	MP-814B		10/49	7991	Retired 3/71, T-I to EMD on SD40's
MP-591	MP-810:2		10/49	7984	Retired 3/70, T-I to EMD
MP-591B	MP-815B		10/49	7992	Retired 1967-1972
MP-592	MP-811:2		10/49	7985	Retired 1970-1971, T-I to EMD
MP-592B	MP-816B		10/49	7993	Retired 1966, T-I to EMD
MP-593	MP-812:2		10/49	7986	Retired 1966, T-I to EMD
MP-593B	MP-817B		10/49	7994	Retired 1972
MP-594	MP-813:2		10/49	7987	Retired 1970-1971, T-I to EMD
MP-594B	MP-818B		10/49	7995	Retired 1970-1971, T-I to EMD
IGN-595	MP-814:1		09/49	8010	Retired 1969-1970, T-I to GE
IGN-595B	MP-819B		09/49	8155	Retired 1970-1971, T-I to EMD
IGN-596	MP-815:2		09/49	8011	Retired 02/72, T-I to EMD on GP38-2's
IGN-596B	MP-820B		09/49	8156	Retired 3/70, T-I to EMD
IGN-597	MP-816:1		09/49	8012	Retired 02/72, T-I to EMD on GP38-2's
IGN-598	MP-817:1		09/49	8013	Retired 1971, T-I to GE, scrapped
IGN-599	MP-818:1		09/49	7964	Retired 02/72, T-I to GE on U30C's
IGN-600	MP-819	MP-1819:1	09/49	7965	Retired 5/73, scrapped
IGN-601	MP-820		09/49	7966	Retired 1970-1971, T-I to EMD
IGN-602	MP-821		09/49	7967	Retired 1972

EMD F7A 1,500 hp 16 units
TE = 61,500 (IGN-603-606) 58,180 (STLB&M-607-610) 60,900 (STLB&M-611-614)
57,255 (STLB&M-615-616) 61,500 (IGN-617-618)
WT = 246,000 (IGN-603-606) 232,720 (STLB&M-607-610)
243,610 (STLB&M-611-614) 229,020 (STLB&M-615-616) 246,000 (IGN-617-618)
Wheels = 40" Fuel = 1,200
Engine: EMD 16-567B V-type 16-cylinder 2-cycle
Min Speed for TE = 11.0 mph
62:15 Gearing 65 mph Max
603-606, 611-614, and 617-618 equipped with steam generator. Scrapped

1st No	2nd No	3rd No	Built	Build#	Notes & Dispositions
IGN-603	MP-822	MP-1822:1	09/49	7968	Retired 3/73, T-I to EMD
IGN-604	MP-823		09/49	7969	Retired 1971, T-I to EMD
IGN-605	MP-824	MP-1824:1	09/49	7970	Retired 02/72, T-I to EMD on GP38-2's
IGN-606	MP-825		09/49	7971	Retired 02/72, T-I to EMD on GP38-2's
STLB&M-607	MP-826		10/49	8002	Retired 02/72, T-I to GE on U30C's
STLB&M-608	MP-827		10/49	8003	Retired 1971, T-I to EMD
STLB&M-609	MP-828		10/49	8004	Retired 1/71, T-I to EMD on SD40's
STLB&M-610	MP-829		10/49	8005	Retired 7/72, T-I to EMD on GP38-2's
STLB&M-611	MP-830	MP-1830	10/49	8006	Retired 5/73, T-I to EMD, to Pielet
STLB&M-612	MP-831		10/49	8007	Retired 1971, T-I to EMD
STLB&M-613	MP-832		10/49	8008	Retired 1970-1971, T-I to EMD
STLB&M-614	MP-833		10/49	8009	Retired 1971, T-I to GE
STLB&M-615	MP-834		04/50	8647	Retired 02/72, T-I to EMD on GP38-2's
STLB&M-616	MP-835		04/50	8648	Retired 1966, T-I to EMD
IGN-617	MP-785:1		04/50	8645	Retired 1970-1971, T-I to EMD
IGN-618	MP-786:1		04/50	8646	Retired 2/71, T-I to EMD on SD40's

EMD F7 series 1,500 hp 10 units
TE = 57,810 (A-units) 57,115 (B-units)
WT = 231,250 (A-units) 228,470 (B-units)
Wheels = 40" Fuel = 1,200
Engine: EMD 16-567B V-type 16-cylinder 2-cycle
Min Speed for TE = 11.0 mph
62:15 Gearing 65 mph Max
Scrapped

1st No	2nd No	3rd No	Built	Build#	Notes & Dispositions
MP-619:1	MP-836		03/51	12521	Retired 1972
MP-619B	MP-821B		03/51	12525	Retired 1972

(this class continued on page 56)

Above: F7A 1549 is at the front of an A-B-B-A lashup at North Little Rock on September 10, 1961. *Louis Marre*

Right: MoPac F7A 842 is on the lead of a train at Sargent Yard in Memphis, Tennessee in May, 1969. *Phil Gosney*

Below: KO&G had four F7A's and two F7B's. The 847 is at Denison, Texas on March 26, 1964. *Joe McMillan*

EMD F7 series (continued from page 55)

1st No	2nd No	3rd No	Built	Build#	Notes & Dispositions
MP-620:1	MP-837	MP-1837:1	03/51	12522	Wore Jenks blue as MP-620. Retired 1/73, T-I to EMD
MP-620B	MP-822B		03/51	12526	Retired 1972
MP-621:1	MP-838	MP-1838:1	03/51	12523	Retired 6/73, T-I to GE on U30C's, to Pielet
MP-622:1	MP-839	MP-1839:1	03/51	12524	Retired 1972
MP-623:1	MP-840		03/51	12527	Retired 02/72, T-I to EMD on GP38-2's
MP-624:1	MP-841		03/51	12528	Retired 02/72, T-I to EMD on GP38-2's
MP-625:1	MP-842	MP-1842:1	03/51	12529	Retired 1/73, T-I to EMD
MP-626:1	MP-843		03/51	12530	Retired 1/71, T-I to EMD on SD40's

EMD F7 series   1,500 hp   6 units
TE = 58,000 (A-units) 58,400 (B-units)
WT = 232,000 (A-units) 233,600 (B-units)
Wheels = 40"   Fuel = 1,200
Engine: EMD 16-567B V-type 16-cylinder 2-cycle
Min Speed for TE = 11.0 mph
62:15 Gearing   65 mph Max

1st No	2nd No	Built	Build#	Notes & Dispositions
KO&G-751	T&P-844	04/49	8404	Retired 3/71, T-I to EMD on SD40's
KO&G-752	T&P-845	04/49	8405	Retired 9/66, T-I to EMD
KO&G-753	T&P-846	04/49	8406	Retired 8/64, T-I to EMD on GP28 KO&G-700
KO&G-754	T&P-847	04/49	8407	Retired 8/64, T-I to EMD on GP28 KO&G-701
KO&G-755B	T&P-846B	04/49	8408	Retired 2/72, T-I to EMD, scrapped
KO&G-756B	T&P-847B	04/49	8409	Retired 2/72, T-I to EMD on GP38-2's

EMD F7 series   1,500 hp   4 units
TE = 61,500 (A-units) 61,850 (B-units)
WT = 246,000 (A-units) 241,400 (B-units)
Wheels = 40"   Fuel = 1,200
Engine: EMD 16-567B V-type 16-cylinder 2-cycle
Min Speed for TE = 11.0 mph
62:15 Gearing   65 mph Max
Purchased from PNC 8/67

1st No	2nd No	3rd No	Built	Build#	Notes & Dispositions
DRGW-5684	TPMPT-848	MP-1848:1	06/50	11412	Retired 2/73, T-I to EMD, to Pielet, scrapped
DRGW-5683	TPMPT-848B	MP-848B	06/50	11422	Retired 1/72, T-I to EMD
DRGW-5694	TPMPT-849		06/50	11414	Retired 1972, T-I to EMD
DRGW-5693	TPMPT-849B	MP-849B	06/50	11424	Retired 2/72, T-I to EMD on GP38-2's, scrapped

EMD F7 series   1,500 hp   72 units
TE = 58,150 (T&P-1500-1519), 61,200 (T&P-1520-1536) 58,545 (T&P-1500B-1515B), 57,275 (T&P-1516B-1517B),
58,000 (T&P-1518B-1523B), 61,500 (T&P-1524B-1534B)
WT = 232,600 (T&P-1500-1519), 244,800 (T&P-1520-1536) 234,180 (T&P-1500B-1515B), 229,100 (T&P-1516B-1517B),
232,000 (T&P-1518B-1523B), 246,000 (T&P-1524B-1534B)
Wheels = 40"   Fuel = 1,200
Engine: EMD 16-567B V-type 16-cylinder 2-cycle
Min Speed for TE = 11.0 mph
62:15 Gearing   65 mph Max
T&P-1500-1501 and T&P-1531B-1534B equipped with steam generators

1st No	2nd No	3rd No	4th No	Built	Build#	Notes & Dispositions
T&P-1500	T&P-850:1	T&P-1850		02/49	8428	Equipped with steam generator. Retired 3/73, T-I to EMD, to Pielet, scrapped
T&P-1500B	T&P-850B			02/49	8440	Retired 1967-1973, scrapped
T&P-1501	T&P-851:1	T&P-1851		11/49	8429	Equipped with steam generator. Retired 1971, T-I to EMD
T&P-1501B	T&P-851B			11/49	8441	Retired 1967-1973, scrapped
T&P-1502	T&P-852	T&P-1852		11/49	8430	Retired 1972, T-I to EMD
T&P-1502B	T&P-852B			11/49	8442	Retired 1964-1965, T-I to EMD on GP35's
T&P-1503	T&P-853	T&P-1853		11/49	8431	Retired 7/73, T-I to EMD
T&P-1503B	T&P-853B			11/49	8443	Retired 1970-1971, T-I to EMD
T&P-1504	T&P-854	T&P-1854		11/49	8432	Retired 3/74, T-I to EMD
T&P-1504B	T&P-854B			11/49	8444	Retired 1964-1965, T-I to EMD on GP35's
T&P-1505	T&P-855	T&P-1855		11/49	8433	Retired 3/74, T-I to EMD on SD40-2's MP-3139-3149
T&P-1505B	T&P-855B			11/49	8445	Retired 1970-1971, T-I to EMD
T&P-1506	T&P-856	T&P-1856		11/49	8434	Retired 1972, T-I to GE
T&P-1506B	T&P-856B			11/49	8446	Retired 1964-1965, T-I to EMD on GP35's
T&P-1507	T&P-857	T&P-1857		11/49	8435	Retired 04/73, T-I to EMD
T&P-1507B	T&P-857B			11/49	8447	Retired 1970-1971, T-I to EMD
T&P-1508	T&P-858	T&P-1858		11/49	8436	Retired 1/73, T-I to EMD
T&P-1508B	T&P-858B			11/49	8448	Retired 02/72, T-I to EMD on GP38-2's, scrapped
T&P-1509	T&P-859:1	T&P-1859	T&P-859:2	11/49	8437	Retired 8/74, T-I to EMD
T&P-1509B	T&P-859B			11/49	8449	Retired 1966, T-I to EMD 10/67
T&P-1510	T&P-860	T&P-1860		11/49	8438	Retired 3/74, T-I to EMD
T&P-1510B	T&P-860B			11/49	8450	Retired 1964-1965, T-I to EMD on GP35's
T&P-1511	T&P-861			11/49	8439	T-I to GE 3/68, sold to Precision, scrapped
T&P-1511B	T&P-861B			11/49	8451	Retired 1967-1973, scrapped
T&P-1512	T&P-862	T&P-1862		11/49	8452	Retired 3/73, T-I to EMD
T&P-1512B	T&P-862B			11/49	8460	Retired 1969-1970, T-I to GE
T&P-1513	T&P-863			11/49	8453	Retired 4/71, T-I to EMD on SD40's
T&P-1513B	T&P-863B			11/49	8461	Retired 11/66, scrapped 11/66
T&P-1514	T&P-864	T&P-1864		11/49	8454	Retired 1/74, T-I to EMD on SD40-2's C&EI-3150-3163
T&P-1514B	T&P-864B			11/49	8462	Retired 6/70, T-I to GE
T&P-1515	T&P-865	T&P-1865		11/49	8455	Retired 3/74, T-I to EMD on SD40-2's MP-3139-3149
T&P-1515B	T&P-865B			11/49	8463	Retired 4/73, T-I to GE, to Pielet, scrapped
T&P-1516	T&P-866	T&P-1866		11/49	8456	Retired 7/73, T-I to EMD, to Pielet, scrapped
T&P-1516B	T&P-866B			07/50	11576	Retired 1964-1965, T-I to EMD on GP35's
T&P-1517	T&P-867			11/49	8457	Retired 1964-1965, T-I to EMD on GP35's
T&P-1517B	T&P-867B			07/50	11577	Retired 1964-1965, T-I to EMD on GP35's
T&P-1518	T&P-868			11/49	8458	Scrapped 11/66
T&P-1518B	T&P-868B			03/51	13516	T-I to EMD 9/66
T&P-1519	T&P-869	T&P-1869		11/49	8459	Retired 2/74, T-I to EMD on SD40-2's C&EI-3150-3163
T&P-1519B	T&P-869B			04/51	13517	Retired 3/73, T-I to EMD
T&P-1520	T&P-870			07/50	11559	Retired 1971, T-I to GE
T&P-1520B	T&P-870B			04/51	13518	T-I to EMD 9/66
T&P-1521	T&P-871			07/50	11560	Retired 1964-1965, T-I to EMD on GP35's
T&P-1521B	T&P-871B			04/51	13519	Retired 1967-1973, scrapped
T&P-1522	T&P-872			07/50	11561	Retired 1964-1965, T-I to EMD on GP35's
T&P-1522B	T&P-872B			04/51	13520	Retired 1967-1973, scrapped
T&P-1523	T&P-873			07/50	11562	Retired 1964-1965, T-I to EMD on GP35's

(This class continued on page 58)

EMD F7 series (continued from page 57)

1st No	2nd No	3rd No	Built	Build#	Notes & Dispositions
T&P-1523B	T&P-873B		04/51	13521	Retired 1967-1973, scrapped
T&P-1524	T&P-874		07/50	11563	Retired 1/71, T-I to EMD on SD40's
T&P-1524B	T&P-874B		07/51	14541	Scrapped 3/67
T&P-1525	T&P-875	T&P-1875	07/50	11564	Retired 5/73, T-I to EMD, to Pielet, scrapped
T&P-1525B	T&P-875B		07/51	14542	Retired 1972, T-I to EMD on GP38-2's, scrapped
T&P-1526	T&P-876		07/50	11565	Retired 1964-1965, T-I to EMD on GP35's
T&P-1526B	T&P-876B		07/51	14543	Retired 1964-1965, T-I to EMD on GP35's
T&P-1527	T&P-877		07/50	11566	Retired 1970-1971, T-I to EMD
T&P-1527B	T&P-877B		07/51	14544	Retired 1967-1973, scrapped
T&P-1528	T&P-878		07/50	11567	Retired 1964-1965, T-I to EMD on GP35's
T&P-1528B	T&P-878B		07/51	14545	Retired 1972, T-I to EMD on GP38-2's, scrapped
T&P-1529	T&P-879	T&P-1879	07/50	11568	Retired 1/74, T-I to EMD on SD40-2's C&EI-3150-3163
T&P-1522B	T&P-879B		07/51	14546	Retired 1/73, T-I to EMD
T&P-1530	T&P-880	T&P-1880	07/50	11569	Retired 1/74, T-I to EMD on SD40-2's C&EI-3150-3163
T&P-1530B	T&P-880B		07/51	14547	Retired 1964-1965, T-I to EMD on GP35's
T&P-1531	T&P-881		07/50	11570	Retired 1964-1965, T-I to EMD on GP35's
T&P-1531B	T&P-881B		01/52	15841	Steam generator. Retired 2/73, T-I to EMD
T&P-1532	T&P-882	T&P-1882	07/50	11571	Retired 11/73, T-I to EMD on C&EI SD40-2's
T&P-1532B	T&P-882B		01/52	15842	Steam generator. Retired 1972, T-I to EMD on GP38-2's, scrapped
T&P-1533	T&P-883	T&P-1883	07/50	11572	Retired 7/73, T-I to EMD, to Pielet, scrapped
T&P-1533B	T&P-883B		01/52	15843	Steam generator. Retired 1967-1973, scrapped
T&P-1534	T&P-884	T&P-1884	07/50	11573	Retired 8/73, T-I to EMD on C&EI SD40-2's, to Pielet, scrapped
T&P-1534B	T&P-884B		01/52	15844	Steam generator. Retired 1/73, T-I to EMD
T&P-1535	T&P-885	T&P-1885	07/50	11574	Retired 7/72, T-I to EMD on GP38-2's, to Pielet, scrapped
T&P-1536	T&P-886		07/50	11575	Retired 1964-1965, T-I to EMD on GP35's

Above: T&P 907 was the last unit of an order for 21 F7's that were delivered in April, 1951. She still looks sharp at the engine facility at Neff Yard in Kansas City, Missouri on November 11, 1964. *Joe McMillan*

EMD F7A   1,500 hp   21 units
TE = 60,000   WT = 240,000
Wheels = 40"   Fuel = 1,200
Engine: EMD 16-567B V-type 16-cylinder 2-cycle
Min Speed for TE = 11.0 mph
62:15 Gearing   65 mph Max

1st No	2nd No	3rd No	Built	Build#	Notes & Dispositions
T&P-1537	T&P-887	T&P-1887	03/51	12029	Retired 3/73, T-I to EMD, to Pielet, scrapped
T&P-1538	T&P-888	T&P-1888	04/51	12030	Retired 3/73, T-I to EMD
T&P-1539	T&P-889		04/51	12031	Retired 1964-1965, T-I to EMD on GP35's
T&P-1540	T&P-890	T&P-1890	04/51	12032	Retired 1/74, T-I to EMD on SD40-2's C&EI-3150-3163
T&P-1541	T&P-891	T&P-1891	04/51	12033	Retired 1/73, T-I to EMD
T&P-1542	T&P-892	T&P-1892	04/51	12034	Retired 7/72, T-I to EMD on GP38-2's, to Pielet, scrapped
T&P-1543	T&P-893		04/51	12035	Retired 1964-1965, T-I to EMD on GP35's
T&P-1544	T&P-894		04/51	12036	Retired 1964-1965, T-I to EMD on GP35's
T&P-1545	T&P-895		04/51	12037	Retired 1968-1970, T-I to EMD 11/68
T&P-1546	T&P-896	T&P-1896	04/51	12038	Retired 02/72, T-I to EMD on GP38-2's, scrapped
T&P-1547	T&P-897		04/51	12039	Retired 1971, T-I to GE
T&P-1548	T&P-898	T&P-1898	04/51	12040	Retired 5/73, T-I to EMD, to Pielet, scrapped
T&P-1549	T&P-899		04/51	12041	Retired 6/70, T-I to GE
T&P-1550	T&P-900	T&P-1900	04/51	12042	Retired 5/73, T-I to EMD, to Pielet, scrapped
T&P-1551	T&P-901	T&P-1901	04/51	12043	Retired 2/74, T-I to EMD
T&P-1552	T&P-902	T&P-1902	04/51	12044	Wrecked 2/21/73 Taft or Luling LA, retired 3/73, T-I to EMD
T&P-1553	T&P-903		04/51	12045	Retired 1964-1965, T-I to EMD on GP35's
T&P-1554	T&P-904		04/51	12046	Retired 1966, T-I to EMD 12/67
T&P-1555	T&P-905	T&P-1905	04/51	12047	Retired 3/73, T-I to EMD, to Pielet, scrapped
T&P-1556	T&P-906	T&P-1906	04/51	12048	Retired 3/73, T-I to EMD
T&P-1557	T&P-907	T&P-1907	04/51	12049	Retired 1/74, T-I to EMD on SD40-2's C&EI-3150-3163

Below: The 849 was one of two F7A's purchased from Precision in August, 1967 for the TPMPT. The two F7A's were purchased with two F7B's, and all four were ex-Denver & Rio Grande Western. They worked the remainder of their careers for the MoPac subsidiary. The 849 is in Dolton, Illinois at Yard Center on September 15, 1968. *Dennis Schmidt*

Above: T&P 1551 basks in the sunshine in El Paso, Texas in 1958. The F7 was perhaps the most attractive carbody freight unit ever built. The blue and white of parent MoPac was also an exceptionally attractive scheme on covered wagons. Unfortunately, the 1551 followed the rest of her sisters on a last trip to the scrapper's torch, for her in February, 1974. *Jerry Pitts collection*

EMD F7A 1,500 hp 25 units
TE = 62,000   WT = 248,000
Wheels = 40" Fuel = 1,200
Engine: EMD 16-567B V-type 16-cylinder 2-cycle
Min Speed for TE = 11.0 mph
62:15 Gearing 65 mph Max
T&P-1581-1582 equipped with steam generators

1st No	2nd No	3rd No	4th No	Built	Build#	Notes & Dispositions
T&P-1558	T&P-908			07/52	14518	Retired 1967-1971, to GE or EMD
T&P-1559	T&P-909	T&P-1909		08/51	14519	Retired 9/73, T-I to EMD on SD40-2's C&EI-3150-3163, to Pielet, scrapped
T&P-1560	T&P-910	T&P-1910		08/51	14520	Retired 2/74, T-I to EMD on SD40-2's C&EI-3139-3149
T&P-1561	T&P-911	T&P-1911		08/51	14521	Retired 1/73, T-I to EMD
T&P-1562	T&P-912	T&P-1912		08/51	14522	Retired 1974, T-I to EMD on GP35's
T&P-1563	T&P-913	T&P-1913		08/51	14523	Retired 12/73, T-I to EMD on SD40-2's C&EI-3150-3163
T&P-1564	T&P-914			08/51	14524	Retired 1964-1965, T-I to EMD on GP35's
T&P-1565	T&P-915	T&P-1915		08/51	14525	Retired 12/73, T-I to EMD on SD40-2's C&EI-3150-3163
T&P-1566	T&P-916	T&P-1916		08/51	14526	Retired 7/73, T-I to EMD
T&P-1567	T&P-917	T&P-1917		08/51	14527	Retired 11/73, T-I to EMD on SD40-2's C&EI-3150-3163
T&P-1568	T&P-918			08/51	14528	Retired 4/69, T-I to GE 4/69, scrapped
T&P-1569	T&P-919	T&P-1919		08/51	14529	Retired 8/73, T-I to EMD, to Pielet, scrapped
T&P-1570	T&P-920	T&P-1920		08/51	14530	Retired 1974, T-I to EMD 10/67
T&P-1571	T&P-921	T&P-1921		08/51	14531	Retired 2/74, T-I to EMD on SD40-2's MP-3139-3149
T&P-1572	T&P-922	T&P-1922		08/51	14532	Retired 11/73, T-I to EMD on SD40-2's C&EI-3150-3163
T&P-1573	T&P-923	T&P-1923		08/51	14533	Retired 4/74, T-I to EMD
T&P-1574	T&P-924	T&P-1924		08/51	14534	Retired 1972, T-I to EMD
T&P-1575	T&P-925			08/51	14535	Retired 1970-1971, T-I to EMD
T&P-1576	T&P-926			08/51	14536	Retired 1964-1965, T-I to EMD on GP35's
T&P-1577	T&P-927			08/51	14537	Retired 4/67, to EMD or GE, scrapped 4/67
T&P-1578	T&P-928			08/51	14538	Retired 1964-1965, T-I to EMD on GP35's
T&P-1579	T&P-929			08/51	14539	Retired 1964-1965, T-I to EMD on GP35's
T&P-1580	T&P-930	T&P-1930		08/51	14540	Retired 2/74, T-I to EMD
T&P-1581	T&P-931	T&P-1931		08/51	15839	Retired 3/73, T-I to EMD, to Pielet, scrapped
T&P-1582	T&P-932:1	T&P-1932	T&P-932:2	08/51	15840	Last F-unit on MoPac, retired 9/4/74, T-I to EMD

EMD
SW7
SW8
SW9
SW1200
Slugs

Baldwin
S-12

After the post-war switcher purchases from Baldwin, Alco, and EMD, the MoPac settled down into consistent purchases from EMD. With the exception of Baldwin S-12's, EMD would get every MoPac switcher order after mid-1950.

In June, 1950, the MoPac received five SW7's (MP-9142-9146), beginning a trend of relying heavily on EMD SW-series units that would not fail throughout the MoPac's diesel purchase years. The SW7 was a relatively popular switcher model, with 493 units produced between October, 1949 and January, 1951, only 15 months. It was powered with a 12-cylinder 567A, and was rated at 1,200 horsepower.

The T&P also went for SW7's, picking up four units (T&P-1020-1023) in July, 1950. In addition to these nine units, the MoPac would inherit five more SW7's from the C&EI. A number of these early switchers were later cut down to slugs, and some are still operating on the UP.

The next group of switchers from EMD were in the form of SW9's. T&P got into the act first, buying two groups of SW9's in February and July-August, 1951. The first group was five units (T&P-1024-1028), and the second was eight units (T&P-1029-1036). The SW9 was essentially identical to the SW7 internally, except that it employed the 567B engine. They

were produced after the SW7, with production running from February, 1951 through December, 1953. There were 805 SW9's produced during this period before they were replaced by the SW1200.

The MoPac bought 17 SW9's in one order (MP-9170-9186), delivered between April and June, 1951. An additional five units were pur-

The SW1200 was the MoPac's overwhelming choice for first generation switcher power. Between January, 1963 and April, 1966 the MoPac and T&P purchased 136 of the functional EMD's, and three were later acquired in trades. The practical switchers worked throughout the MoPac system, handling everything from yard duties to the occasional pusher assignment or local freight.

Above: A pair of SW9's lend a hand in helper service assisting a freight at Fort Worth on March 30, 1980. There were a total of 36 SW9's on the MoPac system. *James Holder*

Opposite page top: SW1200 1156 rolls across Kirkwood Road at Kirkwood, Missouri with the eastbound local 456 in tow on October 2, 1981. *Dan Shroeder*

Opposite page bottom: An SW1200 triple-header is hard at work in Fort Worth, Texas on October 22, 1978. The trio combine for 3,600 horsepower. *James Holder*

Below: T&P SW1200 1280 works the "Town Local" at Alexandria, Louisiana in June, 1970. This was a typical assignment for an SW1200 in this era. *Glenn Anderson*

chased for the STLB&M subsidiary (STLB&M-9187-9191). A final SW9 was acquired in a trade with the Bauxite and Northern, a shortline in Arkansas. The MoPac traded two RS-3's (MP-975, originally MP-4502, and MP-977, originally MP-4504) for B&N-10 (an SW9) and B&N-11 (an SW1200). This brought the SW9 total to 36 units.

A group of smaller switchers were acquired by the T&P in January, 1952, when eight SW8's were purchased from EMD (T&P-811-818). The SW8 like the SW9 employed the 567B engine, but only had 8 cylinders rather than 12. It consequently generated only 800 horsepower. The SW8's were assigned to the TPMPT in New Orleans, and rarely made it up to the northern end of the system. The SW8's were all converted to slugs between 1979 and 1981. All are still on the UP system.

While the SW8's and SW9's were coming from EMD, the MoPac ordered S-12's from Baldwin. The S-12 was a well proportioned switcher that competed well with the EMDs. It utilized the 6-cylinder 606A engine, and generated 1,200 horsepower. The MoPac liked the S-12, and bought them in nearly equal quantities compared to the SW7's and SW9's.

The S-12's were acquired in several orders. The first was placed in early 1951 for 20 units

(MP-9200-9219). They were delivered between May and September, 1951, and immediately went into yard service allowing the MoPac to get rid of a few more 0-6-0 and 0-8-0 steam switchers. MP-9212-9219 later had m-u connections added. The next delivery consisted of units built for the MoPac, STLB&M, and the IGN. This brought the MoPac seven more units (MP-9220-9226), the STLB&M three units (STLB&M-9227-9229) and the IGN an additional three units (IGN-9230-9232). These were all delivered in March and April, 1952. The MP-9225-9226, like the earlier MoPac units, also had m-u connections added.

The last order came a year later, when seven S-12 switchers came from Baldwin for the UT (UT-9233-9239). This brought the grand total to a respectable 40 S-12's from Baldwin. It was the last of the Baldwin switchers for the MoPac. EMD took over from there, with the exception of two Plymouth switchers bought by the NO&LC. The first of these was a 165 horsepower model JDT built in August, 1957, numbered NO&LC-3003. A second Plymouth was purchased by the NO&LC in April, 1961. This was slightly larger, a 240 horsepower model JDT-25.

The final type of first-generation switcher on the MoPac far outnumbered all previous switcher models, and accounted for almost exactly 50% of all switchers purchased up to that time. These were of course the popular SW1200 switchers from EMD. The SW1200 was slightly more popular than the SW9, though a good percentage of the SW1200's built went to Canada.

The MoPac went in for the SW1200 in a big way, and with the eradication of steam, the SW1200 became the standard yard switcher for the MoPac. Though they are classified as "first generation" because of the 567C power plant, many of these units were produced after EMD's introduction of the 645 engine, which is as good a line as can be drawn between first and second generation diesels. In fact, the line between first and second generation gets a little fuzzier if one figures that the GP20, GP30 and GP35 were second generation because they replaced FT's and F3's rather than steam, and the GP20 was powered with the 567 prime mover.

There were numerous batches of SW1200's delivered spanning more than three years, from January, 1963 through April, 1966. The MoPac itself wound up with 122 SW1200's (MP-1100-1201 and MP-1255-1274). The T&P also bought a significant number of SW1200's, placing three orders for a total of 25 (T&P-1275-1299).

Three of the MoPac's SW1200's were second-hand units, one as previously mentioned from the B&N, and two from the Rockdale, Sandow & Southern in exchange for RS-3's MP-978 and 980 (originally MP-4505 and MP-4507). Many of the SW1200's lasted more than twenty years on the MoPac, and many that were sold are still fulfilling what they were built to do; shuffling cars to and fro. All were retired by the MoPac in February and June, 1985.

MoPac Slugs

The concept of converting aging switchers into units that would simply add extra tractive effort had been conceived as far back as the 1940's, when Alco-GE-Ingersoll Rand boxcabs were cut down into slugs and m-u'd to diesels in hump service. The idea of weighted vehicles with traction motors but no locomotion capabilities goes at least back to 1914, when the Butte, Anaconda & Pacific used three 40-ton "tractor trucks" connected to electric locomotives. It wasn't until the arrival of high horse-power diesels that the idea of road slugs became practical, and the MoPac never employed road slugs. Road slugs are only really practical in lower speed ranges, when locomotives have excess electrical capacity due to restrictions in power output related to adhesion. This excess electrical capacity can be used to drive traction motors on road slugs, but beyond a relatively low speed of perhaps 15 mph there is no longer excess electrical capacity to drive slugs. The MoPac never deemed road slugs to be worth the effort, but did utilize slugs for switching and hump duties and transfer service.

Missouri Pacific's slug program began with C&EI SW7 1206, which was cut down into a slug in December, 1978 at North Little Rock. The MoPac classed all the slugs as SL-1, regardless of their origin, and all were "manufactured" at North Little Rock. All were cut down from first generation switchers and ran with "mothers" in yard and hump service. None were built for road service. Slug MP-1400 received an SW1500 mother (MP-1275), but all the rest went with MP15's. Probably the most common assignment was in hump service in the MoPac's major yards.

MoPac SL1 23 units
TE = 64,300   WT = 257,200
Wheels = 40"
62:15 Gearing 65 mph Max

Model	1st No	2nd No	3rd No	1st Slug No	2nd Slug No	Built	Build#	Cut down
SW7	C&EI-130	C&EI-1206		MP-1400	UP-S9	02/50	8886	12/78
SW8	T&P-814	T&P-8003	MP-8003:2	MP-1401	UP-S10	01/52	15833	03/79
SW8	T&P-812	T&P-8001	MP-8001:2	MP-1402	UP-S11	01/52	15831	06/79
SW8	T&P-818:1	T&P-8007	MP-8007:2	MP-1403	UP-S12	01/52	15837	09/79
SW8	T&P-813	T&P-8002	MP-8002:2	MP-1404	UP-S13	01/52	15832	04/80
SW7	MP-9146	MP-1214		MP-1405	UP-S14	06/50	11558	06/80
SW8	T&P-811	T&P-8000	MP-8000	MP-1406	UP-S15	01/52	15830	07/80
SW7	MP-9143	MP-1211		MP-1407	UP-S16	06/50	11555	08/80
SW7	MP-9145	MP-1213		MP-1408	UP-S17	06/50	11557	09/80
SW8	T&P-815	T&P-8004	MP-8004:2	MP-1409	UP-S18	01/52	15834	10/80
SW9	T&P-1033	T&P-1228		MP-1410	UP-S19	07/51	14514	11/80
SW7	MP-9142	MP-1210		MP-1411	UP-S20	06/50	11554	12/80
SW9	T&P-1026	T&P-1221		MP-1412	UP-S21	02/51	14024	12/80
SW9	MP-9173	MP-1235		MP-1413	UP-S22	04/51	12554	04/81
SW8	T&P-817:1	T&P-8006	MP-8006:2	MP-1414	UP-S23	01/52	15836	05/81
SW7	T&P-1023	T&P-1218	T&P-1204	MP-1415	UP-S24	07/50	11999	12/81
SW8	T&P-816:1	T&P-8005	MP-8005:2	MP-1416	UP-S25	01/52	15835	08/81
SW7	T&P-1020	T&P-1215		MP-1417	UP-S26	07/50	11996	09/81
SW7	MP-9144	MP-1212		MP-1418	UP-S27	06/50	11556	10/81
SW9	T&P-1024	T&P-1219		MP-1419	UP-S28	02/51	14022	10/81
SW9	STLB&M-9191	MP-1253:1	MP-1217	MP-1420	UP-S29	04/51	14329	12/81
SW9	B&N-10	MP-1254:1	MP-1218	MP-1421	UP-S30	02/52	15838	12/81
SW9	T&P-1025	T&P-1220		MP-1422	UP-S31	02/51	14023	01/82

Above: Slug 1400 was cut down from a C&EI SW7 and is mated with SW1200 1275 at North Little Rock on January 14, 1979. *J Harlen Wilson*

Right: A slug on the point of an action shot is a relatively rare sight. They most often worked yards, but Slug 1411 is powered by MP15DC 1532 on the front of a run on the high iron in Fort Worth, Texas on January 2, 1983. The 1411 began life as MoPac SW7 9142 in June, 1950. Thirty years later the switcher was cut down into the slug. *James Holder*

EMD SW7   1,200 hp   4 units
TE = 62,025   WT = 248,100
Wheels = 40"   Fuel = 600
Engine: EMD 12-567A V-type 12-cylinder 2-cycle
Min Speed for TE = 11.4 mph
62:15 Gearing   65 mph Max

1st No	2nd No	3rd No	4th No	5th No	Built	Build#	Notes
T&P-1020	T&P-1215	MP-1417	UP-S26		07/50	11996	Note 1
T&P-1021	T&P-1216	T&P-1202			07/50	11997	Note 2
T&P-1022	T&P-1217	T&P-1203			07/50	11998	Note 3
T&P-1023	T&P-1218	T&P-1204	MP-1415	UP-S24	07/50	11999	Note 4

Note 1: Cut down to slug 9/81, r# MP-1417
Note 2: Retired 5/75, to US Steel, Fairfield, AL, 5/75, used for parts, scrapped
Note 3: Retired 4/75, to US Steel, Fairfield, AL, 4/75, r# USS-200
Note 4: Cut down to slug 12/81, r# MP-1421

EMD SW7   1,200 hp   5 units
TE = 61,650   WT = 246,610
Wheels = 40"   Fuel = 600
Engine: EMD 12-567A V-type 12-cylinder 2-cycle
Min Speed for TE = 11.4 mph
62:15 Gearing   65 mph Max
All cut down to Slug SL1's

1st No	2nd No	3rd No	4th No	Built	Build#	Slug	Slug No
MP-9142	MP-1210	MP-1411	UP-S20	06/50	11554	12/80	MP-1411
MP-9143	MP-1211	MP-1407	UP-S16	06/50	11555	08/80	MP-1407
MP-9144	MP-1212	MP-1418	UP-S27	06/50	11556	10/81	MP-1418
MP-9145	MP-1213	MP-1408	UP-S17	06/50	11557	09/80	MP-1408
MP-9146	MP-1214	MP-1405	UP-S14	06/50	11558	06/80	MP-1405

EMD SW9   1,200 hp   5 units
TE = 61,955   WT = 247,830
Wheels = 40"   Fuel = 600
Engine: EMD 12-567B V-type 12-cylinder 2-cycle
Min Speed for TE = 9.0 mph
62:15 Gearing   65 mph Max

1st No	2nd No	3rd No	4th No	Built	Build#	Slug	Notes
T&P-1024	T&P-1219	MP-1419	UP-S28	02/51	14022	10/81	Note 1
T&P-1025	T&P-1220	MP-1422	UP-S31	02/51	14023	01/82	Note 2
T&P-1026	T&P-1221	MP-1412	UP-S21	02/51	14024	12/80	Note 3
T&P-1027	T&P-1222	MP-1222		02/51	14025		Note 4
T&P-1028	T&P-1223	MP-1223		02/51	14026		Note 5

Note 1: Slug# MP-1419
Note 2: Hump control unit, Timken roller bearings on #4 axle. Slug# MP-1422
Note 3: Hump control unit, Timken roller bearings on #4 axle. Slug# MP-1412
Note 4: Hump control unit, Timken roller bearings on #4 axle. Retired 2/85, to PNC 4/85, to Inman, Baytown, TX, scrapped
Note 5: Retired 2/85, to PNC 4/85, to Inman, Baytown, TX, mid/86, to Chevron, Cedar Bayou, TX

EMD SW9   1,200 hp   8 units
TE = 61,625   WT = 246,510
Wheels = 40"   Fuel = 600
Engine: EMD 12-567B V-type 12-cylinder 2-cycle
Min Speed for TE = 9.0 mph
62:15 Gearing   65 mph Max

1st No	2nd No	3rd No	4th No	Built	Build#	Retired	Notes
T&P-1029	T&P-1224	MP-1224		07/51	14510	02/85	Note 1
T&P-1030	T&P-1225	MP-1225		07/51	14511	02/85	Note 2
T&P-1031	T&P-1226	MP-1226	UP-1267	07/51	14512	08/84	Note 3
T&P-1032	T&P-1227	MP-1227		07/51	14513	02/85	Note 4
T&P-1033	T&P-1228	MP-1410	UP-S19	07/51	14514		Note 5
T&P-1034	T&P-1229	MP-1229		07/51	14515	02/85	Note 6
T&P-1035	T&P-1230	MP-1230		08/51	14516	02/85	Note 7
T&P-1036	T&P-1231	MP-1231		08/51	14517	08/87	Note 8

Note 1: To PNC 4/85, to Inman, Baytown, TX, to Himount Ind, Deer Park, TX
Note 2: Tto PNC 4/85, to Inman, scrapped 1986
Note 3: Rebuilt to SW10 UP-1267 10/84. Retired 8/92
Note 4: To PNC 4/85, to Inman, Baytown, TX, to Occidental, Taft, LA
Note 5: Cut down to slug 11/80, r# MP-1410
Note 6: To PNC 4/85, to Inman, Baytown, TX, to Occidental, Taft, LA
Note 7: To PNC 4/85, to Inman, Baytown, TX
Note 8: Leased to Great Southwest 7/84, r# GSW-102, returned to UP 10/85, to Wilson, Des Moines, IA, 6/88, to Farmer's Coop Elevator, MN 6/88

Above: The MoPac acquired 9 SW7's, 8 SW8's, and 35 SW9's before buying a horde of SW1200's. All the SW's were similar, though minor differences in louver placement and the number of stacks differentiate the early SW's. SW9 1217 works piggybacks in Houston, Texas on December 11, 1980. *J Harlen Wilson*

EMD SW9   1,200 hp   17 units
TE = 61,650   WT = 246,610
Wheels = 40"   Fuel = 600
Engine: EMD 12-567B V-type 12-cylinder 2-cycle
Min Speed for TE = 9.0 mph
62:15 Gearing   65 mph Max

1st No	2nd No	3rd No	4th No	Built	Build#	Retired	Notes
MP-9170	MP-1232	UP-1269		04/51	12551	08/84	Note 1
MP-9171	MP-1233	UP-1270		04/51	12552	08/84	Note 2
MP-9172	MP-1234			04/51	12553	02/85	Note 3
MP-9173	MP-1235	MP-1413	UP-S22	04/51	12554		Note 4
MP-9174	MP-1236			04/51	12555	02/85	Note 5
MP-9175	MP-1237			05/51	12556	03/84	Note 6
MP-9176	MP-1238			05/51	12557	03/84	Note 7
MP-9177	MP-1239			05/51	12558	03/84	Note 8
MP-9178	MP-1240			06/51	12559	03/83	Note 9
MP-9179	MP-1241			06/51	12560	03/84	Note 10
MP-9180	MP-1242	UP-1266		06/51	12561	08/84	Note 11
MP-9181	MP-1243	UP-1261		06/51	12562	08/84	Note 12
MP-9182	MP-1244	UP-1262		06/51	12563	08/84	Note 13
MP-9183	MP-1245	UP-1264		06/51	12564	08/84	Note 14
MP-9184	MP-1246	UP-1263		06/51	12565	08/84	Note 15
MP-9185	MP-1247			06/51	12566	02/85	Note 16
MP-9186	MP-1248			06/51	12567	02/85	Note 17

Note 1: Rebuilt to SW10 UP-1269 10/84. Leased to Great Southwest RR, GSRR-1232
Note 2: Rebuilt to SW10 UP-1270 11/84. Leased to Great Southwest RR, GSRR-1233
Note 3: Timken roller bearings on #1 truck. Partially rebuilt as MP-slug 1423, to Gray Supply 4/85, scrapped
Note 4: Cut down to slug 4/81, r# MP-1413
Note 5: To PNC 4/85, to Inman, Baytown, TX, to Contenental Grain CONG-1236
Note 6: To Mid America Car, Kansas City, MO, 3/84, to Kansas City Power & Light, KC, MO, late/84 KCLX-1237
Note 7: To Mid America Car, Kansas City, MO, 3/84, to Amoco Chemicals, Kemmerer, WY, late/84 AMOX-1238
Note 8: To Mid America Car, KC, MO, 3/84, to Superior Tie & Timber, Superior, LA, 9/84, r# ST&T-22, to Rail Switching Service, Camden, AR
Note 9: To Commercial Distributing Center, Independence, MO, CDC-1240, to CPSC-1240, to WATCO 1/91
Note 10: To Mid America Car, Kansas City, MO, 3/84, to Green Hills Redevelopment (Chillicothe & Southern) Maryville, MO, GRHD-1241
Note 11: Rebuilt to SW10 UP-1266 7/84. Retired 1990
Note 12: Rebuilt to SW10 UP-1261 7/84
Note 13: Rebuilt to SW10 UP-1262 7/84
Note 14: Rebuilt to SW10 UP-1264 8/84
Note 15: Rebuilt to SW10 UP-1263 10/84
Note 16: To PNC 4/85, to Inman, Baytown, TX, late/85, to Pittsburg Plate Glass, Lake Charles, LA
Note 17: To Erman 4/85, scrapped

EMD SW9   1,200 hp   5 units
TE = 61,650   WT = 246,610
Wheels = 40"   Fuel = 600
Engine: EMD 12-567B V-type 12-cylinder 2-cycle
Min Speed for TE = 9.0 mph
62:15 Gearing   65 mph Max

1st No	2nd No	3rd No	4th No	5th No	Built	Build#	Notes & Dispositions
STLB&M-9187	MP-1249				04/51	14325	Timken roller bearings on both trucks. Leased to Great Southwest RR, Arlington, TX, 7/84, r# GSW-103, returned to UP-10/85, retired 8/87, to Wilson Locomotive, Des Moines, IA, 6/88, to Farmer's Coop MN, 6/88
STLB&M-9188	MP-1250				04/51	14326	Timken roller bearings on both trucks. Retired 6/84, to Granite Mountain Quarry 6/84, r# GMQ-4744
STLB&M-9189	MP-1251	UP-1268			04/51	14327	Retired 6/84, rebuilt to SW10 UP-1268 10/84
STLB&M-9190	STLB&M-1252	MP-1252	MP-1216		04/51	14328	Retired 02/85, to PNC 4/85, to Exxon, Baton Rouge, LA
STLB&M-9191	MP-1253:1		MP-1217	MP-1420	UP-S29	04/51	14329	Cut down to slug 12/81, r# MP-1420

EMD SW9   1,200 hp   1 unit
TE = 61,500   WT = 246,000
Wheels = 40"   Fuel = 600
Engine: EMD 12-567C V-type 12-cylinder 2-cycle
Min Speed for TE = 9.0 mph
68:14 Gearing   65 mph Max

1st No	2nd No	3rd No	4th No	5th No	Built	Build#	Notes
B&N-10	MP-1254:1	MP-1218	MP-1421	UP-S30	02/52	15838	Note 1

Note 1: Acquired in trade from Bauxite & Northern for RS-3's MP-975 and
MP-977 in 1964. Cut down to slug 12/81, r# MP-1421

Baldwin S-12   1,200 hp   20 units
TE = 58,900   WT = 235,600
Wheels = 40"   Fuel = 650
Engine: Baldwin 606A 6-cylinder 4-cycle Turbocharged
Min Speed for TE = 10.8 mph
68:14 Gearing   60 mph Max
Retired 1966, T-I to EMD

1st No	2nd No	3rd No	Built	Build#
MP-9200	MP-1260:1		05/51	75033
MP-9201	MP-1261:1		05/51	75034
MP-9202	MP-1262:1		05/51	75035
MP-9203	MP-1263:1		05/51	75036
MP-9204	MP-1264:1		05/51	75037
MP-9205	MP-1265:1	MP-1365:1	05/51	75038
MP-9206	MP-1266:1		05/51	75039
MP-9207	MP-1267:1		05/51	75040
MP-9208	MP-1268:1	MP-1368:1	06/51	75041
MP-9209	MP-1269:1	MP-1369:1	06/51	75042
MP-9210	MP-1270:1	MP-1370:2	06/51	75043
MP-9211	MP-1271:1		06/51	75044
MP-9212	MP-1272:1	MP-1372:1	06/51	75045
MP-9213	MP-1273:1	MP-1373:2	06/51	75046
MP-9214	MP-1274:1	MP-1374:2	06/51	75047
MP-9215	MP-1275:1	MP-1375:2	06/51	75048
MP-9216	MP-1276:1		06/51	75049
MP-9217	MP-1277:1	MP-1377:2	07/51	75050
MP-9218	MP-1278:1		09/51	75051
MP-9219	MP-1279:1		09/51	75052

Baldwin S-12   1,200 hp   13 units
TE = 59,505   WT = 238,020
Wheels = 40"   Fuel = 650
Engine: Baldwin 606A 6-cylinder 4-cycle Turbocharged
Min Speed for TE = 10.8 mph
68:14 Gearing   60 mph Max
Retired 1966, T-I to EMD, scrapped

1st No	2nd No	3rd No	Built	Build#
MP-9220	MP-1280:1	MP-1380:2	03/52	75531
MP-9221	MP-1281:1	MP-1381:2	03/52	75532
MP-9222	MP-1282:1	MP-1382:2	03/52	75533
MP-9223	MP-1283:1		03/52	75534
MP-9224	MP-1284:1		04/52	75535
MP-9225	MP-1285:1		04/52	75536
MP-9226	MP-1286:1	MP-1386:2	04/52	75537
STLB&M-9227	MP-1287:1	MP-1387:2	04/52	75313
STLB&M-9228	MP-1288:1		04/52	75314
STLB&M-9229	MP-1289:1		04/52	75315

Above: T&P accounted for a good portion of the MoPac's SW9's, buying 13 out of 35 purchased. SW9 1031 is latched onto a load of poles at Longview, Texas on May 25, 1954. *E M Kahn photo, Louis Marre collection*

Above: SW9 1240 is at KC, MO on April 10, 1965. *Joe McMillan*
Below: MoPac SW9 1250, ex-STLB&M 9188, is at Houston, Texas on June 25, 1974. *Tom Chenoweth photo, Lon Coone collection*

Baldwin S12 (continued)

1st No	2nd No	3rd No	Built	Build#
IGN-9230	MP-1290:1	MP-1390:2	04/52	75528
IGN-9231	MP-1291:1	MP-1391:2	04/52	75529
IGN-9232	MP-1292:1	MP-1392:2	04/52	75530

# Baldwin S-12 1,200 hp 7 units
TE = 60,510   WT = 242,050
Wheels = 40"   Fuel = 750
Engine: Baldwin 606A 6-cylinder
    4-cycle Turbocharged
Min Speed for TE = 10.8 mph
68:14 Gearing   60 mph Max
Retired 1966, T-I to EMD, scrapped

1st No	2nd No	3rd No	Built	Build#
UT-9233	MP-1293:1	MP-1393	04/53	75827
UT-9234	MP-1294:1		04/53	75828
UT-9235	MP-1295:1	MP-1395	04/53	75829
UT-9236	MP-1296:1		04/53	75830
UT-9237	MP-1297:1		05/53	75831
UT-9238	MP-1298:1		05/53	75832
UT-9239	MP-1299:1		05/53	75833

# EMD SW8 800 hp 8 units
TE = 58,500   WT = 234,000
Wheels = 40"   Fuel = 600
Engine: EMD 8-567B V-type 8-cylinder 2-cycle
Min Speed for TE = 9.0 mph
62:15 Gearing   65 mph Max

1st No	2nd No	3rd No	4th No	5th No	Built	Build#	Notes & Dispositions
T&P-811	T&P-8000	MP-8000	MP-1406	UP-S15	01/52	15830	Cut down to slug 7/80, r# MP-1406
T&P-812	T&P-8001	MP-8001:2	MP-1402	UP-S11	01/52	15831	Cut down to slug 6/79, r# MP-1402
T&P-813	T&P-8002	MP-8002:2	MP-1404	UP-S13	01/52	15832	Cut down to slug 4/80, r# MP-1404
T&P-814	T&P-8003	MP-8003:2	MP-1401	UP-S10	01/52	15833	Cut down to slug 3/79, r# MP-1401
T&P-815	T&P-8004	MP-8004:2	MP-1409	UP-S18	01/52	15834	Cut down to slug 10/80, r# MP-1409
T&P-816:1	T&P-8005	MP-8005:2	MP-1416	UP-S25	01/52	15835	Cut down to slug 8/81, r# MP-1416. NLR "block" lettering as UP-S25
T&P-817:1	T&P-8006	MP-8006:2	MP-1414	UP-S23	01/52	15836	Cut down to slug 5/81, r# MP-1414
T&P-818:1	T&P-8007	MP-8007:2	MP-1403	UP-S12	01/52	15837	Cut down to slug 9/79, r# MP-1403

Above: Two of the eight T&P SW8's, 8001 and 8006, work an eastbound way freight through Morganza, Texas at 1:15 in the afternoon on February 22, 1965. The SW8 was the only model type that had all units cut down to slugs. They were "sacrificed" between March, 1979 and May, 1981, becoming just a little more adhesion for the switcher fleet. *Barry Carlson*

Below left: T&P SW8 815 is at New Orleans, Louisiana on March 18, 1956 in the Swamp Holly Orange paint scheme. *E M Kahn photo, Louis Marre collection*

Below: S-12 1370 is battered but still in service at Kansas City, Missouri on January 30, 1965, still in black. *Charles Zieler*

Bottom left: S-12 9239 was purchased for the UT, but only wears MoPac lettering at North Little Rock on September 10, 1961. *Louis Marre*

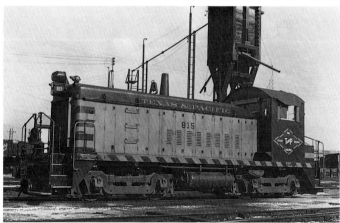

Below: Baldwin S-12 1281 sits at Kansas City, Missouri on October 24, 1964, now wearing blue. Several of the S-12's made it into blue paint before retirement. *Joe McMillan*

EMD SW1200   1,200 hp   26 units
TE = 61,525   WT = 246,100
Wheels = 40"   Fuel = 600
Engine: EMD 12-567C V-type 12-cylinder 2-cycle
Min Speed for TE = 9.0 mph
62:15 Gearing   55 mph Max

1st No	Built	Build#	Notes & Dispositions
MP-1100	01/63	27868	Retired 1/85, to PNC 4/85, to Florida Portland Cement, r# FPC-020
MP-1101	01/63	27869	Retired 6/85, to PNC 7/85, to Wilson Locomotive, Des Moines, IA, 8/86, to US Steel USS-1101, Fairless, PA, 2/87
MP-1102	01/63	27870	Retired 6/85, to PNC 7/85, to Wilson Locomotive, Des Moines, IA, 8/86, to US Steel USS-1102, Geneva, UT, 1/87
MP-1103	01/63	27871	Retired 6/85, to PNC 7/85, to Wilson Locomotive, Des Moines, IA, 8/86, to Granite City Steel 5/87, r# GCS-1188
MP-1104	01/63	27872	Retired 6/85, to PNC 7/85, scrapped
MP-1105	01/63	27873	Retired 2/85, to PNC 4/85, to Sheffield Steel, Kansas City, MO, 6/85, r# SS-SS3
MP-1106	01/63	27874	Retired 6/85, to PNC 7/85, to Wilson Locomotive, Des Moines, IA, 8/86, stored
MP-1107	01/63	27875	Retired 2/85, to PNC 4/85, to Helm, to Wisconsin Central, r# WC-1230
MP-1108	01/63	27876	Retired 2/85, to PNC 4/85, scrapped
MP-1109	02/63	27877	Retired 6/85, to PNC 7/85, to Wilson Locomotive, Des Moines, IA, 8/86, stored
MP-1110	02/63	27878	Retired 2/85, to PNC 4/85, to Wilson Locomotive, Des Moines, IA, 8/86, stored
MP-1111	02/63	27879	Retired 6/85, to PNC 7/85, to Wilson Locomotive, Des Moines, IA, 8/86, stored
MP-1112	02/63	27880	Retired 2/85, to PNC 4/85, scrapped
MP-1113	02/63	27881	Retired 2/85, to PNC 4/85, to Lyondell Petrochemicals, Pasedena, TX, 9/86, r# LP-MKV99
MP-1114	02/63	27882	Retired 6/85, to PNC 7/85, to Wilson Locomotive, Des Moines, IA, 8/86, to US Steel USS-1114, Geneva, UT, 11/86
MP-1115	03/63	27883	Retired 6/85, to PNC 7/85, scrapped
MP-1116	03/63	27884	Retired 2/85, to PNC 4/85, to Wilson Locomotive, Des Moines, IA, 8/86, to Granite Rock, Watsonville, CA, 1986
MP-1117	04/63	27885	Retired 2/85, to PNC 4/85, scrapped
MP-1118	04/63	27886	Retired 2/85, to PNC 4/85, scrapped
MP-1119	04/63	27887	Retired 2/85, to PNC 4/85, scrapped
MP-1120	04/63	27888	Retired 2/85, to PNC 4/85, scrapped
MP-1121	04/63	27889	Retired 2/85, to PNC 4/85, scrapped
MP-1122	04/63	27890	Retired 2/85, to PNC 4/85, scrapped
MP-1123	04/63	27891	Retired 2/85, to PNC 4/85, to Wilson Locomotive, Des Moines, IA, 8/86, to US Steel USS-1123, Fairless, PA
MP-1124	06/63	27892	Retired 6/85, to PNC 7/85, scrapped
MP-1125	04/63	27893	Retired 6/85, to PNC 7/85, to Wilson Locomotive, Des Moines, IA, 6/86, to US Steel USS-1125, Geneva, UT, 11/86

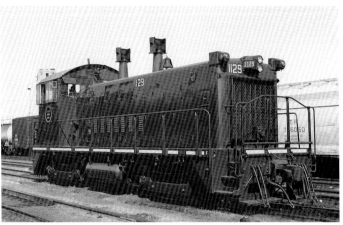

Top: The First order of SW1200's was for 26 units, and by the time all was finished, the MoPac had 139 of the first generation SW1200's. MoPac 1118 was part of the first order, and is at St. Louis, Missouri on October 21, 1981 with a fresh coat of Jenks blue. *Ronald Plazzota*

Middle: The 1129 was part of an order for eight units that came in January and February, 1964. It is at Neff Yard in Kansas City and has just been repainted in April, 1974, just before the re-styling of the Jenks blue. *Tony Fey*

Bottom: SW1200 1138 basks in the summer heat in Carthage, Missouri in June, 1966. It has yet to get MoPac's exhaust treatment. *Britt Graber*

EMD SW1200   1,200 hp   8 units
TE = 61,860   WT = 247,440
Wheels = 40"   Fuel = 600
Engine: EMD 12-567C V-type 12-cylinder 2-cycle
Min Speed for TE = 9.0 mph
62:15 Gearing   55 mph Max

1st No	Built	Build#	Notes & Dispositions
MP-1126	01/64	28747	Retired 6/85, to PNC 7/85, to Inspiration Consol Copper, Miami, AZ, 9/87, r# ICC-24, to Arizona Eastern, r# AZER-24
MP-1127	02/64	28748	Retired 2/85, to Wilson Locomotive, Des Moines, IA, 4/85, to Austin, Todd & Ladd, Watonga, OK, AT&L-1127 5/86
MP-1128	01/64	28749	Retired 2/85, to PNC 4/85, scrapped
MP-1129	01/64	28750	Retired 6/85, to PNC 7/85, to Inspiration Consol Copper, Miami, AZ, 9/87, r# ICC-25, to Arizona Eastern, r# AZER-25
MP-1130	02/64	28751	Retired 2/85, to Wilson Locomotive, Des Moines, IA, 4/85, to US Steel USS-1130, Fairless, PA, to Wilson Locomotive, 5/91, scrapped
MP-1131	02/64	28752	Retired 6/85, to PNC 7/85, to Rail Switching Service, Dothan, AL, r# RSS-901
MP-1132	02/64	28753	Retired 2/85, to Wilson Locomotive, Des Moines, IA, 4/85, to Weyerhauser Paper, Valiant, OK, WEYH-1132 11/86
MP-1133	02/64	28754	Retired 6/85, to PNC 7/85, scrapped

EMD SW1200   1,200 hp   18 units
TE = 62,190   WT = 248,760
Wheels = 40"   Fuel = 930
Engine: EMD 12-567E V-type 12-cylinder 2-cycle
Min Speed for TE = 9.0 mph
62:15 Gearing   55 mph Max

1st No	Built	Build#	Notes & Dispositions
MP-1134	03/66	31094	Retired 6/85, to PNC 7/85, to NRE 12/85, to Con Agra, Denver, CO, CONG-1134 10/86
MP-1135	03/66	31095	Retired 6/85, to PNC 7/85, to NRE 12/85, to Prince Rupert Grain, Prince Rupert, BC, PRGL-1135 4/87
MP-1136	03/66	31096	Retired 6/85, to PNC 7/85, to Crab Orchard & Egyptian, Marion, IL, COER-1136 9/86
MP-1137	03/66	31097	Retired 2/85, to PNC 4/85, scrapped
MP-1138	03/66	31098	Retired 6/85, to PNC 7/85, scrapped
MP-1139	03/66	31099	Retired 6/85, to PNC 7/85, scrapped
MP-1140	03/66	31100	Retired 6/85, to PNC 7/85, to NRE 12/85, to Fort Howard Paper, Green Bay, WI, 12/86, r# FHPX-1
MP-1141	03/66	31101	Retired 6/85, to PNC 7/85, to Elgin Joliet and Eastern 4/86, r# EJE-310
MP-1142	03/66	31216	Retired 6/85, to PNC 7/85, to NRE 12/85, to Fort Howard Paper, Green Bay, WI, 12/86
MP-1143	03/66	31217	Retired 2/85, to PNC 4/85, to Elgin Joliet and Eastern 4/86, r# EJE-320
MP-1144	04/66	31218	Retired 2/85, to PNC 4/85, to Wilson Locomotive, Des Moines, IA, 10/86, to Carolina Rail Service 10/86, r# CRIJ-1201
MP-1145	04/66	31219	Retired 2/85, to PNC 4/85, to NRE, to Shore Fast Line, Pleasantville, NJ, 5/86
MP-1146	04/66	31220	Retired 2/85, to PNC 4/85, to Cedar Rapids & Iowa City, Cedar Rapids, IA, 12/85, r# CIC-99
MP-1147	04/66	31221	Retired 2/85, to PNC 4/85, to Crab Orchard & Egyptian, Marion, IL, COER-1147 9/86, to PNC
MP-1148	04/66	31222	Retired 6/85, to Coast Engine & Equipment, Tacoma, WA, 7/85, r# EEC-203, to Washington Central, Yakima, WA, 9/86 r# WCRC-203
MP-1149	04/66	31223	Retired 2/85, to PNC 4/85, to Elgin Joliet and Eastern 4/86, r# EJE-311
MP-1150	04/66	31224	Retired 2/85, to PNC 4/85, to Rail Switching Service, Dothan, AL, 12/86, r# RSS-904
MP-1151	04/66	31225	Retired 6/85, to PNC 6/85, scrapped

EMD SW1200   1,200 hp   15 units
TE = 61,895   WT = 247,580
Wheels = 40"   Fuel = 930
Engine: EMD 12-567C V-type 12-cylinder 2-cycle
Min Speed for TE = 9.0 mph
62:15 Gearing   55 mph Max

1st No	Built	Build#	Notes & Dispositions
MP-1152	03/65	29790	Retired 2/85, to PNC 4/85, to Elgin Joliet and Eastern 4/86, r# EJE-316
MP-1153	03/65	29791	Wore MP yellow as MP-1153. Retired 6/85, to Shell Oil, Deer Park, TX, 6/85, r# SHO-28704, later 27804
MP-1154	03/65	29792	Retired 6/85, to PNC 4/85, to Rail Switching Service, Dothan, AL, 12/86, r# RSS-903
MP-1155	03/65	29793	Retired 2/85, to PNC 4/85, to Anchor Grain/Bloomer Shippers, Anchor, IL, 10/85
MP-1156	03/65	29794	Retired 6/85, to PNC 6/85, to Wilson Locomotive, IA, to Sabine River & Northern 4/87, r# SRN-1208
MP-1157	03/65	29795	Retired 6/85, to PNC 6/85, to Elgin Joliet and Eastern 4/86, r# EJE-319
MP-1158	03/65	29796	Retired 6/85, to PNC 6/85, scrapped
MP-1159	03/65	29797	Retired 2/85, to PNC 4/85, scrapped
MP-1160	03/65	29798	Retired 2/85, to PNC 4/85, to Wilson Locomotive, 8/86, to US Steel USS-1160, Geneva, UT, 11/86
MP-1161	03/65	29799	Retired 6/85, to PNC 6/85, to Crab Orchard & Egyptian, Marion, IL, 9/86 COER-1161
MP-1162	04/65	29800	Retired 2/85, to PNC 4/85, disposition unknown
MP-1163	04/65	29801	Retired 6/85, to Coast Engine & Equipment, Tacoma, WA, 6/85, r# CEE-202, to Washington Central, Yakima, WA, 10/86 r# WCRC-202
MP-1164	04/65	29802	Retired 6/85, to PNC 6/85, to Elgin Joliet and Eastern 4/86, r# EJE-318
MP-1165	04/65	29803	Retired 6/85, to DOW, Freeport, TX, 6/85, r# DOW-1004
MP-1166	04/65	29804	Retired 2/85, to PNC 4/85, disposition unknown

EMD SW1200   1,200 hp   15 units
TE = 61,860   WT = 247,440
Wheels = 40"   Fuel = 930
Engine: EMD 12-567C V-type 12-cylinder 2-cycle
Min Speed for TE = 9.0 mph
62:15 Gearing   55 mph Max

1st No	Built	Build#	Notes & Dispositions
MP-1175	01/64	28766	Retired 6/85, to Chrome 6/85, to Rail Switching Service, Dothan, AL, 12/85, r# RSS-701
MP-1176	02/64	28767	Hump control unit. Retired 6/85, to Chrome 6/85, to Rail Switching Service, Dothan, AL, 12/85, r# RSS-501
MP-1177	02/64	28768	Hump control unit. Retired 2/85, to PNC 4/85, disposition unknown, possibly scrapped
MP-1178	02/64	28769	Hump control unit. Retired 2/85, to PNC 4/85, to NRE 12/85, disposition unknown, possibly scrapped
MP-1179	02/64	28755	Retired 6/85, to Chrome 6/85, to Rail Switching Service, Dothan, AL, 12/85, r# RSS-602, r# RSS-905
MP-1180	02/64	28756	Retired 6/85, to Chrome 6/85, to Rail Switching Service, Dothan, AL, mid/86, r# RSS 803
MP-1181	03/64	28757	Retired 6/85, to Chrome 6/85, to Rail Switching Service, Dothan, AL, 12/85, r# RSS-502
MP-1182	03/64	28758	Hump control unit. Retired 6/85, to UP for parts 6/85, to Erman 6/85, to Wilson Locomotive, 4/87, scrapped
MP-1183	03/64	28759	Hump control unit. Retired 6/85, to PNC 6/85, disposition unknown, possibly scrapped
MP-1184	03/64	28760	Hump control unit. Retired 6/85, to PNC 6/85, to Brandywine Valley, 12/87, r# BVRY-8204
MP-1185	03/64	28761	Hump control unit. Retired 6/85, to PNC 6/85, to Elgin Joliet and Eastern 4/86, r# EJE-321
MP-1186	03/64	28762	Hump control unit. Retired 6/85, to PNC 6/85, disposition unknown, possibly scrapped
MP-1187	03/64	28763	Hump control unit. Retired 6/85, to PNC 6/85, disposition unknown, possibly scrapped
MP-1188	03/64	28764	Hump helper unit. Retired 6/85, to PNC 6/85, to Elgin Joliet and Eastern 4/86, r# EJE-313
MP-1189	03/64	28765	Hump helper unit. Retired 6/85, to PNC 6/85, to Wilson Locomotive, 8/86, to US Steel, Fairless, PA, 2/87, r# USS-1130

Above: If one looked only at the MoPac roster, they'd be easily convinced that the SW1200 was the most popular switcher in EMD's catalog. This is not the case, however, as the NW2 well outsold everything else, with a total of **1,143** units. The SW1200 comes in second, only because of significant Canadian sales (287 units), with a production total of **1,024.** The SW9 is next with **815,** and the 645-powered SW1500 is right behind the SW9 with a total of **807** units sold. For the MoPac, however, the SW1200 was the 567-powered first generation switcher of choice. Their 139 SW1200's account for almost 20 percent of the U. S. production. The 1181 was part of an order for 15 units delivered between January and March, 1964. It is at North Little Rock on November 11, 1984. *Terry Foshee photo, Kevin EuDaly collection*

EMD SW1200   1,200 hp   10 units
TE = 62,530   WT = 250,120
Wheels = 40"   Fuel = 930
Engine: EMD 12-567C V-type 12-cylinder 2-cycle
Min Speed for TE = 9.0 mph
62:15 Gearing   55 mph Max
Has extra louver sets in slightly raised boxes - custom for MoPac

1st No	Built	Build#	Notes & Dispositions
MP-1190	02/63	27858	Retired 6/85, to PNC 6/85, to Wheeling Pittsburg Steel, Mingo Jct., OH, mid/86, r# WPS-1260
MP-1191	02/63	27859	Retired 6/85, to Coast Engine & Equipment, Tacoma, WA, 7/85, r# CEECO-207, to Tacoma Municipal Belt Line, Tacoma, WA, 12/87, r# TMBL-1204
MP-1192	02/63	27860	Retired 6/85, to PNC 6/85, to Rail Switching Service, Dothan, AL, 12/85, r# RSS-902
MP-1193	02/63	27861	Retired 6/85, to Coast Engine & Equipment, Tacoma, WA, 7/85, to PNC 1988
MP-1194	03/63	27862	Retired 2/85, to PNC 4/85, to Wheeling Pittsburg Steel, Mingo Jct., OH, mid/86, r# WPS-1262
MP-1195	03/63	27863	Retired 6/85, to PNC 6/85, to Wheeling Pittsburg Steel, Mingo Jct., OH, mid/86, r# WPS-1263
MP-1196	03/63	27864	Retired 2/85, to PNC 4/85, to Wheeling Pittsburg Steel, Mingo Jct., OH, mid/86, r# WPS-1264
MP-1197	03/63	27865	Retired 2/85, to PNC 4/85, to Port Jersey Terminal, Bayonne, NJ, 12/87, r# PJR-1197
MP-1198	03/63	27866	Retired 6/85, to PNC 6/85, to Morrison Knudsen, to Blue Diamond Mining, Leatherwood, KY, 5/86
MP-1199	03/63	27867	Retired 2/85, to PNC 4/85, to Wheeling Pittsburg Steel, Mingo Jct., OH, mid/86, r# WPS-1261

EMD SW1200   1,200 hp   7 units
TE = 62,390   WT = 249,560
Wheels = 40"   Fuel = 930
Engine: EMD 12-567E V-type 12-cylinder 2-cycle
Min Speed for TE = 9.0 mph
62:15 Gearing   55 mph Max

1st No	2nd No	Built	Build#	Notes
MP-1200	MP-1253:2	02/66	31226	Note 1
MP-1201	MP-1254:2	02/66	31227	Note 2
MP-1255		02/66	31228	Note 3
MP-1256		02/66	31229	Note 4
MP-1257		02/66	31230	Note 5
MP-1258		02/66	31231	Note 6
MP-1259		02/66	31232	Note 7

Note 1: Renumbered 10/74 to block all 1966-built units together. Retired 2/85, to PNC 4/85, to Elgin Joliet & Eastern 4/86, r# EJE-314
Note 2: Renumbered 10/74 to block all 1966-built units together. Retired 6/85, to PNC 6/85, scrapped
Note 3: Retired 6/85, to Coast Engine & Equipment, Tacoma, WA, 7/85, to SeaLand, Seattle, WA
Note 4: Retired 6/85, to Tri State Concrete, Shreveport, LA, 7/85 TSCC-1256
Note 5: Retired 6/85, to Coast Engine & Equipment, Tacoma, WA, 7/85, r# CEECO-201, to Washington Central, Yakima, WA, 9/86 WCRC-1201
Note 6: Retired 2/85, to PNC 4/85, to Wilson Locomotive, Des Moines, IA, 8/86, to Washington Central, Yakima, WA, 10/86, r# WCRC-1203
Note 7: Retired 2/85, to PNC 4/85, to Chrome, to Terre Haute Brazil & Eastern 11 87, r# TBER-100

EMD SW1200   1,200 hp   3 units
TE = 61,635   WT = 246,540
Wheels = 40"   Fuel = 600
Engine: EMD 12-567C V-type 12-cylinder 2-cycle
Min Speed for TE = 9.0 mph
62:15 Gearing   55 mph Max
Hump helper units

1st No	2nd No	3rd No	Built	Build#	Notes & Dispositions
B&N-11	MP-1260:2		06/54	19530	Note 1
RS&S-8	MP-1261:2		10/55	20702	Note 2
PC&N-4	RS&S-9	MP-1262:2	10/55	20703	Note 3

Note 1: Acquired from Bauxite & Northern in trade for RS-3's MP-975 and MP-977. Retired 6/85, to PNC 6/85, to Columbia Terminal, Columbia, MO, 6/87, r# CTR-1
Note 2: Acquired from Rockdale, Sandow and Southern in trade for RS-3's MP-978 and MP-980. Retired 2/85, to PNC 4/85, to Commonwealth Edison, Peoria, IL, 6/87, rebuilt with Caterpillar engine
Note 3: Originally Point Comfort & Northern, acquired from Rockdale, Sandow and Southern in trade for RS-3's MP-978 and MP-980. Retired 2/85, to PNC 4/85, scrapped

Above: SW1200 1261 was acquired from Rockdale, Sandow and Southern for two RS-3's. It is at North Little Rock on March 30, 1978. *J Harlen Wilson*

EMD SW1200   1,200 hp   12 units
TE = 61,645   WT = 246,580
Wheels = 40"   Fuel = 600
Engine: EMD 12-567C V-type 12-cylinder 2-cycle
Min Speed for TE = 9.0 mph
62:15 Gearing   55 mph Max

1st No	Built	Build#	Notes & Dispositions
MP-1263:2	04/64	28770	Hump helper unit. Retired 2/85, to PNC 4/85, scrapped
MP-1264:2	04/64	28771	Retired 6/85, to Chrome 6/85, disposition unknown
MP-1265:2	01/65	29780	Retired 6/85, to Chrome 6/85, to Rail Switching Service, Dothan, AL, r# RSS-601
MP-1266:2	01/65	29781	Retired 6/85, to Chrome 6/85, to Rail Switching Service, Dothan, AL, r# RSS-702
MP-1267:2	02/65	29782	Retired 2/85, to PNC 4/85, scrapped
MP-1268:2	02/65	29783	Retired 6/85, to Chrome 6/85, resold or scrapped
MP-1269:2	02/65	29784	Retired 6/85, to Coast Engine & Equipment, Tacoma, WA, 7/85, r# CEECO-211, to Washington Central, Yakima, WA, 9/86, r# WCRC-211
MP-1270:2	02/65	29785	Retired 6/85, to Coast Engine & Equipment, Tacoma, WA, 7/85
MP-1271:2	02/65	29786	Retired 6/85, to Coast Engine & Equipment, Tacoma, WA, 7/85, to Tacoma Municipal Belt Line, Tacoma, WA, r# TMBL-1203
MP-1272:2	02/65	29787	Retired 6/85, to Big Rock Stone & Material, Little Rock, AR, 4/86, r# BRSM-212
MP-1273:2	02/65	29788	Retired 6/85, to Coast Engine & Equipment, Tacoma, WA, 7/85, r# CEECO-212, to Washington Central, Yakima, WA, 9/86, r# WCRC-212
MP-1274:2	03/65	29789	Retired 2/85, to PNC 4/85, scrapped

Left: SW1200 1255 was built at the tail end of SW1200 production, coming off the floor at La Grange in February, 1966. SW1200 production ended in May, 1966. The last of its breed is at Memphis, Tennessee on September 27, 1975. *David Johnston*

EMD SW1200   1,200 hp   25 units
TE = 62,390   WT = 249,560
Wheels = 40"   Fuel = 930
Engine: EMD 12-567E V-type 12-cylinder 2-cycle
Min Speed for TE = 9.0 mph
62:15 Gearing   55 mph Max

1st No	2nd No	Built	Build#	Notes & Dispositions
T&P-1275	MP-1275:2	02/66	31233	Upgraded to 1,500 hp, hump control unit. Retired 6/85, to Coast Engine & Equipment, Tacoma, WA, 7/85, to PNC 1988, to Arizona Eastern, r# AZER-1501
T&P-1276	MP-1276:2	02/66	31234	Retired 6/85, to PNC 6/85, to Morrison Knudsen 9/86, to Southern Peru Copper 12/86, r# SPCC-16
T&P-1277	MP-1277:2	02/66	31235	Retired 6/85, to PNC 6/85, to Elgin Joliet and Eastern 4/86, r# EJE-317
T&P-1278	MP-1278:2	02/66	31236	Retired 6/85, to PNC 6/85, to NRE 12/85, to Wisconsin Central 10/87, r# WC-1232
T&P-1279	MP-1279:2	02/66	31237	Retired 6/85, to PNC 6/85, to NRE 12/85, to Vancouver Wharves, Vancouver, BC, 1/87, r# VANW-824
T&P-1280	MP-1280:2	02/66	31110	Retired 2/85, to PNC 4/85
T&P-1281	MP-1281:2	02/66	31111	Retired 2/85, to PNC 4/85, to Wilson Locomotive, Des Moines, IA, to North Carolina Ports 10/86, r# CRIJ-1201
T&P-1282	MP-1282:2	03/66	31112	Hump control unit. Retired 6/85, to PNC 6/85, to Elgin Joliet and Eastern 4/86, r# EJE-312
T&P-1283	MP-1283:2	02/66	31113	Hump helper unit. Retired 2/85, to PNC 4/85, scrapped
T&P-1284	MP-1284:2	02/66	31114	Retired 6/85, to PNC 6/85, to Rail Switching Service, Savannah, GA, mid/86, r# RSS-801
T&P-1285	MP-1285:2	02/66	31115	Retired 2/85, to PNC 4/85, to Elgin Joliet and Eastern 4/86, r# EJE-315
T&P-1286	MP-1286:2	02/66	31116	Retired 2/85, to PNC 4/85, to Peaker Services, Brighton, MI, 4/85, r# PS-1
T&P-1287	MP-1287:2	02/66	31117	Retired 2/85, to PNC 4/85, to Wilson Locomotive, Des Moines, IA, 8/86, to Wilmington Terminal, Wilmington, NC, 10/86, r# WTRY-1204
T&P-1288	MP-1288:2	03/66	31118	Retired 2/85, to PNC 4/85, scrapped
T&P-1289	MP-1289:2	03/66	31119	Retired 2/85, to PNC 4/85, to Wilson Locomotive, Des Moines, IA, 8/86, to Bartlett Grain, Kansas City, MO, 10/86, r# BGC-9600
T&P-1290	MP-1290:2	03/66	31238	Retired 2/85, to PNC 4/85, to Reed Crushed Stone 11/85, r# RCS-2900
T&P-1291	MP-1291:2	03/66	31239	Retired 6/85, to Chrome 6/85, to Cedar Rapids & Iowa City, Cedar rapids, IA, 8/86, r# CIC-97
T&P-1292	MP-1292:2	03/66	31240	Retired 2/85, to PNC 4/85, to Wilson Locomotive, Des Moines, IA, 8/86, to Wilmington Terminal, Wilmington, NC, 10/86, r# WTRY-1205
T&P-1293	MP-1293:2	03/66	31241	Retired 6/85, to Chrome 6/85, to Rail Switching Service, Savannah, GA, r# RSS-802
T&P-1294	MP-1294:2	03/66	31242	Retired 6/85, to PNC 6/85, scrapped
T&P-1295	MP-1295:2	03/66	31243	Retired 6/85, to Chrome 6/85, to DuPont DUPX-1295, Gibbstown, NJ, 8/86
T&P-1296	MP-1296:2	03/66	31244	Retired 2/85, to PNC 4/85, scrapped
T&P-1297	MP-1297:2	03/66	31245	Retired 2/85, to PNC 4/85, to Peaker Services, Brighton, MI, 7/85, r# PS-2, to Great Lakes Steel, r# GLS-55
T&P-1298	MP-1298:2	03/66	31246	Retired 2/85, to PNC 4/85, to Morrison Knudsen 9/86, to Southern Peru Copper 12/86, r# SPCC-17
T&P-1299	MP-1299:2	03/66	31247	Retired 6/85, to Chrome 6/85, leased to Iowa Interstate 5/87, r# IAIS-250

Below: A pair of SW1200's from the first order, 1120 and 1105, are hard at work in St. Louis on May 7, 1981. *Lon EuDaly*

EMD
GP7
GP9
GP18

Baldwin
AS-16

Alco
RS-3
"GP12"
RS-11
"GP16"

Roadswitchers had their start on the MoPac when the RS-2's came for the TPMPT in April, 1948. The M-I and the T&P also each had one RS-2, and the STLB&M had the four previously mentioned DRS-4-4-1500's of February, 1949. After these came the BL2's, which were EMD's first attempt at the roadswitcher idea.

The BL2 was not particularly successful, with only 58 units built, but its immediate replacement in EMD's evolving roadswitcher line was a smashing success. Introduced in October, 1949, the GP7 became the most popular model from any builder ever, until the GP9 passed it by in the late 1950's. GP7 demo 922 was the first "geep" built, introducing EMD's true roadswitcher line to the railroad industry.

It is highly doubtful that any model will ever pass the utilitarian "geeps" of the first generation era in quantity. All variations of GP7's and GP9's combine for a total of nearly 7,000 units, and the GP18's and GP20's add another 725 units, bringing the total to 7,711 first generation geeps.

The geep was designed by Dick Dilworth of Electro-Motive, and was intended as a utilitarian model for branch lines, secondary main lines, and in switcher service. The sales pitch included the idea of buying them for road service and then demoting them to yard and branch line service once they had been superseded by

bigger power. Yard crews never liked using geeps, though, because their throttles had a slow response, which made kicking cars difficult and tedious. The slow response, however, was an advantage to starting heavy trains very gradually. Conversion to the switcher throttle would make them impractical as road units. However, the railroads that wanted road units with branch line capabilities went for the geeps in a big way, the MoPac included.

The standard GP7 was a high-hood roadswitcher powered by EMD's 567B 16-cylinder engine rated at 1,500 horsepower. There were 2,724 GP7's built between October, 1949 and May, 1954. In many ways, these roadswitchers completely ended the era of steam on the high iron. By the end of GP7 and GP9 production, even the Appalachian roads had put out the fires in their steamers. At the beginning of 1949, however, steam still ruled. The MoPac still had a total of 937 steam engines, including subsidiaries, but only 261 diesels.

The GP7 was extremely popular with the MoPac. In early 1950, the railroad saw each purchase of geeps as another group of inefficient steamers that could be taken off the railroad. GP7 production had started and the MoPac folks liked what they saw.

By March, 1950 the T&P was receiving their first GP7's, a group of seven units (T&P-1110-1116). Interestingly, the diesel producers had failed to interest the MoPac in dynamic brakes. The railroad had always viewed itself as a basically flat road, and what hills or grades they had were short enough that the motive power people saw little gain in the dynamic brakes. Though a few units for subsidiaries came with dynamic brakes, and second-genera-

tion units for coal service were dynamic brake equipped, very few units on the roster had them.

The next group of GP7's was purchased for the MoPac and two subsidiaries, the STLB&M and the IGN. Eighteen MoPac units came first (MP-4124-4141), followed by three for the IGN (IGN-4121-4123), and finally followed by five STLB&M units (STLB&M-4116-4120). Of these 26, the first two show builder's dates in June, 1950, and the remainder were all built in July. Another eight units came the same month for the MoPac (MP-4142-4149).

These first geeps made an indelible impression on everyone on the railroad. They were easy to maintain, easy to operate, efficient, and easy to perform switching duties with in branch line service. The crews were sold, and so was management. By March, 1951, more GP7's were arriving on the property, this time six more for the IGN (IGN-4153-4158). More orders in 1951 brought in 32 GP7's for the MoPac (MP-4166-4194 and 4150-4152) between March and May, seven more for the STLB&M (STLB&M-4159-4165) in April, two more for the T&P (T&P-1117-1118) in April and six for the T&P (T&P-1119-1124) in August.

January, 1951 also brought a new roadswitcher model to the MoPac's fold, with a single RS-3 delivered to the M-I (MI-62). The RS-3 was Alco's direct competitor to the GP7, and though the RS-3's certainly didn't outlast the easily rebuilt GP7's, it was a successful model for Alco. The RS-3 utilized Alco's familiar 244 12-cylinder engine, and generated 1,600 horsepower, slightly more than EMD's GP7. There were 1,265 RS-3's built, making it one of Alco's most successful engines. The only Alco to outsell the RS-3 was the S-2. No other Alco model came close.

There were a number of RS-3's purchased during the GP7 acquisition period, but for the most part while GP7's were in production the MoPac was happy to order them, and in quantity. Yet another deviation from the GP7 was an order for two Baldwin AS-16's built in November, 1951 for the IGN (IGN-4195-4196).

The AS-16 was Baldwin's answer to the RS-3 and the GP7, and employed the 1,600 horsepower 8-cylinder 608A engine. There

Left: GP18 401 performs switching duties while U30C 8 looks on at Alexandria, Louisiana on November 16, 1973. Alco FA's were traded in on the GP18's in the 400 class, and consequently the 401 and her sisters ride on Alco trucks. The trade-in of the FA's brought 100 new GP18's onto MoPac rails. *Glenn Anderson*

were 127 AS-16's built between 1950 and 1955, and the MoPac bought two groups. The second group was purchased for the STLB&M (STLB&M-4326-4331), and was delivered in June and July, 1954, shortly after the MoPac's last GP7 purchase. Baldwin's 1954 order book graphically demonstrates why that builder decided to exit the locomotive market. Only 14 AS-series switchers were ordered that year. The AS-16's only lasted 11 years on the MoPac, as again the purge of four-cycle power and the standardization on EMD 2-cycle power killed the Baldwins. While the nearby Katy decided to re-power their Baldwins with EMD 567 power plants, the MoPac didn't. The Baldwin's careers were over on MoPac rails.

In the meantime, the M-I ignored the GP7 and bought RS-3's. They placed six more orders for RS-3's after the initial single unit, and purchased a total of 13 units. The RS-3's were delivered in small groups, the first was another single unit purchase (MI-63) in October, 1951. Another single RS-3 was added in June, 1952 (MI-64), and two more came a year later in June, 1953 (MI-65-66). Two more came in October, 1953 (MI-67-68), and two in March, 1954 (MI-69-70).

The M-I was quite pleased with the versatile RS-3 roadswitcher, as it could handle switching chores and road freights as well. In March, 1955, the M-I received their last group of RS-3's, this time four units (MI-71-74). The only other subsidiary that bought any RS-3's was the

Above: A perfect front-front-back-back lashup of GP18's whirl a northbound freight downgrade into Austin, Texas at sunset on a mid summer's eve in 1965. The geep was the ideal unit for the era, and was one of the most popular engines of its time with the crews who had to work them. The 400 class was delivered in Jenks blue. *J Parker Lamb*

Below: The first 31 GP18's were delivered in blue and white, but didn't carry their original numbers for long. The 515 was originally 4811, and leads the two KO&G GP28's through Osawatomie, Kansas on May 1, 1965. The blue and white could still be found in the mid-1960's, but time was running out on the scheme. *Joe McMillan*

In January, 1953 the MV bought four GP7's (MV-151-154), continuing the trend of the Midwestern roads to acquire the highly versatile roadswitcher from EMD. The MV later re-rated their GP7's to 1,600 horsepower, but after the units were placed under T&P control, their rating was reduced back to 1,500 horsepower.

Two of the MV units were wrecked five years later in April, 1958, and were "exchanged" with EMD for GP9's. These two units are sometimes referred to as "rebuilt" GP7's, but the new serial number indicates that EMD considered them new units, not rebuilds. Obviously some components came from the wrecked GP7's. They were boosted to 1,800 horsepower, but again when the T&P inherited them they were re-rated back to 1,500, a GP7 equivalent.

March, 1953 and March through May, 1954 saw the usual spring purchase of more motive power, again GP7's. In two main orders the MoPac and its subsidiaries acquired an additional 36 GP7's. The STLB&M added eight

A rather odd purchase was the acquisition of two Baldwin AS-16's by the I-GN in November, 1951. Even stranger was MoPac's later purchase of six of the boxy Baldwins. The AS-16 was a direct competitor of the Alco RS-series and EMD's geeps, but it fared poorly.

Above: Not long from the scrapper's torch, the 939's number boards cast long shadows in the Texas sun in Austin in 1963. Her hulk is not worth another coat of paint. *J Parker Lamb*

Below: Builders photo of I-GN 4195 clearly shows the "F" on the long hood end. Baldwin was still thinking like a steam producer. *Charlie Duckworth collection*

TPMPT, which picked up a single unit in April, 1956 (TPMPT-24). The MoPac itself bought RS-3's also, but not until after the massive GP7 acquisitions were over.

From 1952 to 1954 the MoPac continued to buy GP7's from EMD, in quantities that drove steam from the rails. 1952 started with a group of four GP7's for the KO&G (KO&G-801-804) delivered in January. By February the MoPac received a large group split among several subsidiaries. Delivered between February and July, this order consisted of six units for the IGN

(IGN-4197-4202), eight units for the STLB&M (STLB&M-4203-4207 and 4249-4251), and 41 units for the MoPac (MP-4208-4248).

In April, 1952 the T&P expanded their GP7 fleet with the purchase of six more units (T&P-1125-1130), and in October five more geeps came for the KO&G (KO&G-805-809). Between these two orders, in May, 1952, diesels outnumbered steam on US Class I's for the first time. By late 1952, the GP7 had become the dominant type of roadswitcher on the MoPac's rails.

Left: After purchasing something near a legion of GP7's and GP9's, the order for 12 RS-11's in 1959 was out of character for the MoPac. The RS-11's were destined to be the odd-men-out, and wound up orphaned among the 567-powered fleet. A trio of the hefty Alco's work a cut of autoracks at the south end of the yard at Dupo, Illinois in December, 1961. They won't keep their 251 engines for long. *Harold K Vollrath collection*

more geeps, with number series scattered in amongst the MoPac and IGN numbers (STLB&M-4252-4253, 4284-4286, 4298, and 4323-4324). The IGN subsidiary also added more GP7's, a total of 14 came in three number series (IGN-4254-4255, 4287-4297, and 4325).

The MoPac itself added 52 more GP7's, a group in March, 1953 (MP-4256-4283) and another group of 24 in April and May, 1954 (MP-4299-4322) bringing the total GP7 count for the entire system to a staggering 242 units. They were easily the most numerous model on the MoPac, and would remain so until second-hand Rock Island GP38-2's would make that model the most numerous ever on MoPac rails. In fact, C&EI GP7's would add an additional 19 units to the MoPac fleet, with the other 11 C&EI GP7's going to L&N.

The MoPac was content with its motive power situation for the better part of a year, and when the motive power folks went back for more power, they surprisingly went to both Alco and EMD. January, 1955 saw orders arriving from both builders, RS-3's from Alco and GP9's from EMD.

The GP9 was the next evolutionary step for EMD, and utilized the 567C 16-cylinder engine to generate 1,750 horsepower. The GP9 was easily the most popular first generation locomotive in North America. All types combined for a total production of 4,257 GP9's built in six years, from January, 1954 through December, 1959. Of these, 3,436 were standard GP9's sold in the US, while 646 GP9's went to Canada and 10 went to Mexico. An additional 165 GP9B's were built for the Pennsylvania Railroad and the UP. Only the second generation SD40-2 out-sold the GP9.

The MoPac only ordered GP9's once, a total of 40 units (MP-4332-4371) delivered between January and April, 1955. Later, two groups of GP9's totaling 14 units came for the T&P, the first in March, 1957 (T&P-1131-1136) and the second in May of the same year

(T&P-1137-1144). This brought the total GP9 count to 54 units. Two more came via the C&EI when that road was acquired, while four of the C&EI GP9's went to the L&N. The C&EI units were rated at 1,800 horsepower.

Meanwhile, the shop floor at Alco was littered with RS-3's being built for the MoPac at the same time GP9's were coming out of La Grange. Two orders brought 26 RS-3's into the MoPac fold in early 1955, which would eventually be joined by the 13 M-I units and the lone TPMPT RS-3. The first order was delivered in January and February, 1955 (MP-4501-4512) and the second group came in February (MP-4513-4526).

The RS-3 fleet was originally intended for local service, and performed in that capacity for a number of years. Eventually, high maintenance costs and a high failure rate with the 12-244 engine forced them into yard service. Since yard service didn't require or utilize the full 1,500 horsepower, the MoPac decided that these units could be repowered with the less powerful

EMD 12-567 engine. The engines for these rebuilds came from the failing E unit fleet, which supplied 12-567A engines that were rebuilt and plugged into the RS-3's. These conversions were referred to as "EMCO's" by the MoPac, and given the model designation "GP12."

From April, 1955 through mid-1959, no new units came to the MoPac, which in many ways explains the lack of GP9's in any substantial quantity on the MoPac's roster. This four-year gap in diesel purchases was the longest gap between MoPac locomotive purchases in the road's entire diesel history. As a final note to the GP9 purchases, two MV GP7's (MV-152:1 and 153:1) were wrecked and traded in and rebuilt to "GP9m's" (MV-152:2 and 153:2).

The early geep fleet went through numerous rebuildings and alterations, resulting in a multitude of appearances. Many of the 200-series GP7's were rebuilt to 300-series standards, Their noses were chopped, 2,500 gallon

Below: GP7 4169 has the unfortunate distinction of being the first unit to be painted in Jenks blue. The unit only had one nose chevron, and this would be changed to two for the remainder of the units destined for the new scheme. The unlucky geep leads an RS-11 and three FA's through Greenwood Junction, Oklahoma on June 21, 1961. *Louis Marre*

Roadswitchers in action!

Left: GP7 269 was ordered for the I-GN as 4290, and leads GP7 245 and two more geeps through Alexandria, Louisiana on November 12, 1972. Only the MoPac had GP7's built after December, 1953, which came with GP9-like hoods. With a friendly wave from the engineer the geeps roll by. *Glenn Anderson*

Below: The last light of a summer's day strikes rebuilt "GP12" 1075 working in Atchison, Kansas in June, 1971. The 1075 was once a 244-powered RS-3, but has since had a 12-cylinder EMD 567 engine installed. *Bruce Petty*

Opposite page top: Long evening shadows creep across the rails as "GP12" 1086 works the yard at Alexandria, Louisiana on November 26, 1972 under a cloudless sky. The stars will soon be out. *Glenn Anderson*

Opposite page bottom: T&P GP9 394 is almost ready for a night run out of Alexandria, Louisiana on a summer evening in 1970. Thunderclouds build in the distance, adding a rosy hue to the scene just before the light fails. The MoPac bought only a few GP9's, at least compared to the GP7. They wound up with a total of 56, including two for the MV that were rebuilt from the hulks of wrecked GP7's. Fourteen came for the T&P and the MoPac got 40. *Glenn Anderson*

fuel tanks replaced the 1,600 gallon originals, which in turn forced the air reservoirs to be mounted up over the long hood. Their footboards were removed and snow plows were added. Two of the GP18's (MP-480 and MP-488) had "Farr" air filters added. This was an experiment to test the design to take either Paper Filters or Inertial Filters or both. It was not instituted as a program, and the two units were the only GP18's so equipped. Two GP7's (MP-1671 and MP-1672) also got the Farr air filters.

Oddly enough, when a new locomotive purchase was finally approved in 1959, the road went to ALCO rather than EMD. It was the last time. An order for 12 1,800 horsepower RS-11 roadswitchers from ALCO was delivered in October and November (MP-4601-4612). These rode on what remained of the Baldwin DR-4-4-1500 trucks and traction motors, making them a combination unique to the MoPac.

The RS-11 was a direct competitor of the GP9, but by account of the production totals it is apparent that it failed to compete. Though it was modestly successful for ALCO, it's production total of 327 units for U. S. roads and 99 for Mexico pale next to the GP9's success. On the flip side, if one has it in mind to defend ALCO, nothing compared to the GP9's success.

The RS-11's failure on the MoPac is evident in hindsight. A scant six years after their purchase, they were being rebuilt into honorary GP9's in the MoPac's North Little Rock shops. In 1965 the entire 12 units were re-engined with 16-cylinder 1,650 horsepower EMD 567's, and were redesignated as "GP16's."

The MoPac fabricated their own multi-stack manifolds for the rebuilt units, which gave them a unique appearance. EMD radiator fans and shutters were substituted, but the ALCO

long hood remained basically intact, with the exception that the "notches" in the corners were eliminated. They were the only RS-11's repowered by any road, and lasted about another ten years before they were retired. Even as rebuilt units they were disliked by the crews. Their electrical gear was problematic and they failed where the geeps were a success.

At the same time, the RS-3's went through a similar program, and were re-engined with 12-cylinder EMD 567 power plants. The RS-3's were known as "RS-3m's" or more commonly "GP12's." They were also repowered in the North Little Rock shops and also retained much of their Alco character. They had a very distinc-

Above: Frisco and MoPac freights pound the diamonds arriving at Broadway Junction in Memphis, Tennessee side by side in August, 1973. GP7 304 leads the MoPac freight, a geep that was originally steam generator equipped. The air reservoirs have been relocated to the top of the long hood, often referred to as "torpedo tubes." *David Johnston*

Below: A northbound freight off the Brownsville Subdivision arrives in Houston behind GP18 1925, one of the 400-series that rode on FA trade-in trucks. The train is powered with seven units, two of which are switchers. The rather tattered GP18 still has six years of service left when this was taken on the fourth of July, 1978. *George Hamlin*

tive three-stack manifold that was fabricated by the MoPac at North Little Rock, and EMD fans were again substituted.

Three of the MoPac's RS-2's were repowered in a similar fashion. Few other railroads repowered these Alco models. L&N repowered one RS-3 in a similar way, and the Katy, the Frisco, and the Rock Island repowered RS-2's or RS-3's with 16-cylinder 567 EMD power plants.

This was all part of the master plan for the MoPac's motive power put in place by John German. He came from the Great Northern, and became the youngest Vice President - Mechanical in the industry. He put North Little Rock, the MoPac's main diesel shop, on the same playing field as La Grange, being completely sold on the 567 power plant. During this era the MoPac avoided turbochargers, six motor trucks, 645 engines (or anything else besides a 567 for that matter), and even "ordinary" 567 engines. The MoPac fleet at this time began receiving the MoPac-designed intake and exhaust manifolds with their characteristic four exhaust stacks. This gained enormous fuel efficiency and an increase of about 10% in horsepower.

The final model of first generation power that the MoPac purchased was EMD's GP18. The GP18 was powered with EMD's 16-cylinder 567D1 engine, and generated 1,800 horsepower. Though it is difficult to make an absolutely clean break between first and second generation units, the 567 is generally associated with first generation power. The 567 was still the engine in use when the GP28, GP30 and GP35 models rolled out the door at La Grange, though these three models are usually associated

with second generation power. The above logic would then dictate that the GP18 was the last of the first generation power purchased by the MoPac.

In April, May, and June, 1960 the MoPac bought 26 GP18's for the MoPac proper (MP-4801-4826), and an additional five for the T&P (T&P-1145-1149). The final two MoPac units and all five of the T&P units came with low noses, a new look for the MoPac. Within just a few months, the GP18's were experiencing broken exhaust valves and cracked cylinder heads. After studying the problem, the MoPac concluded that the problem was the most serious on units assigned to Kansas City, and determined that the higher altitude on the runs to Pueblo was the culprit. The problem centered around the very high back pressure that these units operated at, and the MoPac's solution was to add two additional exhaust stacks.

The four-stack arrangement reduced the back pressure by about 70%, and added an additional 80 horsepower per unit without any greater fuel consumption. The results from the extra exhaust stacks was so significant that the MoPac began adding stacks to all GP18's, and later added them to GP7's and GP9's. In fact, this program found its way throughout later normally aspirated (non-turbocharged) units, including GP28's, GP38's, GP38-2's, and the GP35's after they were rebuilt to "GP35m's" (with turbochargers removed). The entire group of the MoPac high-hood GP18's were later chopnosed by the MoPac. The 26 GP18's were the MoPac's last units delivered in the attractive blue and white first generation paint scheme.

The MoPac traded in FA's and FB's on more GP18's from EMD, and 100 of the GP18's rode on trade-in Alco AAR type B trucks from the FA's, and had the original GE motors. These were numbered MP-400-499, and arrived between January, 1962 and January, 1963. They were all built with low-noses, and all came in the MoPac's new dress - Jenks blue. An additional 20 GP18's (MP-534-550 and MP-4827-4829) were bought by the MoPac the same year, these all coming with low noses but on standard EMD trucks. This brought the GP18 total to 151 units, which trailed only the GP7 and the F7 in total purchases by the MoPac at the time.

At some point it is interesting to take a step back and do a little explaining on the 567-series engines from EMD. As with all the EMDs, the

Below: The GP18 was not a particularly successful model, perhaps because the earlier diesel purchases had not quite began to wear out. The railroads that bought a lot of F-units typically hung on to them long into the second generation, while those that didn't dieselize with covered wagons bought GP7's and GP9's. The MoPac had the misfortune (financially) of buying a significant number of FA's, and they were shot after a relatively short career. After this, the GP18 was the model of choice for the MoPac, which was not particularly big on turbochargers. The MoPac bought 146 GP18's, and the T&P added another 5. Their fleet accounted for over 43 percent of GP18's built for U. S. roads. Veteran GP18 1928 leads a conglomeration of motive power through Roanoke, Texas on December 9, 1978.
Bill Phillips photo, James Holder collection

model number of the prime mover is its cylinder's displacement in inches, thus each cylinder of the 567 displaces 567 cubic inches. EMD added the letter suffix to identify each subsequent model of engine, distinguishable by a number of characteristics. The original 567, the 567A and its immediate offspring, the 567B have a round air box and oil pan covers. Unfortunately, many changes regularly occur, resulting in a 567B that can have many modifications. It is not unusual at all to see 567B engines with 567C crankcases, or even a mixture of A's, AC's B's, BC's, and C's. Power assemblies were drastically altered be-

tween the 567B and 567C, but they still were somewhat interchangeable. The 567AC and 567BC hybrids are essentially 567A or 567B prime movers with the crankcases modified to take 567C cylinder assemblies (or power assemblies). Derated 645 crankcases and power assemblies can also be used, however, the capacity of the electrical system in the 567 becomes the limiting factor.

The GP18's lasted over 20 years on the MoPac, serving on everything from hotshots to the slowest old local and yard service. All of the geeps turned out to be good investments, as they

Above: In most minds the GP7 is nearly always connected with the local freight, where the geep's versatility could be exploited to the maximum. Such is the case with GP7 221, performing the local duties at Topeka, Kansas on July 20, 1968. *Joe McMillan*

not only performed well over a long duration, but also held a good resale value. Many of their scrapped-out components are still marketable today.

Left: T&P GP7 105 leads GP9 359 and GP18's 420 and 481 through Tioga, Louisiana on November 3, 1973. The geeps were the mainstay of through freight power throughout the early and mid-1960's, until they were supplanted by second generation power. *Glenn Anderson*

Opposite page top: In early 1957 the T&P placed two orders for GP9's, an earlier MoPac order had already brought 40 on the property. One of the T&P units, now wearing 564, swings around the curve at the top of Kirkwood Hill in Kirkwood, Missouri with the Sedalia Subdivision local freight on October 20, 1974. *Paul Dalman photo, James Holder collection*

Opposite page bottom: One of the last order of GP7's, MoPac 287, rolls through Orange, Texas on June 17, 1975. *James Holder*

EMD GP7   1,500 hp   4 units
TE = 61,490   WT = 245,950
Wheels = 40"   Fuel = 1,200
Engine: EMD 16-567B V-type 16-cylinder 2-cycle
Min Speed for TE = 12.0 mph
62:15 Gearing   65 mph Max

1st No	2nd No	3rd No	4th No	Built	Build#	Notes
MV-151	MV-106	T&P-106	T&P-1693	01/53	17847	Note 1
MV-152:1				02/53	17848	Note 2
MV-153:1				02/53	17849	Note 3
MV-154	MV-107	T&P-107	T&P-1694	01/53	17850	Note 4

Note 1: Rerated to 1,600 hp, then back to 1,500 hp under T&P. Retired 1980,
    T-I to EMD
Note 2: Wrecked 4/58, rebuilt 4/58 to "GP9m" MV-152:2
Note 3: Wrecked 4/58, rebuilt 4/58 to "GP9m" MV-153:2
Note 4: Rerated to 1,600 hp, then back to 1,500 hp under T&P. Retired
    1979-1981, T-I to EMD

EMD GP7   1,500 hp   9 units
TE = 61,260   WT = 245,030
Wheels = 40"   Fuel = 1,200
Engine: EMD 16-567B V-type 16-cylinder 2-cycle
Min Speed for TE = 12.0 mph
62:15 Gearing   65 mph Max
Some had 567BC engines
Rerated to 1,600 hp, 1,600 gallon fuel tanks
T-I to EMD

1st No	2nd No	3rd No	4th No	Built	Build#	Retired	Notes
KO&G-801	T&P-97	T&P-1637	MP-637:2	01/52	15632	09/79	
KO&G-802	T&P-98	T&P-1638		01/52	15633	12/75	
KO&G-803	T&P-99	T&P-1639		01/52	15845	11/75	Note 1
KO&G-804	T&P-100	T&P-1640	MP-640	01/52	15846	09/79	
KO&G-805	T&P-101	T&P-1688		10/52	17468	12/79	Note 2
KO&G-806	T&P-102	T&P-1689		10/52	17469	09/79	
KO&G-807	T&P-103	T&P-1690		12/52	17844	79-81	
KO&G-808	T&P-104	T&P-1691		12/52	17845	79-81	
KO&G-809	T&P-105	T&P-1692		01/53	17846	01/76	Note 3

Note 1: Wrecked at Vienna IL 6/12/75
Note 2: T-I on GP38-2's MP-2158-2197
Note 3: Wrecked 12/75, scrapped

EMD GP7   1,500 hp   21 units
TE = 62,185   WT = 245,950
Wheels = 40"   Fuel = 1,200
Engine: EMD 16-567B V-type 16-cylinder 2-cycle
Min Speed for TE = 12.0 mph
62:15 Gearing   65 mph Max
Some had 567BC engines
Rerated to 1,600 hp
T-I to EMD (627, 632, 641 and 643 T-I on GP38-2's MP-2158-2197)

1st No	2nd No	3rd No	4th No	Built	Build#	Retired	Notes
T&P-1110	T&P-110			03/50	11018	1976	Fuel = 1,600
T&P-1111	T&P-111			03/50	11019	03/75	Fuel = 1,600
T&P-1112	T&P-112			03/50	11020	75-79	
T&P-1113	T&P-113			03/50	11021	10/74	
T&P-1114	T&P-114			03/50	11022	1976	
T&P-1115	T&P-115			03/50	11023	75-79	
T&P-1116	T&P-116			03/50	11024	75-79	
T&P-1117	T&P-117			04/51	14020	03/73	Note 1
T&P-1118	T&P-118	MP-1627:1	MP-627:2	04/51	14021	12/79	
T&P-1119	T&P-119	MP-1628:1	MP-628:2	08/51	14550	09/79	
T&P-1120	T&P-120	MP-1629:1		08/51	14551	09/79	
T&P-1121	T&P-121	MP-1630:1		08/51	14552	1976	
T&P-1122	T&P-122	MP-1631:1	MP-631:2	08/51	14553	09/79	
T&P-1123	T&P-123	MP-1632:1	MP-632:2	08/51	14554	12/79	
T&P-1124	T&P-124	MP-1633:1		08/51	14555	75-79	
T&P-1125	T&P-125	MP-1641:1	MP-641	04/52	15824	12/79	Fuel = 1,600
T&P-1126	T&P-126	MP-1642:1	MP-642:1	04/52	15825	09/79	Fuel = 1,600
T&P-1127	T&P-127	MP-1643:1	MP-643	04/52	15826	12/79	Fuel = 1,600
T&P-1128	T&P-128			04/52	15827	10/74	Fuel = 1,600
T&P-1129	T&P-129	MP-1644:1		04/52	15828	75-79	Fuel = 1,600
T&P-1130	T&P-130			04/52	15829	11/74	Fuel = 1,600

Note 1: Wrecked 2/21/73 Taft or Luling LA

EMD GP7   1,500 hp   26 units
TE = 61,005   WT = 244,030
Wheels = 40"   Fuel = 1,200
Engine: EMD 16-567B V-type 16-cylinder 2-cycle
Min Speed for TE = 11.0 mph
62:15 Gearing   65 mph Max
Upgraded to 1,600 hp, T-I to EMD

1st No	2nd No	Built	Build#	Notes & Dispositions
STLB&M-4116	MP-131	07/50	11549	Retired 1975-1979
STLB&M-4117	MP-132	07/50	11550	Retired 1976
STLB&M-4118	MP-133	07/50	11551	Retired 1975-1979
STLB&M-4119	MP-134	07/50	11552	Retired 9/79
STLB&M-4120	MP-135	07/50	11553	Retired 1975-1979
IGN-4121	MP-136	07/50	11546	Retired 1975-1979
IGN-4122	MP-137	07/50	11547	Retired 10/74
IGN-4123	MP-138	07/50	11548	Retired 1975-1979
MP-4124	MP-139	06/50	11528	Wore Jenks blue as 4124. Retired 11/75
MP-4125	MP-140	06/50	11529	Retired 1975-1979
MP-4126	MP-141	07/50	11530	Retired 1975-1979
MP-4127	MP-142	07/50	11531	Retired 1975-1979
MP-4128	MP-143	07/50	11532	Retired 1976
MP-4129	MP-144	07/50	11533	Snow plow front. Chopnose by MoPac, 1,700 gallon fuel tank. Retired 9/79
MP-4130	MP-145	07/50	11534	Retired 12/79, T-I on GP38-2's MP-2158-2197
MP-4131	MP-146	07/50	11535	Retired 1975-1979
MP-4132	MP-147	07/50	11536	Retired 12/79, T-I on GP38-2's MP-2158-2197
MP-4133	MP-148	07/50	11537	Retired 1975-1979, T-I to EMD
MP-4134	MP-149	07/50	11538	Retired 12/79, T-I GP38-2's MP-2158-2197
MP-4135	MP-150	07/50	11539	Retired 1975-1979
MP-4136	MP-151	07/50	11540	Retired 1975-1979
MP-4137	MP-152	07/50	11541	Retired 3/75
MP-4138	MP-153	07/50	11542	Retired 1975-1979
MP-4139	MP-154	07/50	11543	Retired 1975-1979
MP-4140	MP-155	07/50	11544	Retired 1976
MP-4141	MP-156	07/50	11545	Retired 1975-1979

EMD GP7   1,500 hp   8 units
TE = 63,290   WT = 253,160
Wheels = 40"   Fuel = 800
Engine: EMD 16-567B V-type 16-cylinder 2-cycle
Min Speed for TE = 11.0 mph
62:15 Gearing   65 mph Max
Equipped with steam generators
Upgraded to 1,600 hp, T-I to EMD

1st No	2nd No	3rd No	4th No	Built	Build#	Notes & Dispositions
MP-4142	MP-295			07/50	8670	Retired 1979
MP-4143	MP-296			07/50	8671	Note1
MP-4144	MP-297			07/50	8672	Retired 9/79
MP-4145	MP-298			07/50	8673	Retired 1975-1979
MP-4146	MP-299	MP-332:3	MP-1753	07/50	8674	Note 2
MP-4147	MP-300	MP-1750		07/50	8675	Note 3
MP-4148	MP-301:2	MP-1751		07/50	8676	Note 4
MP-4149	MP-302:2	MP-1752		07/50	8677	Note 5

Note 1: Retired 12/79, T-I GP38-2's MP-2158-2197
Note 2: Rebuilt to "GP7u," chopnose by MoPac. Retired 8/81
Note 3: Rebuilt to "GP7u," 1,800 hp 567BC engine, snow plow front, chopnose by MoPac, 2,500 gallon fuel tank. Retired 1980
Note 4: Rebuilt to "GP7u," 1,800 hp 567BC engine, snow plow front, chopnose by MoPac, 2,500 gallon fuel tank. Wrecked at Vienna IL 6/12/75, retired 12/75
Note 5: Rebuilt to "GP7u," 1,800 hp 567BC engine, snow plow front, chopnose by MoPac, 2,500 gallon fuel tank. Retired 1979-1981

Above: In January, 1952 the KO&G took delivery of four GP7's, 801-804. The 804 now wears its second number, T&P-100, and works for its new official owner. It is at Dolton, Illinois on July 25, 1972. *Joe McMillan*

Opposite page top: A very few geeps were repainted into Jenks blue while retaining their 4-digit numbers. GP7 4124 is such a creature, shuffling around in North Little Rock on December 18, 1961. *Louis Marre*

Opposite page bottom: T&P's geeps were delivered in Swamp Holly Orange and black. Highly visible GP7 1130 is at Shreveport, Louisiana in December, 1960. *Harold K Vollrath collection*

EMD GP7   1,500 hp   16 units
TE = 62,745   WT = 250,980
Wheels = 40"   Fuel = 800
Engine: EMD 16-567B V-type 16-cylinder 2-cycle
Min Speed for TE = 11.0 mph
62:15 Gearing   65 mph Max
Equipped with steam generators
Upgraded to 1,600 hp
1754-1759 rebuilt to "GP7u" with 1,800 hp EMD 16-567BC engine, snow plow front, chopnose by MoPac, and 2,500 gallon fuel tank. T-I to EMD

1st No	2nd No	3rd No	4th No	Built	Build#	Notes
MP-4150	MP-303:2	MP-1754		05/51	14350	Retired 8/81
MP-4151	MP-304:2	MP-1755		05/51	14351	Note 1
MP-4152	MP-305:2	MP-1756		05/51	14352	Retired 11/81
IGN-4153	MP-157:2	MP-257:2	MP-1725	03/51	14330	Retired 79-81
IGN-4154	MP-158			03/51	14331	Retired 75-79
IGN-4155	MP-159			03/51	14332	Retired 9/79
IGN-4156	MP-160			03/51	14333	Retired 75-79
IGN-4157	MP-161			03/51	14334	Retired 75-79
IGN-4158	MP-162			03/51	14335	Retired 12/79
STLB&M-4159	MP-163			04/51	14320	Note 2
STLB&M-4160	MP-164			04/51	14321	Retired 75-79
STLB&M-4161	MP-306:2	MP-1757		04/51	14322	Retired 9/79
STLB&M-4162	MP-307:2	MP-1758		04/51	14323	Retired 79-81
STLB&M-4163	MP-308:2	MP-1759		04/51	14324	Retired 1/76
STLB&M-4164	MP-165			04/51	14318	Retired 12/79
STLB&M-4165	MP-166			04/51	14319	Retired 11/74

Note 1: Wrecked 2/3/76 Ward AR, retired
Note 2: Snow plow front. Chopnose by MoPac. Retired 1976

EMD GP7   1,500 hp   29 units
TE = 61,180   WT = 244,725
Wheels = 40"   Fuel = 1,200
Engine: EMD 16-567B V-type 16-cylinder 2-cycle
Min Speed for TE = 11.0 mph
62:15 Gearing   65 mph Max
Upgraded to 1,600 hp. T-I to EMD

1st No	2nd No	3rd No	4th No	Built	Build#	Notes & Dispositions
MP-4166	MP-167			03/51	12571	Retired 9/79
MP-4167	MP-168			03/51	12572	Retired 12/79
MP-4168	MP-169			03/51	12573	Retired 12/79
MP-4169	MP-170	MP-1600:1	MP-600:1	03/51	12574	Retired 12/79
MP-4170	MP-171	MP-1601:1	MP-601	03/51	12575	Retired 9/79
MP-4171	MP-172	MP-1602:1	MP-602	03/51	12576	Retired 9/79
MP-4172	MP-173	MP-1603:1	MP-603:1	03/51	12577	Retired 1979
MP-4173	MP-174	MP-1604:1	MP-604:1	03/51	12578	Retired 12/79
MP-4174	MP-175	MP-1605:1		03/51	12579	Retired 1976
MP-4175	MP-176	MP-1606:1	MP-606:1	03/51	12580	Retired 9/79
MP-4176	MP-177	MP-1607:1	MP-607	05/51	12581	Retired 12/79
MP-4177	MP-178	MP-1608:1	MP-608:1	05/51	12582	Retired 9/79
MP-4178	MP-179	MP-1609:1		05/51	12583	Retired 1976
MP-4179	MP-180	MP-1610:1	MP-610	05/51	12584	Retired 12/79
MP-4180	MP-181	MP-1611:1	MP-611:1	05/51	12585	Retired 12/79
MP-4181	MP-182	MP-1612:1	MP-612:1	05/51	14336	Retired 1979
MP-4182	MP-183	MP-1613:1	MP-613	05/51	14337	Retired 9/79
MP-4183	MP-184	MP-1614:1	MP-614	05/51	14338	Retired 9/79
MP-4184	MP-185	MP-1615:1	MP-615:2	05/51	14339	Retired 9/79
MP-4185	MP-186	MP-1616:1	MP-616:2	05/51	14340	Retired 12/79
MP-4186	MP-187	MP-1617:1	MP-617:2	05/51	14341	Retired 9/79
MP-4187	MP-188	MP-1618:1	MP-618:2	05/51	14342	Retired 9/79
MP-4188	MP-189	MP-1619:1	MP-619:3	05/51	14343	Retired 9/79
MP-4189	MP-190	MP-1620:1	MP-620:3	05/51	14344	Note 1. Retired 9/79
MP-4190	MP-191	MP-1621:1	MP-621:3	05/51	14345	Note 1. Retired 9/79
MP-4191	MP-192	MP-1622:1	MP-622:3	05/51	14346	Note 1. Retired 12/79
MP-4192	MP-193	MP-1623:1	MP-623:3	05/51	14347	Note 1. Retired 9/79
MP-4193	MP-194	MP-1624:1	MP-624:3	05/51	14348	Note 1. Retired 9/79
MP-4194	MP-195	MP-1625:1	MP-625:3	05/51	14349	Note 1. Retired 9/79

Note 1: Snow plow both ends

Left: Sparkling new MoPac GP7 4180 depicts the as-delivered livery in June, 1951. It was the last unit of an order for 15 GP7's that were built at La Grange between March and May, 1951. It is at the beginning of a million-plus mile career. *Ed Hawkins collection*

Right: GP7 310 was part of an order for passenger geeps equipped with steam generators. It was retrofitted with a 2,500 gallon fuel tank. It rests quietly in the engine terminal at Houston, Texas on September 8, 1965, waiting for the next call. *Joe McMillan*

EMD GP7   1,500 hp   44 units
TE = 61,690   WT = 246,755
Wheels = 40"   Fuel = 1,600
Engine: EMD 16-567B V-type 16-cylinder 2-cycle
Min Speed for TE = 11.0 mph
62:15 Gearing   65 mph Max
All except MP-4208 and 4236 upgraded to 1,600 hp.
T-I to EMD (1645, 1649, 1653, 1658, 1665-1667, and 1670 T-I on GP38-2's MP-2158-2197)

1st No	2nd No	3rd No	Built	Build#	Retired	Notes
IGN-4197	MP-196	MP-1682:1	07/52	16126	79-81	Note 1
IGN-4198	MP-197	MP-1683:1	07/52	16127	79-81	Note 1
IGN-4199	MP-198	MP-1684:1	07/52	16128	79-81	Note 1
IGN-4200	MP-199	MP-1685:1	07/52	16129	1980	Note 1
IGN-4201	MP-200	MP-1686:1	07/52	16130	79-81	
IGN-4202	MP-201:2	MP-1687:1	07/52	16131	79-81	
STLB&M-4203	MP-202:2	MP-1645:1	04/52	16118	12/79	
STLB&M-4204	MP-203:2	MP-1646:1	04/52	16119	75-79	Note 3
STLB&M-4205	MP-204:2	MP-1647:1	04/52	16120	79-81	
STLB&M-4206	MP-205:2	MP-1648:1	04/52	16121	79-81	
STLB&M-4207	MP-206:2	MP-1649:1	04/52	16122	12/79	
MP-4208			02/52	16132	05/60	Note 3, 4
MP-4209	MP-207:2	MP-1650:1	02/52	16133	79-81	
MP-4210	MP-208:2	MP-1651:1	02/52	16134	1980	
MP-4211	MP-209	MP-1652:1	02/52	16135	79-81	Note 2, 3 , 5
MP-4212	MP-210	MP-1653:1	02/52	16136	12/79	
MP-4213	MP-211	MP-1654:1	02/52	16137	09/79	
MP-4214	MP-212	MP-1655:1	02/52	16138	09/79	
MP-4215	MP-213	MP-1656:1	02/52	16139	79/81	
MP-4216	MP-214	MP-1657:1	02/52	16140	1980	
MP-4217	MP-215	MP-1658:1	02/52	16141	12/79	Note 2
MP-4218	MP-216	MP-1659:1	03/52	16142	1980	
MP-4219	MP-217	MP-1660:1	03/52	16143	1980	
MP-4220	MP-218	MP-1661:1	03/52	16144	1980	
MP-4221	MP-219	MP-1662:1	03/52	16145	1980	
MP-4222	MP-220	MP-1663:1	03/52	16146	09/79	
MP-4223	MP-221	MP-1664:1	03/52	16147	1980	Note 2, 3, 5
MP-4224	MP-222	MP-1665:1	03/52	16148	12/79	
MP-4225	MP-223	MP-1666:1	03/52	16149	12/79	
MP-4226	MP-224	MP-1667:1	03/52	16150	12/79	
MP-4227	MP-225		03/52	16151	12/73	Note 2, 3,6
MP-4228	MP-226	MP-1668:1	03/52	16152	1976	
MP-4229	MP-227	MP-1669:1	03/52	16153	79-81	
MP-4230	MP-228	MP-1670:1	03/52	16154	12/79	
MP-4231	MP-229	MP-1671:1	03/52	16155	79-81	Note 7
MP-4232	MP-230	MP-1672:1	04/52	16156	1980	Note 7
MP-4233	MP-231	MP-1673:1	04/52	16157	79-81	
MP-4234	MP-232	MP-1674:1	04/52	16158	1980	Note 3
MP-4235	MP-233	MP-1675:1	04/52	16159	79-81	
MP-4236			04/52	16160		Note 3, 8
MP-4237	MP-234	MP-1676:1	04/52	16161	04/79	Note 9
MP-4238	MP-235	MP-1677:1	04/52	16162	79-81	
MP-4239	MP-236	MP-1678:1	04/52	16163	79-81	
MP-4240	MP-237	MP-1679:1	04/52	16164	1980	

Note 1: Snow plow both ends
Note 2: Snow plow front
Note 3: Chopnose by MoPac
Note 4: Wrecked, T-I 5/60 on GP18 1877
Note 5: 2,500 gallon fuel tank
Note 6: Wrecked 12/1/73 Cotulla TX
Note 7: Farr air system applied by MoPac
Note 8: T-I on GP18 1878
Note 9: Wore Jenks blue as 4237

EMD GP7   1,500 hp   11 units
TE = 62,630   WT = 250,535
Wheels = 40"   Fuel = 800
Engine: EMD 16-567B V-type 16-cylinder 2-cycle
Min Speed for TE = 11.0 mph
62:15 Gearing   65 mph Max
Equipped with steam generators. All but 4249 rebuilt to "GP7u" with Chopnose by MoPac snow plow front, 2,500 gallon fuel tank, and 1,800 hp.
Exceptions: 1764 had no snow plow
1766 not chopnose and no snow plow
1681 not chopnose, no snow plow, and1,800 gallon fuel tank
All T-I to EMD

1st No	2nd No	3rd No	4th No	Built	Build#	Retired	Notes
MP-4241	MP-309:2	MP-1760		05/52	16165	79-81	
MP-4242	MP-310:2	MP-1761		05/52	16166	11/81	
MP-4243	MP-311:2	MP-1762		05/52	16167	08/81	
MP-4244	MP-312:2	MP-1763		05/52	16168	08/81	
MP-4245	MP-238	MP-1680:1	MP-1764	05/52	16169	79-81	
MP-4246	MP-313:2	MP-1765		05/52	16170	1980	Note 1
MP-4247	MP-314:2	MP-1766		05/52	16171	08/81	
MP-4248	MP-315:2			05/52	16172	08/81	
STLB&M-4249	MP-239	MP-1681:1		04/52	16123	79-81	
STLB&M-4250	MP-316:2	MP-1767		04/52	16124	1980	
STLB&M-4251	MP-317:2	MP-1768		04/52	16125	08/81	

Note 1: Wrecked 4/2/71 at Paola, rebuilt

EMD GP7   1,500 hp   4 units
TE = 63,700   WT = 254,800
Wheels = 40"   Fuel = 1,100
Engine: EMD 16-567B V-type 16-cylinder 2-cycle
Min Speed for TE = 11.0 mph
62:15 Gearing   65 mph Max
Equipped with steam generators
Rebuilt to "GP7u," rerated to 1,800 hp, 2,500 gallon fuel tanks

1st No	2nd No	3rd No	Built	Build#	Notes & Dispositions
STLB&M-4252	MP-318:2	MP-1769	03/53	18031	Note 1. Retired 8/81
STLB&M-4253	MP-319:2	MP-1770	03/53	18032	Note 1. Retired 1981
IGN-4254	MP-320:2	MP-1771	03/53	18026	Retired 1980
IGN-4255	MP-321:2	MP-1772	03/53	18027	Retired 1980

Note 1: Chopnose by MoPac, snow plow front

Right: GP7 1672 wears its third number and its second paint scheme. It was delivered in blue and white as 4232, and wore 232 for a time. It is one of two GP7's in its class that received a Farr air system applied by the MoPac. The box on the top of the long hood behind the cab houses the unique air system. It is at North Little Rock on December 7, 1977, 35 years since the attack on Pearl Harbor and U. S. involvement in World War II. *J Harlen Wilson*

EMD GP7   1,500 hp   5 units
TE = 63,855   WT = 255,420
Wheels = 40"   Fuel = 1,100
Engine: EMD 16-567B V-type 16-cylinder 2-cycle
Min Speed for TE = 11.0 mph
62:15 Gearing   65 mph Max
Steam generators added
Rebuilt to "GP7u," rerated to 1,800 hp, 2,500 gallon fuel tanks
All T-I to EMD

1st No	2nd No	3rd No	4th No	Built	Build#	Retired	Notes
MP-4256	MP-322:2	MP-1773		03/53	18021	79-81	
MP-4257	MP-323:2	MP-1774		03/53	18022	79-81	
MP-4258	MP-324:2	MP-1775		03/53	18023	79-81	
MP-4259	MP-325:2	MP-1776:1	MP-1639:1	03/53	18024	11/75	Note 1
MP-4260	MP-326:2	MP-1777		03/53	18025	79-81	Note 2

Note 1: Renumbered to make room for Bicentennial GP7 1776:2 (ex C&EI-84)
Note 2: Chopnose by MoPac, snow plow front

Above: GP7 4275 glistens at Dupo, Illinois in March, 1953, having just arrived from EMD. *Joe Collias*

EMD GP7   1,500 hp   23 units
TE = 60,690   WT = 242,760
Wheels = 40"   Fuel = 1,600
Engine: EMD 16-567B V-type 16-cylinder 2-cycle
Min Speed for TE = 11.0 mph
62:15 Gearing   65 mph Max
Rerated to 1,600 hp. All T-I to EMD

1st No	2nd No	3rd No	4th No	5th No	Built	Build#	Notes
MP-4261	MP-240	MP-1697:1			03/53	17998	Note 1
MP-4262	MP-241	MP-1698:1			03/53	17999	Note 2
MP-4263	MP-242	MP-1699:1			03/53	18000	Note 2
MP-4264	MP-243	MP-1700:1			03/53	18001	Note 1
MP-4265	MP-244	MP-1701:1			03/53	18002	Note 2
MP-4266	MP-245	MP-1702:1			03/53	18003	Note 2
MP-4267	MP-246	MP-1703:1			03/53	18004	Note 1
MP-4268	MP-247	MP-1704:1			03/53	18005	Note 1
MP-4269	MP-248	MP-1705:1			03/53	18006	Note 1
MP-4270	MP-249	MP-1706:1			03/53	18007	Note 2
MP-4271	MP-250	MP-1707:1			03/53	18008	Note 1
MP-4272	MP-251	MP-1708:1			03/53	18009	Note 3
MP-4273	MP-252	MP-1709:1			03/53	18010	Note 1
MP-4274	MP-253	MP-1710:1			03/53	18011	Note 1
MP-4275	MP-254	MP-1711:1			03/53	18012	Note 4, 5
MP-4276	MP-255	MP-1712:1			03/53	18013	Note 6
MP-4277	MP-256	MP-1713:1			03/53	18014	Note 1, 5
MP-4278	MP-257:1	MP-157:1	MP-1626:1	MP-626:3	03/53	18015	Note 3, 7
MP-4279	MP-258	MP-1714:1			03/53	18016	Note 1
MP-4280	MP-259	MP-1715:1			03/53	18017	Note 4
MP-4281	MP-260	MP-1716:1			03/53	18018	Note 2
MP-4282	MP-261	MP-1717:1			03/53	18019	Note 1
MP-4283	MP-262	MP-1718:1			03/53	18020	Note 2

Note 1: Retired 1979-1981
Note 2: Retired 1980
Note 3: Retired 12/79, T-I on GP38-2's MP-2158-2197
Note 4: Retired 9/79
Note 5: Snow plow front. Chopnose by MoPac, 2,500 gallon fuel tank
Note 6: Wrecked 1/3/75 at Columbia IL and retired, T-I on MP15's
Note 7: Rebuilt 8/62 by EMD, 1,700 gallon fuel tank

EMD GP7   1,500 hp   6 units
TE = 60,600   WT = 242,400
Wheels = 40"   Fuel = 1,600
Engine: EMD 16-567B V-type 16-cylinder 2-cycle
Min Speed for TE = 11.0 mph
62:15 Gearing   65 mph Max
Rerated to 1,600 hp. All T-I to EMD

1st No	2nd No	3rd No	Built	Build#	Notes & Dispositions
STLB&M-4284	MP-263	MP-1719:1	03/53	18033	Retired 1979-1981
STLB&M-4285	MP-264	MP-1720:1	03/53	18034	Retired 1980
STLB&M-4286	MP-265	MP-1721:1	03/53	18035	Retired 1980
IGN-4287	MP-266	MP-1722:1	03/53	18028	Retired 1979-1981
IGN-4288	MP-267	MP-1723:1	03/53	18029	Retired 1979-1981
IGN-4289	MP-268	MP-1724:1	03/53	18030	Retired 1979-1981

EMD GP7   1,500 hp   26 units
TE = 61,100   WT = 244,400
Wheels = 40"   Fuel = 1,600
Engine: EMD 16-567B V-type 16-cylinder 2-cycle
Min Speed for TE = 11.0 mph
62:15 Gearing   65 mph Max
Rerated to 1,600 hp. All T-I to EMD

1st No	2nd No	3rd No	Built	Build#	Retired	Notes
IGN-4290	MP-269	MP-1726:1	05/54	19418	79-81	
IGN-4291	MP-270	MP-1727:1	05/54	19419	79-81	
IGN-4292	MP-271	MP-1728:1	05/54	19420	1980	
IGN-4293	MP-272	MP-1729:1	05/54	19421	79-81	Note 1, 2
IGN-4294	MP-273	MP-1730:1	05/54	19422	79-81	Note 1, 2, 3
IGN-4295	MP-274		05/54	19423		Wrecked 12/73
IGN-4296	MP-275	MP-1731:1	05/54	19424	79-81	
IGN-4297	MP-276	MP-1732:1	05/54	19425	79-81	
STLB&M-4298	MP-277	MP-1733:1	04/54	19428	1980	
MP-4299	MP-278		04/54	19393		Note 4
MP-4300	MP-279	MP-1734:1	04/54	19394	79-81	
MP-4301	MP-280	MP-1735:1	04/54	19395	79-81	Note 2
MP-4302	MP-281	MP-1736:1	04/54	19396	79-81	Note 1, 2, 3
MP-4303	MP-282	MP-1737:1	04/54	19397	1980	
MP-4304	MP-283	MP-1738:1	04/54	19398	12/79	Note 5
MP-4305	MP-284	MP-1739:1	04/54	19399	79-81	
MP-4306	MP-285	MP-1740:1	04/54	19400	1980	
MP-4307	MP-286	MP-1741:1	04/54	19401	79-81	
MP-4308	MP-287	MP-1742:1	04/54	19402	79-81	
MP-4309	MP-288	MP-1743:1	04/54	19403	79-81	
MP-4310	MP-289	MP-1744:1	05/54	19404	79-81	
MP-4311	MP-290	MP-1745	05/54	19405	79-81	
MP-4312	MP-291	MP-1746	05/54	19406	79-81	
MP-4313	MP-292	MP-1747	05/54	19407	1976	
MP-4314	MP-293	MP-1748	05/54	19408	79-81	
MP-4315	MP-294	MP-1749	05/54	19409	79-81	

Note 1: Snow plow front
Note 2: Chopnose by MoPac
Note 3: 2,500 gallon fuel tank
Note 4: Wrecked 2/74, retired 3/74, T-I on SD40-2's MP-3139-3149
Note 5: T-I on GP38-2's MP-2158-2197

Below: GP7 1741 is a graduate of EMD's class of 1954, graduating in April. It is at Monroe, Louisiana on August 12, 1976. A GP15-1 will later wear its number. Only the MoPac got GP7's built in 1954. *James Holder*

EMD GP7 1,500 hp 10 units
TE = 63,575 WT = 254,300
Wheels = 40" Fuel = 1,100
Engine: EMD 16-567 V-type 16-cylinder 2-cycle
Min Speed for TE = 11.0 mph
62:15 Gearing 65 mph Max
Equipped with steam generators
Rebuilt to "GP7u," rerated to 1,800 hp, 2,500 gallon fuel tanks. All T-I to EMD

1st No	2nd No	3rd No	Built	Build#	Retired	Notes
MP-4316	MP-327:2	MP-1778	03/54	19410	08/81	
MP-4317	MP-328:2	MP-1779	03/54	19411	1980	
MP-4318	MP-329:2	MP-1780	03/54	19412	08/81	
MP-4319	MP-330:2	MP-1781	03/54	19413	08/81	
MP-4320	MP-331:2	MP-1782	03/54	19414	79-81	Note 1, 2
MP-4321	MP-332:2		04/54	19415	1974	Note 1, 2, 3
MP-4322	MP-333:2	MP-1783	04/54	19416	1980	
STLB&M-4323	MP-334:2	MP-1784	04/54	19426	79-81	Note 1, 2
STLB&M-4324	MP-335:2	MP-1785	04/54	19427	1980	Note 1, 2
IGN-4325	MP-336:2	MP-1786	05/54	19417	79-81	Note 1

Note 1: Chopnose by MoPac
Note 2: Snow plow front
Note 3: 567BC engine

Alco-GE RS-3 1,600 hp 14 units
TE = 62,375 WT = 249,500
Wheels = 40" Fuel = 1,800
Engine: Alco 244-H V-type 12-cylinder 4-cycle Turbocharged
Min Speed for TE = 9.0 mph
74:18 Gearing 65 mph Max
MI-69-74 were built by Alco
Rebuilt with GM 12/567 1,200 hp engine, designated "RS-3m" or "GP12"
After rebuilding:
TE = 61,185 WT = 244,740
Wheels = 40" Fuel = 1,400
Engine: EMD 12-567B V-type 12-cylinder 2-cycle
Min Speed for TE = 12.0
74:18 Gearing 65 mph Max

1st No	2nd No	3rd No	Built	Build#	Notes & Dispositions
TPMPT-24	TPMPT-959:1	T&P-1071	04/56	81897	Retired 2/73. Note 1
MI-62	MI-961	MI-1065	01/51	78545	Retired 1/73, T-I to GE 1/73
MI-63	MI-962	MI-1093	10/51	79252	Retired 6/73, T-I to GE
MI-64	MI-963	MI-1067	06/52	79942	Retired 3/74, T-I to GE
MI-65	MI-964	MI-1095	06/53	80512	Retired 1/74, T-I to GE
MI-66	MI-965	MI-1069	06/53	80513	Retired 4/75, T-I to GE
MI-67	MI-966	MI-1070	10/53	80548	Retired 4/75, T-I to GE
MI-68	MI-967	MI-1091	10/53	80551	Retired 6/73, T-I to GE
MI-69	MI-968	MI-1072	03/54	80730	Retired 4/75. Note 2
MI-70	MI-969	MI-1073	03/54	80731	Retired 12/74. Note 3
MI-71	MI-970	MI-1079	03/55	81150	Retired 1976, T-I to GE
MI-72	MI-971	MI-1081	03/55	81151	Retired 3/74, T-I to GE
MI-73	MI-972	MI-1066	03/55	81152	Retired 12/74, T-I to GE
MI-74	MI-973	MI-1092	03/55	81153	Retired 2/74, T-I to GE

Note 1: Rebuilt 9/66, 1,200 gallon fuel tank. T-I to GE 3/73
Note 2: T-I to GE, leased to CR, to Transkentucky Transportation RR, Paris, KY 11/79, chopnose by TTS
Note 3: T-I to GE, retained as chopper electric test bed as LE&RB-1977

Alco RS-3 1,600 hp 26 units
TE = 62,375 WT = 249,500
Wheels = 40" Fuel = 1,800
Engine: Alco 244-H V-type 12-cylinder 4-cycle Turbocharged
Min Speed for TE = 9.0 mph
74:18 Gearing 65 mph Max
Rebuilt with GM 12/567 1,200 hp engine, designated "RS-3m" or "GP12"
After rebuilding:
TE = 60,460 WT = 241,840
Wheels = 40" Fuel = 1,800
Engine: EMD 12-567B V-type 12-cylinder 2-cycle
Min Speed for TE = 12.0 mph
74:18 Gearing 65 mph Max

1st No	2nd No	3rd No	Built	Build#	Notes & Dispositions
MP-4501:1	MP-974:1	MP-1074:2	01/55	80758	Retired 11/74, T-I to GE
MP-4502:1	MP-975:1		01/55	80759	Retired 1975. Note 1
MP-4503:1	MP-976:1	MP-1075:2	01/55	80760	Retired 4/75. Note 2
MP-4504:1	MP-977:1		01/55	80761	Retired 1975. Note 1
MP-4505:1	MP-978:1		01/55	80762	Retired 1964. Note 3
MP-4506:1	MP-979:1		01/55	80763	Sold to PC&N
MP-4507:1	MP-980:1		01/55	80764	Retired 1964. Note 3
MP-4508:1	MP-981:1	MP-1076:2	02/55	80765	Retired 4/75. Note 2
MP-4509:1	MP-982:1	MP-1077:2	02/55	80766	Retired 12/74, T-I to GE
MP-4510:1	MP-983:1	MP-1068:2	02/55	80767	Retired 10/74, T-I to GE
MP-4511:1	MP-984	MP-1062:2	02/55	80768	Retired 03/73, T-I to GE
MP-4512:1	MP-985	MP-1080:2	02/55	80769	Retired 1976, T-I to GE
MP-4513:1	MP-986	MP-1094:2	02/55	81136	Retired 7/73, T-I to GE
MP-4514:1	MP-987	MP-1090:2	02/55	81137	Retired 6/76, T-I to GE
MP-4515:1	MP-988	MP-1083:2	02/55	81138	Retired 1976, T-I to GE
MP-4516:1	MP-989	MP-1084	02/55	81139	Note 4
MP-4517:1	MP-990	MP-1096:2	02/55	81140	Retired 1976, T-I to GE
MP-4518:1	MP-991	MP-1097:2	02/55	81141	Retired 10/74, T-I to GE
MP-4519:1	MP-992	MP-1087	02/55	81142	Retired 1976, T-I to GE
MP-4520:1	MP-993	MP-1063:2	02/55	81143	Retired 1973-1975, T-I to GE
MP-4521:1	MP-994	MP-1078:2	02/55	81144	Retired 1976, T-I to GE
MP-4522:1	MP-995	MP-1085	02/55	81145	Retired 12/74, T-I to GE
MP-4523:1	MP-996	MP-1086	02/55	81146	Retired 1977, T-I to GE
MP-4524:1	MP-997	MP-1088	02/55	81147	Retired 5/74, T-I to GE
MP-4525:1	MP-998	MP-1082:2	02/55	81148	Retired 1976, T-I to GE
MP-4526:1	MP-999	MP-1089:2	02/55	81149	Retired 6/73, T-I to GE

Note 1: To Bauxite & Northern in trade for SW1200's B&N-10 and B&N-11
Note 2: T-I to GE, leased to CR, to Transkentucky RR, Paris, KY 11/79, chopnose by TTS
Note 3: Traded to RS&S for SW1200's MP-1261 and MP-1262
Note 4: Wore Jenks blue as MP-4516. Retired 1976, T-I to GE

BLH AS-16 1,600 hp 2 units
TE = 61,180 WT = 259,500
Wheels = 42" Fuel = 1,900
Engine: Baldwin 608A 8-cylinder 4-cycle Turbocharged
Min Speed for TE = 9.9 mph
63:15 Gearing 70 mph Max
T-I to EMD, scrapped

1st No	Built	Build#
IGN-4195	11/51	75161
IGN-4196	11/51	75162

BLH AS-16 1,600 hp 6 units
TE = 64,500 WT = 258,000
Wheels = 42" Fuel = 1,600
Engine: Baldwin 608A 8-cylinder 4-cycle Turbocharged
Min Speed for TE = 9.9 mph
63:15 Gearing 70 mph Max

1st No	2nd No	3rd No	Built	Build#	Retired	Notes
STLB&M-4326	MP-941:1	MP-935:1	06/54	76004	12/62	To GR Silcott
STLB&M-4327	MP-942:1	MP-936:1	06/54	76005	02/65	To Peabody Coal
STLB&M-4328	MP-943:1	MP-937:1	07/54	76006	07/65	To PNC
STLB&M-4329	MP-944:1	MP-938:1	07/54	76007	02/65	Note 1
STLB&M-4330	MP-945:1	MP-939:1	07/54	76008	02/65	Note 1
STLB&M-4331	MP-946:1	MP-940:1	07/54	76009		Disposition unknown

Note 1: To Birmingham Rail

Left: GP7 1778 has been upgraded to a "GP7u," with a new horsepower rating of 1,800 and a 2,500 gallon fuel tank. It is at Dolton, Illinois in April, 1976.
Richard Panek photo, Brian Jennisen collection

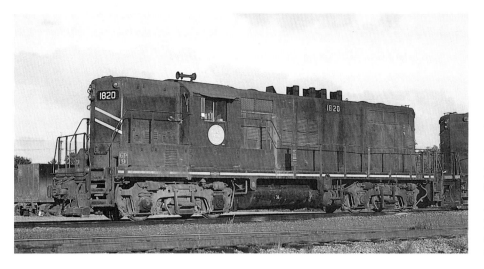

Left: GP9 1820 looks a bit tired on May 1, 1975, at Monroe, Louisiana, but she's still got six more years left. She has the standard liberated exhaust typical of the MoPac's geep fleet. Her prime mover is now long silenced, having gone to EMD in trade in November, 1981. *James Holder*

Below: T&P 108 is one of two GP9's that were a result of MV wrecking a pair of their GP7's in April, 1958. Though the GP7's were officially "rebuilt," in actuality a new GP9 was brought on-line with perhaps a few parts left over from the scrapping of the GP7's. The paper game called "rebuilding" was in this case merely a way to avoid taxes on what would otherwise be termed a new locomotive. The 108 is at St. Louis, Missouri on January 29, 1974. *Raymond Kucaba photo, James Holder collection*

EMD GP9 1,750 hp 40 units
TE = 60,750 WT = 243,000
Wheels = 40" Fuel = 1,600
Engine: EMD 16-567C V-type 16-cylinder 2-cycle
Min Speed for TE = 11.0 mph
62:15 Gearing 65 mph Max
Rerated to 1,800 hp

1st No	2nd No	3rd No	Built	Build#	Notes & Dispositions
MP-4332	MP-346:2	MP-1787	01/55	20242	Retired 1980, T-I to EMD
MP-4333	MP-347:2	MP-1788	01/55	20243	Retired 8/81, T-I to EMD
MP-4334	MP-348:2	MP-1789	01/55	20244	Retired 8/81, T-I to EMD
MP-4335	MP-349:2	MP-1790	01/55	20245	Retired 8/81, T-I to EMD
MP-4336	MP-350:2	MP-1791	01/55	20246	Retired 11/81, T-I to EMD
MP-4337	MP-351:2	MP-1792	02/55	20247	Retired 1980, T-I to EMD
MP-4338	MP-352:2	MP-1793	02/55	20248	Retired 11/81, T-I to EMD
MP-4339	MP-353:2	MP-1794	02/55	20249	Retired 8/81, T-I to EMD
MP-4340	MP-354:2	MP-1795	02/55	20250	Retired 1979-1981, T-I to EMD
MP-4341	MP-355:2		02/55	20251	Wrecked and retired 1966, T-I to EMD on GP38 2007:1
MP-4342	MP-356:2	MP-1796	02/55	20252	Retired 1980, T-I to EMD
MP-4343	MP-357:2	MP-1797	02/55	20253	Retired 11/81, T-I to EMD
MP-4344	MP-358:2	MP-1798	02/55	20254	Retired 11/81, T-I to EMD
MP-4345	MP-359:2	MP-1799	02/55	20255	Retired 1981, T-I to EMD
MP-4346	MP-360:2	MP-1800	02/55	20256	Retired 1979-1981, T-I to EMD
MP-4347	MP-361:2	MP-1801	03/55	20257	Retired 11/81, T-I to EMD
MP-4348	MP-362:2	MP-1802	03/55	20258	Retired 1980, T-I to EMD
MP-4349	MP-363:2	MP-1803	03/55	20259	Retired 11/81, T-I to EMD
MP-4350	MP-364:2	MP-1804	03/55	20260	Retired 11/81, T-I to EMD
MP-4351	MP-365:2	MP-1805	03/55	20261	Retired 11/81, T-I to EMD
MP-4352	MP-366:2	MP-1806	03/55	20262	Retired 11/81, T-I to EMD
MP-4353	MP-367:2	MP-1807	03/55	20263	Retired 1979-1981, T-I to EMD
MP-4354	MP-368:2	MP-1808:2	03/55	20264	Retired 11/81, T-I to EMD
MP-4355	MP-369:2	MP-1809	03/55	20265	Retired 11/81, T-I to EMD
MP-4356	MP-370:2	MP-1810	03/55	20266	Retired 11/81, T-I to EMD
MP-4357	MP-371:2	MP-1811	03/55	20267	Retired 11/81, T-I to EMD
MP-4358	MP-372:2	MP-1812	03/55	20268	Retired 11/81, T-I to EMD
MP-4359	MP-373:2	MP-1813	03/55	20269	Retired 1980, T-I to EMD
MP-4360	MP-374:2	MP-1814	03/55	20270	Retired 11/81, T-I to EMD
MP-4361	MP-375:2	MP-1815	03/55	20271	Retired 9/79, T-I to EMD
MP-4362	MP-376:2	MP-1816	03/55	20272	Retired 11/81, T-I to EMD
MP-4363	MP-377:2	MP-1817	04/55	20273	Note 1
MP-4364	MP-378:2	MP-1818	04/55	20274	Retired 11/81, T-I to EMD
MP-4365	MP-379:2	MP-1819:2	04/55	20275	Retired 11/81, T-I to EMD
MP-4366	MP-380:2	MP-1820	04/55	20276	Retired 11/81, T-I to EMD
MP-4367	MP-381:2	MP-1821	04/55	20277	Retired 9/79, T-I to EMD
MP-4368	MP-382:2	MP-1822:2	04/55	20278	Retired 1980, T-I to EMD
MP-4369	MP-383:2	MP-1823	04/55	20279	Retired 11/81, T-I to EMD
MP-4370	MP-384:2	MP-1824:2	04/55	20280	Retired 1980, T-I to EMD
MP-4371	MP-385:2	MP-1825	04/55	20281	Retired 11/81, T-I to EMD

Note 1: Chopnose by MoPac, snow plow front, 2,500 gallon fuel tank. Retired 11/81, T-I to EMD

EMD GP9 1,750 hp 14 units
TE = 62,100 WT = 250,850
Wheels = 40" Fuel = 1,600
Engine: EMD 16-567C V-type 16-cylinder 2-cycle
Min Speed for TE = 11.0 mph
62:15 Gearing 65 mph Max
Rerated to 1,800 hp. All T-I to EMD except 1842, disposition unknown

1st No	2nd No	3rd No	4th No	Built	Build#	Retired	Notes
T&P-1131	T&P-386	MP-551	MP-1837:2	03/57	22524	1981	Note 1
T&P-1132	T&P-387	MP-552		03/57	22525	11/73	Note 2
T&P-1133	T&P-388	MP-553	MP-1838:2	03/57	22526	11/81	Note 1
T&P-1134	T&P-389	MP-554	MP-1839:2	03/57	22527	11/81	Note 1
T&P-1135	T&P-390	MP-555	MP-1840	03/57	22528	11/81	Note 1
T&P-1136	T&P-391	MP-556	MP-1841	03/57	22529	1980	Note 1
T&P-1137	T&P-392	MP-557	MP-1842:2	05/57	25345		Note 1
T&P-1138	T&P-393	MP-558	MP-1843	05/57	25346	11/81	Note 1
T&P-1139	T&P-394	MP-559	MP-1844	05/57	25347	11/81	Note 1
T&P-1140	T&P-395	MP-560	MP-1845	05/57	25348	11/81	
T&P-1141	T&P-396	MP-561:2	MP-1846	05/57	25349	1980	
T&P-1142	T&P-397	MP-562:2	MP-1847	05/57	25350	11/81	
T&P-1143	T&P-398	MP-563:2	MP-1848:2	05/57	25351	11/81	
T&P-1144	T&P-399	MP-564:2	MP-1849	05/57	25352	11/81	

Note 1: Chopnose by MoPac
Note 2: Wrecked and retired 11/73, T-I to EMD on SD40-2's C&EI-3150-3163

EMD "GP9m" 1,500 hp 2 units
TE = 61,490 WT = 245,950
Wheels = 40" Fuel = 1,700
Engine: EMD 16-567C V-type 16-cylinder 2-cycle
Min Speed for TE = 12.0 mph
62:15 Gearing 65 mph Max
Rerated to 1,800 hp, then back to 1,500 hp under T&P

1st No	2nd No	3rd No	4th No	Built	Build#	Notes
MV-152:2	MV-108	T&P-108	T&P-1695	04/58	24680	Note 1
MV-153:2	MV-109	T&P-109	T&P-1696	04/58	24681	Note 2

Note 1: GP7 MV-152:1 wrecked 4/58, rebuilt by EMD to "GP9m" MV-152:2. Retired 1979-1981, T-I to EMD
Note 2: GP7 MV-153:1 wrecked 4/58, rebuilt by EMD to "GP9m" MV-153:2. Retired 12/79, T-I to EMD on GP38-2's MP-2158-2197

Right: RS-1's, RS-2's, and RS-3's all outsold the RS-11, but the RS-11 was still a respectable competitor. As the builders approached the second generation, however, Alco slowly fell behind, eventually disappearing from the locomotive scene. When the builder's photo was taken of 4611, Alco was still a force to be reckoned with. *Charlie Duckworth collection*

Alco RS-11 1,800 hp 12 units
TE = 61,650 WT = 246,600
Wheels = 42" Fuel = 1,800
Engine: Alco 251-B V-type 12-cylinder 4-cycle Turbocharged
Min Speed for TE = 11.2 mph
63:15 Gearing 65 mph Max
All had DR-4-4-1500 201-208 trucks & traction motors. Repowered with 1,650 hp EMD engines 1964-1965, designated "RS-11m" or "GP16"
After rebuilding:
Wheels = 40" Fuel = 1,800
Engine: EMD 16-567 V-type 16-cylinder 2-cycle
Min Speed for TE = 12.0 mph
74:18 Gearing 65 mph Max. All T-I to GE, scrapped

1st No	2nd No	3rd No	4th No	Built	Build#	Retired	Notes
MP-4601:1	MP-488:1	MP-944:2	MP-68:2	10/59	83492	11/74	
MP-4602:1	MP-489:1	MP-945:2	MP-69:2	10/59	83493	01/74	
MP-4603:1	MP-490:1	MP-946:2	MP-70:2	10/59	83494	12/74	
MP-4604:1	MP-491:1	MP-947:1	MP-71:2	10/59	83495	1976	
MP-4605:1	MP-492:1	MP-948:1	MP-72:2	11/59	83496	1976	
MP-4606:1	MP-493:1	MP-949:1	MP-73:2	11/59	83497	12/74	
MP-4607:1	MP-494:1	MP-950:1	MP-74:2	11/59	83498	09/74	
MP-4608:1	MP-495:1	MP-951:1	MP-75:2	11/59	83499	06/73	Note 1
MP-4609:1	MP-496:1	MP-952:1	MP-76:2	11/59	83500	1976	
MP-4610:1	MP-497:1	MP-953:1	MP-77:2	11/59	83501	1976	
MP-4611:1	MP-498:1	MP-954:1	MP-78:2	11/59	83502	11/74	
MP-4612:1	MP-499:1	MP-955:1	MP-79:2	11/59	83503	03/74	

Note 1: Wrecked 5/21/73, Webster Groves MO, T-I on U30C's

EMD GP18 1,800 hp 26 units
TE = 61,625 WT = 246,500
Wheels = 40" Fuel = 1,700
Engine: EMD 16-567D V-type 16-cylinder 2-cycle
Min Speed for TE = 12.0 mph
62:15 Gearing 65 mph Max
505-528 chopnosed by MoPac, 4825-4826 built new with low nose, all units with snow plows except 517, 520, 524, and 527

1st No	2nd No	3rd No	Built	Build#	Notes & Dispositions
MP-4801:1	MP-505:2	MP-1855	04/60	25798	Note 1
MP-4802:1	MP-506:2	MP-1856	04/60	25799	Retired 4/84, to PNC 7/85
MP-4803:1	MP-507:2		04/60	25800	Note 2
MP-4804:1	MP-508:2	MP-1857	04/60	25801	Retired 4/84, to PNC 7/85
MP-4805:1	MP-509:2	MP-1858	04/60	25802	Retired 4/84, to PNC 7/85
MP-4806:1	MP-510:2	MP-1859	05/60	25803	Retired 11/81, scrapped
MP-4807:1	MP-511:2	MP-1860	05/60	25829	Retired 4/84, to PNC 7/85
MP-4808:1	MP-512:2	MP-1861	05/60	25830	Retired 4/84, to PNC 7/85
MP-4809:1	MP-513:2	MP-1862	05/60	25831	Retired 4/84, to PNC 7/85
MP-4810:1	MP-514:2	MP-1863	05/60	25832	Retired 4/84, to PNC 7/85
MP-4811:1	MP-515:2	MP-1864	05/60	25833	Retired 4/84, to PNC 7/85
MP-4812:1	MP-516:2	MP-1865	05/60	25834	Retired 4/84, to PNC 7/85
MP-4813:1	MP-517:2	MP-1866	05/60	25835	Retired 4/84, to PNC 7/85
MP-4814:1	MP-518:2	MP-1867	05/60	25836	Retired 4/84, to PNC 7/85
MP-4815:1	MP-519:2	MP-1868	06/60	25837	Retired 11/81, scrapped
MP-4816:1	MP-520:2	MP-1869	06/60	25838	Retired 4/84, to PNC 7/85
MP-4817:1	MP-521:2	MP-1870	06/60	25839	Retired 4/84, to PNC 7/85
MP-4818:1	MP-522:2	MP-1871	06/60	25840	Retired 4/84, to PNC 7/85
MP-4819:1	MP-523:2		06/60	25841	Note 3
MP-4820:1	MP-524:2	MP-1872	06/60	25842	Retired 4/84, to PNC
MP-4821:1	MP-525	MP-1873	06/60	25843	Retired 4/84, to PNC 7/85
MP-4822:1	MP-526	MP-1874	06/60	25844	Retired 4/84, to PNC 7/85
MP-4823:1	MP-527	(MP-1875)	06/60	25845	Note 4
MP-4824:1	MP-528	MP-1876	06/60	25846	Retired 4/84, to PNC 7/85
MP-4825:1	MP-529	MP-1877	05/60	26021	Retired 11/81, scrapped
MP-4826:1	MP-530	MP-1878	05/60	26022	Note 5

Note 1: First unit in new five inch stripes (May, 1974). Wrecked at Vienna IL 6/12/75, retired 1/76, T-I to EMD
Note 2: Wrecked 12/1/73 Cotulla TX, T-I to EMD
Note 3: Wrecked 2/21/73 Taft or Luling LA, retired 3/73, T-I to EMD
Note 4: Wrecked before renumbering. Retired 1/75, T-I to EMD
Note 5: Rebuilt with 16- 645 engine, 1,900 hp. Retired 4/84, to PNC 7/85

Above: After the miscue with the RS-11's, the MoPac settled down into the practice of buying 567-powered machines from EMD. Shortly after the RS-11's came on the property, GP18's were being added to the fold. The 503 was among the first, purchased for the T&P. It is at New Orleans, Louisiana on August 31, 1974. *James Holder*

EMD GP18 1,800 hp 3 units
TE = 64,190 WT = 256,750
Wheels = 40" Fuel = 2,000
Engine: EMD 16-567D1 V-type 16-cylinder 2-cycle
Min Speed for TE = 12.0 mph
62:15 Gearing 65 mph Max
Built new with low nose, rebuilt with 16-cylinder 645 engine, 2,000 hp

1st No	2nd No	3rd No	Built	Build#	Notes & Dispositions
MP-4827:1	MP-531	MP-1879	01/62	26953	Wore Jenks blue as 4827. Retired 4/84, to PNC 7/85
MP-4828:1	MP-532	MP-1880	01/62	26954	Retired 4/84, to PNC 7/85
MP-4829:1	MP-533	MP-1881	01/62	26955	Retired 4/84, to PNC 7/85

EMD GP18 1,800 hp 5 units
TE = 62,000 WT = 248,000
Wheels = 40" Fuel = 1,700
Engine: EMD 16-567D1 V-type 16-cylinder 2-cycle
Min Speed for TE = 12.0 mph
62:15 Gearing 65 mph Max
Built new with low nose

1st No	2nd No	3rd No	4th No	Built	Build#	Notes
T&P-1145	T&P-500	MP-500	MP-1850	05/60	25906	Note 1
T&P-1146	T&P-501	MP-501:2	MP-1851	05/60	25907	Note 2
T&P-1147	T&P-502	MP-502:2	MP-1852	05/60	25908	Note 3
T&P-1148	T&P-503	MP-503:2	MP-1853	05/60	25909	Note 4
T&P-1149	T&P-504	MP-504:2	MP-1854	05/60	25910	Note 5

Note 1: Retired 4/84, to PNC 7/85
Note 2: Retired 4/84, to PNC 7/85
Note 3: 2,000 gallon fuel tank. Retired 4/84, to PNC 7/85
Note 4: Retired 11/81, scrapped
Note 5: Repowered with 16-cylinder 645D1 engine, 2,000 gallon fuel tank, snow plow front. Retired 9/79, T-I to EMD

EMD GP18   1,800 hp   47 units
TE = 63,650   WT = 254,600
Wheels = 40"   Fuel = 2,000
Engine: EMD 16-567D1 V-type 16-cylinder 2-cycle
Min Speed for TE = 12.0 mph
74:18 Gearing   65 mph Max
Ride on Alco T-I trucks from FA's and FB's, built new with low nose

1st No	2nd No	Built	Build#	Notes & Dispositions
MP-400	MP-1900	01/62	26956	Retired 4/84. Note 1
MP-401	MP-1901	01/62	26957	Retired 4/84. Note 1
MP-402	MP-1902	01/62	26958	Retired 11/81, scrapped
MP-403	MP-1903	01/62	26959	Retired 4/84. Note 1
MP-404	MP-1904	01/62	26960	Retired 4/84. Note 1
MP-405	MP-1905	01/62	26961	Retired 4/84. Note 1
MP-406	MP-1906	01/62	26962	Retired 4/84. Note 1
MP-407	MP-1907	01/62	26963	Retired 11/81, scrapped
MP-408	MP-1908	01/62	26964	Retired 4/84. Note 1
MP-409	MP-1909	01/62	26965	Retired 4/84. Note 1
MP-410	MP-1910	01/62	26966	Retired 4/84, to PNC 7/85
MP-411	MP-1911	01/62	26967	Retired 4/84. Note 1
MP-412	MP-1912	01/62	26968	Retired 1984, scrapped
MP-413	MP-1913	01/62	26969	Retired 4/84. Note 1
MP-414	MP-1914	01/62	26970	Retired 11/81, scrapped
MP-415	MP-1915	01/62	26971	Retired 1984, scrapped
MP-416	MP-1916	02/62	26972	Retired 4/84. Note 1
MP-417	MP-1917	02/62	26973	Retired 4/84. Note 1
MP-418	MP-1918	02/62	26974	Retired 4/84. Note 1
MP-419	MP-1919	02/62	26975	Retired 11/81, scrapped
MP-420	MP-1920	02/62	26976	Retired 1984, scrapped
MP-421	MP-1921	02/62	26977	Retired 1984, scrapped
MP-422	MP-1922	02/62	26978	Retired 4/84. Note 1
MP-423		02/62	26979	Note 2
MP-424	MP-1923	02/62	26980	Retired 4/84. Note 1
MP-425		02/62	26981	Note 3
MP-426	MP-1924	02/62	26982	Retired 4/84. Note 1
MP-427	MP-1925	02/62	26983	Retired 4/84. Note 1
MP-428	MP-1926	02/62	26984	Retired 1984, scrapped
MP-429	MP-1927	02/62	26985	Retired 4/84, to PNC 7/85
MP-430	MP-1928	02/62	26986	Retired 4/84. Note 1
MP-431	MP-1929	02/62	26987	Retired 4/84. Note 1
MP-432	MP-1930	02/62	26988	Snow plow front. Retired 4/84. Note 1
MP-433	MP-1931	03/62	26989	Retired 4/84. Note 1
MP-434	MP-1932	03/62	26990	Retired 11/81, scrapped
MP-435	MP-1933	03/62	26991	Retired 4/84, to PNC 7/85
MP-436	MP-1934	03/62	26992	Retired 4/84, to PNC 7/85
MP-437	MP-1935	03/62	26993	Retired 4/84. Note 1
MP-438	MP-1936	03/62	26994	Retired 4/84. Note 1
MP-439	MP-1937	03/62	26995	Retired 4/84. Note 1
MP-440	MP-1938	03/62	26996	Retired 1984, scrapped
MP-441	MP-1939	03/62	26997	Retired 4/84, to PNC 7/85
MP-442	MP-1940	03/62	26998	Retired 5/79, T-I to EMD
MP-443	MP-1941	03/62	26999	Retired 4/84. Note 1
MP-444	MP-1942	03/62	27000	Retired 1984, scrapped
MP-445	MP-1943	03/62	27001	Retired 4/84. Note 1
MP-446	MP-1944	03/62	27002	Retired 4/84. Note 1

Note 1: T-I to GE 5/84, to ScrapServ 6/84, scrapped
Note 2: Wrecked 1966, T-I to EMD on GP38 MP-2003
Note 3: Wrecked 1966, T-I to EMD on GP38 MP-2005

Above: As soon as the FA's were deemed to have fulfilled their useful life, they were unceremoniously traded in on GP18's. One hundred of the GP18's came on the FA trade-in trucks. GP18 466 is at Austin, Texas on November 17, 1973, still riding on those old FA trucks. *Jeff Pletcher*

Above: In the order of early 1962, the first three units came in the 4-digit number series, 4827-4829. These had standard Blomberg trucks, but otherwise were identical to the 100 that came in the 400-series. The 1879 is at Little Rock in January, 1977. *James Holder*

Above: The 1853 was one of five GP18's built for the T&P in May, 1960. they came with low noses, as did all the MoPac GP18's except the first 26. The standard road power of the early 1960's rests at Monroe, Louisiana awaiting the next call for service on November 24, 1975. *James Holder*

Left: A number of the GP18's survived long enough to receive the 1974 styling revision, with 5 1/2-inch stripes and the flying eagle buzz-saw on the cab side. Veteran GP18 1934 wears the new image at North Little Rock, Arkansas on December 9, 1977. *J Harlen Wilson*

Above: Storm clouds roll by in the distance as GP18 535 pauses between duties in Alexandria, Louisiana on August 6, 1973. The lonely geep has another decade of dependable service left, and then will follow the fate of many of the MoPac's geeps; the scrapper's torch. *Glenn Anderson*

EMD GP18   1,800 hp   34 units
TE = 64,100   WT = 256,400
Wheels = 40"   Fuel = 2,000
Engine: EMD 16-567D1 V-type 16-cylinder 2-cycle
Min Speed for TE = 12.0 mph
74:18 Gearing   65 mph Max
Rode on Alco T-I trucks from FA's and FB's, built new with low nose

1st No	2nd No	Built	Build#	Notes & Dispositions
MP-447	MP-1945	05/62	27228	Note 1
MP-448	MP-1946	05/62	27229	Retired 1984, scrapped
MP-449	MP-1947	05/62	27230	Note 1
MP-450	MP-1948	05/62	27231	Note 1
MP-451	MP-1949	05/62	27232	Note 1
MP-452	MP-1950	05/62	27233	Note 1
MP-453	MP-1951	05/62	27234	Retired 4/84, to Gachman 12/85, scrapped
MP-454	MP-1952	05/62	27235	Retired 4/84, to PNC 7/85
MP-455	MP-1953	05/62	27236	Retired 1984, scrapped
MP-456	MP-1954	05/62	27237	Retired 4/84, to PNC 7/85
MP-457	MP-1955	05/62	27238	Retired 1984, scrapped
MP-458	MP-1956	05/62	27239	Note 1
MP-459		06/62	27240	Wrecked 1966, T-I to EMD on GP38 MP-2004
MP-460	MP-1957	06/62	27241	Retired 4/84, to PNC 7/85
MP-461	MP-1958	06/62	27242	Note 1
MP-462	MP-1959	06/62	27243	Retired 1984, scrapped
MP-463		06/62	27244	Wrecked 1974, T-I to EMD, scrapped
MP-464	MP-1960	06/62	27245	Note 1
MP-465	MP-1961	06/62	27246	Note 1
MP-466	MP-1962	06/62	27247	Note 1
MP-467		06/62	27248	Wrecked 1974, T-I to EMD, scrapped
MP-468	MP-1963	06/62	27249	Retired 11/81, scrapped
MP-469	MP-1964	06/62	27250	Retired 11/81, scrapped
MP-470	MP-1965	06/62	27251	Note 1
MP-471	MP-1966	06/62	27252	Retired 1984, scrapped
MP-472	MP-1967	06/62	27253	Note 1
MP-473	MP-1968	06/62	27254	Note 1
MP-474	MP-1969	06/62	27255	Note 1
MP-475	MP-1970	06/62	27256	Retired 11/81, scrapped
MP-476	MP-1971	06/62	27257	Retired 4/84, to PNC 7/85
MP-477	(MP-1972)	06/62	27258	Assigned (MP-1972) but wrecked before renumbering. Retired 1/76, T-I to EMD
MP-478	MP-1973	06/62	27259	Retired 4/84, to ARR Test Track
MP-479	MP-1974	06/62	27260	Note 1
MP-480	MP-1975	06/62	27261	Farr air installed by MoPac. Note 1

Note 1: Retired 4/84, T-I to GE 5/84, to ScrapServe 6/84, scrapped

EMD GP18   1,800 hp   17 units
TE = 64,100   WT = 256,400
Wheels = 40"   Fuel = 2,000
Engine: EMD 16-567D1 V-type 16-cylinder 2-cycle
Min Speed for TE = 12.0 mph
62:15 Gearing   65 mph Max
Built new with low nose

1st No	2nd No	Built	Build#	Notes & Dispositions
MP-534	MP-1882	05/62	27262	Rebuilt with 16-cylinder 645 engine, 2,000 hp snow plow front. Retired 4/84, to PNC 7/85
MP-535	MP-1883	05/62	27263	Rebuilt with 16-cylinder 645 engine, 2,000 hp. Retired 4/84, to PNC 7/85
MP-536	MP-1884	05/62	27264	Retired 11/81, scrapped
MP-537	MP-1885	05/62	27265	Retired 11/81, scrapped
MP-538	MP-1886	05/62	27266	Retired 4/84, to PNC 7/85
MP-539	MP-1887	05/62	27267	Retired 4/84, to PNC 7/85
MP-540		05/62	27268	Wrecked 2/21/73 Taft or Luling LA, retired 3/73, T-I to EMD, scrapped
MP-541	MP-1888	06/62	27269	Retired 11/81, scrapped
MP-542	MP-1889	06/62	27270	Retired 4/84, to PNC 7/85
MP-543	MP-1890	06/62	27271	Retired 4/84, to PNC 7/85
MP-544	MP-1891	06/62	27272	Retired 4/84, to PNC 7/85
MP-545	MP-1892	06/62	27273	Retired 11/81, scrapped
MP-546	MP-1893	06/62	27274	Retired 4/84, to PNC 7/85
MP-547		06/62	27275	Wrecked 1966, T-I to EMD on GP38 MP-2006
MP-548	MP-1894	06/62	27276	Retired 4/84, to PNC 7/85
MP-549	MP-1895	06/62	27277	Retired 4/84, to PNC 7/85
MP-550	MP-1896	01/63	28017	Retired 4/84, to PNC 7/85

EMD GP18   1,800 hp   19 units
TE = 64,235   WT = 256,940
Wheels = 40"   Fuel = 2,000
Engine: EMD 16-567D1 V-type 16-cylinder 2-cycle
Min Speed for TE = 12.0 mph
74:18 Gearing   65 mph Max
Ride on Alco T-I trucks from FA's and FB's, built new with low nose

1st No	2nd No	Built	Build#	Notes & Dispositions
MP-481	MP-1976	12/62	27998	Wore bicentennial paint scheme 1/76. Retired 4/84, to PNC 7/85
MP-482	MP-1977	12/62	27999	Retired 4/84, to Gachman 12/85, scrapped
MP-483	MP-1978	12/62	28000	Note 1
MP-484	MP-1979	12/62	28001	Retired 4/84, to PNC 7/85
MP-485	MP-1980	12/62	28002	Retired 11/81, scrapped
MP-486	MP-1981	12/62	28003	Note 1
MP-487	MP-1982	12/62	28004	Note 1
MP-488:2	(MP-1983)	12/62	28005	Note 2
MP-489:2	MP-1984	12/62	28006	Retired 4/84, T-I to EMD 10/84 on SD50's
MP-490:2	MP-1985	12/62	28007	Retired 5/84, T-I to GE 5/84, to ScrapServe 6/84, scrapped
MP-491:2	MP-1986	12/62	28008	Note 1
MP-492:2	MP-1987	12/62	28009	Snow plow front. Retired 11/81, scrapped
MP-493:2	MP-1988	01/63	28010	Retired 1984, scrapped
MP-494:2	MP-1989	01/63	28011	Retired 4/81, scrapped
MP-495:2	MP-1990	01/63	28012	Note 1
MP-496:2	MP-1991	01/63	28013	Retired 4/84, to PNC 7/85
MP-497:2	MP-1992	01/63	28014	Retired 4/84, to PNC 7/85
MP-498:2	MP-1993	01/63	28015	Note 1
MP-499:2	MP-1994	01/63	28016	Note 1

Note 1: Retired 4/84, T-I to GE 5/84, to ScrapServe 6/84, scrapped
Note 2: Farr air installed by MoPac. Wrecked 1/3/75 at Columbia IL before renumbering, retired 1/75, T-I to EMD on MP15's

EMD
GP35
GP28
GP38

The second generation phase of dieseldom began on the MoPac with the purchase of the first group of GP35's in January, 1964, but it had already begun on the C&EI. The C&EI started with GP30's in 1963, and the three units that lofted them into the second generation passed quietly into the L&N when the merger deal was finalized. Though they were owned by the MoPac none of the GP30's ever received MoPac paint, and there would never be a MoPac GP30 in true MoPac dress.

Turbocharging is one of the significant features that distinguishes EMD's first and second generation power from each other. Geared turbocharging was pioneered on the Union Pacific in September, 1955 by adding turbochargers to existing GP9's. EMD jumped into the turbocharger business in 1959 by experimentally applying turbochargers to nine UP GP9's and then to GP20's as

a standard feature. EMD's first turbocharged unit was built in July, 1958; SD24 demonstrator 5579. This unit utilized a geared turbocharger, as opposed to the propeller versions previously offered by Alco and GE.

The GP35, like its immediate predecessor the GP30, introduced a high-horsepower design in a low-hood roadswitcher. It introduced what is referred to as the Spartan car body, and came with turbocharging and dynamic brakes as standard features, but the MoPac bought theirs without the dynamic brakes. It was powered with EMD's 567-D3A 16-cylinder power plant, and generated 2,500 horsepower.

The MoPac's GP35's came in three batches, the first with construction dates in January, 1964. T&P got the first group, adding 15 of the high-horsepower B-B's to their roster (T&P-600-614). Part of this group also went to the MoPac, adding five GP35's to the MoPac fleet (MP-615-619). The MoPac had studied second generation power at some length, and had done detailed comparisons on EMD's GP30, GE's U25B, and Alco's C424. A combination of cost figures, failure rate data, and inspection of the

Above: The now famous "screaming eagle" adorns the side of the first GP35, T&P 600, the first unit to wear the large eagle on the long hood. The sight was worthy enough to commit the new image to film. *Ed Hawkins*

Below: An absolutely stunning lashup for the GP35 fan heads west with one of MoPac's premier auto parts trains, 61, from Lancaster Yard in Fort Worth, Texas for an overnight run to El Paso in August, 1969. The 15,000 horsepower all-GP35 lashup is T&P, MP, C&EI, T&P, C&EI and C&EI. The C&EI units have dynamic brakes. *J Parker Lamb*

units resulted in the decision in favor of GP35's. The U25B and C424 were another pair of might-have-beens.

In February, 1964 the MoPac added an additional five GP35's (MP-620-624), bringing their total to ten. Over in Illinois the C&EI was buying GP35's as well, purchasing 31 of the new EMDs. When the C&EI was folded into the MoPac, 13 of their GP35's were transferred to the L&N, and the remaining 18 units landed on the MoPac roster (these were originally C&EI-242-259, then C&EI-650-667, and when merged became T&P-650-667).

From January through April, 1965, EMD delivered another 25 GP35's to the MoPac and the T&P as part of the same order (MP-625-639 and T&P-640-649). This final purchase brought the GP35 total to 50 units before the C&EI acquisition. The GP35's were quite successful on the MoPac. They lasted well into the 1980's, and many were rebuilt into "GP35m's." Many of the "GP35m" rebuilds are still running off miles on the Wisconsin Central.

While GP35's were arriving on the C&EI and the MoPac, the little KO&G went to EMD for new power. They bought two GP28's (KO&G-700-701), a rather rare model that in essence was a GP18 in a Spartan car body. Only 16 GP28's were built for U.S. customers, and an additional 10 went to Mexico. The general specifications are identical to the GP18; 1,800 horsepower, powered by the 16-cylinder 567-D1 engine, and nonturbocharged. When the KO&G was officially absorbed, these two units became T&P-570-571, then T&P-850-851, then T&P-2000-2001, and finally MP-2000-2001.

They were assigned UP numbers after the merger (UP-2060-2061) but were never renumbered or repainted.

The final model purchased in the early stages of second generation diesels was the GP38. The GP38 was MoPac's first representative of the latest and greatest from EMD; the 645 engine. The GP38 was rated at 2,000 horsepower, and though climbing horsepower continued to be a selling point, the MoPac was content with the lower horsepower nonturbocharged units. The GP38's were nonturbocharged, and packed a 16-cylinder version of the 645.

The GP38's were acquired piecemeal by the MoPac, which replaced wrecked engines with GP38's. They wound up with only six GP38's (MP-572-577) all acquired in 1966. They were, however, a precursor of what was to come, as the Dash-2 version of the GP38 would be the MoPac's most abundant model.

EMD GP35 2,500 hp 25 units
TE = 64,700 WT = 258,800
Wheels = 40" Fuel = 2,600
Engine: EMD 16-567D3A V-type 16-cylinder 2-cycle Turbocharged
Min Speed for TE = 12.0 mph
62:15 Gearing 65 mph Max
"GP35m's" (2600-series) rebuilt with 645 power packs and no turbocharger

1st No	2nd No	3rd No	4th No	Built	Build#	Retired	Notes
T&P-600	T&P-2500	MP-2500	MP-2617	01/64	28772	08/86	Note 1, 16
T&P-601	T&P-2501	MP-2501	MP-2601	01/64	28773	08/87	Note 2
T&P-602	T&P-2502	MP-2502		01/64	28774	02/84	Note 3
T&P-603	T&P-2503	MP-2503	MP-2602	01/64	28775	08/86	Note 4, 16
T&P-604	T&P-2504	MP-2504		01/64	28776	02/84	Note 3
T&P-605	T&P-2505	MP-2505	MP-2603	01/64	28777	08/86	Note 5, 16
T&P-606	T&P-2506	MP-2506	MP-2604	01/64	28778	08/86	Note 6, 16
T&P-607	T&P-2507	MP-2507	MP-2605	01/64	28779	08/86	Note 7, 16
T&P-608	T&P-2508	MP-2508		01/64	28780	02/84	Note 3
T&P-609	T&P-2509	MP-2509		01/64	28781	02/84	Note 3, 8
T&P-610	T&P-2510	MP-2510		01/64	28782	02/84	Note 3
T&P-611	T&P-2511	MP-2511		01/64	28783	02/84	Note 3
T&P-612	T&P-2512	MP-2512	MP-2606	01/64	28784	08/87	Note 8, 9
T&P-613	T&P-2513	MP-2513	MP-2607	01/64	28785	08/86	Note 10, 16
T&P-614				01/64	28786	1967	Note 11
MP-615:1				01/64	28787	12/73	Note 3
MP-616:1	MP-2514			01/64	28788	02/84	Note 3
MP-617:1	MP-2515			01/64	28789	02/84	Note 3
MP-618:1	MP-2516	MP-2608		01/64	28790	08/86	Note 12, 16
MP-619:2	MP-2517			01/64	28791	02/84	Note 3
MP-620:2	MP-2518			02/64	28928	02/84	Note 3, 13
MP-621:2	MP-2519	MP-2609		02/64	28929	08/86	Note 14, 16
MP-622:2	MP-2520			02/64	28930	02/84	Note 3
MP-623:2	MP-2521	MP-2610		02/64	28931	08/86	Note 15, 16
MP-624:2	MP-2522			02/64	28932	02/84	Note 3, 8

Note 1: To Kiamichi RR, r# KRR-3804, to Texas Mexican and r# TM-869 but never shipped, to AZC, r# AZC-3804
Note 2: To Helm, to Kiamichi RR-2601, to BN 2/89, to EMD for BN rebuild
Note 3: T-I to EMD 5/84
Note 4: To Wisconsin Central 10/87, r# WC-4001
Note 5: Wore MP yellow as MP-2603. To Wisconsin Central 10/87, r# WC-4002
Note 6: To Kiamichi RR, r# KRR-3802
Note 7: To Wisconsin Central 10/87, r# WC-4003, r# WC-4013
Note 8: Snow plow
Note 9: Wore MP yellow as MP-2606. To Helm, to Kiamichi RR-2606 4/88, to BN 2/89, to EMD 5/89 for BN rebuild
Note 10: To Kiamichi RR, r# KRR-3803
Note 11: Wrecked and retired 1967, scrapped, 03/68
Note 12: To Wisconsin Central 10/87, r# WC-4004
Note 13: Wore Double-Eagles as MP-2518
Note 14: To Wisconsin Central 10/87, r# WC-4005
Note 15: To Wisconsin Central 10/87, r# WC-4006
Note 16: To Wilson Locomotive, Des Moines, IA, 1/87

EMD GP35 2,500 hp 25 units
TE = 64,450 WT = 257,800
Wheels = 40" Fuel = 2,600
Engine: EMD 16-567D3A V-type 16-cylinder 2-cycle Turbocharged
Min Speed for TE = 12.0 mph
62:15 Gearing 65 mph Max
"GP35m's" (2600-series) rebuilt with 645 power packs and no turbocharger

1st No	2nd No	3rd No	4th No	Built	Build#	Retired	Notes
MP-625:2	MP-2523	MP-2611		01/65	29805	08/86	Note 1, 11
MP-626:2	MP-2524			01/65	29806	02/84	Note 2
MP-627:1	MP-2525			01/65	29807	02/84	Note 2
MP-628:1	MP-2526			01/65	29808	02/84	Note 2
MP-629:1	MP-2527			01/65	29809	02/76	Note 3
MP-630	MP-2007:1	MP-2008	MP-2600	02/65	29810	08/86	Note 4, 11
MP-631:1	MP-2528			02/65	29811	02/84	Note 2
MP-632:1	MP-2529			02/65	29812	02/84	Note 2
MP-633:1	MP-2530	MP-2612		03/65	29813	08/86	Note 5, 11
MP-634:1	MP-2531			03/65	29814	02/84	Note 2
MP-635:1	MP-2532			03/65	29815	02/84	Note 2
MP-636	MP-2533			03/65	29816	02/84	Note 2
MP-637:1	MP-2534			03/65	29817	02/84	Note 6
MP-638	MP-2535			03/65	29818	02/84	Note 2
MP-639:1	MP-2536			03/65	29819	02/84	Note 2, 7
T&P-640	T&P-2537	MP-2537		03/65	29820	02/84	
T&P-641	T&P-2538	MP-2538		03/65	29821	02/84	Note 2
T&P-642	T&P-2539	MP-2539		03/65	29822	02/84	Note 2
T&P-643	T&P-2540	MP-2540		03/65	29823	02/84	Note 2
T&P-644	T&P-2541	MP-2541	MP-2613	03/65	29824	08/86	Note 8, 11
T&P-645	T&P-2542	MP-2542		03/65	29825	02/84	Note 2
T&P-646	T&P-2543	MP-2543	MP-2614	04/65	29826	08/86	Note 9, 11
T&P-647	T&P-2544	MP-2544		04/65	29827	02/84	Note 2
T&P-648	T&P-2545	MP-2545		04/65	29828	02/84	Note 2
T&P-649	T&P-2546	MP-2546		04/65	29829	02/84	Note 10

Note 1: Wrecked at Gorham IL 5/17/78. To Wisconsin Central 10/87, r# WC-4007
Note 2: T-I to EMD 5/84
Note 3: Wrecked 2/3/76 at Ward, AR, retired 2/76, T-I to EMD
Note 4: Wrecked into Intracoastal Canal, Baton Rouge, LA, 9/17/73, rebuilt into "GP35u" (Class 65, GP38). To Kiamichi RR, r# KRR-3801
Note 5: To Wisconsin Central 10/87, r# WC-4008
Note 6: Wrecked by FNM, scrapped
Note 7: Snow plow
Note 8: To Wisconsin Central 10/87, r# WC-4009
Note 9: To Wisconsin Central 10/87, r# WC-4010
Note 10: Wrecked by NdeM, to Gray 8/84
Note 11: To Wilson Locomotive, Des Moines, IA, 1/87

EMD GP28   2,000 hp   2 units
TE = 65,825   WT = 263,600 (KO&G-700)
TE = 65,700   WT = 262,800 (KO&G-701)
Wheels = 40"   Fuel = 2,600
Engine: EMD 16-567D1 V-type 16-cylinder 2-cycle
Min Speed for TE = 12.0 mph
62:15 Gearing   65 mph Max
Rebuilt with 645 power packs

1st No	2nd No	3rd No	4th No	5th No	6th No	Built	Build#	Notes
KO&G-700	T&P-570	T&P-850:2	T&P-2000:2	MP-2000	(UP-2060)	11/64	29632	Note 1
KO&G-701	T&P-571	T&P-851:2	T&P-2001:2	MP-2001	(UP-2061)	11/64	29633	Note 2

Note 1: Wrecked 3/30/89 at Chloride, MO, retired 6/89, to Helm 7/89, to VMV, Paducah, KY, 8/89, to Ashley Drew & Northern, r# AD&N-1815

Note 2: Wore large eagle on long hood sides even though not turbocharged. Retired 1/87, to Helm, to Kyle, r# KYLE-1829

EMD GP38   2,000 hp   6 units
TE = 65,780   WT = 263,120 (MP-572-MP-576)
TE = 64,975   WT = 259,900 (MP-577)
Wheels = 40"   Fuel = 2,600
Engine: EMD 16-645E V-type 16-cylinder 2-cycle
Min Speed for TE = 12.0 mph
62:15 Gearing   65 mph Max
Retired 8/87, to Helm 12/87

1st No	2nd No	3rd No	Built	Build#	Notes & Dispositions
MP-572:2	MP-852	MP-2002	10/66	32495	To Iowa Interstate, r# IAIS-601
MP-573:2	MP-853	MP-2003	10/66	32496	To Bangor and Aroostok, r# BAR-96
MP-574:2	MP-854	MP-2004	10/66	32497	To Bangor and Aroostok, r# BAR-98
MP-575:2	MP-855	MP-2005	10/66	32608	To Iowa Interstate, r# IAIS-602
MP-576:2	MP-856	MP-2006	10/66	32672	To Bangor and Aroostok, r# BAR-95
MP-577:2	MP-857	MP-2007:2	06/66	33174	Note 1

Note 1: Wore large eagle on long hood side even though not turbocharged. Wore MP yellow as MP-2007. To Bangor and Aroostok, r# BAR-97

Above: GP35 2521 swings into the curve at Paola, Kansas with the KSA train in September, 1977 trailed by two more GP35's spliced by a pair of GP18's. The 2521 was later rebuilt into a "GP35m," and was sold to Wisconsin Central after that. *Tony Fey*

Opposite page top: One of the two KO&G GP28's leads a pair of GP38-2's through Unity Village, Missouri on October 2, 1984. The GP28's wore five numbers, and were assigned a sixth. The 2001 is wearing its final MoPac number. *Lon EuDaly*

Opposite page bottom: A trio of GP35's is led by 643, rolling through Alexandria, Louisiana in May, 1969. The 643 was part of the second order of GP35's for the MoPac, an order totaling 25 units delivered between January and April, 1965. The first order had been split between the T&P and the MoPac, with 15 for the T&P and 10 for the MoPac. *Glenn Anderson*

by Ray Curl

EMC
SW

EMD
SW1
NW2
SW7

Alco
HH660
S-1
RS-1

Baldwin
VO660

In May, 1967, the Interstate Commerce Commission awarded the Missouri Pacific control of the C&EI, stipulating that the Evansville-Woodland Junction, Illinois portion be sold to the Louisville and Nashville. Also, the railroad north of Woodland Junction would be jointly owned by the MoPac and the L&N. This declaration by the ICC was the culmination of seven years of corporate wrangling between the L&N, the MoPac, the Illinois Central, and others for control of the C&EI.

The C&EI is an interesting railroad in and of itself, and it is appropriate at this juncture in the MoPac's diesel story to digress back into the history of the C&EI's diesel fleet.

The C&EI purchased its first diesel locomotives in 1937. Orders were placed in June with EMC for two 600 horsepower model SW switchers, and with Alco for one 600 horsepower switcher. These locomotives were delivered in January, 1938, and were assigned to the Chicago Terminal.

The EMC diesels (C&EI-100-101) were each powered with one Winton 201-A, in-line, eight cylinder, normally aspirated, two cycle engine. The switchers weighed 100 tons with full supplies. The Alco switcher was a model HH660 (C&EI-102), which was powered with a McIntosh-Seymore model 531 six cylin-

der, in-line, normally aspirated, four cycle engine. The traction motors were GE, and the loaded weight was just slightly over 100 tons.

The purchase of these locomotives in 1937 was primarily due to an effort to reduce locomotive operating expenses (the railroad was in receivership), and also to meet Chicago's smoke ordinances. Evidently this was accomplished, as new steam power was never purchased subsequently, although two second-hand Wabash 2-10-2's were acquired in 1942 for freight service in southern Illinois due to a power shortage during the World War II oil rush.

Four additional diesels for yard service were ordered on June 8, 1941; an order for an Alco S-1 switcher, and another order to what was now EMD for three SW1 switchers. EMD evidently had a greater backlog of orders than Alco, as the Alco unit (C&EI-103) came first on October 16, 1941. After being set up at Danville, it was shipped to Evansville, Indiana for yard duties. The EMD SW1's (C&EI-97-99) arrived on January 17 and 24, 1942, and like the Alco were set up at Danville and then sent to Evansville. The electrical equipment on the SW1's was all EMD.

The new Alco unit (C&EI-103) differed from the first in that the top of the engine hood was lowered to give the operating crew full forward visibility, similar to that afforded by EMC and EMD locomotives. This was brought about by a new diesel engine design and by lowering the engine mounting from the top of the main longitudinal frame members to between the frame members.

Soon after delivery of the three SW1's, two additional SW1's were ordered. Delivery was made in June, 1942 and the little EMDs (C&EI-

95-96) headed south to Evansville after set up like the previous switchers. They were essentially identical to the previous three SW1's. Three additional switchers were ordered at the same time as the pair of SW1's, two from Alco and one from Baldwin. The two Alcos were S-1's, and were lettered for the Chicago Heights Terminal Transfer (CHTT-104-105). They were delivered in August, 1942 at Chicago Heights, Illinois, where they were set up. They were basically identical to the C&EI-103 except that the draft gear came from a different vendor and they were slightly heavier.

The third purchase order of the group was the lone Baldwin VO660, to be assigned to Vincennes, Indiana. The Baldwin unit (C&EI-110) was delivered in August, 1942, but after set up at Danville was sent to Yard Center in the Chicago terminal area for assignment on August 28. The engine was assigned to Evansville by June, 1944 and later was at Danville, where it was involved in a head-on collision on December 31, 1948. It was repaired after the accident. It was the C&EI's only Baldwin.

The CHTT was a wholly-owned subsidiary of the C&EI, and rostered 12 engines by mid-September, 1942. Some of these units were lettered CHTT and others were lettered for the parent road. All were diesel switchers and were painted black with either a circular emblem (C&EI-97-99 and C&EI-100-102) or the new elliptical oval design (C&EI-95-96, C&EI-103, CHTT-104-105, and C&EI-110) in white enamel paint. C&EI initials were centered in the logo, except for CHTT-104-105 which were lettered for the CHTT. The logo was located on the sides of the engine hood toward the front. Stenciled on the cab sides in 8-inch letters and numbers were the initials C&EI or CHTT, and below the initials was the locomotive number. No numbers or initials were applied on the ends.

Two and a half years passed before another order was placed, and then the C&EI ordered four locomotives from Alco on June 11, 1944. All were RS-1 roadswitchers, a model that the Missouri Pacific never sampled. This was a new design configuration at the time, and boasted Alco's 539 engine with six in-line cylinders that produced 1,000 horsepower. The engine was a four-cycle, turbocharged design, with GE traction motors and generators. The RS-1 was

Left: The C&EI jumped into roadswitchers before the MoPac did, consequently rostering four RS-1's built in April, 1945. Brand new RS-1 116 works the south lead in the North Yard, north of the yard office in Danville, Illinois on April 17, 1945. The paint is barely dry under the lettering "Speed & Service - The CHICAGO Line!" *Paul Moffitt photo, Ray Curl collection*

Above: In late 1949 the C&EI bought six NW2's, originally 119-124. They later renumbered the 119 to 125 to avoid confusing it with the RS-1's. C&EI NW2 1031 is at Neff Yard in Kansas City in September, 1972 in MoPac blue dress, but with a C&EI buzzsaw. She'll be traded in on SW1500's in four months. *Lee Berglund*

Alco's initial plunge into the roadswitcher concept, a concept that Alco had been key in developing. In fact, the RS-1 was the first roadswitcher, and generated a fair sales figure of 353 units during its 19-year production period from March, 1941 through March, 1960. Domestic production ended in 1957, and a number of RS-1's were converted to RSD-1's. Alco sold more RS-1's than any other model except the RS-2 (barely), the extremely popular RS-3 roadswitcher, the FA-1 cab unit, and the S-1 and S-2 switchers.

The four new Alco RS-1's (C&EI-115-118) arrived at Danville on April 16, 1945, about ten months after the date of the order. Although classed as roadswitchers, the C&EI numbered the four new diesels in a yard locomotive series, as they were to be assigned to yard switching and transfer service. After set up, C&EI-115 was moved to Evansville, C&EI-116 was at Danville for a short time, and C&EI-117-118 were assigned to Mitchell Yard in the St. Louis terminal area, and Chicago heights, respectively. Later, RS-1 C&EI-116 was also assigned to Mitchell Yard. These assignments were effective in June, 1945, after the diesel fueling facilities were completed at Mitchell.

Of these four RS-1's, only the C&EI-117 was equipped with m-u, and that was added later as all were delivered without m-u capability. During a severe road locomotive power shortage in 1956, a decision was made to equip the four RS-1's with m-u controls. C&EI-117 was due for heavy overhaul, so material and drawings were secured from ALCO to modify the locomotive. This work required several months and involved many ancillary systems. One was converting the radiator shutter system from manual operation to automatic temperature control operated by air cylinders.

The locomotive ends had to be modified for m-u electrical equipment and for the additional air lines needed for sanding, control air, compressor synchronization, and brake pipe equalization. The engine was overhauled and modernized. After completion of the job, the locomotive was load-tested using meters and resistance grids to determine the power output. Unfortunately, the maximum horsepower output from the generator was about 850, much lower than the builder's nominal rating. After several days of testing, tinkering, and talking, all with no improvement, the C&EI-117 was tested on the Brewer Yard (Danville) to Terre Haute local freight with an EMD GP7. This test quickly brought out several major shortcomings of the RS-1. First, the engine ran hot all the time, and second, the truck journals, which were friction bearings, overheated. All these problems, besides a cost overrun, convinced the Mechanical Department to shelve this idea and return the unit to Evansville to work yard jobs. The remaining three RS-1's were never modified.

The RS-1's were not painted in the C&EI standard black and white styling, but were painted in orange and blue, the University of Illinois school colors. The locomotives were outstanding in appearance and received favorable comments from nearly all who observed them. The trucks, fuel tank, and underframe were painted black, while the side sill, handrails, and handrail stanchions were orange along with the cab roof and the top and ends of the hoods. The end bumper plates and step wells were blue, as well as the cab sides and ends, except to maintain the orange in a continuous horizontal plane. There were 30-inch orange numbers centered on the long hood, and small blue numbers were located directly over the headlight on the hood ends. A new oval emblem advertising the C&EI as "The Chicago Line," and "Speed, Service" graced the cab sides.

The next group of switchers delivered to the C&EI were six EMD 1,000 horsepower NW2's. These were received in November, 1949, and were numbered C&EI-119-124. However, prior to releasing the C&EI-119 to service it was renumbered C&EI-125, evidently

to avoid identifying the unit as part of the C&EI-115-118 class of RS-1's. For reasons unknown, the first two were ordered on April 25, 1948, while the remaining four were ordered February 2, 1949, the same date as ten FP7A's, which are covered later. At any rate the six NW2's were delivered in late November, 1949, and had consecutive builder's numbers.

The NW2's had a new air brake design for the C&EI, a Westinghouse 6-BL, and no provision for m-u operation was furnished. They were delivered in black paint with white numbers on the hood, white emblems on the cab sides, and white striping on the front and rear.

Four months before the delivery of the six new NW2's, eight additional switchers were ordered from EMD on August 7, 1949. When 20 new GP7's were approved for order at the same time, the orders spelled the death blow to steam operations. The eight switchers were SW7's, six for the C&EI (C&EI-126-131) and two for the CHTT subsidiary (CHTT-132-133). Although all were ordered at the same time, the six for the C&EI arrived first in late February, 1950, while the CHTT units were delivered on June 10, 1950. The units were nearly identical to the previous NW2's, except that the units were 1,200 horsepower rather than 1,000, and they came with EMD's latest traction motor. The extra 200 horsepower was obtained by an increase in both the fuel rack setting on the governor and the injector timing.

With the demise of steam operations in May, 1950, the C&EI operated 85 diesels, two less than had been purchased. The two off the roster were oddball switchers, which were sold to locomotive dealers in late 1949. These included the Alco HH660 (C&EI-102) and the lone Baldwin VO660 (C&EI-110).

The two CHTT units were the final switchers delivered new for the C&EI, though they did acquire one more unit. On July 31, 1954, the C&EI purchased the St. Louis & O'Fallon Railroad, which brought an additional Alco S-1 to the C&EI. It was numbered SL&O-51, and was transferred to Danville in early November and placed in yard service. It was renumbered C&EI-106 and repainted in December and was outshopped by December 16, 1954. This was a futile effort, as the locomotive was sold on December 28, 1954 to Inland Steel Company. It had been built in July, 1946.

The switcher fleet was by far the most diverse of the C&EI's three categories of locomotives. Two SW1's (C&EI-98-99) and all the NW2's and SW7's made it onto the MoPac roster on merger day, the rest were all off the roster.

The switchers included three builders and eight models, whereas all the other units were EMD. As with the MoPac, it was generally two or three at a time, especially in the early years. The C&EI's 31-unit switcher fleet was purchased early compared to many roads, SW's, SW1's, the HH660, and S-1's all representing the builder's early designs. They pushed steam out of the yards.

Above: The C&EI bought five SW1's, two of which survived beyond the MoPac takeover. One of the two survivors was SW1 99, which was subsequently renumbered C&EI-6001. It carried that number until it was sold to the Dardanelle & Russellville. Though it was officially owned by the MoPac, it never was lettered for the MoPac but retained its C&EI reporting marks. It is at Oaklawn Shops in Danville, Illinois on November 5, 1967. *Ray Curl*

Right: The last switchers for the C&EI were SW7's purchased in 1950. The 1202 is now owned by the MoPac as she shuffles cars in Danville, Illinois on September 22, 1967. The cab side has been painted over and a C&EI buzz-saw applied, and the large number on the flank has also been blacked out. *Ray Curl*

Left: RS-1 118 had worked for the C&EI for 19 years and had been retired for one when this photo was taken on December 22, 1965 at Dolton, Illinois. All four RS-1's were retired in December, 1964. *K C Henkels photo, Kevin EuDaly collection*

EMC-GE SW   600 hp   2 units
TE = 50,000   WT = 200,000
Wheels = 40"   Fuel = 600
Engine: Winton 8-201A 8-cylinder 2-cycle
Min Speed for TE = Not Available
68:16 Gearing   40 mph Max

1st No	Built	Build#	Notes
C&EI-100	01/38	631	Note 1
C&EI-101	01/38	656	Note 2

Note 1: Retired 9/59, to Lauria Brothers 09/59, to Lipsett, scrapped
Note 2: Retired 8/59, to Lauria Brothers 08/59, to Detroit Marine Terminal,
    r# DMT- 6, to KCS 1991 for slug 4255

Alco HH660   660 hp   1 unit
TE = 50,315   WT = 201,260
Wheels = 40"   Fuel = 400
Engine: McIntosh-Seymore 531 6-cylinder 4-cycle
Min Speed for TE = Not Available
68:16 Gearing   40 mph Max

1st No	Built	Build#	Notes & Disposition
C&EI-102	01/38	69045	Note 1

Note 1: To Export-Import Co. 08/49, to Atkinson Co. 102, to Puget Sound and
    Baker River, r# PSBR-95, to Pine Flat Contractors, to Scott Paper,
    r# SPCO-3. Scrapped 06/71

EMD SW1   600 hp   5 units
TE = 49,375   WT = 197,500
Wheels = 40"   Fuel = 600
Engine: EMD 6-567 V-type 6-cylinder 2-cycle
Min Speed for TE = 5 mph
62:15 Gearing   45 mph Max

1st No	2nd No	Built	Build#	Retired	Notes
C&EI-95:1		05/42	1855	11/65	Note 1. R# IS-L006
C&EI-96:1		05/42	1856	11/65	Note 1. R# IS-L007
C&EI-97		01/42	1378	11/65	Note 1. R# IS-L008
C&EI-98	C&EI-6000	01/42	1379	03/68	Note 2
C&EI-99	C&EI-6001	01/42	1474	03/68	Note 3

Note 1: To Arnold Hughes Co., to Interlake Steel
Note 2: To Whisler, to Granite Mountain Quarries 11/69 r# GMTQ-4742
Note 3: To Dardanelle & Russellville, r# D&R-6

Alco-GE S-1   600 hp   1 unit
TE = 49,400   WT = 197,600
Wheels = 40"   Fuel = 635
Engine: Alco 539 6-cylinder 4-cycle
Min Speed for TE = 6.5 mph
75:16 Gearing   60 mph Max

1st No	Built	Build#	Retired	Notes & Disposition
C&EI-103	10/41	69593	12/64	To Joliet Ry. Equipment Co. 12/64, scrapped

Alco-GE S-1   600 hp   2 units
TE = 50,540   WT = 202,150
Wheels = 40"   Fuel = 635
Engine: Alco 539 6-cylinder 4-cycle
Min Speed for TE = 6.5 mph
75:16 Gearing   60 mph Max

1st No	Built	Build#	Retired	Notes & Dispositions
CHTT 104	08/42	69827	12/64	To Joliet Ry. Equipment Co., scrapped
CHTT 105	08/42	69828	12/64	To Joliet Ry. Equipment Co., scrapped

Alco-GE S-1   660 hp   1 unit
TE = 49,750   WT = 199,000
Wheels = 40"   Fuel = 635
Engine: Alco 539 6-cylinder 4-cycle
Min Speed for TE = 6.5 mph
75:16 Gearing   60 mph Max
Purchased on 7/31/54

1st No	2nd No	Built	Build#	Notes & Disposition
SL&O-51	C&EI-106	07/46	73908	Retired 12/54, to Inland Steel 12/54, r# INS-85. T-I to EMD 08/68

Baldwin VO660   660 hp   1 unit
TE = 49,050   WT = 196,210
Wheels = 40"   Fuel = 600
Engine: Baldwin VO 6-cylinder 4-cycle
Min Speed for TE = 6.5 mph
76:16 Gearing   60 mph Max

1st No	Built	Build#	Notes & Disposition
C&EI-110	08/42	64392	Retired 8/49, to Export-Import Co. 08/49

Alco-GE RS-1   1,000 hp   4 units
TE = 60,000   WT = 240,000
Wheels = 40"   Fuel = 1,600
Engine: Alco 539 6-cylinder 4-cycle Turbocharged
Min Speed for TE = 8.0 mph
75:16 Gearing   60 mph Max
Retired 12/64, to Marfax Steel 12/64

1st No	Built	Build#	Notes & Dispositions
C&EI-115	04/45	73328	To Chatahoochee Industrial RR
C&EI-116	04/45	73329	Scrapped
C&EI-117	04/45	73330	To Chatahoochee Industrial RR
C&EI-118	04/45	73331	Scrapped

EMD NW2   1,000 hp   6 units
TE = 60,905   WT = 243,620
Wheels = 40"   Fuel = 600
Engine: EMD 12-567 V-type 12-cylinder 2-cycle
Min Speed for TE = 5 mph
62:15 Gearing   65 mph Max

1st No	2nd No	3rd No	4th No	Built	Build#	Notes
C&EI-119	C&EI-125	C&EI-1034	L&N-2209	11/49	7830	Note 1
C&EI-120	C&EI-1029	L&N-2207		11/49	7831	Note 1
C&EI-121	C&EI-1030			11/49	7832	Note 2
C&EI-122	C&EI-1031			11/49	7833	Note 2
C&EI-123	C&EI-1032			11/49	7834	Note 2
C&EI-124	C&EI-1033	L&N-2208		11/49	7835	Note 1

Note 1: Transferred to L&N 2/7/68
Note 2: Retired 1/73, T-I to EMD on SW1500's

EMD SW7   1,200 hp   8 units
TE = 60,875   WT = 243,500
Wheels = 40"   Fuel = 600
Engine: EMD 12-567A V-type 12-cylinder 2-cycle
Min Speed for TE = 11.4 mph
62:15 Gearing   65 mph Max

1st No	2nd No	3rd No	4th No	Built	Build#	Notes
C&EI-126	C&EI-1202:2	MP-1202	L&N-2221	02/50	8882	Note 1, 2
C&EI-127	C&EI-1203:2	MP-1203	L&N-2222	02/50	8883	Note 1
C&EI-128	C&EI-1204:2	MP-1204	L&N-2223	02/50	8884	Note 1
C&EI-129	C&EI-1205:2			02/50	8885	Note 3
C&EI-130	C&EI-1206	MP-1400	UP-S9	02/50	8886	Note 4
C&EI-131	C&EI-1207			02/50	8887	Note 5
CHTT-132	CHTT-1208			06/50	10526	Note 6
CHTT-133	CHTT-1209			06/50	10527	Note 7

Note 1: Transferred to L&N 2/7/68
Note 2: To US Steel, Fairfield, AL, 1975 for parts, scrapped
Note 3: Retired 11/77, to Hyman-Michaels, to Birmingham Rail & Locomotive,
    r# BR&L-186, rebuilt 1/79 for St. Joe Zinc, Monaca, PA, r# SJZ-6
Note 4: Cut down to slug 12/78, r# MP-1400
Note 5: Retired 7/75, to US Steel, Leeds, AL, to B&M-1207
Note 6: Retired 5/75, to Dardanelle & Russellville, Dardanelle, AR, r# D&R-17
Note 7: Retired 6/75, to Hyman-Michaels, to Birmingham Rail & Locomotive,
    r# BR&L-130, to Stockham Valve, r# SV-1903, scrapped 04/88

**Left: S-1 105 is one of two S-1's built for the CHTT subsidiary. It rests in
Chicago Heights, Illinois in 1946.** *Bowman photo, Ray Curl collection*

by Ray Curl

EMD
E7
E9
F3
"F5"
FP7
BL1
BL2

During World War II, the C&EI investigated the benefits of operating new streamlined passenger trains between Chicago and Evansville, and between Chicago and southern Illinois. Ever confident about post-war passenger loads, on December 21, 1944 orders were placed with Pullman-Standard for 11 streamlined cars and with EMD for two E7A streamlined diesel road units. This equipment was sufficient for the two trains planned for post-war operation. Several months later, on April 8, 1945, a third E7A passenger unit was ordered as a spare and also to power the *Dixie*

Flagler, an all coach streamliner from Chicago to Miami scheduled every third day, with C&EI power as far as Evansville.

The first two E7A units (C&EI-1100-1101) arrived on the property on May 15, 1946, while the third (C&EI-1102) came on September 12, 1946. The E7A's were designated as "EA7's" by the C&EI, and that designation appears on their drawings from that era. The drawings were later modified to read E7A. The passenger locomotives were geared for 98 mph maximum speed, utilizing a gear ratio of 55:22 and 36-inch wheels.

The C&EI figured locomotive weight at one-half supplies (one-half fuel and water, etc..), which leads to some discrepancy between railroad and builder records where the builder fig-

Below: The C&EI purchased a group of 10 FP7A's in mid-1948 that began arriving on the property in August. The new FP's took over passenger runs and all survived until the MoPac merger. When the merger split the old C&EI between the L&N and the MoPac, about half the C&EI fleet went to the L&N. Eight of the 10 FP7A's went to the L&N, including the 1601. The handsome FP rounds the curve at 47th Street in Chicago on October 31, 1965 under a fabulous sky. The A-B-A lashup was an American classic, now a part of history. *Charles Zeiler*

Above: On February 18, 1973, FP7A 1941 leads a freight through Algoa, Texas, a long way from any former C&EI rails. The passenger unit has long been relegated to freight service, serving out the remainder of her years in glamourless toil, at least compared to the former glory of passenger service. The 1941 was the last active C&EI FP7 on the system, falling from the roster in March, 1974, and heading back from whence she'd come, back to EMD. *Ralph Back*

ures the weight at full supplies. For the E7's, the one-half supply weight was 308,440, while the fully supplied weight was 318,810.

The units were delivered from EMD in blue and orange paint with the C&EI logo appearing on the nose door beneath the headlight. The C&EI initials and "Speed" above and "Service" below were orange. The logo was on an orange diamond cigar band background that narrowed on each side to a 9-inch wide horizontal stripe running the full length of the lower locomotive body with a zig-zag break near the rear. Inside the orange band were two 1 1/4-inch blue stripes, top and bottom, stopping prior to and resuming after a 5 1/2-inch blue letterboard that spelled out the railroad name. An orange unit number was placed on the nose between the Mars light and the headlight. A 2-inch orange number was also

stenciled at the rear bottom corner of each side of the locomotive between the grabirons. The anti-climber on the nose directly above the pilot was orange with blue protruding ribs.

The C&EI management, however, was not satisfied with the styling of the E7's. There was too much blue and therefore low visual recognition, especially at night. In an effort to add more orange to the basic styling, the railroad altered the paint scheme several times over the next 2 and one half years.

The initial revision, only to C&EI-1100, was an attempt to add orange to the nose and sides. The top of the nose was painted orange narrowing around the Mars light and then sweeping down in a large curve into the top of the cigar band. Above the anti-climber an orange area was added to join with the bottom of the cigar band diamond. This area was slightly narrower than the nose door. 3-inch orange stripes at the eaves and bottom side sill ran the full length of the locomotive, merging with the orange anti-climber, and curving about the outer extremes of the windshield, down to the top of the nose.

The next version eliminated the two orange stripes in the cigar band on the nose and back to the rear of the side letterboard. The orange area on the nose between the anti-climber and the cigar band on the C&EI-1100 was widened and then likewise applied to C&EI-1101-1102.

A minor revision to the nose logo was next. The original logo was replaced by the 1940 ellipse design with the *Saturday Evening Post* style letters. The background was blue with orange letters and horizontal bars.

Another touch-up job was later applied to C&EI-1100, when the nose portion received a full blue anti-climber, except for the top rib which became orange along with a new 3-inch stripe directly above the anti-climber. This horizontal stripe continued around to the sides and flowed into the 3-inch bottom side sill stripes.

There has been speculation that the E7A units were at one time painted in a reverse paint scheme, the blue becoming orange and the orange becoming blue. Photographs have been inconclusive, and study on this subject has led to the conclusion that they were not.

During the spring and summer of 1956, two E7A's (C&EI-1100-1101) were completely repainted in the L&N passenger locomotive styling. The body was dark blue with imitation gold lettering on the letterboards and logo. The side ladder handholds were imitation gold, but yellow or orange paint was used if necessary for touch-up. The trucks, fuel tank, and underframe were black. Gold stripes were to be utilized along the body sides above and below the letterboard, but these were never applied.

Faces of the C&EI: These three builder's photos show the variety of paint schemes that were part of the C&EI.

Above: E7A 1100 is at La Grange before going into service in May, 1946.

Above right: F3A 1203 poses for the EMD photographer in February, 1948. It was the final A-unit of a group of four F3A's and two F3B's (1300-1301).

Opposite page: F3A 1401 was part of a group of F3A's that arrived in July, 1948 without steam generators. In 1949 steam generators were added to this class. *EMD three photos, Ray Curl collection*

The first two E7A's entered road service on May 20, 1946 at Evansville, pulling train 88, the *Dixie Express*, to Chicago. The first train south to Evansville behind the E's was number 93, the *Dixie Limited*, on the same day. Both units continued on the heavy-weight trains and the *Dixie Flagler* between Chicago and Evansville until the fall delivery of the two Pullman-Standard built streamliners. Shortly after their deliv-

Below: A snappy F3 A-B combination leads the *Dixie Limited* past Liberty Lane in Danville, Illinois circa late 1940's. This is the northbound train, number 92, and the consist is 11 heavyweight cars. *Ray Curl collection*

ery both train sets went on tour with one diesel each to allow the residents of the various communities which would be served to inspect the trains. By this time C&EI-1102 had arrived and permitted at least one diesel passenger unit to handle revenue trains.

By late summer 1946, following delivery of all three E7A's, the C&EI management still did not seriously consider complete dieselization. The road was spending thousands of dollars annually in 1945, 1946, and 1947 modernizing steam locomotives, constructing new locomotive coaling facilities, and other related improvements. This situation changed on May 9, 1947, as Mr. Holly Stover, president of the C&EI, succeeded to chairman, and Mr. John M. Budd became president. Mr. Budd assumed complete authority on January 1, 1948 with the retirement of Mr. Stover. Budd was a progressive railroader with the foresight to see that diesel motive power was the only solution to the high operating costs associated with steam power.

Another personnel change was made on November 1, 1949 when Downing B. Jenks became general manager. Mr. Jenks was a brilliant young railroader, and went to further fame with the Rock Island and then the MoPac. Together, Budd and Jenks molded the C&EI into a lean, tough, dieselized railroad by May, 1950, bringing the company into the new decade ready to provide the best possible service.

Approximately four weeks prior to Mr. Budd's appointment as president, the C&EI placed an order on April 6, 1947 for four additional 2,000 horsepower E7A's from EMD for delivery in February, 1948. However, on August 27, 1947, the executive committee of the Board of Directors approved the purchase of six 1,500 horsepower locomotives in lieu of the

four E7A's. The reason for the change was the desire to obtain additional horsepower in locomotive consists to maintain a higher speed on grades and more rapid acceleration after stops. A recent ICC ruling, effective June 17, 1948, required the railroad to install train control for speeds 80 mph and above. This necessitated a one mph reduction in the maximum speed to 79 mph between Clinton and Evansville to avoid the cost of installing additional train control. Although the one mph speed reduction was minor, trains could no longer routinely exceed the speed limits because the ICC required the railroad to closely monitor speeds. Previously, management allowed trains to operate on this section of the railroad as fast as the locomotive could move the train, especially northbound steam powered trains coming downhill into Terre Haute, where speeds were rumored to approach 105 mph on occasion.

By maintaining the 80 mph and 79 mph speed limits the railroad could eliminate the extra maintenance on trackage, avoid the costs associated with train control equipment, and reduce passenger discomfort at the higher speeds. Additionally, the six locomotives gave added boiler capacity and extra water storage capacity for generating steam to heat trains in the winter and cool them in the summer. Steam in the summer was required for passenger equipment with steam ejector cooling systems. The increase in cost for the six units was only about $85,600, or roughly 10%, and was deemed justifiable.

The order was for F3's from EMD, four A-units and two B-units, and they were built in February, 1948. The A-units (C&EI-1200-1203) were orange and blue, similar to the then current paint scheme on the E7A's with the exception

that the orange area on the nose was squared off just above the anti-climber rather than having sweeping curves to the sides. The B-units (C&EI-1300-1301) were also blue with an orange horizontal stripe full-length on both sides.

The six units were immediately placed in passenger service between Chicago and Evansville, handling trains 92 and 93, the *Dixie Limited*, and 94 and 95, the *Dixie Flyer*. They usually operated as two-unit A-A or A-B pairs, or three unit A-B-A consists, or with one of the E7's. However they were operated, the locomotives were an immediate success. Normally a round trip was made daily, a total distance of approximately 600 miles including light movements to and from engine terminals.

Approximately two months after receipt of the six passenger F3's, six freight units were ordered. Once again four A-units (C&EI-1400-1403) and two B-units (C&EI-1500-1501) were specified. Plans called for operation of the new locomotives in three unit A-B-A consists; however, often only two units were operated. The new locomotives were delivered on July 28, 1948, and utilized a freight paint scheme rather than the passenger orange and blue. The carbody was blue with an orange C&EI logo on the nose door and three horizontal orange stripes wrapped around the nose. The railroad name was spelled out in 8-inch orange letters on the sides, and 2-inch numbers were located at the rear corners of each side. The B-units were blue with orange letterboards and unit numbers.

The freight F3's were similar to the passenger F3's except that their gearing was 62:15 versus 59:18, limiting freight units to 65 mph while the passenger units were good for 83 mph. This also gave the units a different tractive effort curve, one more suitable for freight service. The

freight F3's were not equipped with steam generators or boiler water tanks, but did have steam lines and couplings to allow them to run between passenger equipment and passenger locomotives.

Four days after ordering the initial freight F3's, the C&EI placed orders with EMD for nine additional freight F3's, two passenger F3A's, two BL2 "Branch Line" locomotives, and two NW2 switchers on April 25, 1948. The nine freight units came in November and December, 1948, and included six A-units (C&EI-1404-1409) and three B-units (C&EI-1502-1504). The units were mechanically similar to the first freight F3's, but the exterior appearance was different due to the use of stainless steel radiator grills versus the "chicken wire" radiator covers on the previous order. Some EMD literature described these as "F5's" but this model designation was dropped and they were officially late F3's. The new grille design became the F7 trade mark. The original freight F3's were equipped with manual transition in the electrical system to control the traction motor current, while this order had automatic-manual transition, a feature that became standard on the F7.

The exterior styling for the C&EI-1404-1409 and C&EI-1502-1504 was the passenger locomotive design identical to the C&EI-1200-1203 styling. The railroad was not satisfied with the solid blue paint on the early 1400- and 1500-series units, as they were difficult to see at night. Motorists had particular problems seeing the blue locomotives at crossings.

The two F3A passenger locomotives that were ordered on April 25, 1948 were delivered on February 5, 1949, and were numbered above the existing passenger F3's as C&EI-1204-1205. In appearance they were identical with C&EI-1401-1409, except for the boiler exhaust stack and vents on the roof. Like the other passenger F3's they were geared at 59:18 for an 83 mph maximum speed.

Prior to the February, 1949 delivery of C&EI-1204-1205, the railroad accepted three combination freight-passenger units from EMD. These units were BL1 and BL2 branch line locomotives. Two of these were part of the April, 1948 acquisition program and were BL2's (C&EI-1600-1601), but the third was an EMD demonstrator numbered EMD-499, and was the only example of the BL1 model. The BL1 was renumbered C&EI-1602, and came from EMD on November 18, 1948. The BL2's arrived on December 14 and 21, 1948.

The purchase of the BL1 was an "off the cuff" agreement with EMD, as the actual purchase order was dated three days after the unit was on the property. The BL-series was developed to compete with Alco's RS-1 and RS-2 roadswitcher design, and was EMD's initial attempt to produce a lightweight locomotive for branch line service, freight or passenger duties, and for local switching, if that was required. Ultimately EMD wisely developed the GP7 locomotive in 1949, and dominated the U.S.

Right: With the split of the C&EI equipment, the two E7A's went to the L&N. On August 31, 1969, ex-C&EI E7A 1101, now in L&N paint as 799, rolls C&EI train 4 through Dolton, Illinois. The L&N retired the two E's in 1971. *Joe McMillan*

Below: On the first day of the L&N passenger engine pool, April 24, 1966, C&EI E7A 1100 leads F3B 1503 and L&N 786 on a 13-car consist on Train 54. It's 8:20 am, and the first light of the day has crept into the sky, at least what light the spring storm clouds will let through. *Ray Curl*

domestic locomotive market for many years with this basic design.

The primary difference between the BL1 and the production BL2 was in the throttle control. The BL1 had an air control throttle, while the BL2 had an electric control throttle. Before the BL1 was shipped from EMD to the C&EI, it was modified to an electric throttle arrangement, thus bringing the unit up to the BL2 design. However, it was always identified as a BL1.

The BL's were basically equipped with the same equipment as the popular F3A cab units. The three C&EI BL's were not equipped with m-

u control, but did have steam generators located in the nose. Shortly after delivery, in February and March, 1949, the units were renumbered from C&EI-1600-1602 to C&EI-200-202. This was due to a new order for ten FP7A's from EMD that were scheduled for delivery in August and September, 1949, which were to be numbered C&EI-1600-1609. This also moved their numbers down into the three digit roadswitcher series, which they had essentially become a part of.

The BL's were assigned to Illinois Division local passenger trains 123 and 124 between Danville and Thebes, and also, during late 1949

and early 1950, to trains 15 and 16, operating between Danville and Watseka. The Danville cars were attached to or detached from the *Meadowlark* at Watseka, an arrangement that was short lived.

The BL's were not well suited to either passenger, local freight, or transfer assignments. Use on passenger trains always brought forth crew complaints concerning gases in the cab compartment, due to steam generator combustion gases being exhausted through the hollow windshield divider. Whether true or not, it was always a bone of contention. Due to their design they were not an ideal local freight or switching

locomotive either, primarily because the engineer could not see crew members boarding or disembarking from the end platforms unless he leaned out the cab window.

With the anticipated delivery of the ten FP7's in late summer 1949, and the planned application of steam generators to all the F3's by late 1949, a decision was made to remove the steam generator from the BL1 and place the unit in local and transfer service, even though safety concerns remained. This assignment lasted approximately six years. The steam generators remained on the BL2's until January, 1955, but the BL2's were seldom utilized on passenger trains.

Late in 1954, and in January, 1955, the three BL's were sent to EMD for conversion to m-u operation. The BL1 was returned to the C&EI in December, 1954, while the BL2's came back on the property in February, 1955. The BL's were then placed in through freight service over the entire railroad, but due to several limitations by the railroad and EMD they were normally operated as B-units and due to their light underframe construction nearly always operated second in a consist. The C&EI would not allow lead unit operation for the BL's except for short-haul transfer service.

Although freight service extended the useful life of the BL units, they were not quite completely satisfactory. The removal of the steam generators reduced the unit's weight from 228,000 pounds to 221,440 and 221,780 pounds

Above: When C&EI wrecked E7A 1102, they sent the remains in to La Grange, and the unit was "rebuilt" into an "E9Am," which still carried the same number, 1102. After integration into the MoPac system, the graceful E was renumbered 43, and painted blue with the C&EI buzz-saw applied. The lady has 'em rolling on the outskirts of Kansas City with a three-car special in July, 1970. *John Wegner*

Below: FP7A 1605 has the *New Dixieland* well in hand at Princeton, Indiana, running as second number 10 on July 10, 1957 in the Hoosier State. Delivered in orange and blue, the simplified solid blue scheme has taken over by this date. The unit was later transferred to the L&N on February 7, 1968, and then retired by the L&N in 1970. It was the first of the 10 FP7's to be retired. *James EuDaly*

for C&EI-200 and 201, respectively, and from 227,000 to 218,340 pounds for the BL1. The fuel capacity was increased from the original 500 gallons to 1,100 gallons by utilizing the water tanks for fuel, but still the weight for adhesion available for starting, for slow speed drag service, and for power braking was inadequate. This was especially critical for the C&EI due to the heavy trains operated; many were in excess of 250 cars, particularly train 83. The BL's were sold to EMD in April, 1963 as trade-ins for the new GP30's then on order, the first of C&EI's second generation diesels.

On February 2, 1949, the C&EI placed its last order for carbody units in the form of 10 FP7A's. Outwardly, the new units had much the same appearance as the previous orders of F3's, with the major difference that there was a four foot increase in length and thus an increase in the truck centers. This enabled the units to carry larger fuel and boiler water tanks. They came with steam generators from the factory and had a gear ratio of 59:18, which allowed 80 mph operation.

The new units (C&EI-1600-1609) were painted in the blue and orange passenger scheme, and were immediately placed in passenger and freight service system-wide. Seldom used as matched sets, they were operated with E7A's and F3's indiscriminately.

At the time the order for the ten FP7A's was placed, the operating department decided to equip the freight F3A's and F3B's with steam

generators, boiler water tanks, and 59:18 gearing. Another feature was the addition of trainline boiler water capacity between locomotives. The C&EI was operating a record number of passenger trains at the time, while freight carloadings were down. This change would allow greater flexibility in motive power operations, higher utilization of diesel road power, and avoid the use of steam power on some of the faster schedules. This program covered C&EI-1400-1403 and C&EI-1500-1501, commenced in the spring of 1949, and was completed in December of that year. All work was performed at the Oaklawn Shop, and the locomotives were repainted to the orange and blue passenger scheme.

Boiler tanks were purchased and one 200 gallon tank was placed beneath the steam generator, inside the carbody. Additional capacity was obtained by installing one roof tank, and the B-units also had a vertical cylindrical tank at the end of the locomotive. This put the diesel engine and electric generator between the boiler and the vertical water tank in the B-units.

The same program was applied to F3A's C&EI-1404-1409 and F3B's C&EI-1502-1504, but their rebuilding was not quite as extensive since they already had the 59:18 gearing. This raised the weights of all units involved by about 15,000 pounds. In the late 1950's and early 1960's many F3's and FP7's had the boilers removed or placed "out of service" on the locomotives. Concrete ballast was added to the locomotives without boilers at the old boiler

location, and several had the gear ratio changed to the 62:15 gearing for freight service.

After the purchase of the 10 FP7A's, the C&EI purchased only switcher or roadswitcher units, including two orders that were placed after MoPac control was in effect. The carbody phase was over, with a grand total of 36 units purchased by the C&EI, which included 3 E7A's, 16 F3A's, 7 F3B's and 10 FP7A's. These units helped dieselize the railroad, and combined with the GP7's resulted in an all-EMD passenger and road freight roster. By the time the MoPac inherited C&EI's diesel fleet, only one F3A (C&EI-1407), four F3B's (C&EI-1501-1504), and the ten FP7A's (C&EI-1600-1609) remained on the roster. All the remaining carbody units as well as the three BL's had been traded in to EMD on newer power.

E7A C&EI-1102 was one of three units involved in a head-on collision near Daisy Lane crossing, just east of the Oaklawn Shops at Danville. It was "upgraded" to an E9A, and sported the name "Eliza Doolittle" when released from EMD along with an orange nose logo. It was technically a new locomotive, with a new builder's number. Both the name and the orange logo were removed after publicity photographs were made. The C&EI-1102 was the 1,000th unit to be upgraded by EMD, and Eliza Doolittle was the flower girl in Shaw's play *Pygmalion (My Fair Lady)*. Thus the C&EI-1102 served as EMD flower girl in 1958.

EMD E7A 2,000 hp 3 units
TE = 51,970   WT = 308,440 (207,890 on powered wheels)
Wheels = 36"   Fuel = 1,200
Engine: Two EMD 12-567A V-type 12-cylinder 2-cycle
Min Speed for TE = 30.0 mph
55:22 Gearing   98 mph Max
Equipped with steam generators

1st No	2nd No	3rd No	Built	Build#	Notes
C&EI-1100	C&EI-27	L&N-798	05/46	3374	Note 1
C&EI-1101	C&EI-28	L&N-799	05/46	3375	Note 1
C&EI-1102:1			09/46	3585	Note 2

Note 1: Transferred to L&N 2/7/68. Retired by L&N 1971
Note 2: Wrecked in 1958, T-I on "E9Am" C&EI-1102:2

EMD "E9Am" 2,400 hp 1 unit
TE = 52,945   WT = 317,660 (211,775 on powered wheels)
Wheels = 36"   Fuel = 1,200
Engine: Two EMD 12-567B V-type 12-cylinder 2-cycle
Min Speed for TE = 21.5 mph
57:20 Gearing   85 mph Max
Equipped with steam generators

1st No	2nd No	Built	Build#	Notes & Disposition
C&EI-1102:2	C&EI-43	08/58	24733	Note 1

Note 1: Rebuilt from wrecked E7A C&EI-1102:1. Retired 4/72, T-I to EMD
on GP38-2's, to Pielet, scrapped

Left: F3B 1301 is at Danville, Illinois circa 1955. The C&EI bought three groups of F3B's totaling eight units. All were purchased in 1948. the 1301 is one of the first two. *Paul Moffitt photo, Ray Curl collection*

EMD F3A 1,500 hp 4 units
TE = 58,310   WT = 233,250
Wheels = 40"   Fuel = 1,200
Engine: EMD 16-567B 16-cylinder 2-cycle
Min Speed for TE = 15.5 mph
59:18 Gearing   83 mph Max
Equipped with steam generator
T-I to EMD on GP35's, scrapped

1st No	Built	Build#	Notes
C&EI-1200	02/48	6018	Retired 8/64
C&EI-1201	02/48	6019	Retired 7/64
C&EI-1202:1	02/48	6020	Retired 7/64
C&EI-1203:1	02/48	6021	Retired 9/64

EMD F3A 1,500 hp 2 units
TE = 58,700   WT = 234,800
Wheels = 40"   Fuel = 1,200
Engine: EMD 16-567B 16-cylinder 2-cycle
Min Speed for TE = 15.5 mph
59:18 Gearing   83 mph Max
Equipped with steam generator
T-I to EMD on GP35's, scrapped

1st No	Built	Build#	Notes
C&EI-1204:1	02/49	6004	Retired 8/64
C&EI-1205:1	02/49	6005	Retired 8/64

EMD F3B 1,500 hp 2 units
TE = 58,670   WT = 234,670
Wheels = 40"   Fuel = 1,200
Engine: EMD 16-567B 16-cylinder 2-cycle
Min Speed for TE = 15.5 mph
59:18 Gearing   83 mph Max
Steam generator added 1949
Retired 11/64, T-I to EMD on GP35's, scrapped

1st No	Built	Build#
C&EI-1300	02/48	6022
C&EI-1301	02/48	6023

EMD F3A   1,500 hp   4 units
TE = 56,130   WT = 224,520
Wheels = 40"   Fuel = 1,200
Engine: EMD 16-567B 16-cylinder 2-cycle
Min Speed for TE = 15.5 mph
62:15 Gearing   65 mph Max
Steam generator added 1949
Rerated to 1,600 hp
T-I to EMD on GP35's, scrapped

1st No	Built	Build#	Notes & Dispositions
C&EI-1400	07/48	6006	Retired 11/63
C&EI-1401	07/48	6007	Retired 12/63
C&EI-1402	07/48	6008	Retired 11/63
C&EI-1403	07/48	6009	Retired 6/64

EMD F3B   1,500 hp   2 units
TE = 54,215   WT = 216,860
Wheels = 40"   Fuel = 1,200
Engine: EMD 16-567B 16-cylinder 2-cycle
Min Speed for TE = 15.5 mph
62:15 Gearing   65 mph Max
Steam generator added 1949

1st No	2nd No	3rd No	Built	Build#	Notes & Dispositions
C&EI-1500			07/48	6010	Retired 9/64, T-I to EMD on GP35's, scrapped
C&EI-1501	C&EI-750B	C&EI-933B	07/48	6011	Retired 3/73, scrapped

EMD F3A ("F5A")   1,500 hp   6 units
TE = 56,275   WT = 225,100
Wheels = 40"   Fuel = 1,200
Engine: EMD 16-567B 16-cylinder 2-cycle
Min Speed for TE = 15.5 mph
59:18 Gearing   83 mph Max
Steam generator added 1949
Rerated to 1,600 hp

1st No	2nd No	3rd No	Built	Build#	Retired	Notes
C&EI-1404			11/48	7850	09/64	Note 1
C&EI-1405	C&EI-750	C&EI-824	11/48	7851	04/72	Scrapped
C&EI-1406			12/48	5998	12/64	Note 1
C&EI-1407	C&EI-751	C&EI-827	12/48	5999	07/71	Note 2
C&EI-1408			12/48	6000	08/64	Note 1
C&EI-1409			12/48	6001	11/64	Note 1

Note 1: T-I to EMD on GP35's, scrapped
Note 2: To GE 07/71, scrapped

EMD F3B ("F5B")   1,500 hp   3 units
TE = 54,370   WT = 217,480
Wheels = 40"   Fuel = 1,200
Engine: EMD 16-567B 16-cylinder 2-cycle
Min Speed for TE = 15.5 mph
59:18 Gearing   83 mph Max
Steam generators added 1949

1st No	2nd No	3rd No	Built	Build#	Notes & Dispositions
C&EI-1502	C&EI-751B	C&EI-934B	11/48	7852	Retired 1/72, scrapped
C&EI-1503	C&EI-752B	C&EI-935B	12/48	6002	Retired 8/72, scrapped
C&EI-1504	C&EI-753B	C&EI-936B	12/48	6003	Retired 1/72, scrapped

EMD BL2   1,500 hp   2 units
TE = 57,000   WT = 228,000
Wheels = 40"   Fuel = 500
Engine: EMD 16-567 16-cylinder 2-cycle
Min Speed for TE = 15.5 mph
62:15 Gearing   65 mph Max
Equipped with steam generators
T-I 04/63 to EMD on GP30's C&EI-239-241

1st No	2nd No	Built	Build#
C&EI-1600:1	C&EI-200	12/48	6012
C&EI-1601:1	C&EI-201	12/48	6013

Right: The first C&EI BL2 was numbered 1600, and later renumbered 200. The BL2 is externally identical to the BL1, and after the BL1's throttle was retrofitted, it was internally identical as well. There was only one BL1, and only 58 BL2's. Neither C&EI nor MoPac BL2's came with steam generators, a feature that only Boston & Maine, Chesapeake & Ohio, and the Rock Island bought on their BL2's. *Ray Curl collection*

EMD BL1   1,500 hp   1 unit
TE = 56,750   WT = 227,000
Wheels = 40"   Fuel = 500
Engine: EMD 16-567 16-cylinder 2-cycle
Min Speed for TE = 15.5 mph
62:15 Gearing   65 mph Max
Equipped with steam generator

1st No	2nd No	3rd No	Built	Build#	Notes
GM/EMD 499	C&EI-1602:1	C&EI-202	09/47	7428	Note 1

Note 1: T-I 02/63 to EMD on GP30's C&EI-239-241, scrapped

EMD FP7A   1,500 hp   10 units
TE = 61,590   WT = 246,385
Wheels = 40"   Fuel = 1,200
Engine: EMD 16-567B 16-cylinder 2-cycle
Min Speed for TE = 15.5 mph
59:18 Gearing   83 mph Max
Steam generators added 1949

1st No	2nd No	3rd No	Built	Build#	Notes & Dispositions
C&EI-1600:2	C&EI-933	L&N-670	08/48	7535	Note 1, 3
C&EI-1601:2	C&EI-934	L&N-671	08/48	7536	Note 1
C&EI-1602:2	C&EI-935	L&N-672	08/48	7537	Note 1
C&EI-1603	C&EI-936	L&N-673	08/48	7538	Note 1
C&EI-1604	C&EI-937	L&N-674	08/48	7539	Note 1, 3
C&EI-1605	C&EI-938	L&N-675	09/48	7540	Note 1, 2
C&EI-1606	C&EI-939	L&N-676	09/48	7541	Note 1
C&EI-1607	C&EI-940	L&N-677	09/48	7542	Note 1, 3
C&EI-1608	C&EI-941	C&EI-1941	09/48	7543	Retired 3/74, T-I to EMD
C&EI-1609	C&EI-942		09/48	7544	Retired 11/71, T-I to EMD

Note 1: Transferred to L&N 2/7/68
Note 2: Retired by L&N 1970
Note 3: Retired by L&N 1971

Below: The BL1 demonstrator was originally numbered EMD-499. The C&EI bought the unit and numbered it 1602, immediately following their two BL2's. The original intent was to number them in with the F3's, which were similar units, but after studying their new creatures, the C&EI decided they fit better with the switcher or roadswitcher fleet, hence the three-digit numbers. It is at Danville, Illinois. *Bowman photo, Ray Curl collection*

by Ray Curl

EMD
GP7
GP9
"GP9m"

Roadswitchers officially began on the C&EI with the purchase of the four RS-1's, but the C&EI didn't consider them as adequate road freight power, and renumbered them in with the switcher fleet. It was five years before another order for roadswitchers was approved, and that naturally went to EMD, the builder of choice for the C&EI.

When the eight SW7's were ordered on August 7, 1949, a large order by C&EI standards was placed for 20 GP7's. These began arriving on April 3, 1950, and on May 9 the final unit arrived. As these units entered service, steam's fires were put out on the C&EI for the last time; 99 years of steam service ended on May 5, 1950. The GP7's were numbered C&EI-203-222, following the three BL's numerically.

Due to a penny-pinching decision by management, the railroad opted for the standard equipment 6-BL single unit brake rather than the extra cost, newer, and more modern m-u road locomotive brake, the 24-RL. This restricted the GP7's to operation in m-u with one or two other GP7's due to the 6-BL's incompatibility with the F3's and FP7's 24-RL brake. An attempt to rectify the problem was later made by applying three H5 Relayair valves and an MU2A valve to the 6-BL brake, which, with other piping changes created a 6-BLC brake. This allowed the 24-RL equipped units to operate with the GP7's either in the lead or in trailing positions in the locomotive consists. Another oversight was that they were not equipped with toilets.

An interesting comparison is the cost per horsepower for the GP7's versus the SW7's purchased on the same day. A GP7's cost was $101 per horsepower, while an SW7's cost was $81.33 per horsepower. Several things caused the price difference. Because the GP7 was a new design, development and tooling costs were not yet recovered by EMD, a situation that would quickly change. Additionally, the GP7 had m-u capability. The 10 FP7's delivered nearly the same time the GP7's were ordered showed a cost of $117 per horsepower, with the higher cost attributable to the steam generator and the 24-RL brake.

The C&EI GP7's were delivered in basic black and white, with the only touch of color being the orange applied to the grabirons, handrails, and step edges. 30-inch white numerals were applied to the long hood for the road numbers. A white C&EI emblem was on the cab side, and 5-inch white stripes were located on each hood end. The overall design was nearly identical to the Chicago and Western Indiana RS-1 paint scheme, except that the C&EI used white rather than gold trim. It was also similar to the paint scheme on the NW2's and SW7's.

Below: A southbound business car extra rolls through LeCompte, Louisiana on October 20, 1973. This is C&EI GP7 84:2, which later became the bicentennial MP-1776:2. By this date the 84:1 was long a part of the L&N fleet. *Glenn Anderson*

By October, 1950, the operating department realized the road had insufficient motive power, so five additional GP7's were ordered. A sixth GP7 had been ordered for the CHTT in July, 1950. An upturn in carloadings due to the Korean conflict and periodic locomotive maintenance programs produced power shortages. The six GP7's were all lettered C&EI and numbered C&EI-223-228, even though the CHTT owned the 227 and 228. Except for weights these locomotives were identical to the earlier group of GP7's. C&EI-227 arrived first, in December, 1950, and the other five arrived in January, 1951.

At mid-year 1951, four additional GP7's were ordered, two for the C&EI and two for the CHTT. Like the previous group they were all lettered for the C&EI and were numbered C&EI-229-232. All four were ordered on June 17, even though the 231 and 232 were owned by the CHTT. The two C&EI units arrived on August 16 and the CHTT units arrived on October 1, 1951. They were also identical to the earlier groups of GP7's.

Another year passed before the C&EI again revised its motive power roster. A purchase order went to EMD for six GP9's in late December, 1955, which was an upgraded version of the GP7. Two of the new GP9's (C&EI-233-234) were delivered in June, 1956, and the remaining four (C&EI-235-238) came in February, 1957. The GP9's were equipped with a Mars signal light on the short hood, an instantaneous visual distinction from the GP7's. The GP9's also had toilets, as did all other road units except the GP7's, which were soon retrofitted. The air brakes on the GP9's were 6-BLC, an improved version of the 6-BL used on the GP7's, and were capable of operating with 6-BL brakes either in the lead or in the trailing position, and were also compatible with the 24-RL road locomotive brake. The GP7 brake modification already discussed was applied in the mid-1960's. The modification provided additional flexibility in motive power utilization, but was not an ideal solution.

Immediately upon receipt of the GP9's, the units were placed in road freight service as B-units or trailing locomotives behind F3A's and FP7A's with the 24-RL brakes. Few C&EI operating personnel were familiar with the operation of the 6-BLC brake trailing a 24-RL lead unit. The first trips of these consists were costly.

Due to several unique problems, the 6-BLC brake would not release and the result after 100 miles of travel was either flat wheels or thermal cracks in the wheel treads. Many were so severe that it was necessary to change wheel sets or make a truck change immediately. The C&EI preferred running with a carbody unit leading, so until the early 1960's, a GP7 or GP9 was seldom found in the lead position of a mixed geep and F-unit lashup. Instructions were issued on July 9, 1956 giving air hose, angle cock, and valve setting positions along with engineer instructions to remedy the critical situation.

However, the problem was never completely eliminated until the 6-BL and 6-BLC equipped locomotives were retired or converted to 24-RL or 26-RL brakes. The C&EI made no conversions, so the problem persisted until the eventual merging of the geep fleet into the MoPac.

After the GP9 deliveries in February, 1957, the C&EI did not purchase new power for over six years. However, there was considerable activity in the locomotive department during this period, primarily due to collisions. Eight damaged locomotives were returned to EMD between January, 1958 and January, 1961. Three of these were classed as new units and the

Above: GP9 236 leads a pair of covered wagons through Vincennes, Indiana as the smoke and dust flies. When this was taken on May 28, 1965, the C&EI was still independent, though time was running out. Time was ticking for the geeps and F's too, as the GP35's were already powering trains all over the C&EI. *Joe McMillan*

EMD GP7   1,500 hp   14 units
TE = 65,175   WT = 260,700
Wheels = 40"   Fuel = 1,200
Engine: EMD 16-567B V-type 16-cylinder 2-cycle
Min Speed for TE = 12.0 mph
62:15 Gearing   65 mph Max
Some had 567BC engines
Rerated to 1,600 hp

1st No	2nd No	3rd No	4th No	Built	Build#	Notes
C&EI-203	C&EI-68	L&N-388		03/50	8872	Note 1
C&EI-204	C&EI-69	C&EI-83:2		03/50	8873	Note 2
C&EI-205	C&EI-70	L&N-389		03/50	8874	Note 1
C&EI-206	C&EI-71	L&N-390		03/50	8875	Rebuilt. Note 1
C&EI-207	C&EI-72	L&N-391		03/50	8876	Note 1
C&EI-208	C&EI-73	L&N-392		03/50	8877	Note 1
C&EI-209	C&EI-74	L&N-393		03/50	8878	Note 1
C&EI-210	C&EI-75	L&N-394		03/50	8879	Note 1
C&EI-211	C&EI-76	L&N-395		04/50	8880	Note 1
C&EI-212	C&EI-77	C&EI-84:2	MP-1776:2	04/50	8881	Note 5
C&EI-213	C&EI-78	L&N-396		04/50	8894	Note 1
C&EI-214	C&EI-79	C&EI-85:2		04/50	8895	Note 2, 3
C&EI-215	C&EI-80			03/50	8896	Note 4
C&EI-216	C&EI-81			04/50	8897	Note 2

Note 1: Transferred to L&N 2/7/68
Note 2: Retired 9/76, T-I to EMD
Note 3: To Guilford, r# GUIL-593
Note 4: Retired 8/74, T-I to EMD
Note 5: 2,500 gallon fuel tank, chopnose by MoPac, renumbered 1776:1 and
       painted in 1/76 for Bicentennial. Retired 9/77, T-I to EMD

EMD GP7   1,500 hp   16 units
TE = 63,875   WT = 255,500
Wheels = 40"   Fuel = 1,200
Engine: EMD 16-567B V-type 16-cylinder 2-cycle
Min Speed for TE = 12.0 mph
62:15 Gearing   65 mph Max
Some had 567BC engines
All except C&EI-229 rerated to 1,600 hp

1st No	2nd No	3rd No	4th No	5th No	Built	Build#	Notes & Dispositions
C&EI-217	C&EI-82				04/50	10245	Retired 9/76, T-I to EMD
C&EI-218	C&EI-83:1	L&N-397			03/50	10246	Transferred to L&N 2/7/68
C&EI-219	C&EI-84:1	L&N-398			03/50	10247	Transferred to L&N 2/7/68
C&EI-220	C&EI-85:1	L&N-399			03/50	10248	Transferred to L&N 2/7/68
C&EI-221:1					04/50	10249	Rebuilt 8/30/58 by EMD as a "GP9m," see C&EI-221:2
C&EI-222	C&EI-87				05/50	10250	Retired 1/76, T-I to EMD
C&EI-223	C&EI-89				01/51	13266	Retired 5/76, T-I to EMD
C&EI-224	C&EI-88				01/51	13267	Retired 11/75, T-I to EMD
C&EI-225	C&EI-90				01/51	13541	Retired 9/76, T-I to EMD
C&EI-226	C&EI-91				03/50	13542	Wrecked, rebuilt by EMD 3/27/59. Retired 9/76, T-I to EMD
CHTT-227	C&EI-92				12/50	13264	Owned by CHTT. Retired 4/74, T-I to EMD
CHTT-228	C&EI-93				01/51	13265	Owned by CHTT. Retired 7/74, T-I to EMD
C&EI-229:1					08/51	14657	Owned by CHTT, wrecked and rebuilt 1959 as a "GP9m," see C&EI-229:2
CHTT-230	C&EI-94	T&P-94	MP-1634:1	MP-634:2	08/51	14658	Owned by CHTT. Retired 9/79, T-I to EMD on GP38-2's MP-2158-2197
C&EI-231	C&EI-95:2	T&P-95	MP-1635:1		09/51	14655	Retired 4/76, T-I to EMD
C&EI-232	C&EI-96:2	T&P-96	MP-1636:1		09/51	14656	Retired 12/76, T-I to EMD

EMD GP9   1,750 hp   2 units
TE = 61,400   WT = 245,600
Wheels = 40"   Fuel = 1,600
Engine: EMD 16-567C V-type 16-cylinder 2-cycle
Min Speed for TE = 11.0 mph
62:15 Gearing   65 mph Max
Rrerated to 1,800 hp
Retired 10/81, T-I to EMD, scrapped

1st No	2nd No	3rd No	4th No	5th No	Built	Build#
C&EI-233	C&EI-340	T&P-340	MP-1826		06/56	22013
C&EI-234	C&EI-341	T&P-341	C&EI-1827	MP-1827	06/56	22014

Above: GP7 213 receives some attention in Chicago in October, 1966. The trustworthy geep has been on the railroad since April, 1950, and will go to the L&N in just a few short years. *James P Harper photo, Kevin EuDaly collection*

EMD GP9   1,750 hp   4 units
TE = 61,400   WT = 245,600
Wheels = 40"   Fuel = 1,700
Engine: EMD 16-567C V-type 16-cylinder 2-cycle
Min Speed for TE = 11.0 mph
62:15 Gearing   65 mph Max
Rerated to 1,800 hp
Transferred to L&N 2/7/68

1st No	2nd No	3rd No	4th No	Built	Build#
C&EI-235	C&EI-342	T&P-342	L&N-542	02/57	22015
C&EI-236	C&EI-343	T&P-343	L&N-543	02/57	22016
C&EI-237	C&EI-344	T&P-344	L&N-544	02/57	23268
C&EI-238	C&EI-345	T&P-345	L&N-545	02/57	23269

Right: The C&EI bought a pair of GP9's in June, 1956, and later went back for four more in 1957. One of the first two, originally the 234, now wears a MoPac number but retains C&EI lettering in the buzz-saw. It is at Monroe, Louisiana on November 7, 1977. *J Harlen Wilson*

remaining five were rebuilt-in-kind. The new locomotives were C&EI-221, 229, and 1102, and the rebuilt-in-kind units were C&EI-206, 209, 214, 226, and 1609. Roster notes outline these activities.

C&EI-1609 was rebuilt-in-kind twice, once in 1951 and again in 1958. The 1951 accident was a major disaster near Mode, Illinois on June 28, when heavy rains caused the sinking of a fill on the Illinois Division near the trestle over Brush Creek. Train 11, the southbound *Meadowlark*, tumbled into the creek bed 46 feet below when it ran over the soft roadbed. After another rebuilding in 1958, the C&EI-1609 was readily identified by the orange C&EI insignia on the front nose door. The orange remained until MoPac control in 1967, soon after which a red buzz-saw emblem took its place.

EMD "GP9m" 1,500 hp 1 unit
TE = 64,130 WT = 256,520
Wheels = 40" Fuel = 1,600
Engine: EMD 16-567C V-type 16-cylinder 2-cycle
Min Speed for TE = 11.0 mph
62:15 Gearing 65 mph Max
Rerated to 1,800 hp

1st No	2nd No	Built	Build#	Notes
C&EI-221:2	C&EI-86	08/58	24753	Note 1

Note 1: Rebuilt from wrecked GP7 221:1. Retired 4/76, T-I to EMD

EMD "GP9m" 1,500 hp 1 unit
TE = 63,110 WT = 252,450
Wheels = 40" Fuel = 1,600
Engine: EMD 16-567C V-type 16-cylinder 2-cycle
Min Speed for TE = 11.0 mph
62:15 Gearing 65 mph Max
Rerated to 1,800 hp

1st No	Built	Build#	Notes & Disposition
C&EI-229:2	08/58	25460	Note 1

Note 1: Rebuilt from wrecked GP7 229:1. T-I to EMD on GP35 242

Three of the GP7 rebuilds, C&EI-221, 226, and 229, were nearly identical to the six GP9's (C&EI-233-238) in outward appearance after rebuilding, including the Mars light on the short hood. C&EI-221 and 229 were upgraded to "GP9's," although still rated at 1,500 horsepower.

Below: One of the GP9's in the second group (built in 1957), rests outside Oaklawn Shops in Danville, Illinois on October 22, 1967. The C&EI later acquired two more GP9's, though they referred to them as "GP9m's" due to the fact that wrecked GP7's were traded in on them. *Ray Curl*

Right: The builder's photo of GP7 232 shows the as-built appearance of the C&EI's GP7's. That white won't be spotless for long. *EMD photo, Ray Curl collection*

Below: One of the two "GP9m's" leads a pair of F3's leaving Brewer Yard at Danville, Illinois in December, 1959. *J Parker Lamb*

by Ray Curl

The second generation on the C&EI started when the railroad ordered three EMD GP30's on February 3, 1963. The GP30 was a comparatively new design by EMD and had several features new to the C&EI. In appearance the low short hood presented a dramatic change, and enabled the engine crew to have forward visibility equal to or superior to that of EMD's F-units and E-units. Mechanically, there was a new 16-cylinder turbocharged diesel engine, model 16-567D3, with a traction output rated at 2,250 horsepower. The gear ratio was the standard 62:15 for 65 mph operation. An electrical feature was the accelerated start, only used if one unit was switching or kicking cars in a yard.

The GP30 also featured a centralized air system that set it apart from its first generation predecessors, and the air system and the dynamic brake resistors were housed in the pronounced top blister that leaves no confusion in its identity. The GP30 was fairly popular, with 908 units sold, two of which were sold in Canada. The GP35 and GP40 both outsold the GP30. C&EI's GP30's were all standard units, with no special features that set them apart from any other members of the GP30 production period, which lasted two years and four months, from July, 1961 to November, 1963.

The GP30's also came with extended range dynamic brakes, an option which later parent MoPac had avoided. Dynamic brakes are a feature that is unique to diesel engines. Dynamic brakes reverse the traction motor field currents, converting them into generators, with the current transmitted to resistance grids (similar to a toaster) where it is converted to heat and dissipated to the atmosphere. Train momentum turns the wheels and speed is controlled by varying the field currents to induce resistance in the motors. Very low speed means little dynamic braking power, whereas intermediate speeds results in higher dynamic braking power.

The dynamic brake was a tremendous benefit to railroads such as the Chesapeake & Ohio, Baltimore &

Ohio, Pennsy, Union Pacific, and the Southern Pacific where steep mountain grades were common. Savings were realized in reduced brake shoe replacements, fewer wheel problems, and improved running times. Until the C&EI's fleet of GP35's were in service, however, the monetary return on their dynamic brake investment was microscopic, as the units seldom operated together in the same consist. A single unit in the consist was not the ideal utilization of dynamic brakes.

Prior to the delivery of their own GP30's the C&EI leased four new GP30's from EMD for a two-week test. The test was conducted in the second half of April, 1963, and the locomotives were Reading Railroad 5505-5508, but were EMD property. Several road trips were operated between Yard Center and Mitchell, and between Yard Center and Evansville. After testing, the locomotives were delivered to the B&OCT at Barr Yard near Riverdale, Illinois, where the Baltimore & Ohio worked the units east for delivery to the Reading. The C&EI evidently was pleased with the units as no adverse comments surfaced.

Above: C&EI GP35 664 swings into the curve in Alexandria, Louisiana with a long string of hoppers in tow on February 3, 1973. The C&EI bought four batches of GP35's, and the 664 was part of the third group, a group of 10 that were built in October and November, 1964. In MoPac days it became the 2561. *Glenn Anderson*

The GP30's were delivered in late June, 1963, and were numbered above the GP9's as C&EI-239-241. Their trucks and other main components were taken from trade-in units, in this instance, the three BL's. This transaction was the first of its type for the C&EI, and ushered in the second generation diesel era.

The GP30's came in the standard black and white scheme of the roadswitchers. They also had the touch of orange on the handrails, stanchions, and step edges.

Another trade-in agreement was signed in November, 1963, involving three units (C&EI-229, 1400, and 1402) that had all been in a major collision. By this time the F-units had seen better days and it was decided not to rebuild them. GP7 C&EI-229 was only four years old, but was so severely damaged it was scrapped, and the major components were utilized from these trade-ins wherever that was possible.

The new units from EMD were GP35's, similar to the previous GP30's except that they had no bulge on the cab roof. The first three GP35's (C&EI-242-244) arrived on March 31 and April 1, 1964, and the first unit was officially owned by the CHTT, though lettered for the C&EI. This unit replaced the wrecked C&EI-229 which had been a CHTT locomotive. Like the GP30's, the C&EI GP35's also came with dynamic brakes. They were painted like their predecessor GP30's, black and white with orange trim.

Four days following the delivery of the first three GP35's, the road placed two orders totaling ten additional GP35's. The orders were split because the first five were obtained with trade-ins while the remaining five were purchased as new units. The first five (C&EI-245-249) were added with trade-in components from C&EI-1200-1202, 1403, and 1408, all F3A's. The first unit, C&EI-245, arrived on June 30, 1964, and the remaining nine all came in early July. There was a minor change in these ten units versus the previous three; their overspeed trip was set for 71 mph instead of 69 mph.

On July 19, 1964, before the ten new GP35's were all in service, ten more GP35's were ordered, all with trade-in components. This order was identical to the previous one, and the units traded in included C&EI-1203-1205, 1300, 1301, 1401, 1404, 1406, 1409, and 1500. The new units were numbered above the existing GP35 fleet, and deliveries were made on October 30, 1964 (C&EI-255-257), November 17, 1964 (C&EI-258-260 and C&EI-263-264), and November 19 (C&EI-261-262).

The result of these purchases was that the C&EI had a fleet of 26 high horsepower roadswitchers for heavy freight service at the beginning of 1965. Utilization was high as no problems appeared in the new EMDs. With this new influx of freight power the road had surplus GP7's, so in December, 1964 all seven Alcos were sold. All had been assigned at Evansville's Wansford Yard for nearly ten years. These sales included S-1's C&EI-103-105 and RS-1's C&EI-115-118. With the Alcos gone the railroad moved NW2's, SW7's, and GP7's to Wansford. Most of these came from Yard Center, where GP7's then became the predominant switching power.

The C&EI needed additional freight power in early 1965, so on March 7, 1965 eight additional GP35's were ordered. These units were new as no trade-in units were offered. All eight (C&EI-265-272) were delivered during the last half of June. With the arrival of the final group of GP35's, the C&EI was able to operate solid consists of like model roadswitchers, especially on the unit coal trains coming off the L&N at Evansville, and originating at Mt. Vernon, Indi-

ana that hauled West Virginia and eastern Kentucky coal from barges. Coal trains coming out of southern Illinois also could be adequately powered, where an upsurge in business was in progress. Also, solid piggyback trains were being operated between Mitchell or Evansville and Chicago, which required high horsepower and reliability in motive power.

The roadswitcher fleet of the C&EI consisted of only four models (not counting the RS-1's), all from EMD. Though the BL's were in the same numbering sequence as the roadswitchers, they really weren't roadswitchers, but relied on the same principles of construction as the F3's from which they were designed. This type of standardization paid off as EMD intentionally built the GP7 and later models with high

Above: Though officially a MoPac engine, GP35 2560 wears C&EI sublettering rolling through Memphis, Tennessee in October, 1974. It was later rebuilt into a "GP35m" (MP-2616), and then retired in August, 1986 and sold to Wisconsin Central, becoming the 4011. *Steve Forrest*

Below: C&EI 652 wheels a northbound freight through Conroe, Texas on September 26, 1973. This was the final unit of the first order for three GP35's, which came in March, 1964, being born as C&EI-244. The crewman hooks the orders as the units pound the diamonds. *Joe McMillan*

accessibility and easy exchange of parts. The C&EI was not alone in EMD standardization, as later parent MoPac did essentially the same thing in the early 1960's. The MoPac's transition to all EMD was simply on a grander scale.

On November 19, 1965 three SW1's (C&EI-95-97) were sold to Arnold Hughes Company, therefore on December 31, 1965, the C&EI operated 104 locomotives, including six CHTT units. No further changes were made to the roster until May, 1967, and that had nothing to do with the purchase of new motive power, but rather with merger events that had been unfolding over the previous seven years.

Above: C&EI bought a total of 31 GP35's, making the GP35 their most popular model by a margin of a single unit, since there were 30 GP7's. The last GP35, 272, is at South Holland, Illinois on a cold January 15, 1967. *Owen Leander photo, Gary Zuters collection*

EMD GP30 2,250 hp 3 units
TE = 62,435   WT = 249,750
Wheels = 40"   Fuel = 2,600
Engine: EMD 16-567D3 V-type 16-cylinder 2-cycle
Min Speed for TE = 12.0 mph
62:15 Gearing   65 mph Max
Transferred to L&N 2/7/68

1st No	2nd No	3rd No	Built	Build#
C&EI-239	C&EI-590	L&N-1058	06/63	28345
C&EI-240	C&EI-591	L&N-1059	06/63	28346
C&EI-241	C&EI-592	L&N-1060	06/63	28347

EMD GP35 2,500 hp 1 unit
TE = 61,870   WT = 247,480
Wheels = 40"   Fuel = 2,600
Engine: EMD 16-567D3A V-type 16-cylinder 2-cycle Turbocharged
Min Speed for TE = 12.0 mph
62:15 Gearing   65 mph Max
Originally equipped with dynamic brakes, inoperative under MoPac.

1st No	2nd No	3rd No	4th No	Built	Build#	Notes
C&EI-242	C&EI-650	T&P-650	MP-2547	03/64	28958	Note 1

Note 1: Owned by CHTT. Retired 2/84, T-I to EMD 5/84

EMD GP35 2,500 hp 2 units
TE = 61,845   WT = 247,380
Wheels = 40"   Fuel = 2,600
Engine: EMD 16-567D3A V-type 16-cylinder 2-cycle Turbocharged
Min Speed for TE = 12.0 mph
62:15 Gearing   65 mph Max
Originally equipped with dynamic brakes, inoperative under MoPac.

1st No	2nd No	3rd No	4th No	Built	Build#	Notes
C&EI-243	C&EI-651	T&P-651	MP-2548	03/64	28959	Note 1
C&EI-244	C&EI-652	T&P-652	MP-2549	03/64	28960	Note 2

Note 1: Retired 2/84, T-I to EMD 5/84
Note 2: Wrecked at Itaska TX 3/24/70, rebuilt. Rebuilt in 1967, snow plow. Retired 2/83, T-I to EMD 5/84, scrapped

EMD GP35 2,500 hp 10 units
TE = 61,830   WT = 247,320
Wheels = 40"   Fuel = 2,600
Engine: EMD 16-567D3A V-type 16-cylinder 2-cycle Turbocharged
Min Speed for TE = 12.0 mph
62:15 Gearing   65 mph Max
Originally equipped with dynamic brakes, inoperative under MoPac.

1st No	2nd No	3rd No	4th No	5th No	Built	Build#	Notes
C&EI-245	C&EI-653	T&P-653	MP-2550		06/64	29546	Note 1
C&EI-246	C&EI-654	T&P-654	MP-2551	MP-2615	06/64	29547	Note 2
C&EI-247	C&EI-655	T&P-655	MP-2552		06/64	29548	Note 1
C&EI-248	C&EI-656	T&P-656	MP-2553		06/64	29549	Note 1
C&EI-249	C&EI-657	T&P-657	MP-2554		06/64	29550	Note 1, 3
C&EI-250	C&EI-658	T&P-658	MP-2555		07/64	29551	Note 1
C&EI-251	C&EI-659	T&P-659	MP-2556		07/64	29552	Note 1, 3
C&EI-252	C&EI-660	T&P-660	MP-2557		07/64	29553	Note 1
C&EI-253	C&EI-661	T&P-661	MP-2558		07/64	29554	Note 1, 3
C&EI-254	C&EI-662	T&P-662	MP-2559		07/64	29555	Note 1, 3

Note 1: Retired 2/84, T-I to EMD 5/84
Note 2: Rebuilt 1967. Rebuilt to "GP35m" MP-2615. Retired 6/85, to Wilson Locomotive, Des Moines, IA
Note 3: Wore Double-Eagles in 2500-number series

EMD GP35 2,500 hp 10 units
TE = 61,850   WT = 247,415
Wheels = 40"   Fuel = 2,600
Engine: EMD 16-567D3A V-type 16-cylinder 2-cycle Turbocharged
Min Speed for TE = 12.0 mph
62:15 Gearing   65 mph Max
Originally equipped with dynamic brakes, inoperative under MoPac.

1st No	2nd No	3rd No	4th No	5th No	Built	Build#	Notes
C&EI-255	C&EI-663	T&P-663	MP-2560	MP-2616	10/64	29648	Note 1
C&EI-256	C&EI-664	T&P-664	MP-2561		10/64	29649	Note 2
C&EI-257	C&EI-665	T&P-665	MP-2562		10/64	29650	Note 2, 3
C&EI-258	C&EI-666	T&P-666	MP-2563		11/64	29651	Note 2
C&EI-259	C&EI-667	T&P-667	MP-2564		11/64	29652	Note 2, 4
C&EI-260	C&EI-668	L&N-1116			11/64	29653	Note 5
C&EI-261	C&EI-669	L&N-1117			11/64	29654	Note 5
C&EI-262	C&EI-670	L&N-1118			11/64	29655	Note 5
C&EI-263	C&EI-671	L&N-1119			11/64	29656	Note 5
C&EI-264	C&EI-672	L&N-1120			11/64	29657	Note 5

Note 1: Retired 8/86, to Wilson Locomotive, Des Moines, IA, 1/87, to Wisconsin Central 10/87, r# WC-4011
Note 2: Retired 2/84, T-I to EMD 5/84
Note 3: Wrecked
Note 4: Wore Double-Eagles as MP-2564
Note 5: Transferred to L&N 2/7/68

EMD GP35 2,500 hp 8 units
TE = 63,780   WT = 255,130
Wheels = 40"   Fuel = 2,600
Engine: EMD 16-567D3A V-type 16-cylinder 2-cycle Turbocharged
Min Speed for TE = 12.0 mph
62:15 Gearing   65 mph Max
Transferred to L&N 2/7/68

1st No	2nd No	3rd No	Built	Build#
C&EI-265	C&EI-673	L&N-1121	06/65	30491
C&EI-266	C&EI-674	L&N-1122	06/65	30492
C&EI-267	C&EI-675	L&N-1123	06/65	30493
C&EI-268	C&EI-676	L&N-1124	07/65	30494
C&EI-269	C&EI-677	L&N-1125	07/65	30495
C&EI-270	C&EI-678	L&N-1126	07/65	30496
C&EI-271	C&EI-679	L&N-1127	07/65	30497
C&EI-272	C&EI-680	L&N-1128	07/65	30498

Above: The units that ushered in the second generation for the C&EI were a trio of GP30's delivered in June, 1963. The middle unit of the trio, 240, is at Dolton, Illinois on July 1, 1966. *Louis Marre*

Above right: As soon as the merger was finalized and the renumbering plan went into effect, the GP30's were renumbered into the 590-series, becoming 590-592. The new look involved the eradication of the large numbers off of the long hood by simply painting over the number with black paint, and the placement of the C&EI buzz-saw under the cab window on the cab side. The 592 has the new look, which will last a short while until the unit goes to the L&N as part of the merger deal. It is at Dolton, Illinois on November 16, 1968. *K L Douglas photo, Louis Marre collection*

Right: The fate of 13 of the GP35's was to be sent to the L&N as part of the split-up of the C&EI. This turned out to be the last 13 units, one of which was the 674, which became L&N-1122. The L&N unit got the same treatment as the other units did with the MoPac. After carrying its MoPac number (C&EI-674) for a short time, that number was in turn eradicated and replaced with L&N markings. The 1122 is on the L&N in August, 1969. *Kevin EuDaly collection*

Left: C&EI 652 swings through the curve past Tower 55 in Fort Worth in December 1970 leading three F-units and a geep. It had been rebuilt twice by this time, the last time after a wreck at Itaska, Texas on March 24, 1970. It wore a snow plow between the wrecks, the previous wreck having been in 1967. After the second wreck the plow was removed. *Robert Seale collection*

113

by Ray Curl

As previously stated, the May, 1967 declaration awarding the C&EI to the MoPac was the result of seven years of corporate disputes between several railroads for control of the C&EI. Due to several traffic pattern changes in the early 1960's, the patient nearly died before the operation commenced.

Upon control by the MoPac becoming effective in May, 1967, one of the first actions by the MoPac was a locomotive renumbering program. It was to commence on June 15, 1967, but the program moved slowly. By November 10 only 34 units had been renumbered, and the last unit was not

Opposite page top: In the interim stage after the C&EI had been absorbed into the MoPac but before it completely lost its corporate identity, the fleet was painted MoPac Jenks blue and a C&EI buzz-saw adorned the cab side. During this period GP35 658 pulls past Tower 55 in Fort Worth leading a pair of F-units and another EMD unit in December, 1970. In about six years the C&EI will lose its identity altogether. *Robert Seale collection*

Opposite page bottom: C&EI GP35 2559 swings through the curve at Tullos, Louisiana on March 15, 1975. The C&EI name would hold out for another 19 months, until official obliteration on October 15, 1976. *James Holder*

Right: At the height of C&EI's second generation, a trio of light GP35's, 248, 265, and 247, glide through Brewer Yard in Danville, Illinois flying the white extra flags. Their sharp black and white dress will soon be exchanged for a coat of Jenks blue, and then the C&EI buzz-saw will vanish forever under a MoPac buzz-saw, with the exception of the 265, which will go to the L&N. *Ray Curl*

Below: In a scene that makes you wish you were there, a pair of GP35's roll past the brick depot at Salem, Indiana with white flags fluttering on a frigid February 4, 1966. The last gasp for the C&EI is approaching at this date, and the longtime image of Illinois railroading will change again when the C&EI flag falls. With each fallen flag, the railroad scene gets perhaps a little less interesting, certainly the variety of paint schemes is in a downward spiral. *James EuDaly*

renumbered until March 18, 1968. At the same time, the C&EI name or letterboard on the E-units and F-units and the C&EI oval logo on all locomotives was removed and the MoPac style buzz-saw decal with the familiar C&EI initials was applied. In many cases this change took place prior to renumbering. At least three units, C&EI-127, 129, and 1407, were repainted and renumbered at Oaklawn Shop. In the rush to repaint, C&EI blue was used rather than the MoPac blue because the MoPac paint was not yet available at Danville. To regress a bit, in 1955 the C&EI adapted a cheap, simple paint scheme for the EMD cab-units, including B-units, that was similar to the one in use at the time by the L&N. Due to the deteriorating financial condition of the C&EI, not all units were re-painted into this simple scheme. Three units (C&EI-1407, 1503, and 1504) were still in orange and blue when MoPac control commenced. A number of trade-ins were sent to EMD still wearing the orange and blue.

The three E7A's, C&EI-1100-1102, were renumbered and repainted at the St. Louis shop of the MoPac. The remaining units, including some later sold to the L&N in June, 1969, were repainted at various MoPac facilities, though all were renumbered at Danville. All the C&EI GP35's were reassigned to Fort Worth, Texas and repainted at the T&P Lancaster Shop.

On June 6, 1969, the eastern leg of the C&EI was sold to the L&N, which gained title to the line from Woodland Junction to Evansville.

The portion from Woodland Junction to Dolton Junction (Chicago) was equally owned by the C&EI and the L&N, but with C&EI management. The C&EI also retained all local traffic originating on the line south of Thornton Junction to Woodland Junction. The Oaklawn Shop at Danville was divided in ownership, the L&N got the west half and the C&EI retained the east half. The MoPac portion was soon leased to a private freight car repair operation.

C&EI's diesel fleet was split, and a number of the locomotives were sold to the L&N with the eastern portion of the railroad. These units included 3 NW2's, 3 SW7's, 2 E7A's, 8 FP7A's, 12 GP7's, 4 GP9's, 3 GP30's, and 13 GP35's. At least three of these had been repainted into the MoPac paint scheme including MP-27 (ex C&EI-1100), MP-28 (ex C&EI-1101), and MP-1203 (ex C&EI-127). Instructions were issued on February 9, 1970 to renumber three C&EI GP7's to fill gaps in numbers. C&EI-69 (ex C&EI-204) was renumbered C&EI-83:2, C&EI-77 (ex C&EI-212) was renumbered C&EI-84:2, and C&EI-79 (ex C&EI-214) was renumbered C&EI-85:2. The older C&EI units were traded in on new MoPac power between this time and the next new locomotive purchase for the C&EI.

For the first time since MoPac control new locomotives were purchased under C&EI ownership in 1974. All were EMD's popular SD40-2, the first C-C units ever for the C&EI. Fourteen units (C&EI-3150-3163) were built in March, 1974, and came without dynamic brakes,

as the MoPac mechanical department did not believe the dynamic brake feature was a justified expense considering the profiles encountered on their mainlines. These new units were painted in the standard Jenks blue dress of the time, with 3-inch white Scotchlite stripes and 8-inch numbers on the long hood. The buzz-saw under the cab had C&EI lettering.

The final motive power acquisition for the C&EI was five EMD GP15-1's (C&EI-1570-1574), delivered in July, 1976, just three months before the complete demise of the C&EI name. They came in Jenks blue with 5-inch white Scotchlite striping and large 20-inch numbers, and the new 24-inch flying eagle buzz-saw on the cab side.

Another interesting event transpired in 1976 surrounding the bicentennial of the United States. Many railroads painted locomotives in patriotic red, white, and blue, and because the MoPac was a host road to the special train that was touring the country, a decision was made in late 1975 to

Below: In the spring of 1974, the MoPac bought 14 SD40-2's for the C&EI, 3150-3163. The units were delivered in the standard Jenks blue, but with "C&EI" across the buzz-saw. The 3158 is in the lineup at Hoisington, Kansas in January, 1976. The C&EI buzz-saw will later be replaced with a flying eagle buzz-saw, creating one of the Double-Eagles; an engine with two eagles, one under the cab window and one on the long hood. *Lee Berglund*

paint two units in a red, white, and blue design. One unit selected was MP-1976, a GP18, and naturally the MP-1776 was to be the other unit. However, this unit was not in good condition, did not have a cut-down low short hood, and was therefore rejected. A C&EI locomotive, C&EI-84, was a GP7 in good mechanical condition and had a low short hood that had been cut down in North Little Rock in 1975. It was selected to become the MP-1776, and both units were re-painted in February, 1976. The styling design was developed by the MoPac Mechanical Department and was primarily the work of Daryl W. Favignano in the Mechanical Engineer's office.

On October 15, 1976, word trickled down from the 15th floor of the Missouri Pacific building in St. Louis that the C&EI and the T&P would be merged into parent Missouri Pacific on that date. That fast the C&EI quietly ended

Renumbering the C&EI Fleet

When the C&EI fell under the MoPac flag, there was an immediate need to renumber the C&EI fleet into the MoPac fleet to avoid any confusion. The plan was adopted on May 23, 1967, and was completed on March 18, 1968 when NW2 C&EI-121 was renumbered C&EI-1030. All were renumbered at Danville, Illinois except the three E7A's, which were repainted and renumbered at St. Louis. The complete C&EI renumbering dates were as follows:

nearly 100 years of corporate existence, having begun in 1877. There were 43 C&EI locomotives that officially became the MoPac's including 2 SW7's, 3 GP7's, 2 GP9's, 17 GP35's, 5 GP15-1's, and 14 SD40-2's. One GP35, C&EI-242, remained with the CHTT, which now was a wholly-owned MoPac subsidiary. The C&EI

owned a total of 162 locomotives during its diesel career. Sadly, the engines and what remained of the C&EI vanished into the MoPac, and another fascinating smaller road had been consumed by a giant. Not too many years later, that giant would itself be lost.

Above: The final C&EI units were five GP15-1's, 1570-1574, purchased in July, 1976. The only thing that identified them as C&EI units were the small initials to the upper right of the flying eagle buzz-saw. Within a very short time-frame, the C&EI initials were scraped off, and the units "became" MoPac. Brand new GP15-1 1573 is at North Little Rock on July 24, 1976. *J Harlen Wilson*

C&EI No	New No	Mod	Date r#
C&EI-98	C&EI-6000	SW1	01/10/68
C&EI-99	C&EI-6001	SW1	01/10/68
C&EI-120	C&EI-1029	NW2	03/15/68
C&EI-121	C&EI-1030	NW2	03/18/68
C&EI-122	C&EI-1031	NW2	12/04/67
C&EI-123	C&EI-1032	NW2	08/31/67
C&EI-124	C&EI-1033	NW2	01/13/68
C&EI-125	C&EI-1034	NW2	10/06/67
C&EI-126	C&EI-1202:2	SW7	09/14/67
C&EI-127	C&EI-1203:2	SW7	01/25/68
C&EI-128	C&EI-1204:2	SW7	02/07/68
C&EI-129	C&EI-1205:2	SW7	03/15/68
C&EI-130	C&EI-1206	SW7	02/26/68
C&EI-131	C&EI-1207	SW7	08/14/67
CHTT-132	CHTT-1208	SW7	01/10/68
CHTT-133	CHTT-1209	SW7	10/06/67
C&EI-203	C&EI-68	GP7	12/27/67
C&EI-204	C&EI-69	GP7	10/30/67
C&EI-205	C&EI-70	GP7	01/14/68
C&EI-206	C&EI-71	GP7	10/30/67
C&EI-207	C&EI-72	GP7	10/06/67
C&EI-208	C&EI-73	GP7	12/15/67
C&EI-209	C&EI-74	GP7	11/28/67
C&EI-210	C&EI-75	GP7	12/26/67
C&EI-211	C&EI-76	GP7	12/15/67
C&EI-212	C&EI-77	GP7	10/31/67
C&EI-213	C&EI-78	GP7	12/15/67
C&EI-214	C&EI-79	GP7	11/28/67
C&EI-215	C&EI-80	GP7	11/28/67
C&EI-216	C&EI-81	GP7	02/02/68
C&EI-217	C&EI-82	GP7	09/26/67
C&EI-218	C&EI-83:1	GP7	01/11/68
C&EI-219	C&EI-84:1	GP7	12/04/67

C&EI No	New No	Mod	Date r#
C&EI-220	C&EI-85:1	GP7	10/30/67
C&EI-221:2	C&EI-86	GP9m	10/18/67
C&EI-222	C&EI-87	GP7	11/21/67
C&EI-223	C&EI-88	GP7	09/21/67
C&EI-224	C&EI-89	GP7	10/31/67
C&EI-225	C&EI-90	GP7	11/10/67
C&EI-226	C&EI-91	GP7	01/17/68
CHTT-227	CHTT-92	GP7	12/04/67
CHTT-228	CHTT-93	GP7	12/27/67
CHTT-230	CHTT-94	GP7	09/26/67
C&EI-231	C&EI-95:2	GP7	12/07/67
C&EI-232	C&EI-96:2	GP7	12/26/67
C&EI-233	C&EI-340	GP9	02/05/68
C&EI-234	C&EI-341	GP9	09/09/67
C&EI-235	C&EI-342	GP9	12/07/67
C&EI-236	C&EI-343	GP9	02/26/68
C&EI-237	C&EI-344	GP9	11/10/67
C&EI-238	C&EI-345	GP9	11/28/67
C&EI-239	C&EI-590	GP30	12/15/67
C&EI-240	C&EI-591	GP30	10/11/67
C&EI-241	C&EI-592	GP30	01/22/68
C&EI-242	C&EI-650	GP35	11/21/67
C&EI-243	C&EI-651	GP35	12/07/67
C&EI-244	C&EI-652	GP35	02/10/68
C&EI-245	C&EI-653	GP35	11/21/67
C&EI-246	C&EI-654	GP35	12/26/67
C&EI-247	C&EI-655	GP35	12/15/67
C&EI-248	C&EI-656	GP35	08/09/67
C&EI-249	C&EI-657	GP35	11/21/67
C&EI-250	C&EI-658	GP35	12/15/67
C&EI-251	C&EI-659	GP35	01/15/68
C&EI-252	C&EI-660	GP35	01/05/68
C&EI-253	C&EI-661	GP35	12/04/67
C&EI-254	C&EI-662	GP35	01/05/68
C&EI-255	C&EI-663	GP35	01/19/68
C&EI-256	C&EI-664	GP35	12/15/67
C&EI-257	C&EI-665	GP35	12/07/67
C&EI-258	C&EI-666	GP35	08/07/67

C&EI No	New No	Mod	Date r#
C&EI-259	C&EI-667	GP35	02/08/68
C&EI-260	C&EI-668	GP35	11/17/67
C&EI-261	C&EI-669	GP35	12/04/67
C&EI-262	C&EI-670	GP35	12/07/67
C&EI-263	C&EI-671	GP35	11/10/67
C&EI-264	C&EI-672	GP35	08/15/67
C&EI-265	C&EI-673	GP35	12/26/67
C&EI-266	C&EI-674	GP35	10/16/67
C&EI-267	C&EI-675	GP35	11/21/67
C&EI-268	C&EI-676	GP35	12/26/67
C&EI-269	C&EI-677	GP35	11/21/67
C&EI-270	C&EI-678	GP35	10/30/67
C&EI-271	C&EI-679	GP35	11/10/67
C&EI-272	C&EI-680	GP35	11/17/67
C&EI-1100	C&EI-27	E7A	09/20/67
C&EI-1101	C&EI-28	E7A	09/28/67
C&EI-1102:2	C&EI-43	E7A	09/14/67
C&EI-1405	C&EI-750	F3A	11/28/67
C&EI-1407	C&EI-751	F3A	12/26/67
C&EI-1501	C&EI-750B	F3B	01/21/68
C&EI-1502	C&EI-751B	F3B	10/30/67
C&EI-1503	C&EI-752B	F3B	10/19/67
C&EI-1504	C&EI-753B	F3B	02/12/68
C&EI-1600:2	C&EI-933	FP7A	10/11/67
C&EI-1601:2	C&EI-934	FP7A	12/04/67
C&EI-1602:2	C&EI-935	FP7A	11/28/67
C&EI-1603	C&EI-936	FP7A	09/26/67
C&EI-1604	C&EI-937	FP7A	10/19/67
C&EI-1605	C&EI-938	FP7A	10/24/67
C&EI-1606	C&EI-939	FP7A	09/26/67
C&EI-1607	C&EI-940	FP7A	12/07/67
C&EI-1608	C&EI-941	FP7A	11/17/67
C&EI-1609	C&EI-942	FP7A	10/16/67

EMD
SD40

GE
U30C

While EMD was in the transitional phases of the conversion from the 567 to the 645 engine, another builder was moving into large size locomotive production - GE. Though GE had long been involved as a supplier of electrical traction equipment, the "new" builder had not been involved in domestic locomotive sales. Beginning as early as 1925, GE had been a partner with Ingersoll Rand and Alco, which produced 300 and 600 horsepower boxcab electric switchers.

Right: The MoPac ordered SD40's five times, acquiring 90 of the big 3,000 horsepower EMDs. 783 is from the last order, delivered in March, 1971. The heavy-haul SD leads a pair of its siblings through Alexandria, Louisiana on February 2, 1973. *Glenn Anderson*

Opposite page top: SD40 3066 wears its second number, originally delivered as 766. It leads a pair of brand new "coal" SD40-2's, designated "SD40-2c's" by the MoPac, through Osawatomie, Kansas on September 22, 1976. *Tony Fey*

Opposite page bottom: MoPac ordered six batches of U30C's, but never in the quantity of the EMDs, accumulating only 35 of the "Screaming Eagle" U-Boats. The last unit of the third order, 3318, is at the headend of a trio of the GEs running westbound through Hoisington, Kansas in December, 1974. The unit is only three years old but wears its third number. A fourth number will follow shortly, 2983. *Lee Berglund*

Below: The first MoPac U30C was delivered as 960, but was afterward renumbered into the spot series, becoming number 1. Big road power wearing the spot series on a Class I railroad is rare, UP SD45 number 1 comes to mind as another. The big GE leads a pair of the competition's SD40's through Pearland, Texas on July 1, 1973. *Ralph Back*

GE continued in the switcher market in the 1930's, producing a wide range of industrial-sized switchers. They used a variety of diesel engines, and while in production of small locomotives GE and Alco formed a marketing partnership for large road locomotives. This lasted from 1940 to 1953, when Alco took over its own marketing and sales again.

GE produced heavy electric locomotives on its own during this entire period, and began the development of its own line of diesel road locomotives for export in the 1950's. In 1960 GE jumped into the North American market with the introduction of the U25B.

The U25B was a 2,500 horsepower roadswitcher that employed a number of design improvements over the locomotives then on the market from EMD and ALCO. Three years later GE overtook ALCO for second place in sales behind EMD, long the industry leader. The U25B utilized the FDL-16 engine from Cooper-Bessemer, an engine whose direct descendants still power GE units to this day.

The MoPac eyed the new builder with suspicion, and perhaps because they were still feeling the sting from their RS-11 purchase and subsequent repowering they stayed with EMD. In early 1967 the MoPac went to EMD for heavy-duty road freight power. The MoPac had long avoided the C-C truck configuration at the headend of freights, and in fact had never purchased any C-C freight power.

The only six-axle power the MoPac had owned were E-units and PA's, and those were all A-1-A wheel arrangements, where the middle axle of each truck was an unpowered idle axle. This changed when an order was placed for 20 SD40's from EMD, each rated at 3,000 horsepower. After having avoided first generation SD's, which were first introduced when EMD outshopped demonstrator SD7 990 in March, 1952, one would think that the obvious choice was the SD45, which was first produced in February, 1965.

Above: One of five U30C's built in June, 1973, the 3324 adds 3,000 horsepower to the consist at Fort Worth on Christmas day in 1975. The big GE would later be retired two months before its sixteenth birthday, and head for the scrapper in September, 1989. *Bill Phillips photo, James Holder collection*

In its first few years the SD45 dominated sales, as railroads were looking for higher-horsepower units to gain unit reduction. But the 20-cylinder engine in the SD45, along with its associated large radiators, resulted in an increased maintenance cost; and while the 20-cylinder SD45 sold well, its successor, the SD45-2, generated few sales for EMD.

With this in mind, the MoPac went for the SD40. Even though the SD45 outsold the SD40 by 50%, its successor, the SD40-2, far outsold the 20-cylinder higher horsepower models. This indicates that the MoPac was at the forefront of the trend for 16-cylinder EMD power within the time frames involved.

The first 20 SD40's (MP-700-719) arrived in March and April, 1967, bringing the high-horsepower six-axle unit to MoPac rails to stay for the first time. The SD40's success was immediately apparent, as the 700's stomped across the system lugging tonnage like no other unit. It was especially well-suited to the task of hauling heavy coal and grain trains, which the MoPac had in ever increasing quantities.

Within a year, more SD40's were on the way from EMD, but this time the order had been split between EMD and GE. The MoPac had effectively skipped GE's introductory phase,

Left: SD's and GE's line up as if to race south out of Dupo, Illinois on October 1, 1983. Both are on empty coal trains headed for southern Illinois and another load of coal for the power plant at West Labadie, Missouri. As the photo depicts, EMD was always slightly in front in the sales department for SD40's verses U30C's. *Lon EuDaly*

having never purchased any U25 or U28 series engines because studies indicated that the EMDs were more reliable and thus less expensive in the long run, and likewise avoided all the early EMD C-C's, from the SD7 through the SD35. The 3,000 horsepower U30C represented a rerating of the U28C in GE C-C evolution, and early U30C's and late U28C's were housed in identical roadswitcher bodies. These had a small fillet at the top of the unit in front of the air intakes at the rear of the unit. Only the MoPac's first order had the fillet.

Fourteen SD40's (MP-720-733) arrived in January and February, 1968, bringing the total to 34. Also delivered in early 1968 were six U30C's from GE (MP-960-965). The U30C's were added primarily because the heavy iron ore drags and coal trains could take advantage of the lower minimum continuous speed. These units were initially assigned to the coal trains running from southern Illinois to the power plant at West Labadie, Missouri. It was apparent that the MoPac liked the C-C concept and the U30C was proving to be an effective competitor of the SD40, generating about half the number of sales as the SD40. Over the following four years the SD40 and the U30C accounted for 100% of the MoPac's purchases for road-freight locomotives. The big C-C's were here to stay.

In 1969 both builders again produced C-C's for the MoPac. First were 20 more SD40's (MP-734-753) delivered in February. These were followed by eight U30C's, four for the MoPac and four for the T&P (MP-966-969 and T&P-970-973).

EMD captured the MoPac for 1970, which brought in another order for SD40's, this time for

Above: After the line-up at Dupo, the 3061 is released and rolls southbound for the coalfields on October 1, 1983. This train has an equal compliment of GE's and EMD's, which was usually not the case. The U30C's were the mainstay of the Labadie coal train pool for a number of years after their purchase. There was nothing quite like a brace of four U30C's fighting it out up the east slope of Kirkwood Hill with a train of loads for West Labadie. Smoke and noise and that glubbing chug unique to GE's FDL power plant. *Lon EuDaly*

Below: U30C 2979 stomps by the tower at South Holland, Illinois in September, 1979. The big GE wore three previous numbers, 974, 15, and 3314, and will be assigned one more (UP-2979) that it will never wear. All the units from its order went back to GE in trade for UP Dash 8-40C's in June, 1987, and from there went to Pielet to scrap. The turbocharged eagle is but a memory. *Paul Meyer*

121

16 additional units (MP-754-769) delivered in January. This order brought the total to 70 SD40's on the roster compared to 14 U30C's.

The MoPac's buying trend for 3,000 horsepower C-C units continued in 1971. An initial order with EMD resulted in the delivery of 20 more SD40's (MP-770-789) in March and April. This brought the SD40 total to its final quantity of 90 units. Meanwhile, over at GE, another token 5 U30C's (MP-974-978) were delivered in August and September, bringing the U30C total to 19.

After purchasing the first of the GP38-2's, the MoPac returned to GE for yet another batch of U30C's, which arrived in February, 1972. The order was for another five units (MP-979-983), doing their part to support GE and keep competition alive. It seems somewhat more than circumstantial that just as ALCO was failing, the MoPac chose to support GE to some degree, albeit somewhat limited. Either way, a quartet of the big U-boats made an indelible impression pounding up Kirkwood Hill or flying across the prairie on the way to Pueblo.

In 1973 the MoPac ordered seven U23B's (MP-668-674), which were delivered in January and February, 1973, and by mid-year they were getting five more U30C's (MP-984-988) and would soon be getting their first SD40-2's.

In August and September, 1973, the MoPac was receiving 20 SD40-2's, and these were delivered side by side with another order, this time for six U30C's for the T&P (T&P-3329-3334), the final U30C purchase. The T&P U30C's completed the MoPac purchases of that model, and brought the total to 35 of the big GEs with the "screaming eagles." The U30C's all went back to GE between November, 1980 and January, 1981 for some Dash-7 modifications,

but were otherwise not rebuilt. They lasted an average economic life of 15 years, but were deemed not worth the expense to rebuild, unlike the first generation geeps and other EMD products. When they were renumbered into the 3300-series in June, 1974, their rear number boards were painted out.

The MoPac continued to purchase C-C road freight power throughout the remainder of its career. For the MoPac, the U30C and the SD40 were at the beginning of the trend of purchasing the larger, turbocharged, higher horsepower locomotives for road freight service.

Above: EMD C-C power has only been on the MoPac for two years as SD40 720 pulls through Kirkwood, Missouri with 705 and U30C 964 on May 10, 1969. The MoPac will soon standardize on the C-C power for heavy freights. *R R Wallin photo, James Holder collection*

Below: U30C 2991 rolls piggybacks through Memphis, Tennessee in November, 1983. Though the unit has worn four numbers, it still is in its original paint scheme - the large screaming eagle and buzz-saw. *Steve Forrest*

EMD SD40   3,000 hp   20 units
TE = 97,475   WT = 389,910
Wheels = 40"   Fuel = 4,000
Engine: EMD 16-645E3 V-type 16-cylinder 2-cycle Turbocharged
Min Speed for TE = 12.0 mph
62:15 Gearing   65 mph Max

1st No	2nd No	3rd No	Built	Build#	Retired	Notes & Dispositions
MP-700:2	MP-3000:2	(UP-4000)	03/67	32968	01/89	Note 1, 2, 3
MP-701:2	MP-3001	(UP-4001)	03/67	32969	09/88	Note 2, 4
MP-702:2	MP-3002	(UP-4002)	03/67	32970	05/92	To Helm 7/92
MP-703:2	MP-3003	(UP-4003)	03/67	32971	10/88	Note 2, 5
MP-704:2	MP-3004	(UP-4004)	03/67	32972	01/89	Note 2, 6
MP-705:2	MP-3005	(UP-4005)	03/67	32973	0 1/91	Note 13
MP-706:2	MP-3006	(UP-4006)	03/67	32974	03/88	Note 7
MP-707:2	MP-3007	(UP-4007)	03/67	32975	01/91	Note 1, 13
MP-708:2	MP-3008	(UP-4008)	03/67	32976	06/91	Note 1, to NRE 10/91
MP-709:2	MP-3009	(UP-4009)	03/67	32977	06/89	Note 7
MP-710:2	MP-3010	(UP-4010)	03/67	32978	01/91	Note 8, stored
MP-711:2	MP-3011	(UP-4011)	03/67	32979	11/88	Note 8, to VMV 2/89
MP-712:2	MP-3012	(UP-4012)	03/67	32980	01/91	Note 1, 13
MP-713:2	MP-3013	(UP-4013)	03/67	32981	10/88	Note 2, 9
MP-714:2	MP-3014	(UP-4014)	04/67	32982	03/88	To Gray 3/88
MP-715:2	MP-3015	UP-4015	04/67	32983	03/88	To Helm 6/88
MP-716:2	MP-3016	UP-4016	04/67	32984	09/88	Note 2, 11
MP-717:2	MP-3017	(UP-4017)	04/67	32985	10/91	Note 13
MP-718:2	MP-3018	(UP-4018)	04/67	32986	10/91	To Helm 3/93
MP-719:2	MP-3019	(UP-4019)	04/67	32987	03/90	Note 12

Note 1: Wore MP yellow in 3000-series
Note 2: To Wilson Locomotive, Des Moines, IA
Note 3: To PLM-3000 8/89, rebuilt by MK as SD40-2 9/90, leased to CP
Note 4: To Wisconsin Central, r# WC-4001
Note 5: To Wisconsin Central, r# WC-4003
Note 6: To PLM-3004 8/89, rebuilt by MK as SD40-2 9/90, leased to CP
Note 7: To Helm 6/88, to NRE 3/89
Note 8: Wore Double-Eagles in 3000-series
Note 9: To Wisconsin Central, r# WC-4013
Note 10: NLR "block" lettering as UP-4016
Note 11: To Wisconsin Central, r# WC-4016
Note 12: To MK 3/90, to CSXT as SD40-2 6/90, r# CSXT-8448
Note 13: To Southwest 8/93

EMD SD40   3,000 hp   14 units
TE = 96,975   WT = 387,900
Wheels = 40"   Fuel = 4,000
Engine: EMD 16-645E3 V-type 16-cylinder 2-cycle Turbocharged
Min Speed for TE = 12.0 mph
62:15 Gearing   65 mph Max

1st No	2nd No	3rd No	Built	Build#	Retired	Notes & Dispositions
MP-720:2	MP-3020	(UP-4020)	01/68	33771	10/91	To Helm 5/92
MP-721:2	MP-3021	(UP-4021)	01/68	33772	11/88	To PNC 2/89
MP-722:2	MP-3022	(UP-4022)	01/68	33773	12/90	Note 1
MP-723:2	MP-3023	(UP-4023)	01/68	33774	06/90	Note 2, stored
MP-724:2	MP-3024	(UP-4024)	01/68	33775	03/88	To Helm 6/88
MP-725:2	MP-3025	(UP-4025)	01/68	33776	10/88	Note 3, 4
MP-726:2	MP-3026	(UP-4026)	02/68	33777	02/89	Note 5, to PNC 2/89
MP-727:2	MP-3027	UP-4027	02/68	33778	10/91	
MP-728:2	MP-3028	(UP-4028)	02/68	33779	10/91	To Azcon 3/93
MP-729:2	MP-3029	(UP-4029)	02/68	33780	01/89	Note 3, 5, 6
MP-730:2	MP-3030	(UP-4030)	02/68	33781	10/91	To Pielet 4/92
MP-731:2	MP-3031	(UP-4031)	02/68	33782	10/91	To Pielet 7/92
MP-732:2	MP-3032	(UP-4032)	02/68	33783	08/91	Note 7
MP-733:2	MP-3033	UP-4033	02/68	33784	10/91	Stored

Note 1: Wrecked while on lease to NdeM, to NRE 6/91
Note 2: Wore Double-Eagles as MP-3023
Note 3: To Wilson Locomotive, Des Moines, IA
Note 4: To Wisconsin Central, r# WC-4025
Note 5: Wore MP yellow in 3000-series
Note 6: To PLM-3029 9/89, rebuilt by MK as SD40-2 9/90, leased to CP
Note 7: To Azcon, Alton, IL, 10/91, scrapped

Right: The 3052 was part of the third order for SD40's, the middle order of five for SD40's delivered early in the year for five consecutive years, 1967-1971. The unit is in its as-delivered scheme at Dolton, Illinois on June 14, 1975. *Dennis Schmidt*

EMD SD40   3,000 hp   20 units
TE = 98,130   WT = 392,520
Wheels = 40"   Fuel = 4,000
Engine: EMD 16-645E3 V-type 16-cylinder 2-cycle Turbocharged
Min Speed for TE = 12.0 mph
62:15 Gearing   65 mph Max
Retired 7/84, to USL, to VMV (all but 3036, 3038, 3045, 3048 and 2053 to MK)

1st No	2nd No	Built	Build#	Notes & Dispositions
MP-734:2	MP-3034	02/69	34506	To CSXT as SD40-2 9/90, r# CSXT-8475
MP-735:2	MP-3035	02/69	34507	To CSXT as SD40-2 9/90, r# CSXT-8468
MP-736:2	MP-3036	02/69	34508	To FNM as SD40-2 6/88, r# FNM-13061
MP-737:2	MP-3037	02/69	34509	To CSXT as SD40-2 7/90, r# CSXT-8457
MP-738:2	MP-3038	02/69	34510	R# VMV-3038, in lease service
MP-739:2	MP-3039	02/69	34511	To CSXT as SD40-2 9/90, r# CSXT-8474
MP-740:2	MP-3040	02/69	34512	To CSXT as SD40-2 8/90, r# CSXT-8462
MP-741:2	MP-3041	02/69	34513	To CSXT as SD40-2 7/90, r# CSXT-8458
MP-742:2	MP-3042	02/69	34514	To CSXT as SD40-2 10/90, r# CSXT-8480
MP-743:2	MP-3043	02/69	34515	To CSXT as SD40-2 8/90, r# CSXT-8467
MP-744:2	MP-3044	02/69	34516	Wore Double-Eagles as MP-3044. To CSXT as SD40-2 8/90, r# CSXT-8464
MP-745:2	MP-3045	02/69	34517	To FNM as SD40-2 6/88, r# FNM-13059
MP-746:2	MP-3046	02/69	34518	To CSXT as SD40-2 8/90, r# CSXT-8465
MP-747	MP-3047	02/69	34519	To CSXT as SD40-2 7/90, r# CSXT-8459
MP-748	MP-3048	02/69	34520	To FNM as SD40-2 6/88, r# FNM-13062
MP-749	MP-3049	02/69	34521	Wrecked at Itaska TX 3/24/70, rebuilt. To CSXT as SD40-2 7/90, r# CSXT-8460
MP-750	MP-3050	02/69	34522	To CSXT as SD40-2 8/90, r# CSXT-8461
MP-751	MP-3051	02/69	34523	Wore Double-Eagles as MP-3051. To CSXT as SD40-2 10/90, r# CSXT-8483
MP-752	MP-3052	02/69	34524	Wrecked at Itaska TX 3/24/70, rebuilt. To CSXT as SD40-2 8/90, r# CSXT-8466
MP-753	MP-3053	02/69	34525	To FNM as SD40-2 6/88, r# FNM-13060

Below: The first MoPac C-C order was for 20 SD40's from EMD built in March and April, 1967. They followed the tradition set by the GP35's with screaming eagles and without dynamic brakes. The 15th unit of the order is at Dolton, Illinois on May 16, 1984. It wears its second paint scheme: the screaming eagle has fallen to large numbers and the small flying eagle buzz-saw. *Ronald A Plazzotta*

Above: Wrecked U30C 3319 ran around for some time as a makeshift B-unit, and was later rebuilt with a GE cab. It is at St. Louis on December 18, 1976. *J Harlen Wilson*

EMD SD40   3,000 hp   16 units
TE = 97,850   WT = 391,400
Wheels = 40"   Fuel = 4,000
Engine: EMD 16-645E3 V-type 16-cylinder 2-cycle Turbocharged
Min Speed for TE = 12.0 mph
62:15 Gearing   65 mph Max

1st No	2nd No	3rd No	Built	Build#	Retired	Notes & Dispositions
MP-754	MP-3054	UP-4054	01/70	35725	06/90	Note 1
MP-755	MP-3055	(UP-4055)	01/70	35726	11/88	To VMV 2/89
MP-756	MP-3056	UP-4056	01/70	35727	10/91	Stored
MP-757	MP-3057	UP-4057	01/70	35728	06/90	Stored
MP-758	MP-3058	(UP-4058)	01/70	35729	11/88	Note 2
MP-759	MP-3059	(UP-4059)	01/70	35730	08/91	To NRE 10/91
MP-760	MP-3060	UP-4060	01/70	35731	10/91	Stored
MP-761	MP-3061	UP-4061	01/70	35732	01/89	Note 3
MP-762	MP-3062	UP-4062	01/70	35733	11/89	Stored
MP-763	MP-3063	UP-4063	01/70	35734	10/91	To SW Car Parts
MP-764	MP-3064	(UP-4064)	01/70	35735		Note 4
MP-765:2	MP-3065	(UP-4065)	01/70	35736	0 2/91	To Southwest 8/93
MP-766:2	MP-3066	UP-4066	01/70	35737	07/90	Stored
MP-767:2	MP-3067	UP-4067	01/70	35738	10/91	To Phoenix 2/92, to Pielet
MP-768:2	MP-3068	UP-4068	01/70	35739	0 4/90	Note 5
MP-769:2	MP-3069	UP-4069	01/70	35740	03/88	Note 6

Note 1: Wrecked while on lease to FNM, to Smith 2/90
Note 2: To Wilson Locomotive, Des Moines, IA, 3/89, to PLM-3058 8/89, rebuilt by MK as SD40-2 9/90, leased to CP
Note 3: NLR "block" lettering as UP-4061. Retired 11/89, stored
Note 4: Wore Double-Eagles as MP-3064. Leased to FNM 10/89
Note 5: To MK 4/90, to CSXT as SD40-2 6/90, r# CSXT-8449
Note 6: To Helm 3/88, to VMV 3/89, to IAIS

Below: Unlike the 3319, when the 3311 was wrecked the cab was rebuilt with an EMD Spartan cab, a situation unique to the MoPac. There were a number of GEs that got the EMD-style cabs. 3311 is at North Little Rock, Arkansas on November 12, 1976, right after emerging with the new cab. *J Harlen Wilson*

EMD SD40   3,000 hp   20 units
TE = 97,880   WT = 391,520
Wheels = 40"   Fuel = 4,000
Engine: EMD 16-645E3 V-type 16-cylinder 2-cycle Turbocharged
Min Speed for TE = 12.0 mph
62:15 Gearing   65 mph Max
Retired 6/86, to GATX 6/86

1st No	2nd No	Built	Build#	Notes & Dispositions
MP-770:2	MP-3070	03/71	37543	Note 1
MP-771:2	MP-3071	03/71	37544	Note 2
MP-772:2	MP-3072	03/71	37545	Note 3
MP-773:2	MP-3073	03/71	37546	Note 4
MP-774:2	MP-3074	03/71	37547	Note 5
MP-775	MP-3075	03/71	37548	Note 6
MP-776	MP-3076	03/71	37549	Note 7
MP-777	MP-3077	03/71	37550	Note 8
MP-778	MP-3078	03/71	37551	Note 9
MP-779	MP-3079	03/71	37552	Note 10
MP-780	MP-3080	03/71	37553	Note 11
MP-781	MP-3081	03/71	37554	Note 12
MP-782	MP-3082	03/71	37555	Note 13
MP-783	MP-3083	03/71	37556	Note 14
MP-784	MP-3084	04/71	37557	Note 15
MP-785:2	MP-3085	04/71	37558	Note 16
MP-786:2	MP-3086	04/71	37559	Note 17
MP-787	MP-3087	04/71	37560	Note 18
MP-788	MP-3088	04/71	37561	Note 19
MP-789	MP-3089	04/71	37562	Note 20

Note 1: Wrecked 4/2/71 at Paola KS on maiden trip, repaired. R# GATX-5070, to MK, to BN/GATX as "SD40G" 4/89, r# BN-7300
Note 2: To EMD, to FNM as SD40-2 1988, r# FNM-13051
Note 3: R# GATX-5072, to MK, to BN/GATX as "SD40G" 5/89, r# BN-7301
Note 4: R# GATX-5073, to MK, to BN/GATX as "SD40G" 6/89, r# BN-7302
Note 5: To EMD, to FNM as SD40-2 1988, r# FNM-13049
Note 6: R# GATX-5075, to MK, to BN/GATX as "SD40G" 4/89, r# BN-7303
Note 7: R# GATX-5076, to MK, to BN/GATX as "SD40G" 5/89, r# BN-7304
Note 8: Received an air starter. r# GATX-5077, to MK, to BN/GATX as "SD40G" 5/89, r# BN-7305
Note 9: To EMD, to FNM as SD40-2 1988, r# FNM-13057
Note 10: To EMD, to FNM as SD40-2 1988, r# FNM-13055
Note 11: To EMD, to FNM as SD40-2 5/88, r# FNM-13053
note 12: R# GATX-5081, to MK, to BN/GATX as "SD40G" 5/89, r# BN-7306
Note 13: To EMD, to FNM as SD40-2 1988, r# FNM-13052
Note 14: Wrecked 1972, outshopped 4/5/72 with sheet metal windowless cab, standard cab added a short time later. Wore MP yellow as MP-3083. To MK, to BN/GATX as "SD40G" 6/89, r# BN-7307
Note 15: To EMD, to FNM as SD40-2 1988, r# FNM-13056
Note 16: To EMD, to FNM as SD40-2 5/88, r# FNM-13054
Note 17: Wore MP yellow as MP-3086. R# GATX-5086, to MK, to BN/GATX as "SD40G" 7/89, r# BN-7308
Note 18: Wrecked by NdeM, repaired and repainted NdeM. Repainted to MoPac with backwards screaming eagle. To EMD, to FNM as SD40-2 1988, r# FNM-13058
Note 19: R# GATX-5088, to MK, to BN/GATX as "SD40G" 7/89, r# BN-7309
Note 20: To EMD, to FNM as SD40-2 1988, r# FNM-13050

GE U30C   3,000 hp   6 units
TE = 97,000   WT = 388,000
Wheels = 40"   Fuel = 4,000
Engine: GE FDL16 V-type 16-cylinder 4-cycle Turbocharged
Min Speed for TE = 9.6 mph
74:18 Gearing   65 mph Max
Hump control units
Retired 5/85, T-I to GE 5/85 on C36-7's

1st No	2nd No	3rd No	4th No	Built	Build#	Notes
MP-960	MP-1	MP-3300:1	MP-2965	03/68	36700	Note 1
MP-961	MP-2	MP-3301:1	MP-2966	03/68	36701	
MP-962	MP-3	MP-3302:1	MP-2967	03/68	36702	Note 1
MP-963	MP-4	MP-3303:1	MP-2968	04/68	36703	Note 1
MP-964	MP-5	MP-3304:1	MP-2969	04/68	36704	
MP-965	MP-6	MP-3305:1	MP-2970	04/68	36705	Note 1, 2

Note 1: Wore MP yellow in 2900-series
Note 2: Wore MP yellow as MP-2970. To Enterprise Coal 10/85, rebuilt at GE Cleveland with Caterpillar engine and remote control in 1987

GE U30C   3,000 hp   4 units
TE = 97,900   WT = 391,600
Wheels = 40"   Fuel = 4,000
Engine: GE FDL16 V-type 16-cylinder 4-cycle Turbocharged
Min Speed for TE = 9.6 mph
74:18 Gearing   65 mph Max
Hump control units

1st No	2nd No	3rd No	4th No	Built	Build#	Retired	Notes
MP-966	MP-7	MP-3306:1	MP-2971	05/69	37022	07/84	
MP-967	MP-8	MP-3307:1	MP-2972	05/69	37023	07/84	Note 1
MP-968	MP-9	MP-3308:1	MP-2973	06/69	37024	05/84	Note 2
MP-969	MP-10	MP-3309:1	MP-2974	06/69	37025	05/84	Note 2

Note 1: Scrapped by MP at NLR 1985
Note 2: To American Iron & Metal 6/85, scrapped

GE U30C   3,000 hp   4 units
TE = 98,510   WT = 394,040
Wheels = 40"   Fuel = 4,000
Engine: GE FDL16 V-type 16-cylinder 4-cycle Turbocharged
Min Speed for TE = 9.6 mph
74:18 Gearing   65 mph Max
Hump control units
Retired 5/85, T-I to GE 5/85 on C36-7's

1st No	2nd No	3rd No	4th No	5th No	Built	Build#	Notes
T&P-970	T&P-11	T&P-3310	MP-3310	MP-2975	06/69	37559	
T&P-971	T&P-12	T&P-3311	MP-3311	MP-2976	06/69	37560	Note 1
T&P-972	T&P-13	T&P-3312	MP-3312	MP-2977	06/69	37561	
T&P-973	T&P-14	T&P-3313	MP-3313	MP-2978	07/70	37562	

Note 1: Wrecked 1975, rebuilt with EMD cab as MP-3311 11/76, later MP-2976

GE U30C   3,000 hp   5 units
TE = 97,950   WT = 391,800
Wheels = 40"   Fuel = 4,000
Engine: GE FDL16 V-type 16-cylinder 4-cycle Turbocharged
Min Speed for TE = 9.6 mph
74:18 Gearing   65 mph Max
Hump control units
Retired 6/87, T-I to GE 6/87 on Dash 8-40C's UP-9100-9149, to Pielet 7/87, scrapped

1st No	2nd No	3rd No	4th No	5th No	Built	Build#	Notes
MP-974:2	MP-15:2	MP-3314:1	MP-2979	(UP-2979)	08/71	38011	
MP-975:2	MP-16:2	MP-3315:1	MP-2980	(UP-2980)	08/71	38012	
MP-976:2	MP-17:2	MP-3316:1	MP-2981	(UP-2981)	08/71	38013	Note 1
MP-977:2	MP-18:2	MP-3317:1	MP-2982	(UP-2982)	08/71	38014	
MP-978:2	MP-19:2	MP-3318:1	MP-2983	(UP-2983)	09/71	38015	

Note 1: Wore Double-Eagles as MP-2981

GE U30C   3,000 hp   5 units
TE = 97,445   WT = 389,780
Wheels = 40"   Fuel = 4,000
Engine: GE FDL16 V-type 16-cylinder 4-cycle Turbocharged
Min Speed for TE = 9.6 mph
74:18 Gearing   65 mph Max
Hump control units

1st No	2nd No	3rd No	4th No	5th No	Built	Build#	Notes
MP-979:2	MP-20:2	MP-3319:1	MP-2984	(UP-2984)	02/72	38261	Note 1
MP-980:2	MP-21:2	MP-3320:1	MP-2985	(UP-2985)	02/72	38262	Note 2
MP-981:2	MP-22:2	MP-3321:1	MP-2986	(UP-2986)	02/72	38263	Note 3
MP-982:2	MP-23:2	MP-3322	MP-2987	(UP-2987)	02/72	38264	Note 4
MP-983:2	MP-24:2	MP-3323	MP-2988	(UP-2988)	02/72	38265	Note 5

Note 1: Wrecked 6/76, rebuilt without cab or short hood temporarily, then rebuilt with GE cab. Retired 9/87
Note 2: Retired 5/88, T-I to GE 6/88
Note 3: Retired 5/89, wrecked, to Southwest 5/89
Note 4: Wrecked and operated as a B-unit as MP-3322. Retired 6/89, wrecked, to Southwest 7/89
Note 5: Retired 3/88, T-I to GE 6/88

GE U30C   3,000 hp   5 units
TE = 97,445   WT = 389,780
Wheels = 40"   Fuel = 4,000
Engine: GE FDL16 V-type 16-cylinder 4-cycle Turbocharged
Min Speed for TE = 9.6 mph
74:18 Gearing   65 mph Max
Hump control units

1st No	2nd No	3rd No	4th No	5th No	Built	Build#	Notes
MP-984	MP-25:2	MP-3324	UP-2989	(UP-2989)	06/73	39210	Note 1
MP-985	MP-26:2	MP-3325	MP-2990	(UP-2990)	06/73	39211	Note 1
MP-986	MP-27	MP-3326	MP-2991	(UP-2991)	06/73	39212	Note 1
MP-987	MP-28	MP-3327	MP-2992	(UP-2992)	06/73	39213	Note 1
MP-988	MP-29	MP-3328	MP-2993	(UP-2993)	06/73	39214	Note 2

Note 1: Retired 4/89, to Southwest 9/89
Note 2: Retired 3/88, T-I to GE 6/88

GE U30C   3,000 hp   6 units
TE = 97,920   WT = 391,680
Wheels = 40"   Fuel = 4,000
Engine: GE FDL16 V-type 16-cylinder 4-cycle Turbocharged
Min Speed for TE = 9.6 mph
74:18 Gearing   65 mph Max
Hump control units
T-I to GE 6/87 on Dash 8-40C's UP-9100-9149, to Pielet 7/87

1st No	2nd No	3rd No	4th No	Built	Build#	Retired	Notes
T&P-3329	MP-3329	MP-2994	(UP-2994)	01/74	39500	06/87	
T&P-3330	MP-3330	MP-2995	(UP-2995)	01/74	39501	01/87	
T&P-3331	MP-3331	MP-2996	(UP-2996)	01/74	39502	06/87	
T&P-3332	MP-3332	MP-2997	(UP-2997)	01/74	39503	06/87	
T&P-3333	MP-3333	MP-2998	(UP-2998)	01/74	39504	01/87	
T&P-3334	MP-3334	MP-2999	(UP-2999)	01/74	39505	06/87	Note 1

Note 1: Wore Double-Eagles as MP-2999

Below: This is the as-built appearance of the first order of U30C's for the MoPac. This first order had the small fillet in front of the rear radiator screens at the top of the unit. The brand new unit glistens in April, 1968. Notice the black on white number boards, a feature that didn't last long. *John Phillips*

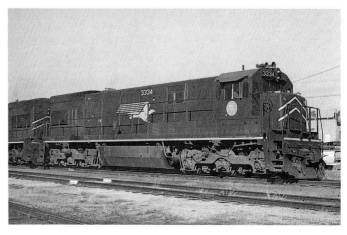

Right: The last U30C, 3334, sits at Hoisington, Kansas in November, 1974. In a few years SD40-2's will climb into the 3300-series, and force the U30C's to be renumbered into the 2965-series. *Lee Berglund*

EMD
SW1500
MP15DC

By late 1972 the MoPac needed to add a few units to the switcher fleet, and naturally turned to EMD. The 567-powered SW1200 had proven to be a great success on the MoPac. When the MoPac motive power people opened the EMD catalog, the obvious choice was the second generation 645-powered 12-cylinder switcher - the SW1500. They only ordered four (MP-1518-1521), however, and they were the only SW1500's the MoPac would own.

The new units arrived in December, 1972, making them late units in SW1500 production. The SW1500 was somewhat successful for EMD, with 808 units of this model sold over its seven and one-half year production run. For over five years of this production run there was essentially no competition for the SW1500. For switcher production at La Grange, only the NW2 had a higher production run. There were more SW1200's, but a percentage of these were built in Canada for Canadian roads. Like the

SW8's, the SW1500's were assigned to the TPMPT in New Orleans, rarely roving to other parts of the system.

Within 18 months the re-engined RS-3's were beginning to fail and were falling from the roster, as well as some of the earlier SW's such as the SW7's. This time though, the MoPac wanted a little more versatility. Switchers had little use in road service, and didn't work well in even the most rickety branch line service, and EMD was now offering a new model that was road compatible. The SW1500 could have been adapted for road service, but its 22-foot frame prevented the substitution of EMD's popular Blomberg-M truck. Sixty lengthened SW1500's were built for Mexico to in essence test the concept of road trucks under a switcher, and these were called SW1504's.

In 1974 EMD introduced a lengthened switcher with 24-foot 2-inch truck centers; a switcher on road trucks - the MP15. Slightly over a year later the designation was changed to MP15DC after the alternating current MP15AC was introduced. The MP15 was aimed at markets that were being fulfilled by aging geeps being utilized in local and switcher service. Some states had laws that required toilets on

units that were used outside of yards or in the lead of road freight lashups. The MoPac's MP15's came with toilets and snow plows, making them available for road and branch service.

The MoPac liked the idea and placed an initial order for five of the road-trucked MP15's (MP-1530-1534) which arrived in March, 1974. The first of these, MP-1530, was the first MP15 built by EMD. These came with front snow plows, and the MoPac quickly added rear snow plows. The rear snow plows were removed by December, 1974 due to the lack of need for snow plows because the engines most often ran back-to-back in pairs in branch line service. In late 1974 more MP15's arrived and by early 1975 three more orders had arrived on the property, the first two for five units each (MP-1535-1544) and the final order for 10 units (MP-1545-1554).

By mid-1976 the MoPac was getting the first of numerous batches of GP15-1's, which EMD classified as a light roadswitcher. The GP15's for most railroads circumvented the need to buy switchers, and specifically the MP15's, but the MoPac continued to buy both, one of the few roads to do so. In a lot of ways the GP15-1's could handle many of the tasks previously assigned to the switcher fleet, but by late 1981

Left: The MoPac bought only four SW1500's, which were built in December, 1972. The SW1500 was a fairly popular model, but MoPac essentially missed the SW1500's production period due to the massive purchases of SW1200's. They instead purchased MP15's. The first of the four SW1500's, 1518, is mated with slug 1418 which was once an SW7, at Neff Yard in Kansas City in October, 1984. *Mark Hall*

Below: A pair of MP15DC's is rolling through South Holland, Illinois with the Ford Run on April 26, 1986. The MoPac bought 65 MP15's, a large number compared to most roads. As built these were originally termed MP15's, but after the MP15AC was introduced in 1975, the designation was changed to MP15DC. *David Fasules*

Opposite page: A trio of MP15DC's pulls a pair of cabooses at New Orleans, Louisiana on June 18, 1975. These three were all part of the third MP15 order, delivered in February and March, 1975. The later MP15's had to be numbered in the 1356-series due to the numbering of the GP15-1's above the original MP15's. *James Holder*

Below: Whether road-trucked or not, switchers are found most often in the service for which they were designed; switching in the yards or in transfer service. The latter is the case on October 22, 1980, as a pair of MP15DC's roll past Busch Stadium and the Arch in St. Louis, Missouri. *Daniel Schroeder*

the MoPac decided more switchers were needed. They hated to tie up any of their light roadswitcher fleet exclusively in yard service.

They placed an order for another 20 MP15DC's (MP-1356-1375), which couldn't be numbered above the existing fleet of MP15DC's because they had numbered the GP15-1's immediately above them. These 20 MP15DC's arrived in January, 1982 and brought the MP15DC total to 45 units. A final order for 20 more MP15DC's (MP-1376-1392) was quickly placed, and by October, 1982 they were arriving on the property.

The delivery was completed in November, and resulted in a total of 62 MP15DC's for the MoPac. The last three of the 20 units of this order for MP15DC's were assigned to the Texas City Terminal (which was MoPac controlled), and were numbered TCT-35-37. They carried a different builder's number than the previous 17 units for accounting purposes when they were purchased. They were otherwise identical. They were all originally part of order number 827018, but the three units were later split off.

When the last MP15DC, MP-1392, arrived on the property, it represented the MoPac's final switcher. Over the course of more than half a century, the MoPac and its subsidiaries (not counting C&EI units that were off the roster by the merger, and also excluding A&S units) acquired 461 switchers, the lion's share from EMD.

The SW1200 was easily the most abundant switcher in the MoPac's fleet, with 147 units rostered. The next most abundant model was a distant second; the 62 MP15DC's. The MoPac rostered 12 different EMC or EMD models, dwarfing all other builders with 322 of 461 switcher units or almost 70%. The rarest switchers for the MoPac above 44 tons were the NC2, the SW, and the NW4, each with two units on the roster. Eight of the EMDs were ex-C&EI acquired as a result of the merger in 1967.

Interestingly, the third most abundant switcher model was the Baldwin S-12, and Baldwin follows EMD on the switcher roster with 85 of the remaining 139 units. Alco falls well behind with 33 switchers on the roster of the MoPac and its subsidiaries, 25 of which were S-2's. Five small Plymouth switchers for the NO&LC that were less than 44 tons and 16 44-Tonners from four builders make up the balance of the switcher roster. Porter's lone 44-Tonner is the MoPac's rarest engine, the only one Porter ever built.

Below: Four brand new MP15DC's are on the property on October 5, 1974 at Little Rock. With builder's dates the same month, the versatile switchers have yet to turn a wheel in revenue service. *James Holder*

EMD SW1500 1500 hp 4 units
TE = 65,290 WT = 261,160
Wheels = 40" Fuel = 1,100
Engine: EMD 12-645E V-type 12-cylinder 2-cycle
Min Speed for TE = 10.7 mph
62:15 Gearing 55 mph Max
Hump control units
Retired 1/88, to Helm

1st No	2nd No	Built	Build#	Notes & Dispositions
MP-1518	UP-1318	12/72	7343-1	Note 1, to Chicago Rail Link 2/88, r# CRL-18
MP-1519	UP-1319	12/72	7343-2	Note 2, to Chicage Rail Link 2/88, r# CRL-19
MP-1520	UP-1320	12/72	7343-3	To UP, r# UP-1320, retired 3/94
MP-1521	UP-1321	12/72	7343-4	To UP, r# UP-1321, retired 3/94

Note 1: Wore MP yellow as MP-1518. NLR "block" lettering as UP-1318
Note 2: NLR "block" lettering as UP-1319

EMD MP15DC 1,500 hp 5 units
TE = 66,700 WT = 266,800
Wheels = 40" Fuel = 1,400
Engine: EMD 12-645E V-type 12-cylinder 2-cycle
Min Spccd for TE = 9.6 mph
62:15 Gearing 65 mph Max
Hump Control units

1st No	2nd No	Built	Build#	Notes
MP-1530	UP-1330	03/74	73749-1	
MP-1531	UP-1331	03/74	73749-2	
MP-1532	UP-1332	03/74	73749-3	Wore MP yellow as MP-1532, NLR "block" lettering as UP-1332
MP-1533	UP-1333	03/74	73749-4	
MP-1534	UP-1334	03/74	73749-5	

EMD MP15DC 1,500 hp 10 units
TE = 66,575 WT = 266,300
Wheels = 40" Fuel = 1,400
Engine: EMD 12-645E V-type 12-cylinder 2-cycle
Min Speed for TE = 9.6 mph
62:15 Gearing 65 mph Max
Hump control units

1st No	2nd No	Built	Build#	Notes
MP-1535	UP-1335	10/74	73678-1	Wore MP yellow as MP-1535
MP-1536	UP-1336	10/74	73678-2	
MP-1537	UP-1337	10/74	73678-3	
MP-1538	UP-1338	10/74	73678-4	
MP-1539	UP-1339	10/74	73678-5	
MP-1540	UP-1340	09/74	73778-1	Wore MP yellow as MP-1540
MP-1541	UP-1341	09/74	73778-2	
MP-1542	UP-1342	10/74	73778-3	Wore MP yellow as MP-1542
MP-1543	UP-1343	10/74	73778-4	
MP-1544	UP-1344	10/74	73778-5	

EMD MP15DC 1,500 hp 10 units
TE = 66,520 WT = 266,080
Wheels = 40" Fuel = 1,400
Engine: EMD 12-645E V-type 12-cylinder 2-cycle
Min Speed for TE = 9.6 mph
62:15 Gearing 65 mph Max
Hump Control units

1st No	2nd No	Built	Build#	Notes
MP-1545	UP-1345	02/75	74791-1	
MP-1546	UP-1346	02/75	74791-2	
MP-1547	UP-1347	02/75	74791-3	
MP-1548	UP-1348	02/75	74791-4	
MP-1549	UP-1349	02/75	74791-5	NLR "block" lettering as UP-1349
MP-1550	UP-1350	03/75	74791-6	
MP-1551	UP-1351	03/75	74791-7	
MP-1552	UP-1352	03/75	74791-8	Wore MP yellow as MP-1552
MP-1553	UP-1353	03/75	74791-9	Wore MP yellow as MP-1553
MP-1554	UP-1354	03/75	74791-10	

EMD MP15DC 1,500 hp 20 units
TE = 66,750 WT = 267,000
Wheels = 40" Fuel = 1,400
Engine: EMD 12-645E3 V-type 12-cylinder 2-cycle
Min Speed for TE = 9.3 mph
62:15 Gearing 65 mph Max
Hump Control units

1st No	2nd No	Built	Builder #	Notes & Dispositions
MP-1356	UP-1356	01/82	817019-1	
MP-1357	UP-1357	01/82	817019-2	Wore MP yellow as MP-1357
MP-1358	UP-1358	01/82	817019-3	
MP-1359	UP-1359	01/82	817019-4	
MP-1360	UP-1360	01/82	817019-5	NLR "block" lettering as UP-1360
MP-1361	UP-1361	01/82	817019-6	NLR "block" lettering as UP-1361
MP-1362	UP-1362	01/82	817019-7	Wore MP yellow as MP-1362
MP-1363	UP-1363	01/82	817019-8	NLR "block" lettering as UP-1363
MP-1364	UP-1364	01/82	817019-9	
MP-1365:2	UP-1365	01/82	817019-10	
MP-1366	UP-1366	01/82	817019-11	
MP-1367	UP-1367	01/82	817019-12	
MP-1368:2	UP-1368	01/82	817019-13	NLR "block" lettering as UP-1368
MP-1369:2	UP-1369	01/82	817019-14	NLR "block" lettering as UP-1368
MP-1370:3	UP-1370	01/82	817019-15	Wore MP yellow as MP-1370
MP-1371	UP-1371	01/82	817019-16	Wore MP yellow as MP-1371
MP-1372:2	UP-1372	01/82	817019-17	Wore MP yellow as MP-1372
MP-1373:3	UP-1373	01/82	817019-18	Wore MP yellow as MP-1373
MP-1374:3	UP-1374	01/82	817019-19	NLR "block" lettering as UP-1374
MP-1375:3	UP-1375	01/82	817019-20	NLR "block" lettering as UP-1375

EMD MP15DC 1,500 hp 20 units
TE = 67,000 WT = 268,000
Wheels = 40" Fuel = 1,400
Engine: EMD 12-645E3 V-type 12-cylinder 2-cycle
Min Speed for TE = 9.3 mph
62:15 Gearing 65 mph Max
Hump Control units

1st No	2nd No	Built	Builder #	Notes
MP-1376:2	UP-1376	10/82	827018-1	
MP-1377:3	UP-1377	10/82	827018-2	Wore MP yellow
MP-1378:2	UP-1378	10/82	827018-3	
MP-1379:2	UP-1379	10/82	827018-4	Wore MP yellow
MP-1380:3	UP-1380	10/82	827018-5	
MP-1381:3	UP-1381	10/82	827018-6	
MP-1382:3	UP-1382	10/82	827018-7	Wore MP yellow
MP-1383:2	UP-1383	10/82	827018-8	
MP-1384:2	UP-1384	11/82	827018-9	
MP-1385:2	UP-1385	11/82	827018-10	
MP-1386:3	UP-1386	11/82	827018-11	
MP-1387:3	UP-1387	11/82	827018-12	
MP-1388:2	UP-1388	11/82	827018-13	
MP-1389:2	UP-1389	11/82	827018-14	
MP-1390:3	UP-1390	11/82	827018-15	
MP-1391:3	UP-1391	11/82	827018-16	NLR "block" lettering as UP-1391
MP-1392:3	UP-1392	11/82	827018-17	
TCT-35		11/82	827028-1	
TCT-36		11/82	827028-2	
TCT-37		11/82	827028-3	

Opposite page bottom: After a 7-year absence in switcher purchases, the MoPac finally went back to EMD for more MP15's in January, 1982. The 1368 is one of 20 that came in January, and another 20 would arrive in October and November. The trio is at North Little Rock on March 5, 1985. *Steve Forrest*

Right: MP15DC 1380 poses at Dolton, Illinois on December 11, 1982. *A Vanier photo, Kevin EuDaly collection*

Alco
RS-2
RS-3

EMD
SW1500
MP15DC
GP38-2

GE
44-Tonner

The Alton and Southern was originally owned by the Aluminum Company of America (Alcoa), and was a believer in Alco for their switcher fleet. In June, 1947 they began diesel operations by purchasing four RS-2's from Alco (A&S-28-31). The RS-2 was fairly successful for Alco, but came nowhere close to the RS-3 production total of 1,380 units. Only 366 RS-2's were sold in the U.S. and 17 in Canada. The RS-2 came with Alco's familiar 12-cylinder 244 engine, and was produced from October, 1946 through May, 1950. Most RS-2's came under specification E-1661A, or E-1661B, which were rated at 1,500 horsepower, but the last 31 produced were built under Specification E-1661C and were rated at 1,600 horsepower. The 1,600 horsepower units were built from February through May, 1950.

The RS-2 seemed to fit the bill, so the railroad went back to Alco later in 1947 for another group of the Alco road switchers. Four more arrived in late September and early October (A&S-32-35), and three more came in November (A&S-36-38). They continued their allegiance to Alco, and by June, 1949 they had 24 of the handsome Alco road switchers, which had now climbed up to number 54, with the A&S-43-45 group left out.

In 1967 RS-2 A&S-33 was wrecked and replaced by TPMPT RS-2 958, which had been slated to become T&P-1063. It never received the new T&P number, however, and was sent to the A&S instead, becoming A&S-33:2. The missing number slots (43-45) were filled by one unit orders in November, 1950, June, 1953, and February, 1956, all for RS-3's.

On May 9, 1968 the C&NW and the MoPac bought the A&S from Alcoa, and began renumbering the fleet. A&S-28 became A&S-1034, and the rest counted up from there, but were not renumbered quite in perfect order. By 1969 the MoPac and C&NW influence resulted in the replacement of the Alcos with a fleet of EMD SW1500's. There were 18 of the new switchers purchased in three groups of six each. The first batch of six was built in May, 1969 (A&S-1500-1505), and the second and third groups were built in February, 1970 (A&S-1506-

Left: In later years the A&S replaced their aging Alco fleet with 18 SW1500's from EMD in three orders of six each. In October, 1979, a pair of almost 10-year-old SW's work through Granite City, Illinois. *Ed Hawkins*

Below: A&S RS-2 38 is at the C&EI yard in Mitchell, Illinois on October 26, 1966. The A&S rostered 25 RS-2's, by far their most popular model. Most of the aging Alcos, including the 38, went to EMD as trade-in material on SW1500's in 1969, 1970, and 1971. *Ray Curl*

Bottom: The A&S was owned by the MoPac and the C&NW, which explains the yellow and blue scheme. On March 26, 1988, A&S SW1500 1513 is working a grain local at East St. Louis, Missouri. *Terry Chicwak*

Opposite page top: the A&S was originally owned by Alcoa, and before the MoPac and C&NW influence their fleet of RS-2's wore this yellow and green scheme. The handsome Alco roadswitcher is at East St. Louis, Illinois on March 16, 1963. *R R Wallin photo, Kevin EuDaly collection*

Opposite page bottom: RS-2 1046 blasts through Dupo, Illinois with a transfer for the MoPac on March 8, 1970. The unit has less than a year left before going to EMD for new SW1500's. *J David Ingles photo, Kevin EuDaly collection*

1511) and April, 1971 (A&S-1512-1517), respectively. The Alcos were quickly retired, with the exception of A&S-1040 and 1057, which served their owners for nearly 30 years. The C&NW later sold its interest in the A&S to the Cotton Belt (SSW), a Southern Pacific subsidiary. One MP15DC was purchased in October, 1980 (A&S-1522), replacing the last of the Alcos.

In late 1993, the A&S finally was in need of more power and purchased two ex-MoPac GP38-2's to supplement their fleet. The two units were UP-2081 and UP-2086, which had both carried the same numbers as MoPac units (MP-2081 and MP-2086). They were renumbered A&S-2000 and A&S-2001 and placed in service in the St. Louis area. They were the first low-hood road units the A&S had ever owned.

The A&S all-time diesel fleet consisted of six models and 50 units from three builders, a fairly diverse roster for a small switching line. Their roster included one 44-Tonner picked up second-hand from the Point Comfort & Northern (A&S-1), 25 RS-2's, three RS-3's, 18 SW1500's, one MP15DC, and two GP38-2's. Their second generation units still serve in switching in and around the St. Louis area, a last holdout among the MoPac subsidiaries.

Above: In December, 1993, the UP retired two ex-MoPac GP38-2's that went to the A&S. The first, ex-MoPac 2081, was painted in the standard A&S scheme and numbered 2000. An A&S herald was applied to the nose, a first for the A&S. The newly painted A&S 2000 is at East St. Louis, Illinois on February 6, 1994. *Lon Coone photo, Tony Fey collection*

Below: Spotless 44-Tonner number 1 is in Cahokia, Illinois on October 5, 1978. the center cab GE was purchased second hand from the Point Comfort & Northern, originally numbered A&S-629, and then the one-spot. *Mike Wise photo, J Harlen Wilson collection*

Right: The first SW1500 was a member of the first of three groups of six units, and was delivered in May, 1969. The unit is at North Little Rock on March 11, 1979, a long way from A&S rails. It is interesting that the MoPac subsidiary had so many SW1500's compared to the parent road. The long lifespan of the Alcos was the major factor in the SW1500 purchase. *J Harlen Wilson*

GE 44-Ton   350 hp   1 unit
TE = 22,000   WT = 88,000
Wheels = 35"   Fuel = 250
Engine: Two Hercules DFXD 6-cylinder 4-cycle
Min Speed for TE = Not Available
74:15 Gearing   35 mph Max

1st No	2nd No	3rd No	4th No	Built	Build#	Retired	Notes
PC&N-2	A&S-629	A&S-1	(A&S-380)	11/48	29990	1983	Note 1

Note 1: Leased to Cooper Terminal, Cahokia, IL, to Fox Terminal, Cahokia, IL

Alco-GE RS-2   1,500 hp   25 units
TE = 61,000   WT = 244,000
Wheels = 40"   Fuel = 1,200
Engine: Alco 244-H V-type 12-cylinder 4-cycle Turbocharged
Min Speed for TE = 9.0 mph
74:18 Gearing   65 mph Max

1st No	2nd No	Built	Build#	Notes & Dispositions
A&S-28	A&S-1034	06/47	75255	Retired 1970, T-I to EMD on SW1500's
A&S-29	A&S-1035	06/47	75256	Retired 1/71, to PNC, scrapped
A&S-30	A&S-1036	07/47	75257	Retired 1/71, to PNC, scrapped
A&S-31	A&S-1037	07/47	75260	Retired 6/69, T-I to EMD on SW1500's
A&S-32	A&S-1038	09/47	75271	Retired 1971, T-I to EMD on SW1500's
A&S-33:1		09/47	75272	Wrecked 1967, scrapped, replaced by A&S-33:2
A&S-33:2	A&S-1053	01/49	76633	Note 1
A&S-34	A&S-1039	09/47	75273	Retired 6/69, T-I to EMD on SW1500's
A&S-35	A&S-1040	10/47	75274	T-I to EMD
A&S-36	A&S-1041	11/47	75411	Retired 1970, T-I to EMD on SW1500's
A&S-37	A&S-1042	11/47	75412	Retired 6/69, T-I to EMD on SW1500's
A&S-38	A&S-1043	11/47	75413	Retired 6/69, T-I to EMD on SW1500's
A&S-39	A&S-1044	11/47	75565	Retired 10/71, to PNC, scrapped
A&S-40	A&S-1047	04/48	75701	Retired 1971, to PNC, scrapped
A&S-41	A&S-1048	04/48	75702	Retired 3/70, T-I to EMD on SW1500's
A&S-42	A&S-1052	11/48	75961	Retired 3/70, T-I to EMD on SW1500's
A&S-46	A&S-1046	03/48	75697	Retired 1970, T-I to EMD on SW1500's
A&S-47	A&S-1049	03/48	75698	Retired 1970, T-I to EMD on SW1500's
A&S-48	A&S-1050	03/48	75699	Retired 1970, T-I to EMD on SW1500's
A&S-49	A&S-1054	05/49	76829	Retired 1970, T-I to EMD on SW1500's
A&S-50	A&S-1045	02/48	75574	Retired 10/71, T-I to EMD on SW1500's
A&S-51	A&S-1055	06/49	76972	Retired 1970, T-I to EMD on SW1500's
A&S-52	A&S-1051	04/48	75700	Note 2
A&S-53	A&S-1056	05/49	76830	Retired 5/71, T-I to EMD on SW1500's
A&S-54	A&S-1057	06/49	76971	Retired 1980, to PNC, scrapped

Note 1: Originally T&P-1100, then TPMPT-23, then TPMPT-958:1. Retired 8/67, traded to PNC for F7A DRGW-5694, to A&S as A&S-33:2 (replaced wrecked A&S-33:1). Retired 6/69, T-I to EMD on SW1500's
Note 2: Retired 1967, to PNC 4/77, to Scotia Coal, Oven Fork, KY

Alco-GE RS-3   1,600 hp   3 units
TE = 62,375   WT = 249,500
Wheels = 40"   Fuel = 1,800
Engine: Alco 244-H V-type 12-cylinder 4-cycle Turbocharged
Min Speed for TE = 9.0 mph
74:18 Gearing   65 mph Max
A&S-45 was built by Alco
Rebuilt with GM 12/567 1,200 hp engine, designated "RS-3m" or "GP12."
After rebuilding:
TE = 61,185   WT = 244,740
Wheels = 40"   Fuel = 1,400
Engine: EMD 12-567B V-type 12-cylinder 2-cycle
Min Speed for TE = 12.0
74:18 Gearing   65 mph Max

1st No	2nd No	Built	Build#	Notes & Dispositions
A&S-43	A&S-1058	11/50	78366	Note 1
A&S-44	A&S-1059	06/53	80504	Retired 1970, T-I to EMD on SW1500's
A&S-45	A&S-1060	02/56	81849	Retired 1971, to PNC, scrapped

Note 1: Retired 1972, to GRS/Birmingham Rail & Locomotive, Birmingham, AL, to Scotia Coal, to Southern Rails, rebuilt with Cummins engine 1979-1980, to Minnesota Power & Electric, r# MPE-1

EMD SW1500   1,500 hp   6 units
TE = 65,210   WT = 260,840
Wheels = 40"   Fuel = 1,100
Engine: EMD 12-645E V-type 12-cylinder 2-cycle
Min Speed for TE = 10.7 mph
62:15 Gearing   55 mph Max
Hump Control units

1st No	Built	Build#
A&S-1500	05/69	34873
A&S-1501	05/69	34874
A&S-1502	05/69	34875
A&S-1503	05/69	34876
A&S-1504	05/69	34877
A&S-1505	05/69	34878

EMD SW1500   1500 hp   12 units
TE = 64,950   WT = 259,800
Wheels = 40"   Fuel = 1,100
Engine: EMD 12-645E V-type 12-cylinder 2-cycle
Min Speed for TE = 10.7 mph
62:15 Gearing   55 mph Max
Hump Control units

1st No	Built	Build#
A&S-1506	02/70	35297
A&S-1507	02/70	35298
A&S-1508	02/70	35299
A&S-1509	02/70	35300
A&S-1510	02/70	35301
A&S-1511	02/70	35302
A&S-1512	04/71	36855
A&S-1513	04/71	36856
A&S-1514	04/71	36857
A&S-1515	04/71	36858
A&S-1516	04/71	36859
A&S-1517	04/71	36860

EMD MP15DC   1,500 hp   1 unit
TE = 64,925   WT = 259,700
Wheels = 40"   Fuel = 1,100
Engine: EMD 12-645E3 V-type 12-cylinder 2-cycle
Min Speed for TE = 9.3 mph
62:15 Gearing   65 mph Max

1st No	Built	Build#
A&S-1522	10/80	796374-1

EMD GP38-2   2,000 hp   2 units
TE = 66,600   WT = 266,420
Wheels = 40"   Fuel = 2,600
Engine: EMD 16-645E V-type 16-cylinder 2-cycle
Min Speed for TE = 12.0 mph
62:15 Gearing   65 mph Max

1st No	2nd No	3rd No	4th No	Built	Build#	Notes
MP-930	MP-2081	UP-2081	A&S-2000	01/73	71702-8	Note 1
MP-935:2	MP-2086	UP-2086	A&S-2001	02/73	71702-13	Note 2

Note 1: Retired by UP 12/93, T-L, to A&S, r# A&S-2000
Note 2: Retired by UP 12/93, T-L, to A&S, r# A&S-2001

EMD
GP38-2
GP15-1
GP15AC

GE
U23B

Right: There were seven GE's that were outfitted with EMD cabs after wrecks. One of the unique hybrids, 4506, is on the point of an eastbound that has just crested Kirkwood Hill at Kirkwood, Missouri on November 13, 1981. *Dan Schroeder*

Opposite page top: The GP38-2 became MoPac's power of choice for medium horsepower road freight and local freight duties. By the time all was said and done, the MoPac had 326 of the EMD B-B GP38-2's, easily the MoPac's most abundant model. The 2169 swings through the junction at Congo, Missouri on the northeast side of Kansas City, running westbound on Santa Fe trackage where the MoPac has trackage rights to access the River Subdivision. The river local is almost to Neff Yard, his day almost done on August, 29, 1986. *Kevin EuDaly*

Opposite page bottom: A trio of GP38-2's led by the 875 roll past the depot at Alexandria, Louisiana on March 11, 1973. The lead unit is 14 months old, having come on the property in January, 1972. *Glenn Anderson*

Below: GP38-2 2255 leads another GP38-2 and a rebuilt GP35 on the high iron south of Little Rock on new year's day, 1981. Only the SD40-2 accompanies the GP38-2 on MoPac's roster with more than 300 units; 306 for the SD40-2. *Steve Glischinski*

In 1972 the MoPac's buying trend for heavy-duty high-horsepower C-C's had slightly changed. By this time EMD's Dash 2 line of locomotives was on the market, and the MoPac liked what it saw. The Dash 2 line of 645 engines was introduced in January, 1972, and the MoPac was one of the first to receive the new Dash 2's.

The Dash-2's were placed in production on January 1, 1972, and from a nomenclature viewpoint merely added "-2" to the previous model designations in the catalog. Though Dash 2 changes were mainly internal, a few spotting features were consistent to the entire line. These included battery box covers without hinges or latches (bolted on instead), a water level sight glass on the long hood on the right side of the carbody, a sloping cab roof that extended slightly beyond the rear of the cab, and on four-axle units most came with new B-B high adhesion trucks. The six-axle Dash 2 units were on a longer frame and came with the HT-C truck with a dampening strut on the center axle, as well as the previously mentioned features. All Dash 2's also came with two possible positions for the marker lights on the rear of the units, with one set blanked out, a decision that was made by each purchaser.

The MoPac placed an order for 45 GP38-2's, which arrived in January and February, 1972 (MP-858-902). These were the first MoPac units delivered with four exhaust stacks, which had previously been a MoPac modification.

These continued to replace an aging fleet of F-units that were slowly giving up the fight, and combined with GP35's were the main replacements of the F's. The 2,000 horsepower GP38-2 employed the 16-cylinder 645E engine, and went on to become the most popular B-B roadswitcher of its time. It quickly gained an exceptional reputation for having high availability coupled with low operating costs. Within a few years it would dominate the B-B side of the MoPac's roster.

The MoPac was quickly impressed with the GP38-2, and placed two more orders for the versatile B-B roadswitcher almost immediately after receiving their first batch. The orders were for 10 units each (MP-903-922) and were delivered sequentially in September and October, 1972. All of a sudden there were 65 GP38-2's on the roster, and they began to invade local, branchline and mainline service across the system.

In early 1973 the MoPac was again acquiring B-B power, but this time it was from both GE and EMD. The EMDs came as more GP38-2's, this time 37 units (MP-923-959). These were delivered between January and May, and brought the GP38-2 total to over 100 units; 102 total. When the MoPac went to GE this time, the U23B was the direct competitor of EMD's GP38-2.

When GE raised the rating of its FDL-16 engine to 3,000 horsepower, they were suddenly without an intermediate size locomotive in their catalog. In response to the GP38's success, GE decided they had better offer something to compete. The design was based on the 12-cylinder 2,250 horsepower FDL-12 engine, and basically adopted the U30B body. Production of this competitor, the U23B, had begun in 1968, and sales were somewhat respectable.

The MoPac placed an order for seven U23B's (MP-668-674), which were delivered in January and February, 1973, confirming again the MoPac's interest in both builders. Most U23B's came with a cyclone inertial primary air filter and secondary oil-bath filters. These units have the forward inlet radiator section down low. The MoPac's first order was equipped with Farr "Dynavane" inertial engine primary filters and paper secondary filters. This resulted in a different appearance in the inlet, which was also down low. By mid-year they were getting five more U30C's (MP-984-988) and right behind those were the first SD40-2's for the MoPac.

Below: By the time GP38-2 2158 arrived on the property, there were already 149 GP38-2's on the MoPac system. It was the first of 40 GP38-2's built for the MoPac in January and February, 1980. Six months later the MoPac went back for more, another 40 delivered in late summer, 1980. Brand new 2158 has 'em rolling with some additional horses from Conrail at Maplewood, Missouri on the east slope of Kirkwood Hill on a sunny March 22, 1980. *Paul DeLuca*

EMD Cabs on GE's

In the late 1970's, the MoPac found a unique solution to cab repair jobs for a number of GEs that were involved in accidents where their cabs were damaged. On May 17, 1978, brand new B23-7 MP-2296 was wrecked at Gorham, and the cab was substantially damaged. Little Rock shop forces had an EMD Spartan cab on hand, and decided to apply it to the new GE to get it into service quickly. They didn't have time to place an order with GE for a new cab, which would have resulted in the unit sitting idle for a rather long period of time.

The result was a unit that had a hybrid appearance, looking like both an EMD and a GE. The end result was a success, and the unit went back into service with the new cab. A

Top: Hybrid U23B 4528 leads an empty Labadie coal train south out of Dupo, Illinois on October 9, 1981. *Kevin EuDaly*

Left: A different face at North Little Rock on June 22, 1977. *J Harlen Wilson*

Below: Spartan cabbed 2282 passes U30C 2972 at Maplewood, Missouri in March, 1980. *Mike Wise photo, David Johnston collection*

number of other GEs were wrecked and rebuilt with EMD cabs, though some of these might have actually been fabricated by the North Little Rock shop forces, rather than coming off older EMDs. The first unit done was U30C 3311, which was outshopped in November, 1976.

Three models received the EMD cabs, including the B23-7, U23B and U30C. There were seven GEs that were rebuilt with EMD cabs. There was one U30C (MP-3311, later renumbered MP-2976), five U23B's (MP-2256, later renumbered MP-4506, MP-4521, MP-4528, MP-2282, later renumbered MP-4531, and MP-4534), and the one B23-7 (MP-2296, later renumbered MP-4607).

By mid-year 1974 there was a need for more B-B power, and there is little surprise in the fact that more GP38-2's were on the way. This time, however, a rarity occurred - the orders were for more GEs than EMDs, as GE continued to get their slice of MoPac power. Ten GP38-2's came in September and October, 1974 (MP-2111-2120) and 11 U23B's arrived in November (MP-2257-2267). Both number series were reflective of the latest renumbering plan. This order of U23B's also had the different air filter scheme. Starting the U23B's numbers at MP-2250 in this plan led to their being renumbered yet again. MP-2257 was the first MoPac GE unit to come on the dramatic floating bolster (FB-2) trucks, which became the standard for later GE power.

The MoPac continued with more of the same in 1975. January and February brought 12 more GP38-2's (MP-2121-2132). Thirty eight more SD40-2's came in February and March. Also in March came six more GE U23B's (MP-2268-2273), bringing the U23B total to 24. These and all subsequent U23B's came with the standard air filter package offered by GE. Besides the MP15DC's that came in February and March, 14 more SD40-2's came in August (MP-3202-3215).

In 1976 the MoPac's locomotive purchases slowed. By mid-year some new power was finally arriving. Joining the ranks of the GEs were five more U23B's (MP-2274-2278) which seemed destined to be added only a handful at a time. These five brought the U23B total to 29, still no comparison to the increasing horde of EMD power in blue.

While the U23B's were coming from GE, EMD was delivering the first of a new model for

the MoPac - the GP15-1, which was destined to be as popular for the MoPac in the second generation as the F7 had been in the first. The GP15-1 was produced by EMD with the idea that it would use components from trade-in GP7's and GP9's, which were about at the end of their usefulness without rebuilding. The MoPac's GP7 and GP9 fleets fit in with this idea nicely, and the MoPac took advantage of the trade-in arrangement. The GP15-1 evolved from the MP15AC, and with the trade-in offer and tax advantages the GP15-1 was competitive with the price of rebuilding old geeps. The five feet in extra length provided room for a typical EMD roadswitcher style front end, and also provided better tracking and operation at road speeds

Above: The MoPac bought 160 GP15-1's and another 30 GP15AC's, making the GP15 a very prevalent model on the MoPac's roster. GP15-1 1654 rolls through Fort Worth, Texas on a sunny fall day in October, 1982. *Keith Wilhite*

Below: A pair of GP15-1's are making a run up Lee's Summit Hill at Unity Village, Missouri on February 14, 1984. They are in charge of the eastbound local this particular day. With only three cars their horsepower per ton ratio is more than just a little on the high side. *Lon EuDaly*

Above: GP15-1 1637 leads a GP38-2 through Webster Groves, Missouri on a work train on July 21, 1984. The GP15's were put in the same local and branch service that was left vacant when the geeps were retired in the 1970's. *Daniel Schroeder*

compared to the MP15. The "Dash 1" terminology indicates the lack of complete "Dash 2" components, due to the reuse of the GP7 and GP9 components. In many ways, these are almost 645E "GP7-2's."

The GP15-1 trade-ins never really materialized for EMD, and generated only modest sales at 368 units including all variations. This is perhaps due to the fact that the service for which the GP15-1's were intended generally doesn't warrant the purchase of new locomotives, regardless of the good trade-in deal. Most railroads figured old GP7's and GP9's would do.

Missouri Pacific's GP15-1's all came with inertial air filters, whereas the Chicago & North Western and Frisco bought theirs without. Chesapeake & Ohio's GP15T's (turbocharged) came with inertial air filters as well. The initial order was for 20 GP15-1's, delivered in June and July, 1976. This order was split between the MoPac, which got 15 GP15-1's (MP-1555-1569), and the C&EI, which got five (C&EI-1570-1574). Over the next 6 1/2 years, the GP15-1 would become one of the MoPac's most abundant model, and would only trail the SD40-2 and GP38-2 in second generation purchases.

EMD dominated MoPac purchases in 1976, when more GP38-2's for medium roadswitcher duties and SD40-2's for heavy road haul service were purchased. The GP38-2 order was small in 1976, only five units built in July and August (MP-2133-2137). The SD40-2 order was for five units with dynamic brakes, one of the only groups of MoPac engines to have them (some of T&P's geeps had dynamic brakes).

By the end of 1976 another 15 GP15-1's were on the way (MP-1575-1589), all built in

December, 1976. Right behind these was the final order for the U23B's, 10 units this time (MP-2279-2288), delivered in January and February, 1977. This brought the U23B total to a somewhat respectable 39 units, though EMD purchases still far outnumbered the GEs, and the SD40-2's were dominating the road freight roster.

In 1977 the MoPac went strictly for B-B power, buying only GP38-2's and GP15-1's. The GP15-1's were first, an order for 25 units (MP-1590-1614) delivered in July that brought the total to 60. The GP38-2's came in October, consecutive orders for 10 units each (MP-2138-2157), bringing the GP38-2 total to 149 and making them one of the MoPac's most prevalent four-axle roadswitcher model. The first ten of this batch were delivered with front and rear snow plows (MP-2138-2147), and were intended to be used on locals on branchlines as single units. The earlier orders had all been intended to be mainline power, and thus did not come with rear snow plows. The GP15-1's were also set up

for single unit operation, with rear snow plows and rear stripes.

The buying trends during the previous five years would continue in 1978, except that the MoPac would return to GE for new B-B road power - the B-Boats.

Before adding the final group of EMD C-C's for 1979, the MoPac first added some more EMD B-B's, going back for another 30 GP15-1's (MP-1615-1644). This was the last group of GP15-1's for two years. The B-Boats were coming at regular intervals as well, and in fact were competing quite well with the EMDs. Ten more non-dynamic brake equipped SD40-2's came in December, 1979 (MP-3302-3311), finishing out the year's purchases.

In the meantime, the older geeps in the 100 and 600 number series were being traded to EMD on GP38-2's. The last three-digit numbered geep left the system in December, 1979, leaving only four-digit numbers on the system for the new decade, a decade of tremendous change for the MoPac.

Early 1980 saw the return of the GP38-2, which hadn't been ordered since mid-1977. Two large orders for 40 units each were delivered in January and February, and July and August, respectively. These 80 units (MP-2158-2237) brought the GP38-2 total to 229 units - which was becoming a dominant model on the MoPac.

The MoPac still had three more GP38-2 purchases in the future. The first of these purchases was a unique move for the MoPac, especially considering the scope of the purchase, involving the purchase of second-hand units. This was not just a handful of units, either,

Below: A pair of GP15-1's from the first order work the yard at South Omaha, Nebraska on May 27, 1978. The lead unit was the first of the order that was for the C&EI, originally it had C&EI lettering above the eagle on the cab side. Not too many years before this would have been a pair of geeps. *Don Wallworth*

but numbered 52 units. They were Chicago, Rock Island & Pacific units, orphaned by a railroad in bankruptcy. Few of the Rock's owned assets were sold, partially due to the anti-negotiating stance of the trustee, but the units that were leased nearly all found other homes. The Rock units helped the MoPac acquire a large number of units in a hurry in late 1980. They were originally CRI&P-4300-4351, and the MoPac painted them up quickly and

numbered them above the existing GP38-2 fleet (MP-2238-2289).

Grand Trunk Western also bought 12 of the ex-CRI&P GP38-2's, while five that were owned by the Rock outright went with all other owned units to Chrome Crankshaft, and these five later went to the Pittsburgh and Lake Erie. The Rock Island GP40's went to UP, and later some of these were assigned MoPac numbers in the post merger era. They never, however, wore MoPac

blue, instead spending the remainder of their UP careers in yellow.

The 1980 purchases of GP38-2's caused their number series to run over into the 2250 series U23B's. As a result, the U23B's were renumbered into the 4500 series, and the B23-7's were renumbered into their final MoPac numbers in the 4600 series.

On the medium horsepower side of things, another group of GP38-2's came in February and

March, 1981, confirming again the MoPac's dependence on the medium horsepower B-B roadswitcher. This group of 30 (MP-2290-2319) brought the GP38-2 total to 311 units. The final GP38-2 order for 15 units (MP-2320-2334) later that year clinched the "most popular single model" title on the MoPac for all time, with a whopping 326 GP38-2's on the roster.

The MoPac's blue era was completed from August, 1981 to December, 1982 with a single model from EMD - the GP15-1, and likewise a single model from GE - the B30-7A. One order of 20 GP15-1's came in August, 1981 (MP-1645-1664), putting the versatile B-B light roadswitcher over 100 units. The rest of the regular DC GP15-1's all came between February and April, 1982 in two orders, one for 40 units (MP-1665-1704) and one for 10 final units (MP-1705-1714). These two orders brought the total number of GP15-1's on the roster to 160.

The final GP15-1 order was for 30 more units (MP-1715-1744), but these were ordered as AC units. The MoPac was the only railroad to buy the GP15AC. Normally, trade-ins achieve the objective of reusing a maximum number of components, but these were outfitted with new AR10 alternators instead of the trade-in DC generators. This final purchase in late 1982 of GP15-1's, albeit GP15AC's, brought the GP15 total to 190, the same quantity that the F7 had attained in the first generation. MP-1744 has the distinction of being the last Missouri Pacific locomotive delivered in solid blue. Another era had passed.

Above: GP38-2 2022 adds a little muscle to a westbound freight on Boyd Hill near Hoisington, Kansas in November, 1977. The 2022 was part of the unusually large first order for GP38-2's, an order for 45 units. Most of MoPac's orders were for substantially less. *Lee Berglund*

Below: An odd lashup, GP38-2 2287 rumbles through Conway Springs, Kansas with an ICG Paducah Rebuild and sister GP38-2 2193 on June 10, 1982. 2287 started life as a Rock Island unit, wore MoPac blue, UP yellow with MoPac lettering, and finally went into full UP dress. *Jerry Alexander*

EMD GP38-2   2,000 hp   45 units
TE = 67,240   WT = 268,960
Wheels = 40"   Fuel = 2,600
Engine: EMD 16-645E V-type 16-cylinder 2-cycle
Min Speed for TE = 12.0 mph
62:15 Gearing   65 mph Max
Delivered with 4 exhaust stacks
All except MP-2031 retired 7/87, to lessor

1st No	2nd No	3rd No	4th No	Built	Build#	Notes
MP-858	MP-2009	(UP-2335)	UP-1800	01/72	7344-1	Note 1
MP-859	MP-2010	(UP-2336)	UP-1801	01/72	7344-2	Note 1
MP-860	MP-2011	UP-2337	UP-1802	01/72	7344-3	Note 1, 2
MP-861	MP-2012	UP-2338	UP-1803	01/72	7344-4	Note 1, 2
MP-862	MP-2013	(UP-2339)	UP-1804	01/72	7344-5	Note 1
MP-863	MP-2014	(UP-2340)	UP-1805	01/72	7344-6	Note 1
MP-864	MP-2015	(UP-2341)	UP-1806	01/72	7344-7	Note 1
MP-865	MP-2016	(UP-2342)	UP-1807	01/72	7344-8	Note 1
MP-866	MP-2017	(UP-2343)	GTW-5708	01/72	7344-9	Note 3
MP-867	MP-2018	(UP-2344)	GTW-5728	01/72	7344-10	Note 4
MP-868	MP-2019	(UP-2345)	GTW-5726	01/72	7344-11	Note 5
MP-869	MP-2020	(UP-2346)	UP-1808	01/72	7344-12	Note 1
MP-870	MP-2021	(UP-2347)	GTW-5732	01/72	7344-13	Note 6
MP-871	MP-2022	(UP-2348)	GTW-5729	01/72	7344-14	Note 7
MP-872	MP-2023	(UP-2349)	UP-1809	01/72	7344-15	Note 1
MP-873	MP-2024	(UP-2350)	UP-1810	01/72	7344-16	Note 1
MP-874	MP-2025	(UP-2351)	GTW-5730	01/72	7344-17	Note 7
MP-875	MP-2026	(UP-2352)	GTW-5706	01/72	7344-18	Note 4
MP-876	MP-2027	(UP-2353)	GTW-5707	01/72	7344-19	Note 4
MP-877	MP-2028	(UP-2354)	GTW-5712	01/72	7344-20	Note 8
MP-878	MP-2029	(UP-2355)	UP-1811	01/72	7344-21	Note 1
MP-879	MP-2030	(UP-2356)	GTW-5714	01/72	7344-22	Note 10
MP-880	MP-2031	(UP-2357)			7344-23	Note 11
MP-881	MP-2032	(UP-2358)	UP-1812	01/72	7344-24	Note 1
MP-882	MP-2033	(UP-2359)	UP-1813	01/72	7344-25	Note 1
MP-883	MP-2034	(UP-2360)	UP-1814	01/72	7344-26	Note 1
MP-884	MP-2035	(UP-2361)	GTW-5725	01/72	7344-27	Note 10
MP-885	MP-2036	UP-2362	UP-1815	01/72	7344-28	Note 1, 2
MP-886	MP-2037	(UP-2363)	GTW-5731	01/72	7344-29	Note 11
MP-887	MP-2038	(UP-2364)	UP-1816	01/72	7344-30	Note 1
MP-888	MP-2039	(UP-2365)	GTW-5733	01/72	7344-31	Note 12
MP-889	MP-2040	(UP-2366)	GTW-5710	01/72	7344-32	Note 13
MP-890	MP-2041	(UP-2367)	GTW-5703	01/72	7344-33	Note 14
MP-891	MP-2042	(UP-2368)	GTW-5711	02/72	7344-34	Note 13
MP-892	MP-2043	UP-2369	GTW-5709	02/72	7344-35	Note 15, 16
MP-893	MP-2044	(UP-2370)	GTW-5705	02/72	7344-36	Note 17
MP-894	MP-2045	(UP-2371)	GTW-5734	02/72	7344-37	Note 18
MP-895	MP-2046	(UP-2372)	GTW-5700	02/72	7344-38	Note 19
MP-896	MP-2047	(UP-2373)	GTW-5701	02/72	7344-39	Note 19
MP-897	MP-2048	UP-2374	UP-1817	02/72	7344-40	Note 1, 2, 15
MP-898	MP-2049	UP-2375	UP-1818	02/72	7344-41	Note 1, 2, 15
MP-899	MP-2050	(UP-2376)	GTW-5702	02/72	7344-42	Note 19
MP-900:1	MP-2051	UP-2377	UP-1819	02/72	7344-43	Note 1, 2, 15
MP-901:1	MP-2052	(UP-2378)	GTW-5727	02/72	7344-44	Note 4
MP-902	MP-2053	(UP-2379)	GTW-5704	02/72	7344-45	Note 17

Note 1: To Helm/GTC, to HL, to UP 2/89
Note 2: Wore MoPac number as HL
Note 3: To Helm, to Grand Trunk Western 12/87
Note 4: To Helm, to Grand Trunk Western 4/91
Note 5: To Helm, to Grand Trunk Western 2/91
Note 6: To Helm, to Grand Trunk Western 9/91
Note 7: To Helm, to Grand Trunk Western 6/91
Note 8: To Helm, to Grand Trunk Western 6/88
Note 9: Wrecked 1/86, frame to Durbano 5/88
Note 10: To Helm, to Grand Trunk Western 2/90
Note 11: To Helm, to Grand Trunk Western 8/91
Note 12: To Helm, to Grand Trunk Western 11/91
Note 13: To Helm, to Grand Trunk Western 4/88
Note 14: To Helm, to Grand Trunk Western 10/87
Note 15: Wore Jenks blue in UP number series
Note 16: To Helm, to Grand Trunk Western 3/88
Note 17: To Helm, to Grand Trunk Western 11/87
Note 18: To Helm, to Grand Trunk Western 12/91
Note 19: To Helm, to Grand Trunk Western 9/87

EMD GP38-2   2,000 hp   20 units
TE = 66,800   WT = 267,200
Wheels = 40"   Fuel = 2,600
Engine: EMD 16-645E V-type 16-cylinder 2-cycle
Min Speed for TE = 12.0 mph
62:15 Gearing   65 mph Max
Retired 1/88, to lessor 1/88, to Helm/GTC

1st No	2nd No	3rd No	4th No	Built	Build#	Notes
MP-903	MP-2054	(UP-2380)	GTW-5713	09/72	72759-1	Note 5
MP-904:1	MP-2055	(UP-2381)	UP-1820	09/72	72759-2	Note 1
MP-905	MP-2056	(UP-2382)	GTW-5718	09/72	72759-3	Note 6
MP-906	MP-2057	(UP-2383)	GTW-5724	09/72	72759-4	Note 7
MP-907:1	MP-2058	UP-2384	UP-1821	09/72	72759-5	Note 1, 2, 3
MP-908	MP-2059	UP-2385	UP-1822	09/72	72759-6	Note 1, 2, 3
MP-909	MP-2060	UP-2060	(UP-2386)	10/72	72759-7	Note 8
MP-910	MP-2061	(UP-2387)	GTW-5719	10/72	72759-8	Note 9
MP-911	MP-2062	UP-2062	(UP-2388)	10/72	72759-9	Note 3, 10
MP-912	MP-2063	(UP-2389)	GTW-5722	10/72	72759-10	Note 11
MP-913	MP-2064	(UP-2390)	GTW-5720	10/72	72659-1	Note 12
MP-914	MP-2065	(UP-2391)	UP-1823	10/72	72659-2	Note 1
MP-915	MP-2066	(UP-2392)	GTW-5723	10/72	72659-3	Note 11
MP-916	MP-2067	(UP-2393)	GTW-5717	10/72	72659-4	Note 6
MP-917	MP-2068	UP-2068	(UP-2394)	10/72	72659-5	Note 3, 13
MP-918	MP-2069	(UP-2395)	UP-1824	10/72	72659-6	Note 1
MP-919	MP-2070	(UP-2396)	UP-1825	10/72	72659-7	Note 1
MP-920	MP-2071	(UP-2397)	UP-1826	10/72	72659-8	Note 1, 4
MP-921	MP-2072	(UP-2398)	UP-1827	10/72	72659-9	Note 1, 3
MP-922	MP-2073	(UP-2399)	UP-1828	10/72	72659-10	Note 1, 3

Note 1: To UP 2/89
Note 2: Wore MoPac number as HL
Note 3: Wore Jenks blue in UP number series
Note 4: Wore MP yellow in MoPac number series
Note 5: To Grand Trunk Western 6/88
Note 6: To Grand Trunk Western 9/88
Note 7: To Grand Trunk Western 1/89
Note 8: To Grand Trunk Western 7/88, r# GTW-5715
Note 9: To Grand Trunk Western 11/88
Note 10: To Grand Trunk Western 11/88, r# GTW-5721
Note 11: To Grand Trunk Western 12/88
Note 12: To Grand Trunk Western 10/88
Note 13: To Grand Trunk Western 8/88, r# GTW-5716

Below: Two brand new GP38-2's are ready for action in Alexandria, Louisiana. They have perhaps made only a run or two by this date, but soon enough their plows will be battered. They are both from the third GP38-2 order, an order for ten that resulted in there being 65 GP38-2's on MoPac's roster. The 918 ultimately went back to the lessor, was sold to Helm, and then wound up back on the UP as 1824. All this was a long ways off when the photographer tripped the shutter on October 20, 1972, capturing the new units at the beginning of their dynasty. *Glenn Anderson*

EMD GP38-2   2,000 hp   37 units
TE = 66,600   WT = 266,420
Wheels = 40"   Fuel = 2,600
Engine: EMD 16-645E V-type 16-cylinder 2-cycle
Min Speed for TE = 12.0 mph
62:15 Gearing   65 mph Max

1st No	2nd No	3rd No	Built	Build#	Notes
MP-923	MP-2074	UP-2074	01/73	71702-1	
MP-924	MP-2075	UP-2075	01/73	71702-2	
MP-925	MP-2076	UP-2076	01/73	71702-3	
MP-926	MP-2077	UP-2077	01/73	71702-4	
MP-927	MP-2078	UP-2078	01/73	71702-5	
MP-928	MP-2079	UP-2079	01/73	71702-6	
MP-929	MP-2080	UP-2080	01/73	71702-7	
MP-930	MP-2081	UP-2081	01/73	71702-8	Note 1
MP-931	MP-2082	UP-2082	01/73	71702-9	
MP-932	MP-2083	UP-2083	01/73	71702-10	
MP-933	MP-2084	UP-2084	02/73	71702-11	
MP-934	MP-2085	UP-2085	02/73	71702-12	
MP-935:2	MP-2086	UP-2086	02/73	71702-13	Note 2
MP-936:2	MP-2087	UP-2087	02/73	71702-14	
MP-937:2	MP-2088	UP-2088	02/73	71702-15	
MP-938:2	MP-2089	UP-2089	02/73	71702-16	
MP-939:2	MP-2090	UP-2090	02/73	71702-17	
MP-940:2	MP-2091	UP-2091	02/73	71702-18	
MP-941:2	MP-2092	UP-2092	02/73	71702-19	
MP-942:2	MP-2093	UP-2093	02/73	71702-20	
MP-943:2	MP-2094	UP-2094	03/73	71702-21	
MP-944:3	MP-2095	UP-2095	03/73	71702-22	Note 3
MP-945:3	MP-2096	UP-2096	03/73	71702-23	
MP-946:3	MP-2097	UP-2097	03/73	71702-24	Note 4
MP-947:2	MP-2098	UP-2098	03/73	71702-25	Note 3, 5
MP-948:2	MP-2099	UP-2099	03/73	71702-26	
MP-949:2	MP-2100	UP-2100	03/73	71702-27	
MP-950:2	MP-2101	UP-2101	05/73	71702-28	
MP-951:2	MP-2102	UP-2102	05/73	71702-29	
MP-952:2	MP-2103	UP-2103	05/73	71702-30	
MP-953:2	MP-2104	UP-2104	05/73	71702-31	Note 5
MP-954:2	MP-2105	UP-2105	05/73	71702-32	
MP-955:2	MP-2106	UP-2106	05/73	71702-33	
MP-956:2	MP-2107	UP-2107	05/73	71702-34	
MP-957:2	MP-2108	UP-2108	05/73	71702-35	
MP-958:2	MP-2109	UP-2109	05/73	71702-36	
MP-959:2	MP-2110	UP-2110	05/73	71702-37	

Note 1: Retired 12/93, T-L, to A&S, r# A&S-2000
Note 2: Retired 12/93, T-L, to A&S, r# A&S-2001
Note 3: Retired 12/93, T-L, to Montana Western
Note 4: Wrecked into Intracoastal Canal, Baton Rouge, LA, 9/17/73, rebuilt
Note 5: Wore MP yellow in MP number series

Above: The first part of 1973 saw the delivery of another 37 GP38-2's, quickly becoming the dominant type of B-B road power on the MoPac. In October, 1982, 2079 leads 2058 through the bridge over the Mississippi River at Memphis, Tennessee. The medium-horsepower non-turbocharged GP38-2 could perform almost any task on the system, from lowly yard jobs and local freight service to mainline through freights on the high iron. *Steve Forrest*

Below: Spotless GP38-2 is fresh from the builder on January 26, 1975 at Riverdale, Illinois. The 1974, 1975, and 1976 orders of GP38-2's were relatively small, 10, 12, and 5 units respectively. The 2127 is one of the 12 units delivered in January and February 1975. *Paul Hunnell photo, Dennis Schmidt collection*

Bottom: In 1977 the MoPac ordered 20 more GP38-2's bringing the total to 149. They came in October, and were the last GP38-2's until more were ordered almost three years later in 1980. The 2144 has some miles under her belt when photographed at Neff Yard in Kansas City, Missouri in September, 1984. *Mark Hall*

Below: The first order of GP38-2's to be delivered in the new scheme with the flying eagle buzz-saw came on-line in September and October, 1974, reflecting the latest image change of the era. The 2118 is at Memphis, Tennessee in December, 1980. It will wear UP yellow in a few years. *Lon Coone*

EMD GP38-2   2,000 hp   10 units
TE = 66,310   WT = 265,240
Wheels = 40"   Fuel = 2,600
Engine: EMD 16-645E V-type 16-cylinder 2-cycle
Min Speed for TE = 12.0 mph
62:15 Gearing   65 mph Max

1st No	2nd No	Built	Build#	Notes
MP-2111	UP-2111	09/74	73679-1	
MP-2112	UP-2112	09/74	73679-2	
MP-2113	UP-2113	09/74	73679-3	Wore MP yellow as MP-2113
MP-2114	UP-2114	09/74	73679-4	Wore MP yellow as MP-2114
MP-2115	UP-2115	09/74	73679-5	
MP-2116	UP-2116	09/74	73679-6	
MP-2117	UP-2117	09/74	73679-7	Wore MP yellow as MP-2117
MP-2118	UP-2118	09/74	73679-8	Wore MP yellow as MP-2118
MP-2119	UP-2119	09/74	73679-9	
MP-2120	UP-2120	10/74	73679-10	

EMD GP38-2   2,000 hp   12 units
TE = 66,180   WT = 264,720
Wheels = 40"   Fuel = 2,600
Engine: EMD 16-645E V-type 16-cylinder 2-cycle
Min Speed for TE = 12.0 mph
62:15 Gearing   65 mph Max

1st No	2nd No	Built	Build#	Notes
MP-2121	UP-2121	01/75	74689-1	
MP-2122	UP-2122	01/75	74689-2	NLR "block" lettering as UP-2122
MP-2123	UP-2123	01/75	74689-3	
MP-2124	UP-2124	01/75	74689-4	
MP-2125	UP-2125	01/75	74689-5	
MP-2126	UP-2126	01/75	74689-6	
MP-2127	UP-2127	01/75	74689-7	
MP-2128	UP-2128	01/75	74689-8	
MP-2129	UP-2129	01/75	74689-9	NLR "block" lettering as UP-2129
MP-2130	UP-2130	01/75	74689-10	NLR "block" lettering as UP-2130
MP-2131	UP-2131	01/75	74689-11	
MP-2132	UP-2132	02/75	74689-12	

EMD GP38-2   2,000 hp   5 units
TE = 66,530   WT = 266,120
Wheels = 40"   Fuel = 2,600
Engine: EMD 16-645E V-type 16-cylinder 2-cycle
Min Speed for TE = 12.0 mph
62:15 Gearing   65 mph Max

1st No	2nd No	Built	Build#	Notes
MP-2133	UP-2133	07/76	766004-1	
MP-2134	UP-2134	08/76	766004-2	
MP-2135	UP-2135	08/76	766004-3	
MP-2136	UP-2136	08/76	766004-4	NLR "block" lettering as UP-2136
MP-2137	UP-2137	08/76	766004-5	

Below: 2137 is a member of the smallest GP38-2 order, an order for only five units placed in mid-1976. The five units were delivered in July and August, and all survived until the UP merger and now work for their new parent. The unit is at Little Rock on March 6, 1977. *James Holder*

EMD GP38-2   2,000 hp   20 units
TE = 66,450   WT = 265,800
Wheels = 40"   Fuel = 2,600
Engine: EMD 16-645E V-type 16-cylinder 2-cycle
Min Speed for TE = 12.0 mph
62:15 Gearing   65 mph Max

1st No	2nd No	Built	Build#	Notes
MP-2138	UP-2138	10/77	776034-1	
MP-2139	UP-2139	10/77	776034-2	
MP-2140	UP-2140	10/77	776034-3	
MP-2141	UP-2141	10/77	776034-4	Wore MP yellow as MP-2141
MP-2142	UP-2142	10/77	776034-5	
MP-2143	UP-2143	10/77	776034-6	
MP-2144	UP-2144	10/77	776034-7	NLR "block" lettering as UP-2144
MP-2145	UP-2145	10/77	776034-8	
MP-2146	UP-2146	10/77	776034-9	
MP-2147	UP-2147	10/77	776034-10	
MP-2148	UP-2148	10/77	777035-1	
MP-2149	UP-2149	10/77	777035-2	
MP-2150	UP-2150	10/77	777035-3	
MP-2151	UP-2151	10/77	777035-4	
MP-2152	UP-2152	10/77	777035-5	
MP-2153	UP-2153	10/77	777035-6	
MP-2154	UP-2154	10/77	777035-7	
MP-2155	UP-2155	10/77	777035-8	NLR "block" lettering as UP-2155
MP-2156	UP-2156	10/77	777035-9	
MP-2157	UP-2157	10/77	777035-10	

EMD GP38-2   2,000 hp   40 units
TE = 68,875   WT = 275,500
Wheels = 40"   Fuel = 3,600
Engine: EMD 16-645E V-type 16-cylinder 2-cycle
Min Speed for TE = 12.0 mph
62:15 Gearing   65 mph Max

1st No	2nd No	Built	Builder #	Notes
MP-2158	UP-2158	01/80	787270-1	
MP-2159	UP-2159	01/80	787270-2	NLR "block" lettering as UP-2159
MP-2160	UP-2160	01/80	787270-3	Wore MP yellow as MP-2160
MP-2161	UP-2161	01/80	787270-4	Wore MP yellow as MP-2161
MP-2162	UP-2162	01/80	787270-5	Wore MP yellow as MP-2162
MP-2163	UP-2163	01/80	787270-6	
MP-2164	UP-2164	01/80	787270-7	
MP-2165	UP-2165	01/80	787270-8	NLR "block" lettering as UP-2165
MP-2166	UP-2166	01/80	787270-9	Wore MP yellow as MP-2166
MP-2167	UP-2167	01/80	787270-10	
MP-2168	UP-2168	01/80	787270-11	
MP-2169	UP-2169	01/80	787270-12	
MP-2170	UP-2170	01/80	787270-13	Wore MP yellow as MP-2170
MP-2171	UP-2171	01/80	787270-14	
MP-2172	UP-2172	01/80	787270-15	
MP-2173	UP-2173	01/80	787270-16	
MP-2174	UP-2174	01/80	787270-17	Wore MP yellow as MP-2174
MP-2175	UP-2175	01/80	787270-18	
MP-2176	UP-2176	01/80	787270-19	NLR "block" lettering as UP-2176
MP-2177	UP-2177	01/80	787270-20	
MP-2178	UP-2178	01/80	787270-21	
MP-2179	UP-2179	01/80	787270-22	NLR "block" lettering as UP-2179
MP-2180	UP-2180	01/80	787270-23	Wore MP yellow as MP-2180
MP-2181	UP-2181	01/80	787270-24	
MP-2182	UP-2182	01/80	787270-25	
MP-2183	UP-2183	01/80	787270-26	NLR "block" lettering as UP-2183
MP-2184	UP-2184	01/80	787270-27	
MP-2185	UP-2185	01/80	787270-28	
MP-2186	UP-2186	01/80	787270-29	
MP-2187	UP-2187	01/80	787270-30	Wore MP yellow as MP-2187
MP-2188	UP-2188	01/80	787270-31	
MP-2189	UP-2189	01/80	787270-32	
MP-2190	UP-2190	01/80	787270-33	
MP-2191	UP-2191	01/80	787270-34	
MP-2192	UP-2192	01/80	787270-35	Wore MP yellow as MP-2192
MP-2193	UP-2193	01/80	787270-36	
MP-2194	UP-2194	01/80	787270-37	Wore MP yellow as MP-2194
MP-2195	UP-2195	01/80	787270-38	
MP-2196	UP-2196	01/80	787270-39	NLR "block" lettering as UP-2196
MP-2197	UP-2197	02/80	787270-40	NLR "block" lettering as UP-2197

EMD GP38-2   2,000 hp   40 units
TE = 68,750   WT = 275,000
Wheels = 40"   Fuel = 3,600
Engine: EMD 16-645E V-type 16-cylinder 2-cycle
Min Speed for TE = 12.0 mph
62:15 Gearing   65 mph Max

1st No	2nd No	Built	Builder #	Notes
MP-2198	UP-2198	07/80	796323-1	Wore MP yellow as MP-2198
MP-2199	UP-2199	07/80	796323-2	
MP-2200	UP-2200	07/80	796323-3	NLR "block" lettering as UP-2200
MP-2201	UP-2201	07/80	796323-4	
MP-2202	UP-2202	07/80	796323-5	
MP-2203	UP-2203	07/80	796323-6	
MP-2204	UP-2204	07/80	796323-7	
MP-2205	UP-2205	07/80	796323-8	
MP-2206	UP-2206	07/80	796323-9	
MP-2207	UP-2207	07/80	796323-10	Wore MP yellow as MP-2207
MP-2208	UP-2208	07/80	796323-11	
MP-2209	UP-2209	07/80	796323-12	
MP-2210	UP-2210	07/80	796323-13	
MP-2211	UP-2211	07/80	796323-14	
MP-2212	UP-2212	07/80	796323-15	
MP-2213	UP-2213	07/80	796323-16	
MP-2214	UP-2214	07/80	796323-17	Wore MP yellow as MP-2214
MP-2215	UP-2215	07/80	796323-18	
MP-2216	UP-2216	07/80	796323-19	
MP-2217	UP-2217	07/80	796323-20	
MP-2218	UP-2218	07/80	796323-21	
MP-2219	UP-2219	07/80	796323-22	Wore MP yellow as MP-2219
MP-2220	UP-2220	08/80	796323-23	NLR "block" lettering as UP-2220
MP-2221	UP-2221	08/80	796323-24	
MP-2222	UP-2222	08/80	796323-25	
MP-2223	UP-2223	08/80	796323-26	
MP-2224	UP-2224	08/80	796323-27	
MP-2225	UP-2225	08/80	796323-28	NLR "block" lettering as UP-2225
MP-2226	UP-2226	08/80	796323-29	
MP-2227	UP-2227	08/80	796323-30	
MP-2228	UP-2228	08/80	796323-31	NLR "block" lettering as UP-2228
MP-2229	UP-2229	08/80	796323-32	NLR "block" lettering as UP-2229
MP-2230	UP-2230	08/80	796323-33	
MP-2231	UP-2231	08/80	796323-34	
MP-2232	UP-2232	08/80	796323-35	
MP-2233	UP-2233	08/80	796323-36	
MP-2234	UP-2234	08/80	796323-37	
MP-2235	UP-2235	08/80	796323-38	NLR "block" lettering as UP-2235
MP-2236	UP-2236	08/80	796323-39	
MP-2237	UP-2237	08/80	796323-40	

Below right: In the spring of 1981 the MoPac ordered 30 additional GP38-2's, on top of 92 that had come the year before, 52 of which were ex-Rock Island units. The 30 new units brought the total to 311 units, surpassing all previous models on MoPac's roster. The GP38-2 became the most abundant model on the MoPac for all time. The 2295 is at Dolton, Illinois on March 9, 1985. *Doug Edwards photo, Kevin EuDaly collection*

Below: 2232 is one unit of the summer, 1980 purchase of 40 GP38-2's. It is at St. Louis, Missouri on June 2, 1984. *Randy Keller*

EMD GP38-2   2,000 hp   52 units   TE = 65,500   WT = 262,000
Wheels = 40"   Fuel = 2,600
Engine: EMD 16-645E V-type 16-cylinder 2-cycle
Min Speed for TE = 12.0 mph
62:15 Gearing   65 mph Max

1st No	2nd No	3rd No	Built	Build#	Notes
CRI&P-4300	MP-2238	UP-2238	09/76	756136-1	
CRI&P-4301	MP-2239	UP-2239	09/76	756136-2	
CRI&P-4302	MP-2240	UP-2240	09/76	756136-3	Wore MP yellow
CRI&P-4303	MP-2241	UP-2241	09/76	756136-4	
CRI&P-4304	MP-2242	UP-2242	09/76	756136-5	
CRI&P-4305	MP-2243	UP-2243	09/76	756136-6	
CRI&P-4306	MP-2244	UP-2244	09/76	756136-7	
CRI&P-4307	MP-2245	UP-2245	09/76	756136-8	
CRI&P-4308	MP-2246	UP-2246	09/76	756136-9	
CRI&P-4309	MP-2247	UP-2247	09/76	756136-10	
CRI&P-4310	MP-2248	UP-2248	09/76	756136-11	
CRI&P-4311	MP-2249	UP-2249	09/76	756136-12	
CRI&P 4312	MP 2250:2	UP 2250	09/76	756136-13	
CRI&P-4313	MP-2251:2	UP-2251	09/76	756136-14	
CRI&P-4314	MP-2252:2	UP-2252	09/76	756136-15	
CRI&P-4315	MP-2253:2	UP-2253	09/76	757136-1	Wore MP yellow
CRI&P-4316	MP-2254:2	UP-2254	10/76	757136-2	
CRI&P-4317	MP-2255:2	UP-2255	10/76	757136-3	
CRI&P-4318	MP-2256:2	UP-2256	10/76	757136-4	
CRI&P-4319	MP-2257:2	UP-2257	10/76	757136-5	
CRI&P-4320	MP-2258:2	UP-2258	10/76	757136-6	
CRI&P-4321	MP-2259:2	UP-2259	10/76	757136-7	
CRI&P-4322	MP-2260:2	UP-2260	10/76	757136-8	
CRI&P-4323	MP-2261:2	UP-2261	10/76	757136-9	
CRI&P-4324	MP-2262:2	UP-2262	10/76	757136-10	Wore MP yellow
CRI&P-4325	MP-2263:2	UP-2263	10/76	757136-11	
CRI&P-4326	MP-2264:2	UP-2264	10/76	757136-12	Wore MP yellow
CRI&P-4327	MP-2265:2	UP-2265	10/76	757136-13	
CRI&P-4328	MP-2266:2	UP-2266	10/76	757136-14	
CRI&P-4329	MP-2267:2	UP-2267	10/76	757136-15	
CRI&P-4330	MP-2268:2	UP-2268	10/76	757136-16	
CRI&P-4331	MP-2269:2	UP-2269	10/76	757136-17	
CRI&P-4332	MP-2270:2	UP-2270	10/76	757136-18	
CRI&P-4333	MP-2271:2	UP-2271	11/76	757136-19	
CRI&P-4334	MP-2272:2	UP-2272	11/76	757136-20	Wore MP yellow
CRI&P-4335	MP-2273:2	UP-2273	11/76	757136-21	
CRI&P-4336	MP-2274:2	UP-2274	11/76	757136-22	
CRI&P-4337	MP-2275:2	UP-2275	11/76	757136-23	
CRI&P-4338	MP-2276:2	UP-2276	11/76	757136-24	
CRI&P-4339	MP-2277:2	UP-2277	11/76	757136-25	
CRI&P-4340	MP-2278:2	UP-2278	11/76	757136-26	
CRI&P-4341	MP-2279:2	UP-2279	11/76	757136-27	
CRI&P-4342	MP-2280:2	UP-2280	11/76	757136-28	
CRI&P-4343	MP-2281:2	UP-2281	11/76	757136-29	
CRI&P-4344	MP-2282:2	UP-2282	11/76	757136-30	
CRI&P-4345	MP-2283:2	UP-2283	11/76	757136-31	
CRI&P-4346	MP-2284:2	UP-2284	11/76	757136-32	Note 1
CRI&P-4347	MP-2285:2	UP-2285	11/76	757136-33	
CRI&P-4348	MP-2286:2	UP-2286	11/76	757136-34	
CRI&P-4349	MP-2287:2	UP-2287	11/76	757136-35	Wore MP yellow
CRI&P-4350	MP-2288:2	UP-2288	11/76	757136-36	
CRI&P-4351	MP-2289:2	UP-2289	11/76	757136-37	

Note 1: NLR "block" lettering as UP

EMD GP38-2   2,000 hp   30 units
TE = 68,810   WT = 275,250
Wheels = 40"   Fuel = 3,600
Engine: EMD 16-645E V-type 16-cylinder 2-cycle
Min Speed for TE = 12.0 mph
62:15 Gearing   65 mph Max

1st No	2nd No	Built	Build#	Notes
MP-2290:2	UP-2290	02/81	807047-1	
MP-2291:2	UP-2291	02/81	807047-2	
MP-2292:2	UP-2292	02/81	807047-3	
MP-2293:2	UP-2293	02/81	807047-4	NLR "block" lettering as UP-2293
MP-2294:2	UP-2294	02/81	807047-5	NLR "block" lettering as UP-2294
MP-2295:2	UP-2295	02/81	807047-6	NLR "block" lettering as UP-2295
MP-2296:2	UP-2296	02/81	807047-7	
MP-2297:2	UP-2297	02/81	807047-8	
MP-2298:2	UP-2298	02/81	807047-9	Wore MP yellow as MP-2298
MP-2299:2	UP-2299	02/81	807047-10	
MP-2300:2	UP-2300	02/81	807047-11	
MP-2301:2	UP-2301	02/81	807047-12	
MP-2302:2	UP-2302	02/81	807047-13	
MP-2303:2	UP-2303	02/81	807047-14	
MP-2304:2	UP-2304	02/81	807047-15	NLR "block" lettering as UP-2304
MP-2305:2	UP-2305	02/81	807047-16	
MP-2306:2	UP-2306	02/81	807047-17	Wore MP yellow as MP-2306
MP-2307:2	UP-2307	02/81	807047-18	Wore MP yellow as MP-2307
MP-2308:2	UP-2308	02/81	807047-19	Wore MP yellow as MP-2308
MP-2309:2	UP-2309	02/81	807047-20	
MP-2310:2	UP-2310	02/81	807047-21	
MP-2311:2	UP-2311	02/81	807047-22	
MP-2312:2	UP-2312	02/81	807047-23	Wore MP yellow as MP-2312
MP-2313:2	UP-2313	02/81	807047-24	Wore MP yellow as MP-2313
MP-2314:2	UP-2314	02/81	807047-25	
MP-2315:2	UP-2315	02/81	807047-26	
MP-2316:2	UP-2316	02/81	807047-27	
MP-2317:2	UP-2317	03/81	807047-28	
MP-2318:2	UP-2318	03/81	807047-29	
MP-2319:2	UP-2319	03/81	807047-30	

EMD GP38-2   2,000 hp   15 units
TE = 69,000   WT = 276,000
Wheels = 40"   Fuel = 3,600
Engine: EMD 16-645E V-type 16-cylinder 2-cycle
Min Speed for TE = 12.0 mph
62:15 Gearing   65 mph Max

1st No	2nd No	Built	Build#	Notes
MP-2320:2	UP-2320	07/81	807052-1	Wore MP yellow as MP-2320
MP-2321:2	UP-2321	07/81	807052-2	
MP-2322:2	UP-2322	07/81	807052-3	
MP-2323:2	UP-2323	07/81	807052-4	
MP-2324:2	UP-2324	07/81	807052-5	
MP-2325:2	UP-2325	07/81	807052-6	
MP-2326:2	UP-2326	07/81	807052-7	
MP-2327:2	UP-2327	07/81	807052-8	
MP-2328:2	UP-2328	07/81	807052-9	Wore MP yellow as MP-2328
MP-2329:2	UP-2329	07/81	807052-10	
MP-2330:2	UP-2330	07/81	807052-11	Wore MP yellow as MP-2330
MP-2331:2	UP-2331	07/81	807052-12	
MP-2332:2	UP-2332	07/81	807052-13	
MP-2333:2	UP-2333	08/81	807052-14	
MP-2334:2	UP-2334	08/81	807052-15	

GE U23B   2,250 hp   7 units
TE = 66,375   WT = 265,500
Wheels = 40"   Fuel = 3,250
Engine: GE FDL-12 V-type 12-cylinder 4-cycle Turbocharged
Min Speed for TE = 10.0 mph
74:18 Gearing   65 mph Max
AAR-B trucks

1st No	2nd No	3rd No	4th No	Built	Build#	Notes
MP-668	MP-2250:1	MP-4500	(UP-534)	01/73	38758	Note 1
MP-669	MP-2251:1	MP-4501:2	(UP-535)	01/73	38759	Note 2
MP-670	MP-2252:1	MP-4502:2	(UP-536)	01/73	38760	Note 3
MP-671	MP-2253:1	MP-4503:2	(UP-537)	01/73	38761	Note 4
MP-672	MP-2254:1	MP-4504:2	(UP-538)	01/73	38762	Note 5
MP-673	MP-2255:1	MP-4505:2	(UP-539)	01/73	38763	Note 6
MP-674	MP-2256:1	MP-4506:2	(UP-540)	02/73	38764	Note 7

Note 1: To NRE 12/88, to Central Michigan, r# CMGN-8903
Note 2: To NRE 12/88, to Central Michigan, r# CMGN-8904
Note 3: To NRE 12/88, to Central Michigan
Note 4: Wore Double-Eagles as MP-4503. Retired 3/88, T-I to GE 03/88 on Dash 8-40C's
Note 5: To NRE 12/88, to Central Michigan, r# CMGN-8905
Note 6: To NRE 12/88, to Central Michigan for parts
Note 7: Wore Double-Eagles as MP-2256. Rebuilt with EMD cab 11/75 as MP-2256, later MP-4506. To NRE 12/88, to Central Michigan, r# CMGN-8902

GE U23B   2,250 hp   11 units
TE = 66,875   WT = 267,500
Wheels = 40"   Fuel = 3,250
Engine: GE FDL-12 V-type 12-cylinder 4-cycle Turbocharged
Min Speed for TE = 10.0 mph
74:18 Gearing   65 mph Max
FB-2 (floating bolster) trucks

1st No	2nd No	3rd No	Built	Build#	Retired	Notes & Dispositions
MP-2257:1	MP-4507:2	UP-541	11/74	39905	03/90	Note 1
MP-2258:1	MP-4508:2	UP-542	11/74	39906	01/91	Note 2
MP-2259:1	MP-4509:2	(UP-543)	11/74	39907	01/91	Note 3
MP-2260:1	MP-4510:2	(UP-544)	11/74	39908	03/88	Note 4
MP-2261:1	MP-4511:2	UP-545	11/74	39909	01/91	Note 5
MP-2262:1	MP-4512:2	UP-546	11/74	39910	01/89	T-I to GE 8/89
MP-2263:1	MP-4513:2	UP-547	11/74	39911	01/91	Note 6
MP-2264:1	MP-4514:2	UP-548	11/74	39912	01/91	Note 7
MP-2265:1	MP-4515:2	(UP-549)	11/74	39913	01/91	Note 8
MP-2266:1	MP-4516:2	(UP-550)	11/74	39914	03/88	Note 9
MP-2267:1	MP-4517:2	UP-551	11/74	39915	05/90	Note 10

Note 1: To Southwest 4/90, scrapped
Note 2: To GATX 1/91, to NRE-542
Note 3: To GATX 1/91, to NRE-4509
Note 4: T-I to GE 3/88 on Dash 8-40C's
Note 5: To GATX 1/91, to NRE, to TUM 2/91
Note 6: To GATX 1/91, to NRE-547
Note 7: NLR "block" lettering as UP-548. To GATX 1/91, to NRE-548
Note 8: To GATX 1/91, to NRE-4515
Note 9: T-I to GE 6/88 on Dash 8-40C's
Note 10: To Azcon, Alton, IL, 5/90

Right: The final purchase of GP38-2's was delivered in July and August, 1981, an order that totaled 15 units and brought the GP38-2 total to its final number on the MoPac: 326. After this order the MoPac turned to higher horsepower B-Boats and GP50's for road freight service, and continued buying GP15's for branch and local duties. The 2327 has just been born, and has yet to run in revenue service, resting at Dolton, Illinois on July 29, 1981. *Ronald Plazzotta*

Opposite page bottom: The MoPac ordered U23B's five times between 1973 and 1977, ordering once each year. No two orders were for the same number of units, and in the end there were 39 U23B's purchased. 4518 is at North Little Rock on November 22, 1984, the first of an order for six of the medium-horsepower turbocharged GEs. *J Harlen Wilson*

GE U23B 2,250 hp 6 units
TE = 67,400   WT = 269,600
Wheels = 40"   Fuel = 3,250
Engine: GE FDL-12 V-type 12-cylinder 4-cycle Turbocharged
Min Speed for TE = 10.0 mph
74:18 Gearing   65 mph Max
FB-2 (floating bolster) trucks

1st No	2nd No	3rd No	Built	Build#	Retired	Notes & Dispositions
MP-2268:1	MP-4518:2	(UP-552)	03/75	40356	08/87	Note 1
MP-2269:1	MP-4519:2	(UP-553)	03/75	40357	08/87	Note 1
MP-2270:1	MP-4520:2	(UP-554)	03/75	40358	08/87	Note 1
MP-2271:1			03/75	40359	11/78	Note 2
MP-2272:1	MP-4521:2	(UP-555)	03/75	40360	03/88	Note 3
MP-2273:1	MP-4522:2	(UP-556)	03/75	40361	07/89	T-I to GE 1/90

Note 1: To Southwest 4/88, scrapped
Note 2: Wrecked in Texas 10/78, scrapped
Note 3: Rebuilt with EMD cab as MP-4521. T-I to GE 5/88, to Pielet 12/91, scrapped

GE U23B 2,250 hp 5 units
TE = 67,230   WT = 268,920
Wheels = 40"   Fuel = 3,250
Engine: GE FDL-12 V-type 12-cylinder 4-cycle Turbocharged
Min Speed for TE = 10.0 mph
74:18 Gearing   65 mph Max
FB-2 (floating bolster) trucks and snow plows

1st No	2nd No	3rd No	Built	Build#	Notes
MP-2274:1	MP-4523:2	UP-557	06/76	40920	
MP-2275:1	MP-4524:2	UP-558	06/76	40921	
MP-2276:1	MP-4525:2	UP-559	06/76	40922	Note 1
MP-2277:1	MP-4526:2	UP-560	06/76	40923	
MP-2278:1	MP-4527:2	UP-561	06/76	40924	NLR "block" lettering as UP-561

Note 1: Retired 5/90, to Azcon, Alton, IL, 10/91

Below: The U23B like the U30C was never purchased in any large quantity. The second order was for 11 units, resulting in 18 U23B's on the roster. U23B 2260 is not quite five years old, at Dolton, Illinois on September 23, 1979.
George Horna photo, Gary Zuters collection

GE U23B 2,250 hp 10 units
TE = 67,100   WT = 268,400
Wheels = 40"   Fuel = 3,250
Engine: GE FDL-12 V-type 12-cylinder 4-cycle Turbocharged
Min Speed for TE = 10.0 mph
74:18 Gearing   65 mph Max
FB-2 (floating bolster) trucks
Retired 8/89, all but 571 T-I to GE 8/89

1st No	2nd No	3rd No	Built	Build#	Notes & Dispositions
MP-2279:1	MP-4528	(UP-562)	01/77	41523	Note 1
MP-2280:1	MP-4529	UP-563	01/77	41524	
MP-2281:1	MP-4530	(UP-564)	01/77	41525	
MP-2282:1	MP-4531	UP-565	02/77	41526	Note 2
MP-2283:1	MP-4532	UP-566	02/77	41527	
MP-2284:1	MP-4533	(UP-567)	02/77	41528	
MP-2285:1	MP-4534	UP-568	02/77	41529	Note 3
MP-2286:1	MP-4535	UP-569	02/77	41530	Note 4
MP-2287:1	MP-4536	UP-570	02/77	41531	
MP-2288:1	MP-4537	UP-571	02/77	41532	To Azcon, Alton, IL, 10/91

Note 1: Rebuilt with EMD cab as MP-4528
Note 2: Rebuilt with EMD cab as MP-2282, later MP-4531
Note 3: Rebuilt with EMD cab as MP-4534
Note 4: To RS as Super 7-23B 2/91, r# RS-52

EMD GP15-1 1,500 hp 20 units
TE = 64,210   WT = 256,840
Wheels = 40"   Fuel = 2,400
Engine: EMD 12-645E V-type 12-cylinder 2-cycle
Min Speed for TE = 9.6 mph
62:15 Gearing   65 mph Max

1st No	2nd No	3rd No	Built	Builder #	Notes
MP-1555	UP-1555		06/76	757138-1	
MP-1556	UP-1556		06/76	757138-2	
MP-1557	UP-1557		06/76	757138-3	
MP-1558	UP-1558		07/76	757138-4	
MP-1559	UP-1559		07/76	757138-5	
MP-1560	UP-1560		07/76	757138-6	Wore MP yellow as MP-1560
MP-1561	UP-1561		07/76	757138-7	
MP-1562	UP-1562		07/76	757138-8	
MP-1563	UP-1563		07/76	757138-9	
MP-1564	UP-1564		07/76	757138-10	
MP-1565	UP-1565		07/76	757138-11	
MP-1566	UP-1566		07/76	757138-12	
MP-1567	UP-1567		07/76	757138-13	Wore MP yellow as MP-1567
MP-1568	UP-1568		07/76	757138-14	
MP-1569	UP-1569		07/76	757138-15	
C&EI-1570	MP-1570	UP-1570	07/76	757138-16	
C&EI-1571	MP-1571	UP-1571	07/76	757138-17	Wore MP yellow as MP-1571
C&EI-1572	MP-1572	UP-1572	07/76	757138-18	NLR "block" lettering as UP-1572
C&EI-1573	MP-1573	UP-1573	07/76	757138-19	
C&EI-1574	MP-1574	UP-1574	07/76	757138-20	

EMD GP15-1 1,500 hp 15 units
TE = 65,270   WT = 261,080
Wheels = 40"   Fuel = 2,400
Engine: EMD 12-645E V-type 12-cylinder 2-cycle
Min Speed for TE = 9.6 mph
62:15 Gearing   65 mph Max

1st No	2nd No	Built	Builder #	Notes
MP-1575	UP-1575	12/76	767037-1	NLR "block" lettering as UP-1575
MP-1576	UP-1576	12/76	767037-2	Wore MP yellow as MP-1576
MP-1577	UP-1577	12/76	767037-3	Wore MP yellow as MP-1577
MP-1578	UP-1578	12/76	767037-4	
MP-1579	UP-1579	12/76	767037-5	
MP-1580	UP-1580	12/76	767037-6	Wore MP yellow as MP-1580
MP-1581	UP-1581	12/76	767037-7	
MP-1582	UP-1582	12/76	767037-8	
MP-1583	UP-1583	12/76	767037-9	
MP-1584	UP-1584	12/76	767037-10	NLR "block" lettering as UP-1584
MP-1585	UP-1585	12/76	767037-11	NLR "block" lettering as UP-1585
MP-1586	UP-1586	12/76	767037-12	
MP-1587	UP-1587	12/76	767037-13	NLR "block" lettering as UP-1587
MP-1588	UP-1588	12/76	767037-14	Wore MP yellow as MP-1588
MP-1589	UP-1589	12/76	767037-15	

EMD GP15-1 1,500 hp 25 units
TE = 65,490 WT = 261,960
Wheels = 40" Fuel = 2,400
Engine: EMD 12-645E V-type 12-cylinder 2-cycle
Min Speed for TE = 9.6 mph
62:15 Gearing 65 mph Max

1st No	2nd No	Built	Builder #	Notes
MP-1590	UP-1590	07/77	767038-1	Wore MP yellow as MP-1590
MP-1591	UP-1591	07/77	767038-2	
MP-1592	UP-1592	07/77	767038-3	NLR "block" lettering as UP-1592
MP-1593	UP-1593	07/77	767038-4	
MP-1594	UP-1594	07/77	767038-5	
MP-1595	UP-1595	07/77	767038-6	Wore MP yellow as MP-1595
MP-1596	UP-1596	07/77	767038-7	Wore MP yellow as MP-1596
MP-1597	UP-1597	07/77	767038-8	
MP-1598	UP-1598	07/77	767038-9	
MP-1599	UP-1599	07/77	767038-10	
MP-1600:2	UP-1600	07/77	767038-11	Wore MP yellow as MP-1600
MP-1601:2	UP-1601	07/77	767038-12	NLR "block" lettering as UP-1601
MP-1602:2	UP-1602	07/77	767038-13	
MP-1603:2	UP-1603	07/77	767038-14	
MP-1604:2	UP-1604	07/77	767038-15	
MP-1605:2	UP-1605	07/77	767038-16	
MP-1606:2	UP-1606	07/77	767038-17	
MP-1607:2	UP-1607	07/77	767038-18	
MP-1608:2	UP-1608	07/77	767038-19	
MP-1609:2	UP-1609	07/77	767038-20	
MP-1610:2	UP-1610	07/77	767038-21	
MP-1611:2	UP-1611	07/77	767038-22	
MP-1612:2	UP-1612	07/77	767038-23	
MP-1613:2	UP-1613	07/77	767038-24	
MP-1614:2	UP-1614	07/77	767038-25	NLR "block" lettering as UP-1614

EMD GP15-1 1,500 hp 30 units
TE = 65,450 WT = 261,800
Wheels = 40" Fuel = 2,400
Engine: EMD 12-645E V-type 12-cylinder 2-cycle
Min Speed for TE = 9.6 mph
62:15 Gearing 65 mph Max

1st No	2nd No	Built	Builder #	Notes
MP-1615:2	UP-1615	09/79	787183-1	
MP-1616:2	UP-1616	09/79	787183-2	
MP-1617:2	UP-1617	09/79	787183-3	
MP-1618:2	UP-1618	09/79	787183-4	
MP-1619:2	UP-1619	09/79	787183-5	Wore MP yellow as MP-1619
MP-1620:2	UP-1620	09/79	787183-6	Wore MP yellow as MP-1620
MP-1621:2	UP-1621	09/79	787183-7	Wore MP yellow as MP-1621. Wore small red eagle buzz-saw on nose as MP-1621 in yellow
MP-1622:2	UP-1622	09/79	787183-8	
MP-1623:2	UP-1623	09/79	787183-9	
MP-1624:2	UP-1624	09/79	787183-10	
MP-1625:2	UP-1625	09/79	787183-11	NLR "block" lettering as UP-1625
MP-1626:2	UP-1626	09/79	787183-12	
MP-1627:2	UP-1627	09/79	787183-13	
MP-1628:2	UP-1628	10/79	787183-14	Wore MP yellow as MP-1628
MP-1629:2	UP-1629	10/79	787183-15	
MP-1630:2	UP-1630	10/79	787183-16	
MP-1631:2	UP-1631	10/79	787183-17	NLR "block" lettering as UP-1631
MP-1632:2	UP-1632	09/79	787183-18	
MP-1633:2	UP-1633	10/79	787183-19	
MP-1634:2	UP-1634	10/79	787183-20	
MP-1635:2	UP-1635	11/79	787183-21	Wore MP yellow as MP-1635
MP-1636:2	UP-1636	11/79	787183-22	
MP-1637	UP-1637	11/79	787183-23	NLR "block" lettering as UP-1637
MP-1638	UP-1638	11/79	787183-24	NLR "block" lettering as UP-1638
MP-1639:2	UP-1639	11/79	787183-25	
MP-1640	UP-1640	11/79	787183-26	NLR "block" lettering as UP-1640
MP-1641:2	UP-1641	11/79	787183-27	NLR "block" lettering as UP-1641
MP-1642:2	UP-1642	11/79	787183-28	Wore MP yellow as MP-1642
MP-1643:2	UP-1643	11/79	787183-29	
MP-1644:2	UP-1644	11/79	787183-30	Wore MP yellow as MP-1644

EMD GP15-1 1,500 hp 20 units
TE = 65,290 WT = 261,150
Wheels = 40" Fuel = 2,400
Engine: EMD 12-645E V-type 12-cylinder 2-cycle
Min Speed for TE = 9.6 mph
62:15 Gearing 65 mph Max

1st No	2nd No	Built	Builder #	Notes
MP-1645:2	UP-1645	08/81	807019-1	Wore MP yellow as MP-1645
MP-1646:2	UP-1646	08/81	807019-2	
MP-1647:2	UP-1647	08/81	807019-3	
MP-1648:2	UP-1648	08/81	807019-4	
MP-1649:2	UP-1649	08/81	807019-5	NLR "block" lettering as UP-1649
MP-1650:2	UP-1650	08/81	807019-6	Wore MP yellow as MP-1650
MP-1651:2	UP-1651	08/81	807019-7	Wore MP yellow as MP-1651
MP-1652:2	UP-1652	08/81	807019-8	
MP-1653:2	UP-1653	08/81	807019-9	
MP-1654:2	UP-1654	08/81	807019-10	NLR "block" lettering as UP-1654
MP-1655:2	UP-1655	08/81	807019-11	Wore MP yellow as MP-1655
MP-1656:2	UP-1656	08/81	807019-12	
MP-1657:2	UP-1657	08/81	807019-13	
MP-1658:2	UP-1658	08/81	807019-14	
MP-1659:2	UP-1659	08/81	807019-15	
MP-1660:2	UP-1660	08/81	807019-16	
MP-1661:2	UP-1661	08/81	807019-17	
MP-1662:2	UP-1662	08/81	807019-18	NLR "block" lettering as UP-1662
MP-1663:2	UP-1663	08/81	807019-19	NLR "block" lettering as UP-1663
MP-1664:2	UP-1664	08/81	807019-20	NLR "block" lettering as UP-1664

Above: The smallest order for U23B's came in 1976, when five were added to the roster, 2274-2278. All but the first order came on the FB-2 trucks - GE's classic floating bolster. The middle unit of the five poses at Houston, Texas in September, 1979. *Dave Beach*

Below: The 1586, resting in the sun at Fort Worth, Texas on September 19, 1982, was part of the third order for GP15-1's. The 1,500 horsepower of the B-B unit is equivalent to the GP7's that were traded in for it. *Bill Phillips photo, Kevin EuDaly collection*

EMD GP15-1   1,500 hp   50 units
TE = 65,090   WT = 260,350
Wheels = 40"   Fuel = 2,400
Engine: EMD 12-645E V-type 12-cylinder 2-cycle
Min Speed for TE = 9.6 mph
62:15 Gearing   65 mph Max

1st No	2nd No	Built	Builder #	Notes
MP-1665:2	UP-1665	02/82	817017-1	NLR "block" lettering as UP-1665
MP-1666:2	UP-1666	02/82	817017-2	
MP-1667:2	UP-1667	02/82	817017-3	
MP-1668:2	UP-1668	02/82	817017-4	
MP-1669:2	UP-1669	02/82	817017-5	
MP-1670:2	UP-1670	02/82	817017-6	
MP-1671:2	UP-1671	02/82	817017-7	NLR "block" lettering as UP-1671
MP-1672:2	UP-1672	02/82	817017-8	
MP-1673:2	UP-1673	02/82	817017-9	NLR "block" lettering as UP-1673
MP-1674:2	UP-1674	02/82	817017-10	
MP-1675:2	UP-1675	02/82	817017-11	
MP-1676	UP 1676	02/82	817017 12	
MP-1677:2	UP-1677	02/82	817017-13	
MP-1678:2	UP-1678	02/82	817017-14	NLR "block" lettering as UP-1678
MP-1679:2	UP-1679	02/82	817017-15	
MP-1680:2	UP-1680	02/82	817017-16	
MP-1681:2	UP-1681	02/82	817017-17	
MP-1682:2	UP-1682	02/82	817017-18	
MP-1683:2	UP-1683	02/82	817017-19	
MP-1684:2	UP-1684	02/82	817017-20	
MP-1685:2	UP-1685	02/82	817017-21	
MP-1686:2	UP-1686	02/82	817017-22	
MP-1687:2	UP-1687	02/82	817017-23	
MP-1688	UP-1688	02/82	817017-24	
MP-1689	UP-1689	02/82	817017-25	Wore MP yellow as MP-1689
MP-1690	UP-1690	02/82	817017-26	Wore MP yellow as MP-1690 (switcher size lettering)
MP-1691	UP-1691	02/82	817017-27	
MP-1692	UP-1692	02/82	817017-28	
MP-1693	UP-1693	02/82	817017-29	Wore MP yellow as MP-1693
MP-1694	UP-1694	02/82	817017-30	Wore MP yellow as MP-1694
MP-1695	UP-1695	03/82	817017-31	
MP-1696	UP-1696	03/82	817017-32	NLR "block" lettering as UP-1696
MP-1697:2	UP-1697	03/82	817017-33	
MP-1698:2	UP-1698	03/82	817017-34	
MP-1699:2	UP-1699	03/82	817017-35	
MP-1700:2	UP-1700	03/82	817017-36	
MP-1701:2	UP-1701	03/82	817017-37	
MP-1702:2	UP-1702	03/82	817017-38	Wore MP yellow as MP-1702
MP-1703:2	UP-1703	03/82	817017-39	
MP-1704:2	UP-1704	03/82	817017-40	
MP-1705:2	UP-1705	03/82	817035-1	
MP-1706:2	UP-1706	03/82	817035-2	Wore MP yellow as MP-1706
MP-1707:2	UP-1707	03/82	817035-3	
MP-1708:2	UP-1708	03/82	817035-4	Wore MP yellow as MP-1708
MP-1709:2	UP-1709	03/82	817035-5	
MP-1710:2	UP-1710	03/82	817035-6	
MP-1711:2	UP-1711	03/82	817035-7	
MP-1712:2	UP-1712	04/82	817035-8	Wore MP yellow as MP-1712
MP-1713:2	UP-1713	04/82	817035-9	
MP-1714:2	UP-1714	04/82	817035-10	NLR "block" lettering as UP-1714

EMD GP15AC   1,500 hp   30 units
TE = 65,090   WT = 260,350
Wheels = 40"   Fuel = 2,400
Engine: EMD 12-645E V-type 12-cylinder 2-cycle
Min Speed for TE = 9.6 mph
62:15 Gearing   65 mph Max

1st No	2nd No	Built	Builder #	Notes
MP-1715:2	UP-1715	11/82	827016-1	NLR "block" lettering as UP-1715
MP-1716:2	UP-1716	11/82	827016-2	
MP-1717:2	UP-1717	11/82	827016-3	NLR "block" lettering as UP-1717
MP-1718:2	UP-1718	11/82	827016-4	
MP-1719:2	UP-1719	11/82	827016-5	
MP-1720:2	UP-1720	11/82	827016-6	NLR "block" lettering as UP-1720
MP-1721:2	UP-1721	11/82	827016-7	
MP-1722:2	UP-1722	11/82	827016-8	
MP-1723:2	UP-1723	11/82	827016-9	
MP-1724:2	UP-1724	11/82	827016-10	
MP-1725:2	UP-1725	11/82	827016-11	
MP-1726:2	UP-1726	11/82	827016-12	
MP-1727:2	UP-1727	12/82	827016-13	
MP-1728:2	UP-1728	12/82	827016-14	
MP-1729:2	UP-1729	12/82	827016-15	
MP-1730:2	UP-1730	12/82	827016-16	Wore MP yellow as MP-1730
MP-1731:2	UP-1731	12/82	827016-17	NLR "block" lettering as UP-1731
MP-1732:2	UP-1732	12/82	827016-18	
MP-1733:2	UP-1733	12/82	827016-19	
MP-1734:2	UP-1734	12/82	827016-20	
MP-1735:2	UP-1735	12/82	827016-21	
MP-1736:2	UP-1736	12/82	827016-22	
MP-1737:2	UP-1737	12/82	827016-23	NLR "block" lettering as UP-1737
MP-1738:2	UP-1738	12/82	827016-24	
MP-1739:2	UP-1739	12/82	827016-25	Wore MP yellow as MP-1739
MP-1740:2	UP-1740	12/82	827016-26	
MP-1741:2	UP-1741	12/82	827016-27	
MP-1742:2	UP-1742	12/82	827016-28	
MP-1743:2	UP-1743	12/82	827016-29	
MP-1744:2	UP-1744	12/82	827016-30	Wore MP yellow as MP-1744

Above right: The 1977 GP15-1 order was for 25 units, 1590-1614. The 1611 is at Kansas City, Kansas at the Quindaro Yard in Fairfax on November 14, 1990, long in the employ of the UP. *James DuBose photo, Kevin EuDaly collection*

Right: The final order for GP15's was for 30 AC units, GP15AC's in EMD parlance. The AC alternator is an indication that the geep fleet that was being traded in on the GP15's was gone. These units did not utilize anything from the old geeps. 1742 idles quietly on November 11, 1984. *Kevin EuDaly collection*

EMD
SD40-2
"SD40-2c"

The SD40-2 was the successor to the SD40 in the EMD catalog, and turned out to be the standard high-horsepower C-C roadswitcher of the late 1970's and early 1980's. Based on the 645E3 power plant, the 3,000 horsepower 16-cylinder SD40-2 in many ways represented the optimum road unit - lots of power, not too slippery, and low maintenance costs. It was the optimum road unit of that era, and came very close to matching the GP9 production total. In fact, if the 310 SD40T-2 tunnel motors bought by the Rio Grande and the Southern Pacific are added to the SD40-2 total, the SD40-2 outsold the GP9 by ten units, making it the most popular diesel model of all time, and probably for all eternity. One of the most significant features that functionally changed the SD40-2 from its pre-Dash 2 equivalent was the HT-C truck (High Traction C-C). It was a significant change from the previous C-C truck under the SD40's.

Two orders went through to EMD, the first for 20 SD40-2's and the second for an additional five, numbered immediately above the existing SD40's. The additional five came first (MP-790-794) followed by the other 20 (MP-795-814). They were delivered in August and September, 1973. Before the year was out, the T&P was also getting SD40-2's, and though they were supposed to be numbered as part of the MoPac fleet, one number was accidentally omitted - the 815 was never built. The 24 new units (T&P-816-839) were delivered in December, 1973 and January, 1974.

They were delivered side by side with another order, six U30C's for the T&P (T&P-3329-3334), the final U30C purchase. The MoPac got 11 more SD40-2's in February, 1974 (MP-3139-3149) and the C&EI also got SD40-2's in 1974. These came in February and March and amounted to 14 units (C&EI-3150-3163). The SD40-2 was quickly becoming one of the more prevalent units on the MoPac, with 74 now on the MoPac's roster.

1975 brought more of the same, GP38-2's in January, and in February and March 38 more SD40-2's arrived on the property (MP-3164-

3201), and this model was becoming the standard road freight power, with 112 of the big SD40-2's now on the roster (along with the previous 90 SD40's). Also in March came six more GE U23B's (MP-2268-2273) and in addition to the MP15DC's that came in February and March, August saw the final group of units for 1975 in the form of 14 SD40-2's (MP-3202-3215).

Besides U23B's and GP15-1's, the two other models for 1976 both came from EMD, more GP38-2's for medium roadswitcher duties and SD40-2's for heavy road haul service. The GP38-2 order was for only five units (MP-2133-2137). The SD40-2 order was a step in a different direction; the units were ordered with dynamic brakes, one of the only groups of MoPac engines so equipped. In fact, they were the first MoPac order that had dynamic brakes, though a number of T&P and C&EI units were purchased with dynamics. They were ordered essentially matching Burlington Northern specifications and arrived in two groups.

The first order was for five units (MP-3216:1-3220:1) and the second was for 15 units (MP-3221:1-3235:1). These units were

Right: SD40-2 3260 leads sister 3308 through Kirkwood on a partly cloudy May 31, 1987. By the time 3260 was ordered and on the property, there were 176 SD40-2's on the MoPac without dynamic brakes, and another 54 with dynamics. The group that 3260 was part of pushed the SD40-2 into second place on the all-time MoPac diesel roster for quantity, and easily resulted in the SD40-2 being MoPac's most popular C-C. *Scott Muskopf*

Opposite page: Two faces of EMD line up side by side at San Antonio, Texas on December 1, 1984. On the left is SD40 3082, one of 90 on MoPac's roster, and on the right is SD40-2 3294, a five-year veteran by this time. 3294 was part of an order for 10 SD40-2's that were built in July, 1979, one of five orders for SD40-2's that year. Two of the five orders were for "SD40-2c's," which put 34 of the coal units on the railroad. *Curtis Wagner*

Below: SD40-2 3180 leads an SD40 on a mixed freight at Texarkana, Arkansas in April, 1984. The 3180 was in the fifth order for SD40-2's, an order for 38 units that arrived in February and March, 1975. After the order was on the property there were 112 SD40-2's in MoPac's employ. *Paul DeLuca*

Locomotive Assignments

The idea of locomotive assignments goes back almost to the very beginning of railroading in America. In the very early steam years, locomotives were built one at a time, and each steamer was unique in and of itself, even though it might be very similar to other steamers much like it. The steam engine was a machine that lended itself to the whims of any particular shop foreman, and could be re-plumbed with about anything that would fit in the necessary space.

Later, as Class I railroads developed fleets of engines, a class would be built to the same specifications. Though these were very nearly identical, there were often minor differences between units of the same class. Steam power tended to be assigned to shops according to where a particular class was needed. Road freight power would be assigned to shops near the major terminals where these engines were serviced.

Local freight power, on the other hand, wound up assigned for maintenance at the nearest facility that could accomplish the routine maintenance required. There were often sections of the railroad where a particular class would never be seen, because its intended service was not applicable. High speed, large-drivered, passenger engines would never be seen up the branches in the coal fields of southern Illinois, for example. Many of the branch engines would only be seen on their branch line territory except for the occasional trip into the larger terminal for maintenance or repair.

When the diesel came along, nearly all railroads assigned them to a particular terminal, mostly out of habit, since that's what they'd always done with the steam power. The MoPac was no exception, and nearly from day one for the diesel, the MoPac assigned each diesel unit to a particular maintenance and repair facility. As the diesel fleet progressed, the motive power from a particular builder would be assigned to a shop that specialized in that builder's engines. This was originally contrived as a cost-cutting measure, but was also driven by the desire to carry less inventory at each major shop. It was a logical progression.

The MoPac always assigned their diesel fleet to particular shops. For the photographer or diesel spotter at trackside in recent years, this would become apparent when standing at South Dupo south of St. Louis as opposed to Harlingen in southern Texas. At South Dupo, a relatively high percentage of the mainline trains were powered by big GEs, a direct result of the fact that the entire GE fleet was assigned to either Little Rock or St. Louis. At Harlingen, a GE was a much more rare sighting. After UP took over, the B-Boats all wound up in Texas and Louisiana, a direct result of moving their shop assignments.

At the end of the MoPac, locomotives were assigned to one of five major shops for maintenance and repair. These were, in order of the number of units assigned, Fort Worth, North Little Rock, Kansas City, St. Louis, and finally Houston. An important deviation from shop assignments would also occur when a unit was significantly damaged. Certain types of repair were only done at one or maybe two of the main shops. Most of the major wreck repair, for example, was done at North Little Rock, so almost anything could be seen there.

The following tabulation is a list of locomotive models and their respective quantities that were assigned to the five major shops on the MoPac system as of June 23, 1983.

Fort Worth - 467 assigned units
(415 road units and 52 switchers)

Road:		Switchers:	
GP15-1	35 units	MP15DC	15 units
GP18	36 units	SW9	12 units
GP35	12 units	SW1200	20 units
GP35m	2 units	SL1 slug	5 units
GP38-2	118 units		
SD40-2	182 units		
GP50	30 units		

North Little Rock - 430 assigned units
(372 road units and 58 switchers)

Road:		Switchers:	
SD40	90 units	MP15DC	24 units
SD40-2	50 units	SW1500	1 unit
SD40-2c	20 units	SW1200	28 units
GP15-1	15 units	SL1 slugs	5 units
GP18	37 units		
GP28	2 units		
GP38	6 units		
GP38-2	73 units		
GP35	23 units		
GP35m	16 units		
B23-7	40 units		

Kansas City - 249 assigned units
(194 road units and 55 switchers)

Road:		Switchers:	
GP15-1	60 units	MP15DC	8 units
GP38-2	80 units	SW9	11 units
SD40-2c	54 units	SW1200	30 units
		SL1 slugs	6 units

St. Louis - 242 assigned units
(203 road units and 39 switchers)

Road:		Switchers:	
GP15-1	30 units	MP15DC	8 units
U23B	38 units	SW1200	27 units
B23-7	45 units	SL1 slugs	4 units
U30C	35 units		
B30-7A	55 units		

Houston - 201 assigned units
(149 road units and 52 switchers)

Road:		Switchers:	
GP15-1	50 units	MP15DC	7 units
GP18	44 units	SW9	5 units
GP38-2	55 units	SW1200	34 units
		SW1500	3 units
		SL1 slugs	3 units

It is interesting that only the GP15-1 had units of that model assigned to all the shops, while all the GEs were only assigned to two shops, with all U30C's, U23B's and B30-7A's at St. Louis. In the switcher fleet, all shops carried responsibilities for MP15DC's, SW1200's, and slugs, an opposing trend to the road freight power.

Left: SD40-2 3208 is north of Aldine, Texas on February 10, 1980. The unit was one of 182 SD40-2's assigned to Fort Worth, Texas. *George Hamlin*

Opposite page: "SD40-2c" 6066 blasts out of the east portal of the tunnel at West Labadie, Missouri like a blowtorch on April 23, 1985 leading SD40-2 3249 and GP50 3528. The train is roaring up the grade to Gray Summit, where it will sail through another double-track bore on its way to St. Louis. *Kevin EuDaly*

numbered above existing SD40-2's but were designated as "SD40-2c" by the MoPac, the "c" symbolizing the service for which they were intended - coal. They were purchased to run in unit coal train service to the Powder River Basin in Wyoming, a service for which everyone else used units with dynamic brakes. This made these units compatible with the other fleets,

Opposite page top: 3173 and two siblings from EMD are rolling through Memphis, Tennessee in October, 1982. The UP inherited the 3173, and later sold it to Grand Trunk Western, where it became their 5930. It wears MoPac blue no more. *Steve Forrest*

Opposite page bottom: SD40-2 3161 leads a GP15-1 and another SD40-2 across the deck bridge at Momence, Illinois with the CH train. The lead unit wears the double-eagle paint scheme, with both a large turbocharger eagle and the flying eagle buzz-saw under the cab window. It is one of the ex-C&EI SD40-2's, of which eight wore the double-eagle scheme. *Paul Meyer*

Below: Another double-eagle, 3092, splits the signals south of Watseka, Illinois in August, 1983. There were a total of 14 SD40-2's that wore the unique scheme. The 3092 is the lowest numbered SD40-2 double-eagle. *Paul Meyer*

including the Burlington Northern, the UP, and the Chicago & North Western, who were accessing the Powder River Basin. They also had a headlight package that was unique on the MoPac, with headlights between the number boards as well as in the low nose on the short hood. Their 3200-series numbers would be short lived, as later purchase decisions would result in a renumbering to keep them separate from their non-dynamic brake equipped brethren.

In mid-1978, after the initial B-Boat order, the MoPac again bolstered their six-axle fleet by adding 50 non-dynamic brake equipped SD40-2's (MP-3216:2-3235:2 and MP-3236-3265) in two consecutive orders. The first order was for 36 units, the first 20 of which were numbered MP-3216:2-3235:2 right on top of the "SD40-2c's" numbers (MP-3216:1-3235:1). The "SD40-2c's" were consequently renumbered MP-6000-6019, isolating them from the other SD40-2's and making room for the new units. The two orders were built sequentially, and were delivered in August and September, 1978.

The orders in 1979 again only added more units of models already on the roster. In May and June another group of SD40-2's were added (MP-3266-3291). This order of 26 units brought the SD40-2 total to 202 units on the roster without dynamic brakes and an additional 20 with dynamic brakes. Right after the non-dynamic brake equipped SD40-2 order was an-

other order for SD40-2's, this time adding 30 additional units with dynamic brakes for coal service (MP-6020-6049), which brought the SD40-2c total to 50.

EMD's next order from the MoPac was another group of non-dynamic brake equipped SD40-2's, this time 10 units (MP-3292-3301). This group forced a renumbering of the U30C fleet into the 2900-series from the 3300-number series they were in at the time. The MoPac was fast becoming the owner of a very large fleet of SD40-2's, and added yet another four units in June, 1979 (MP-6050-6053), obviously dynamic brake equipped since they were numbered in the 6000-series. The last batch of EMD C-C's for 1979 came in December, another 10 non-dynamic brake equipped SD40-2's (MP-3302-3311).

In April, 1980 two final groups of SD40-2's were delivered, 10 without dynamic brakes (MP-3312-3321) and 20 with dynamic brakes (SD40-2c's) (MP-6054-6073). This brought the total SD40-2 count to 306, 232 without dynamic brakes and 74 with the dynamics for coal service. As a general group, the SD40 type (SD40, SD40-2, and SD40-2c) was only outnumbered on the MoPac by the geeps (GP7, GP9, and GP18) by a margin of 483 to 396. F-units (FT, F3, FP7, "F5," and F7) fall third on the MoPac's all-time roster with 333 units, edging out GP38 types (GP38 and GP38-2) by a single unit.

Opposite page top: SD40-2 3167 leads GP38 2003 and another EMD on train 762 at Gads Hill, Missouri on May 19, 1976. A lucky catch. *J Harlen Wilson*

Opposite page bottom: A trio of coal SD40-2's swing through the Rockies on the Rio Grande at Minturn, Colorado on April 17, 1983. A luckier catch. *David Busse photo, David Johnston collection*

Above: SD40-2 3134 leads train LAF westbound through Mesquite, Texas on a mostly clear April 26, 1979. 3134 was one unit of the second order for SD40-2's, an order for 20 built in August and September, 1973. The MoPac was in the C-C groove by this time, as the SD40 had paved the way for Dash 2 C-C sales. They all proved to be great heavy-haul freight units. *Bill Phillips*

Below: East of Russellville, Arkansas on a cloudless blue-sky day, SD40-2 3230 and an SD40 roll along the water westbound with a typical manifest in March, 1980. This was the second 3230, the first one had dynamic brakes and was later renumbered 6014. There were 20 "SD40-2c's" that were numbered 3216-3235. When the new order of non-dynamic brake equipped units arrived, the coal units were renumbered 6000-6019. *Paul Walters*

EMD SD40-2   3,000 hp   25 units
TE = 98,100   WT = 392,400
Wheels = 40"   Fuel = 4,000
Engine: EMD 16-645E3 V-type 16-cylinder 2-cycle Turbocharged
Min Speed for TE = 12.0 mph
62:15 Gearing   65 mph Max
"B" in number indicates conversion to B-unit by removing appliances

1st No	2nd No	3rd No	4th No	Built	Build#	Notes
MP-790:2	MP-3090	UP-4090		08/73	73713-1	
MP-791:2	MP-3091	UP-4091		08/73	73713-2	Note 1
MP-792:2	MP-3092	UP-4092		08/73	73713-3	Note 2
MP-793:2	MP-3093	UP-4093		08/73	73713-4	Note 3
MP-794:2	MP-3094	UP-4094		08/73	73713-5	Note 4
MP-795:2	MP-3095	UP-4095		08/73	73613-1	
MP-796:2	MP-3096	UP-4096		08/73	73613-2	
MP-797:2	MP-3097	UP-4097		08/73	73613-3	Note 1
MP-798:2	MP-3098	UP-4098		08/73	73613-4	
MP-799:2	MP-3099	UP-4099		08/73	73613-5	Note 2, 5
MP-800:3	MP-3100	UP-4100		08/73	73613-6	
MP-801:3	MP-3101	UP-4101		08/73	73613-7	
MP-802:3	MP-3102	UP-4102		08/73	73613-8	Note 6
MP-803:3	MP-3103	UP-4103	UP-B4103	08/73	73613-9	
MP-804:3	MP-3104	UP-4104		08/73	73613-10	Note 1
MP-805:3	MP-3105	UP-4105		08/73	73613-11	Note 7
MP-806:3	MP-3106	UP-4106		08/73	73613-12	
MP-807:3	MP-3107	UP-4107		09/73	73613-13	Note 1
MP-808:3	MP-3108	UP-4108		09/73	73613-14	
MP-809:3	MP-3109	UP-4109		09/73	73613-15	Note 1
MP-810:3	MP-3110	UP-4110		09/73	73613-16	Note 2
MP-811:3	MP-3111	UP-4111		09/73	73613-17	Note 1
MP-812:3	MP-3112	UP-4112		09/73	73613-18	
MP-813:3	MP-3113	UP-4113		09/73	73613-19	Note 1
MP-814:2	MP-3114	UP-4114		09/73	73613-20	

Note 1: Wore MP yellow in 3000 or 3100-series
Note 2: Wore Double-Eagles in 3000 or 3100-series
Note 3: Had large "3093" right on top of screaming eagle on right side only
Note 4: NLR "block" lettering in 4000-series
Note 5: Wore large "3099" below and to the right of the screaming eagle
Note 6: Retired 1989, to Wisconsin Central WC-3102
Note 7: Wrecked 11/18/88 at San Antonio, retired 9/89, scrapped by UP at NLR

EMD SD40-2   3,000 hp   24 units
TE = 97,650   WT = 390,600
Wheels = 40"   Fuel = 4,000
Engine: EMD 16-645E3 V-type 16-cylinder 2-cycle Turbocharged
Min Speed for TE = 12.0 mph
62:15 Gearing   65 mph Max
"B" in number indicates conversion to B-unit by removing appliances

1st No	2nd No	3rd No	4th No	5th No	Built	Build#	Notes
T&P-816:2	T&P-3115	MP-3115	UP-4115	UP-B4115	12/73	73648-1	Note 1
T&P-817:2	T&P-3116	MP-3116	UP-4116	UP-B4116	12/73	73648-2	
T&P-818:2	T&P-3117	MP-3117	UP-4117	UP-B4117	12/73	73648-3	
T&P-819	T&P-3118	MP-3118	UP-4118	UP-B4118	12/73	73648-4	
T&P-820	T&P-3119	MP-3119	UP-4119	UP-B4119	12/73	73648-5	
T&P-821	T&P-3120	MP-3120	UP-4120		01/74	73648-6	Note 1
T&P-822	T&P-3121	MP-3121	UP-4121	UP-B4121	01/74	73648-7	
T&P-823	T&P-3122	MP-3122	UP-4122	UP-B4122	01/74	73648-8	Note 1
T&P-824	T&P-3123	MP-3123	UP-4123	UP-B4123	01/74	73648-9	Note 1
T&P-825	T&P-3124	MP-3124	UP-4124	UP-B4124	01/74	73648-10	
T&P-826	T&P-3125	MP-3125	UP-4125	UP-B4125	01/74	73648-11	
T&P-827	T&P-3126	MP-3126	UP-4126	UP-B4126	01/74	73648-12	
T&P-828	T&P-3127	MP-3127	UP-4127	UP-B4127	01/74	73648-13	
T&P-829	T&P-3128	MP-3128	UP-4128	UP-B4128	01/74	73648-14	
T&P-830	T&P-3129	MP-3129	UP-4129	UP-B4129	01/74	73648-15	Note 2
T&P-831	T&P-3130	MP-3130	(UP-4130)		01/74	73648-16	Note 1, 3
T&P-832	T&P-3131	MP-3131	UP-4131	UP-B4131	01/74	73648-17	
T&P-833	T&P-3132	MP-3132	UP-4132		01/74	73648-18	Note 1, 2
T&P-834	T&P-3133	MP-3133	UP-4133	UP-B4133	01/74	73648-19	
T&P-835	T&P-3134	MP-3134	UP-4134	UP-B4134	01/74	73648-20	
T&P-836	T&P-3135	MP-3135	UP-4135		01/74	73648-21	
T&P-837	T&P-3136	MP-3136	UP-4136	UP-B4136	01/74	73648-22	Note 1
T&P-838	T&P-3137	MP-3137	UP-4137	UP-B4137	01/74	73648-23	
T&P-839	T&P-3138	MP-3138	UP-4138	UP-B4138	01/74	73648-24	

Note 1: Wore MP yellow in 3100-series
Note 2: Wore Double-Eagles in 3100-series
Note 3: Wrecked 1989, retired 5/90, to NRE 10/91

EMD SD40-2   3,000 hp   11 units
TE = 97,810   WT = 391,240
Wheels = 40"   Fuel = 4,000
Engine: EMD 16-645E3 V-type 16-cylinder 2-cycle Turbocharged
Min Speed for TE = 12.0 mph
62:15 Gearing   65 mph Max
"B" in number indicates conversion to B-unit by removing appliances

1st No	2nd No	3rd No	Built	Build#	Notes
MP-3139	UP-4139	UP-B4139	02/74	73748-1	
MP-3140	UP-4140	UP-B4140	02/74	73748-2	Note 1
MP-3141	UP-4141	UP-B4141	02/74	73748-3	Note 1
MP-3142	UP-4142	UP-B4142	02/74	73748-4	
MP-3143	UP-4143	UP-B4143	02/74	73748-5	
MP-3144	UP-4144	UP-B4144	02/74	73748-6	Note 1
MP-3145	UP-4145	UP-B4145	02/74	73748-7	
MP-3146	UP-4146		02/74	73748-8	Note 2
MP-3147	UP-4147	UP-B4147	02/74	73748-9	
MP-3148	UP-4148	UP-B4148	02/74	73748-10	Note 1
MP-3149	UP-4149		02/74	73748-11	

Note 1: Wore MP yellow in 3100-series
Note 2: Wore Double-Eagles in 3100-series

Below right: 3092 was one SD40-2 from the second order, a small order for five delivered simultaneously with a first order for 20. It wears the double-eagle paint scheme in Council Bluffs, Iowa on March 13, 1988. The 15-year veteran has held up quite well, and will soon become UP 4092 under a coat of yellow and gray. *Ken Church*

Below: SD40-2 828 displays her as-delivered appearance, thin frame stripe and chevrons, T&P sublettering under the buzz-saw under the cab window, the large screaming eagle, and a brass-colored bell. The unit has only barely been dusted in road service, and is not yet a month old on February 2, 1974 at Little Rock, Arkansas. *James Holder*

EMD SD40-2   3,000 hp   14 units
TE = 97,905   WT = 391,620
Wheels = 40"   Fuel = 4,000
Engine: EMD 16-645E3 V-type 16-cylinder 2-cycle Turbocharged
Min Speed for TE = 12.0 mph
62:15 Gearing   65 mph Max
"B" in number indicates conversion to B-unit by removing appliances

1st No	2nd No	3rd No	4th No	Built	Builder #	Notes
C&EI-3150	MP-3150	UP-4150	UP-B4150	03/74	73748-12	Note 1
C&EI-3151	MP-3151	UP-4151		03/74	73748-13	Note 1
C&EI-3152	MP-3152	UP-4152	UP-B4152	03/74	73748-14	Note 1, 2
C&EI-3153	MP-3153	UP-4153	UP-B4153	03/74	73748-15	
C&EI-3154	MP-3154	UP-4154		03/74	73748-16	Note 1
C&EI-3155	MP-3155	UP-4155		03/74	73748-17	Note 1
C&EI-3156	MP-3156	UP-4156		03/74	73748-18	Note 1
C&EI-3157	MP-3157	UP-4157	UP-B4157	03/74	73748-19	
C&EI-3158	MP-3158	UP-4118	UP-4158	03/74	73748-20	Note 1, 3
C&EI-3159	MP-3159	UP-4159	UP-B4159	03/74	73748-21	Note 2
C&EI-3160	MP-3160	UP-4160		03/74	73748-22	Note 4
C&EI-3161	MP-3161	UP-4161		03/74	73748-23	Note 1
C&EI-3162	MP-3162	UP-4162:2	UP-B4162	03/74	73748-24	
C&EI-3163	MP-3163	UP-4163:2	UP-B4163	03/74	73748-25	Note 2, 5

Note 1: Wore Double-Eagles in 3100-series
Note 2: Wore MP yellow in 3100-series
Note 3: NLR "block" lettering as UP-4118 and UP-4158
Note 4: NLR "block" lettering as UP-4160
Note 5: Delivered with large number scheme

EMD SD40-2   3,000 hp   38 units
TE = 97,800   WT = 391,200
Wheels = 40"   Fuel = 4,000
Engine: EMD 16-645E3 V-type 16-cylinder 2-cycle Turbocharged
Min Speed for TE = 12.0 mph
62:15 Gearing   65 mph Max
Retired 4/90, to GATX

1st No	2nd No	Built	Build#	Notes & Dispositions
MP-3164	UP-4164:2	02/75	74690-1	R# GATX-2000, leased to DH
MP-3165	UP-4165:2	02/75	74690-2	R# GATX-7359
MP-3166	UP-4166	02/75	74690-3	R# GATX-2001, leased to DH
MP-3167	UP-4167:2	02/75	74690-4	
MP-3168	UP-4168:2	02/75	74690-5	Note 1, R# GATX-7360
MP-3169	(UP-4169)	02/75	74690-6	R# GATX-7361
MP-3170	UP-4170	02/75	74690-7	R# GATX-2002, leased to DH
MP-3171	UP-4171	02/75	74690-8	Wore MP yellow as MP-3171
MP-3172	UP-4172	02/75	74690-9	R# GATX-2003, leased to DH
MP-3173	UP-4173	02/75	74690-10	To Grand Trunk Western, r# GTW-5930
MP-3174	UP-4174	02/75	74690-11	To Grand Trunk Western, r# GTW-5931
MP-3175	UP-4175	02/75	74690-12	R# GATX-2004, leased to DH
MP-3176	(UP-4176)	02/75	74690-13	Note 1, R# GATX-7362
MP-3177	UP-4177	02/75	74690-14	To Grand Trunk Western, r# GTW-5932
MP-3178	UP-4178	02/75	74690-15	To Grand Trunk Western, r# GTW-5933
MP-3179	(UP-4179)	02/75	74690-16	Note 1
MP-3180	UP-4180	02/75	74690-17	To Grand Trunk Western, r# GTW-5934
MP-3181	UP-4181	02/75	74690-18	R# GATX-7363
MP-3182	UP-4182	03/75	74690-19	Note 2, to Grand Trunk Western, r# GTW-5935
MP-3183	(UP-4183)	03/75	74690-20	R# GATX-7364
MP-3184	UP-4184	03/75	74690-21	R# GATX-7365
MP-3185	(UP-4185)	03/75	74690-22	R# GATX-7366
MP-3186	UP-4186	03/75	74690-23	Note 1
MP-3187	UP-4187	03/75	74690-24	R# GATX-2005, leased to DH
MP-3188	UP-4188	03/75	74690-25	R# GATX-2006, leased to DH
MP-3189	UP-4189	03/75	74690-26	
MP-3190	UP-4190	03/75	74690-27	Note 1
MP-3191	UP-4191	03/75	74690-28	R# GATX-7367
MP-3192	UP-4192	03/75	74690-29	To Grand Trunk Western, r# GTW-5936
MP-3193	UP-4193	03/75	74690-30	
MP-3194	(UP-4194)	03/75	74690-31	Note 1, R# GATX-2007, leased to DH
MP-3195	(UP-4195)	03/75	74690-32	Note 1, R# GATX-2008, leased to DH
MP-3196	UP-4196	03/75	74690-33	To Grand Trunk Western, r# GTW-5937
MP-3197	UP-4197	03/75	74690-34	R# GATX-2009, leased to DH
MP-3198	UP-4198	03/75	74690-35	First "Canary" painted in UP yellow as MP-3198
MP-3199	UP-4199	03/75	74690-36	
MP-3200	(UP-4200)	03/75	74690-37	Note 1

1st No	2nd No	Built	Build#	Notes & Dispositions
MP-3201	UP-4201	03/75	74690-38	To GATX, r# GATX-7368

Note 1: Wore MP yellow in 3100 or 3200-series
Note 2: NLR "block" lettering in 4100-series

EMD SD40-2   3,000 hp   14 units
TE = 97,650   WT = 390,600
Wheels = 40"   Fuel = 4,000
Engine: EMD 16-645E3 V-type 16-cylinder 2-cycle Turbocharged
Min Speed for TE = 12.0 mph
62:15 Gearing   65 mph Max
"B" in number indicates conversion to B-unit by removing appliances

1st No	2nd No	3rd No	4th No	Built	Build#	Notes
MP-3202	UP-4162:1	UP-4202		08/75	75616-1	Note 1, 2
MP-3203	UP-4163:1	UP-4203		08/75	75616-2	Note 1, 2
MP-3204	UP-4164:1	UP-4204		08/75	75616-3	Note 1, 2, 3
MP-3205	UP-4165:1	UP-4205	UP-B4205	08/75	75616-4	Note 1, 2
MP-3206	UP-4206			08/75	75616-5	Note 2, 3
MP-3207	UP-4167:1	UP-4207	UP-B4207	08/75	75616-6	Note 1, 2
MP-3208	UP-4168:1	UP-4208		08/75	75616-7	Note 1, 2
MP-3209	UP-4169	UP-4209		08/75	75616-8	Note 1, 2
MP-3210	UP-4210			08/75	75616-9	Note 2
MP-3211	UP-4211			08/75	75616-10	Note 3
MP-3212	UP-4212			08/75	75616-11	Note 3
MP-3213	UP-4213			08/75	75616-12	Note 3
MP-3214	UP-4214			08/75	75616-13	Note 2
MP-3215	UP-4215			08/75	75616-14	Note 2, 3

Note 1: NLR "block" lettering in 4100-series
Note 2: NLR "block" lettering in 4200-series]
Note 3: Wore MP yellow in 3200-series

EMD SD40-2   3,000 hp   50 units
TE = 98,330   WT = 393,320
Wheels = 40"   Fuel = 4,000
Engine: EMD 16-645E3 V-type 16-cylinder 2-cycle Turbocharged
Min Speed for TE = 12.0 mph
62:15 Gearing   65 mph Max
"B" in number indicates conversion to B-unit by removing appliances

1st No	2nd No	3rd No	Built	Builder #	Notes
MP-3216:2	UP-4216	UP-B4216	08/78	776099-1	
MP-3217:2	UP-4217	UP-B4217	08/78	776099-2	
MP-3218:2	UP-4218	UP-B4218	08/78	776099-3	
MP-3219:2	UP-4219	UP-B4219	08/78	776099-4	
MP-3220:2	UP-4220		08/78	776099-5	
MP-3221:2	UP-4221	UP-B4221	08/78	776099-6	
MP-3222:2	UP-4222	UP-B4222	08/78	776099-7	
MP-3223:2	UP-4223	UP-B4223	08/78	776099-8	
MP-3224:2	UP-4224	UP-B4224	08/78	776099-9	
MP-3225:2	UP-4225	UP-B4225	08/78	776099-10	Note 1
MP-3226:2	UP-4226	UP-B4226	08/78	776099-11	Note 2
MP-3227:2	UP-4227	UP-B4227	08/78	776099-12	
MP-3228:2	UP-4228		08/78	776099-13	Note 2
MP-3229:2	UP-4229	UP-B4229	08/78	776099-14	
MP-3230:2	UP-4230	UP-B4230	08/78	776099-15	
MP-3231:2	UP-4231	UP-B4231	09/78	776099-16	
MP-3232:2	UP-4232	UP-B4232	09/78	776099-17	Note 1
MP-3233:2	UP-4233		09/78	776099-18	
MP-3234:2	UP-4234		09/78	776099-19	Note 1
MP-3235:2	UP-4235	UP-B4235	09/78	776099-20	
MP-3236	UP-4236	UP-B4236	09/78	776099-21	
MP-3237	UP-4237	UP-B4237	09/78	776099-22	
MP-3238	UP-4238		09/78	776099-23	Note 2, 3
MP-3239	UP-4239	UP-B4239	09/78	776099-24	Note 2
MP-3240	UP-4240	UP-B4240	09/78	776099-25	
MP-3241	UP-4241	UP-B4241	09/78	776099-26	Note 2
MP-3242	UP-4242	UP-B4242	09/78	776099-27	
MP-3243	UP-4243	UP-B4243	09/78	776099-28	
MP-3244	UP-4244	UP-B4244	09/78	776099-29	
MP-3245	UP-4245	UP-B4245	09/78	776099-30	Note 2
MP-3246	UP-4246		09/78	776099-31	Note 2
MP-3247	UP-4247	UP-B4247	09/78	776099-32	
MP-3248	UP-4248		09/78	776099-33	
MP-3249	UP-4249	UP-B4249	09/78	776099-34	
MP-3250	UP-4250	UP-B4250	09/78	776099-35	

(This class continued on page 160)

EMD SD40-2 (continued from page 159)

1st No	2nd No	3rd No	Built	Builder #	Notes
MP-3251	UP-4251	UP-B4251	09/78	776099-36	Note 1
MP-3252	UP-4252	UP-B4252	08/78	777100-1	
MP-3253	UP-4253	UP-B4253	08/78	777100-2	
MP-3254	UP-4254	UP-B4254	08/78	777100-3	
MP-3255	UP-4255	UP-B4255	08/78	777100-4	
MP-3256	UP-4256	UP-B4256	08/78	777100-5	
MP-3257	UP-4257	UP-B4257	08/78	777100-6	
MP-3258	UP-4258		08/78	777100-7	Note 2
MP-3259	UP-4259	UP-B4259	08/78	777100-8	Note 2
MP-3260	UP-4260	UP-B4260	08/78	777100-9	
MP-3261	UP-4261	UP-B4261	08/78	777100-10	
MP-3262	UP-4262	UP-B4262	08/78	777100-11	
MP-3263	UP-4263	UP-B4263	08/78	777100-12	
MP-3264	UP-4264		08/78	777100-13	
MP-3265	UP-4265	UP-B4265	08/78	777100-14	Note 2

Note 1: NLR "block" lettering in 4200-series
Note 2: Wore MP yellow in 3200-series
Note 3: Painted as "Operation Roadblock" as UP-4238

Opposite page top: SD40-2 3274 and older sister 3243 race past the lush Illinois farmland at Papineau, Illinois on July 6, 1985. The 3274 was part of order number 786178 for 26 units, and four EMD orders later was another group of MoPac SD40-2's, an order for 10 that carried order number 786182. There was only a month spacing delivery of the last of the 26 units and the first of the 10. *Terry Chicwak*

Right: The nearly barren Kansas hills near Herington witness the passage of SD40-2 3265 leading four other C-C's with a heavy grain train on February 24, 1982. The 3265 was the last SD40-2 of 1978, bringing the non-dynamic total to 176. *Dan Schroeder*

Opposite page bottom: A pair of SD40-2's, 3282 and 3095, lean hard into an S-curve at Lansing, Texas on December 14, 1979. The piggybacks in tow are typical of the assignments for the big SD's. *Richard Yremko*

Below: Like a scene from a science fiction novel, the torches from the refinery at Sugar Creek, Missouri loom behind SD40-2 813 and an EMD companion heading eastbound in the late afternoon glow on May 4, 1974. The SD is but eight months old, and was part of the first order for SD40-2's. Standardization of the road-freight fleet on the SD40-2 has just begun. *Joe McMillan*

EMD SD40-2 3,000 hp 36 units
TE = 98,275   WT = 393,100
Wheels = 40"   Fuel = 4,000
Engine: EMD 16-645E3 V-type 16-cylinder 2-cycle Turbocharged
Min Speed for TE = 12.0 mph
62:15 Gearing   65 mph Max
"B" in number indicates conversion to B-unit by removing appliances

1st No	2nd No	3rd No	Built	Builder #	Notes
MP-3266	UP-4266	UP-B4266	05/79	786178-1	
MP-3267	UP-4267	UP-B4267	05/79	786178-2	Note 1
MP-3268	UP-4268		05/79	786178-3	
MP-3269	UP-4269	UP-B4269	05/79	786178-4	Note 1
MP-3270	UP-4270		05/79	786178-5	Note 1
MP-3271	UP-4271	UP-B4271	05/79	786178-6	
MP-3272	UP-4272	UP-B4272	05/79	786178-7	
MP-3273	UP-4273	UP-B4273	05/79	786178-8	
MP-3274	UP-4274	UP-B4274	05/79	786178-9	
MP-3275	UP-4275	UP-B4275	05/79	786178-10	
MP-3276	UP-4276	UP-B4276	05/79	786178-11	Note 2
MP-3277	UP-4277	UP-B4277	05/79	786178-12	
MP-3278	UP-4278	UP-B4278	05/79	786178-13	Note 3
MP-3279	UP-4279	UP-B4279	05/79	786178-14	
MP-3280	UP-4280		05/79	786178-15	Note 1
MP-3281	UP-4281	UP-B4281	05/79	786178-16	Note 2
MP-3282	UP-4282	UP-B4282	05/79	786178-17	
MP-3283	UP-4283	UP-B4283	05/79	786178-18	
MP-3284	UP-4284	UP-B4284	05/79	786178-19	
MP-3285	UP-4285		05/79	786178-20	
MP-3286	UP-4286		05/79	786178-21	Note 1
MP-3287	UP-4287	UP-B4287	05/79	786178-22	
MP-3288	UP-4288	UP-B4288	05/79	786178-23	
MP-3289	UP-4289		05/79	786178-24	Note 1
MP-3290	UP-4290	UP-B4290	05/79	786178-25	
MP-3291	UP-4291	UP-B4291	06/79	786178-26	Note 1
MP-3292	UP-4292	UP-B4292	07/79	786182-1	
MP-3293	UP-4293		07/79	786182-2	
MP-3294	UP-4294	UP-B4294	07/79	786182-3	Note 1
MP-3295	UP-4295	UP-B4295	07/79	786182-4	Note 2
MP-3296	UP-4296	UP-B4296	07/79	786182-5	
MP-3297	UP-4297	UP-B4297	07/79	786182-6	Note 1
MP-3298	UP-4298	UP-B4298	07/79	786182-7	Note 1
MP-3299	UP-4299	UP-B4299	07/79	786182-8	
MP-3300:2	UP-4300	UP-B4300	07/79	786182-9	
MP-3301:2	UP-4301	UP-B4301	07/79	786182-10	

Note 1: Wore MP yellow in 3200-series
Note 2: NLR "block" lettering in 4200-series
Note 3: Wore "2378" on long hood left side as MP-3278

Below: SD40-2 3139 was the first unit of MoPac's fourth order for the 3,000 horsepower EMDs, an order that brought the total to 60. The SD leads a westbound on Boyd Hill near Hoisington, Kansas in March, 1974. *Lee Berglund*

Below right: The SD40 series was by far the most popular EMD model, and if all versions of SD40's and SD40-2's are added together the production total reached an astounding 5,567 units. The MoPac contributed its share, buying 90 SD40's, 232 SD40-2's and 74 "SD40-2c's." The 3302 is from one of four orders in 1979, and is at Dolton, Illinois on March 26, 1986. *Ronald Plazzotta*

EMD SD40-2 3,000 hp 10 units
TE = 98,300   WT = 393,200
Wheels = 40"   Fuel = 4,000
Engine: EMD 16-645E3 V-type 16-cylinder 2-cycle Turbocharged
Min Speed for TE = 12.0 mph
62:15 Gearing   65 mph Max
"B" in number indicates conversion to B-unit by removing appliances

1st No	2nd No	3rd No	Built	Builder #	Notes
MP-3302:2	UP-4302		12/79	796308-1	Note 2
MP-3303:2	UP-4303	UP-B4303	12/79	796308-2	
MP-3304:2	UP-4304	UP-B4304	12/79	796308-3	Note 1
MP-3305:2	UP-4305	UP-B4305	12/79	796308-4	
MP-3306:2	UP-4306		12/79	796308-5	Note 1
MP-3307:2	UP-4307		12/79	796308-6	Note 2
MP-3308:2	UP-4308		12/79	796308-7	
MP-3309:2	UP-4309	UP-B4309	12/79	796308-8	Note 1
MP-3310	UP-4310	UP-B4310	12/79	796308-9	Note 1
MP-3311	UP-4311	UP-B4311	12/79	796308-10	Note 1

Note 1: Wore MP yellow in 3300-series
Note 2: NLR "block" lettering in 4300-series

EMD SD40-2 3,000 hp 10 units
TE = 98,225   WT = 392,900
Wheels = 40"   Fuel = 4,000
Engine: EMD 16-645E3 V-type 16-cylinder 2-cycle Turbocharged
Min Speed for TE = 12.0 mph
62:15 Gearing   65 mph Max
"B" in number indicates conversion to B-unit by removing appliances

1st No	2nd No	3rd No	Built	Builder #	Notes
MP-3312	UP-4312	UP-B4312	04/80	786269-1	
MP-3313	UP-4313	UP-B4313	04/80	786269-2	
MP-3314:2	UP-4314		04/80	786269-3	
MP-3315:2	UP-4315	UP-B4315	04/80	786269-4	
MP-3316:2	UP-4316	UP-B4316	04/80	786269-5	
MP-3317:2	UP-4317	UP-B4317	04/80	786269-6	
MP-3318:2	UP-4318	UP-B4318	04/80	786269-7	
MP-3319:2	UP-4319		04/80	786269-8	Note 1
MP-3320:2	UP-4320		04/80	786269-9	
MP-3321:2	UP-4321	UP-B4321	04/80	786269-10	

Note 1: Wore MP yellow in 3300-series

EMD "SD40-2c" 3,000 hp 5 units
TE = 104,230   WT = 416,920
Wheels = 40"   Fuel = 4,000
Engine: EMD 16-645E3 V-type 16-cylinder 2-cycle Turbocharged
Min Speed for TE = 8.5 mph
62:15 Gearing   65 mph Max
Designated as "c" for coal service, with dynamic brakes
3216-3220 renumbered 6000-6004 in May 1978
Equipped with Pacesetter control. Retired 2/94

1st No	2nd No	3rd No	Built	Build#	Notes
MP-3216:1	MP-6000	UP-3900	07/76	756145-1	
MP-3217:1	MP-6001	UP-3901	07/76	756145-2	Note 1
MP-3218:1	MP-6002	UP-3902	07/76	756145-3	Wore MP yellow as MP-6002
MP-3219:1	MP-6003	UP-3903	07/76	756145-4	
MP-3220:1	MP-6004	UP-3904	07/76	756145-5	

Note 1: Wore large BN style number under grille (put on by BN). NLR "block" lettering in 3900-series

EMD "SD40-2c" 3,000 hp 15 units
TE = 104,230 WT = 416,920
Wheels = 40" Fuel = 4,000
Engine: EMD 16-645E3 V-type 16-cylinder 2-cycle Turbocharged
Min Speed for TE = 8.5 mph
62:15 Gearing 65 mph Max
Designated as "c" for coal service, with dynamic brakes
3221-3235 renumbered 6005-6019 in May 1978
Equipped with Pacesetter control

1st No	2nd No	3rd No	Built	Builder #	Notes
MP-3221:1	MP-6005:2	UP-3905	08/76	766005-1	Note 1
MP-3222:1	MP-6006:2	UP-3906	08/76	766005-2	
MP-3223:1	MP-6007:2	UP-3907	08/76	766005-3	
MP-3224:1	MP-6008:2	UP-3908	09/76	766005-4	
MP-3225:1	MP-6009:2	UP-3909	09/76	766005-5	Note 2
MP-3226:1	MP-6010:2	UP-3910	09/76	766005-6	Note 1, 2
MP-3227:1	MP-6011:2	UP-3911	09/76	766005-7	
MP-3228:1	MP-6012:2	UP-3912	09/76	766005-8	
MP-3229:1	MP-6013:2	UP-3913	09/76	766005-9	
MP-3230:1	MP-6014:2	UP-3914	09/76	766005-10	Note 2
MP-3231:1	MP-6015:2	UP-3915	09/76	766005-11	
MP-3232:1	MP-6016:2	UP-3916	09/76	766005-12	Note 2
MP-3233:1	MP-6017:2	UP-3917	09/76	766005-13	
MP-3234:1	MP-6018	UP-3918	09/76	766005-14	Note 2
MP-3235:1	MP-6019	UP-3919	09/76	766005-15	Note 1

Note 1: Wore MP yellow in 6000-series
Note 2: NLR "block" lettering in 3900-series

EMD "SD40-2c" 3,000 hp 34 units
TE = 103,525 WT = 414,100
Wheels = 40" Fuel = 4,000
Engine: EMD 16-645E3 V-type 16-cylinder 2-cycle Turbocharged
Min Speed for TE = 8.5 mph
62:15 Gearing 65 mph Max
Designated as "c" for coal service, with dynamic brakes
Equipped with Pacesetter control

1st No	2nd No	Built	Builder #	Notes
MP-6020	UP-3920	06/79	786181-1	Wore MP yellow as MP-6020
MP-6021	UP-3921	06/79	786181-2	
MP-6022	UP-3922	06/79	786181-3	
MP-6023	UP-3923	06/79	786181-4	NLR "block" lettering as UP-3923
MP-6024	UP-3924	06/79	786181-5	NLR "block" lettering as UP-3924
MP-6025	UP-3925	06/79	786181-6	
MP-6026	UP-3926	06/79	786181-7	Wore MP yellow as MP-6026
MP-6027	UP-3927	06/79	786181-8	
MP-6028	UP-3928	06/79	786181-9	
MP-6029	UP-3929	06/79	786181-10	
MP-6030	UP-3930	06/79	786181-11	
MP-6031	UP-3931	06/79	786181-12	
MP-6032	UP-3932	06/79	786181-13	
MP-6033	UP-3933	06/79	786181-14	Wore MP yellow as MP-6033
MP-6034	UP-3934	06/79	786181-15	NLR "block" lettering as UP-3934
MP-6035	UP-3935	06/79	786181-16	
MP-6036	UP-3936	06/79	786181-17	Wore MP yellow as MP-6036
MP-6037	UP-3937	06/79	786181-18	
MP-6038	UP-3938	06/79	786181-19	
MP-6039	UP-3939	06/79	786181-20	
MP-6040	UP-3940	06/79	786181-21	NLR "block" lettering as UP-3940
MP-6041	UP-3941	06/79	786181-22	
MP-6042	UP-3942	06/79	786181-23	
MP-6043	UP-3943	06/79	786181-24	
MP-6044	UP-3944	06/79	786181-25	Wore MP yellow as MP-6044
MP-6045	UP-3945	06/79	786181-26	Wore MP yellow as MP-6045
MP-6046	UP-3946	06/79	786181-27	
MP-6047	UP-3947	06/79	786181-28	
MP-6048	UP-3948	06/79	786181-29	
MP-6049	UP-3949	06/79	786181-30	
MP-6050	UP-3950	06/79	786274-1	
MP-6051	UP-3951	06/79	786274-2	
MP-6052	UP-3952	06/79	786274-3	
MP-6053	UP-3953	06/79	786274-4	NLR "block" lettering as UP-3953

Top: The first two orders of dynamic brake equipped SD40-2's arrived in the 3200-series, beginning with the 3216. The 3232 is part of the second order, an order for 20 units that arrived in August and September, 1976. They later were renumbered into the 6000-series. The 3232 carries some road dust at Little Rock on December 28, 1977. *James Holder*

Above: Coal SD40-2 6003 is at Fort Worth, Texas on February 3, 1980. It was one of five delivered in July, 1976, the first units that the MoPac itself ordered with dynamic brakes. *Bill Phillips photo, James Holder collection*

EMD "SD40-2c" 3,000 hp 20 units
TE = 103,600 WT = 414,400
Wheels = 40" Fuel = 4,000
Engine: EMD 16-645E3B V-type 16-cylinder 2-cycle Turbocharged
Min Speed for TE = 8.5 mph
62:15 Gearing 65 mph Max
Designated as "c" for coal service, with dynamic brakes
Equipped with Pacesetter control

1st No	2nd No	Built	Builder #	Notes
MP-6054	UP-3954	04/80	796311-1	
MP-6055	UP-3955	04/80	796311-2	
MP-6056	UP-3956	04/80	796311-3	
MP-6057	UP-3957	04/80	796311-4	Wore MP yellow as MP-6057
MP-6058	UP-3958	04/80	796311-5	
MP-6059	UP-3959	04/80	796311-6	Wore MP yellow as MP-6059
MP-6060	UP-3960	04/80	796311-7	
MP-6061	UP-3961	04/80	796311-8	
MP-6062	UP-3962	04/80	796311-9	
MP-6063	UP-3963	04/80	796311-10	
MP-6064	UP-3964	04/80	796311-11	
MP-6065	UP-3965	04/80	796311-12	
MP-6066	UP-3966	04/80	796311-13	
MP-6067	UP-3967	04/80	796311-14	
MP-6068	UP-3968	04/80	796311-15	Wore MP yellow as MP-6068
MP-6069	UP-3969	04/80	796311-16	
MP-6070	UP-3970	04/80	796311-17	Wore MP yellow as MP-6070
MP-6071	UP-3971	04/80	796311-18	Last blue SD40-2c
MP-6072	UP-3972	04/80	796311-19	NLR "block" lettering as UP-3972
MP-6073	UP-3973	04/80	796311-20	

Nine Thousand Horses

EMD
GP50

GE
B23-7
B30-7A

The leaves tumble by in the crisp autumn air, some in hurried flight and others seeming to slowly crawl along the ground. The late afternoon blue sky begs to be photographed, a crystal clear hue that extends into infinity. Squirrels are busy scampering about in the crisp air, searching and gathering a store for the winter that now lies just around the corner. The birds overhead are drifting effortlessly south, pushed by the stiff northerly breeze above the treetops.

The soft breeze at ground level carries the sounds of distant traffic, children playing, and the creak of the

Below: A trio of B30-7A's roars out of one of the eastbound departure tracks and up onto the Big Blue high line, a bridge over the MoPac's Kansas City Subdivision and the Kansas City Southern mainline. The three B-Boats are headed for St. Louis on a day much like the inside of a deep freeze, January 12, 1985. *Kevin EuDaly*

Below: B30-7A 4824 leads a three-unit lashup on the CHZ train on August 18, 1984 at Texarkana, Arkansas. The B30-7A only had 12 cylinders, yet generated 3,000 horsepower, pushing the horsepower per cylinder figure to a new level, 250. The MoPac's 55 B30-7A's are the only examples of that model, though Burlington Northern did buy 120 cabless versions, denoted as B30-7AB's. Though the B30-7A was in the catalog from June, 1980 through February, 1982, the units all came between November, 1981 and February, 1982. *Paul DeLuca*

Above: B23-7 4655 is solely in charge at Little Rock on November 16, 1984. The B23-7's came in six orders, the first delivered in January, 1978 and the last in April and May, 1981. There was a total of 85 of the sleek B23-7's on the railroad, and though three were boosted from their normal 2,250 horsepower to 3,000, the MoPac never classed these as B30-7A's. There was only six months between the arrival of the last B23-7 and the first B30-7A. The B23-7 was fairly successful for GE, with a production run from September, 1977 through December, 1984. Even during those economically slow times, there were still 411 B23-7's sold in the U. S. and another 125 in Mexico. *Paul DeLuca*

Right: Immediately after the fifth order for B23-7's the MoPac went to EMD for similar power, and the result was three orders for GP50's totaling 30 units. The three orders all came between November, 1980 and January, 1981. They had a relatively short lifespan in blue, and were the only class completely repainted to the UP scheme with MoPac lettering. Stocky GP50 3526 leads a sister unit GP50 in yellow at Kirkwood, Missouri on a beautiful fall day, November 3, 1984. *Ken Albrecht*

monstrous oak nearby. The sunshine brings a warmth to the skin, making the fall air seem a perfect temperature. A short distance to the west, perhaps a half mile, Kirkwood Station stands against the cloudless sky, a 100-year-old majestic monument left from a simpler era. To the east the cool ribbons of steel curl endlessly downhill and out of sight on one of the MoPac's most famous grades: Kirkwood Hill.

Mingled amid the sounds of the town, a low throb grows, barely perceptible in the whispering breeze. At first it is a challenge to be convinced that it really exists, like an airplane just before it comes within the audible range. It grows, then fades, then grows some more. Soon it is a distinct thug, thug, thug, and the conclusion is obvious: GEs.

Very quickly the volume increases, and within just a few moments it drowns out all other sound. The engineer sets the horn blaring for a grade crossing, the only one that they blow at in this area. A gust of wind blows more leaves over the close rail on the right-of-way, as if preparing a path for the beast still out of sight on the hill. Then there is a glimmer of light on the inside rail on the curve as the headlight reflects off the polished steel.

He storms around the curve at a steady 20 mph, 9,000 horses in the form of B30-7A's fighting against the tonnage of the hot manifest in tow. The three blue units with the distinctive nose stripes fight into the curve with exhaust blasting skyward, sending the leaves pell-mell into upward flight. They roar past, sand billowing off the rail, each locomotive with 12 cylinders of GE muscle pitted in the timeless duel against gravity.

The three units are now past, heading toward the distant depot and their successful appointment with the top of the hill. The cars glide past, their polished wheels singing on the rail-

Above: B23-7 4649 and a GP15-1 provide the power for an eastbound local on the Sedalia Subdivision at Pacific, Missouri in October, 1987. The B23-7's were used in a different type of service than the B30-7A's. They were usually on low priority trains while the B30-7A's were in high-speed service. *Dan Tracy*

Below: B30-7A 4835 roars out of the east portal of the tunnel at West Labadie with a hot eastbound on April 6, 1985. Plenty of muscle is up front; four GEs and a pair of EMDs. He'll be rolling down the far side of Kirkwood Hill within the hour. *Lon EuDaly*

head. An occasional flange screams in protest on the curve, oblivious to the drama with which it is associated.

The short red caboose on the tail end approaches, as the train gains speed after cresting the grade. The conductor waves as the MoPac eagle under the window sails past, as if sending the train on its way to good fortune. The leaves rustle and drop, their motion at an end for the moment, and the last sounds of the westbound drift back over the lawn of the box plant where the last hour has been spent. The crossing gate bells at Kirkwood ring for a few last moments, then the normal city sounds replace the roar of the last few minutes.

For what now seems a brief moment in time, two or three B30-7A's was the standard power for the westbound afternoon hotshots out of St. Louis, but they've now faded into a gigantic yellow and gray roster working for a new master, with new three-digit numbers and a new coat of paint. Their classic lines, stubby noses, and dramatic floating bolster trucks will soon fade even from the rails they've just sanded, and will fall into the obscurity associated with being but one model on a roster of dozens. But to the MoPac fans who watched their passing, they are etched forever into the webs of memory, and thankfully will be preserved for some time to come on small pieces of plastic in two by two inch mounts.

The B30-7A and its immediate predecessor, the B23-7, came to the MoPac over a more than four-year span beginning in January, 1978. They came to a power-short MoPac desperately in need of new power, and were used in the MoPac's hottest service, exemplifying the latest technology of the era. They helped replace 60 N&W units, 50 Chessie GP40's, and even four Grand Trunk SD40's that had been leased to alleviate the power crunch. In fact, many of the B-Boats, as GE's B-series units were nicknamed, would be part of a massive motive power acquisition period seeing the purchase of 312 units in only 14 months.

The ultimate purchase of 140 of the B-Boats was much in keeping with the high-speed railroading philosophy of the time that chose to utilize high-horsepower B-B units for high speed service, rather than their six-axle counterparts. It was a philosophy that is best applied in the flat lands, but would ultimately be proven to be a miscalculation for railroads with significant grades. There were easily more B23-7's on the MoPac than any other GE model, with a final total that reached 85 units.

The B-Boats began on the MoPac with the purchase of 10 B23-7's rated at 2,250 horsepower, built in January, 1978. Conrail had already ordered B23's, making the MoPac the second railroad to roster the unique GEs. The new units were numbered MP-2289-2298, continuing the numbering sequence above the U23B's, which were numbered MP-2250-2288. All of the MoPac's B-Boats were delivered in the standard Jenks blue with 5 1/2-inch frame and

nose stripes, and the small flying eagle buzz-saw under the cab.

The B-Boats on the MoPac were essentially all identical, all with floating bolster trucks, six power assembly access doors on the long hood (as opposed to eight on the standard B30-7), and all decorated with the standard Jenks blue paint scheme. Though their appearance was identical, somehow the 4800-series B30-7A's seemed more impressive, perhaps just because of the knowledge of the higher horsepower figure. They were treated differently by the railroad too, perhaps because of their higher gear ratio. The B23-7's were equipped with 74:18 gearing, while the B30-7A's are geared at 83:20. The treatment the B30-7A's got seemed to indicate that the higher gearing was no accident. They routinely ran on hotter traffic than the B23-7's did.

The GEs were assigned to St. Louis for maintenance purposes, and were therefore very common on the hotshots that plied the rails between the Gateway City and Kansas City to the west. They constantly ate up the miles on this corridor, and often two or three consecutive trains would roll by in the sole charge of the MoPac's magnificent B-Boats. They also frequently operated in Illinois to Chicago, and down to Little Rock and Fort Worth. They also ran off a lot of miles to and from Pueblo.

On May 17, 1978, the new B-Boats experienced their first casualty when a stopped Cotton Belt train was rear-ended near Gorham, Illinois. The lead unit on the MoPac freight was nearly brand-new B23-7 MP-2296. It and trailing GP35 MP-2523 were both heavily damaged. The resultant repair put an EMD Spartan cab on the new B-Boat, which would be the only B23-7 or B30-7A so equipped.

A second order was placed with GE for an additional 20 B23-7's in the summer of 1978, with delivery scheduled for late in the year. They began rolling off the shop floor in mid-

October, and had builder's dates in October and November. They were numbered MP-2299-2318, bringing the MoPac total to 30 B23-7's.

These were some of the units that came during the power-short period from late 1978 through 1980. By November, 1978, they had begun to show up in St. Louis, which was the maintenance base for the MoPac's GE fleet. They helped replace 60 N&W units that were on the MoPac during a long strike on the N&W. The N&W units included not only GP's and SD's, but U30B's, at least one SD9 (N&W-2340), and high-nose GP30 N&W-539. During the same year the MoPac was receiving 50 of the incredibly popular SD40-2's. A large batch of ex-Rock Island GP38-2's also have builder's dates in 1978, but those were acquired second-hand after the demise of the Rock in 1980. GE was certainly getting a share of locomotive orders from the MoPac, though the majority of the MoPac fleet had always been from EMD.

The orders in 1979 added another group of SD40-2's (MP-3266-3291) and 30 more units with dynamic brakes for coal service (MP-6020-6049). EMD's next order from the MoPac was another 10 non-dynamic brake equipped SD40-2's (MP-3292-3301), and another four units were added in June, 1979 (MP-6050-6053).

In late 1979, the MoPac also once again went to GE for more units, and again opted for the B23-7. They had been leasing about 50 Chessie System GP40's and four Grand Trunk SD40's, and the new GEs helped send these back to their home rails. They bought 20 more of the

Below: Two GP50's lead a B23-7 through Texarkana, Texas on November 24, 1982. The GP50 was mildly successful, with a production total of 278 units. It was primarily purchased for high speed service where reduced locomotive weight was an advantage. They were commonly purchased for TOFC and COFC duties. *Paul DeLuca photo, David Johnston collection*

B23-7's, numbered MP-2319-2338, which brought the total number of B23-7's to 50 units, MP-2289-2338. They were delivered in November and December.

The GP38-2's were not all on the roster in 1980, as the MoPac would buy three more groups of GP38-2's. Also among the locomotive orders for 1980 were two groups of 10 B23-7's, which were originally to be numbered MP-2339-2358. However, by delivery of the first group in April, the ex-Rock Island GP38-2's were already climbing above the 2250 mark, so they were numbered above the previous B23-7's, which had been renumbered in the 4600 series. The second group of 10 came in June, 1980. The 20 new units were numbered MP-4650-4669.

The final three units of the last 1980 group, MP-4667-4669, were boosted to 3,000 horsepower, pushing the horsepower per cylinder to a new plateau of 250, the highest achieved at the time. These tested as a set for some time, and ultimately were deemed successful and generated orders for additional 3,000 horsepower 12-cylinder units from GE.

Though it was speculated that the MP-4667-4669 might be renumbered in with the later and similar B30-7A fleet, this never occurred, at least not in MoPac days. The main reason they chose not to renumber them with the B30-7A's was that the MP-4667-4669 were not equipped with Sentry Wheel Slip, and also that the engine governors were different. Interestingly, the UP renumbered these three units above the B30-7A's, but oddly skipped two numbers. The B30-7A's currently end at UP number 254,

and the ex-MP-4667-4669 are numbered UP-257-259.

In November, 1980 there was finally the purchase of a new EMD model for the MoPac - the GP50. The GP50 represented the next horsepower step for EMD in its B-B roadswitcher series. Oddly, the GP40-2 (which the MoPac never purchased, opting for the lower horsepower nonturbocharged GP38-2 instead) was in production side by side with the GP50. Over 100 GP40-2's were built during the GP50's mildly successful production period. In fact, the Florida East Coast bought two GP40-2's after even GP50 production had already ceased. The primary problem with the GP50 perhaps was a general uneasiness within the industry about the increased horsepower and the associated maintenance. A secondary factor was the desire of some roads to complete their fleets with compatible power. Earlier in dieseldom this kind of flexibility from a builder would not have existed, but as sales declined in the 1980's the builders were searching for ways to cater to the railroad's motive power needs. The GP40-2 and the GP50 were both cataloged for high speed service with reduced locomotive weight as compared to an SD40-2.

EMD sold 278 GP50's in the U. S. from May, 1980 to November, 1985, not particularly impressive. It was powered with the 645F engine which generated 3,500 horsepower. The MoPac's GP50's naturally came without dynamic brakes. The GP60 knocked both the GP40-2 and the GP50 out of the catalog in late 1986, having begun production in October, 1985 using EMD's new 710 prime mover.

The MoPac was the third purchaser of the GP50, behind the Chicago & North Western and the Southern. They bought 10 units (MP-3500-3509) in late 1980, delivered in November and December. These in a lot of ways were direct competition to the B30-7A's, though GE would win the battle this time. The B30-7A would overtake and eventually outnumber the GP50 on the MoPac. The rest of the MoPac's GP50's came one month later in January, 1981, when two orders, one for 16 units (MP-3510-3525) and one for four units (MP-3526-3529) were delivered. When the MoPac went back for high horsepower B-B roadswitchers, the tables would finally be turned and GE would get the edge in orders for this type of unit.

Meanwhile, at EMD another group of GP38-2's was outshopped for delivery in February and March, 1981. Before being completely sold on the 3,000 horsepower figure for 12-cylinder GEs, the MoPac would place one last order for the 2,250 horsepower B23-7. Fifteen were built in April, May, and June, 1981, and numbered MP-4670-4684 above the existing fleet, bringing the B23-7 roster to its final total of 85 units.

By November, 1981, the MoPac was receiving more B-Boats from GE, this time in the form of the 3,000 horsepower B30-7A. The "A" was used to indicate that the units had only 12 cylinders rather than the standard 16 for the B30-7. They were numbered in the 4800 series, perhaps because the MoPac wanted to leave some room above the B23-7's in case they went back for more of the lower horsepower units. Whatever the case, the 4800 number series seemed to be the right series for these high-horsepower B-Boats.

The order was originally announced to be for 35 units, but by the time delivery began it stood at 55 units, one of the larger single model orders of the last few years. The MoPac must have liked how the MP-4667-4669 performed. It was, however, the last B-Boat purchase by the MoPac, bringing the B-Boat total to 140 units, 85 B23-7's and 55 B30-7A's. The B30-7A's were built from November, 1981 through February, 1982, and the chapter on the acquisition of the B-Boats was closed. Interestingly, the builder's numbers are scattered in three groups, MP-4800-4834 are in one sequence, MP-4835-4848 are in a different (and lower numbered) sequence, and the final six, MP-4849-4854, have yet a third numbering sequence.

Even as these units were arriving, the pending merger with the UP was beginning to influence the MoPac, and the final group of GP15-1's delivered in late 1982 would draw the acquisition of blue and white power to a close.

Opposite page top: The MoPac only bought 30 GP50's, and acquired 55 B30-7A's within a year. It was one of the only times that GE got a larger share of MoPac's orders in a given era. In April, 1981, three-month-old GP50 3501 blasts up Kirkwood Hill at Kirkwood, Missouri with a pair of her siblings. *Dan Schroeder*

Opposite page bottom: A mixed bag of GE power pulls train XCH-1 through Texarkana, Arkansas on August 18, 1984. Led by B30-7A 4830, B23-7 4643, and a U30C, the three units total 8,250 horsepower. The only spotting feature that differentiates B30-7A's from B23-7's is the larger exhaust stack, though the last group of B23-7's (MP-4670-4684) also had the larger stack. *Paul DeLuca*

Left: B23-7 4626 fulfills typical B23 duties on the point of Local number 938 at Roanoke, Texas in September, 1985. The trio of B23-7's supplies plenty of horses for local duties, 6,750 total. *John Leopard*

EMD B23-7 2,250 hp 10 units
TE = 66,950 WT = 267,800
Wheels = 40" Fuel = 3,250
Engine: GE FDL-12 12-cylinder 4-cycle
Min Speed for TE = 10.8 mph
74:18 Gearing 65 mph Max

1st No	2nd No	3rd No	Built	Build#	Notes
MP-2289:1	MP-4600	UP-100	01/78	41772	Note 1
MP-2290:1	MP-4601:2	UP-101	01/78	41773	
MP-2291:1	MP-4602:2	UP-102	01/78	41774	
MP-2292:1	MP-4603:2	UP-103	01/78	41775	
MP-2293:1	MP-4604:2	UP-104	01/78	41776	Wore MP yellow as MP-4604
MP-2294:1	MP-4605:2	UP-105	01/78	41777	
MP-2295:1	MP-4606:2	UP-106	01/78	41778	
MP-2296:1	MP-4607:2	UP-107	01/78	41779	Note 2
MP-2297:1	MP-4608:2	UP-108	01/78	41780	Wore MP yellow as MP-4608
MP-2298:1	MP-4609:2	UP-109	01/78	41781	

Note 1: NLR "block" lettering as UP-100
Note 2: Wrecked at Gorham IL 5/17/78, rebuilt with EMD cab as MP-2296, later MP-4607.

EMD B23-7 2,250 hp 20 units
TE = 66,325 WT = 265,300
Wheels = 40" Fuel = 3,250
Engine: GE FDL-12 12-cylinder 4-cycle
Min Speed for TE = 10.8 mph
74:18 Gearing 65 mph Max

1st No	2nd No	3rd No	4th No	Built	Build#	Notes
MP-2299:1	MP-4610:2	UP-110		10/78	42148	
MP-2300:1	MP-4611:2	UP-111		10/78	42149	Note 1
MP-2301:1	MP-4612:2	UP-112		10/78	42150	
MP-2302:1	MP-4613	UP-113		10/78	42151	
MP-2303:1	MP-4614	UP-114		10/78	42152	
MP-2304:1	MP-4615	UP-115		10/78	42153	
MP-2305:1	MP-4616	UP-4616	UP-116	10/78	42154	
MP-2306:1	MP-4617	UP-117		10/78	42155	
MP-2307:1	MP-4618	UP-118		10/78	42156	
MP-2308:1	MP-4619	UP-119		10/78	42157	Note 1
MP-2309:1	MP-4620	UP-120		10/78	42158	
MP-2310:1	MP-4621	UP-121		10/78	42159	
MP-2311:1	MP-4622	UP-122		10/78	42160	
MP-2312:1	MP-4623	UP-123		11/78	42161	Note 1
MP-2313:1	MP-4624	UP-124		11/78	42162	
MP-2314:1	MP-4625	UP-125		11/78	42163	
MP-2315:1	MP-4626	UP-126		11/78	42164	
MP-2316:1	MP-4627	UP-127		11/78	42165	Note 1
MP-2317:1	MP-4628	UP-128		11/78	42166	
MP-2318:1	MP-4629	UP-129		11/78	42167	

Note 1: Wore MP yellow in 4600-series

Below: Glowing B23-7 2306 rests at GE's Erie, Pennsylvania plant prior to delivery to the MoPac on October 30, 1978. The first 50 B23-7's were delivered in the 2289-2338 series, while the remainder came as 4650-4684. *Warren Opalk photo, James Holder collection*

Below right: GP50 3509 is ready for its first trip on December 13, 1980 at North Little Rock. *J Harlen Wilson*

EMD B23-7 2,250 hp 20 units
TE = 66,475 WT = 265,900
Wheels = 40" Fuel = 3,250
Engine: GE FDL-12 12-cylinder 4-cycle
Min Speed for TE = 10.8 mph
74:18 Gearing 65 mph Max

1st No	2nd No	3rd No	Built	Build#	Notes & Dispositions
MP-2319:1	MP-4630	UP-130	11/79	42680	
MP-2320:1	MP-4631	UP-131	11/79	42681	
MP-2321:1	MP-4632	UP-132	11/79	42682	
MP-2322:1	MP-4633	UP-133	11/79	42683	
MP-2323:1	MP-4634	UP-134	11/79	42684	
MP-2324:1	MP-4635	UP-135	11/79	42685	
MP-2325:1	MP-4636		11/79	42686	Wrecked 6/23/84, retired 1/85
MP-2326:1	MP-4637	UP-137	11/79	42687	
MP-2327:1	MP-4638	UP-138	11/79	42688	
MP-2328:1	MP-4639	UP-139	11/79	42689	
MP-2329:1	MP-4640	UP-140	11/79	42690	
MP-2330:1	MP-4641	UP-141	11/79	42691	
MP-2331:1	MP-4642	UP-142	12/79	42692	
MP-2332:1	MP-4643	UP-143	12/79	42693	
MP-2333:1	MP-4644	UP-144	12/79	42694	Wore MP yellow as MP-4644
MP-2334:1	MP-4645	UP-145	12/79	42695	
MP-2335	MP-4646	UP-146	12/79	42696	
MP-2336	MP-4647	UP-147	12/79	42697	
MP-2337	MP-4648	UP-148	12/79	42698	
MP-2338	MP-4649	UP-149	12/79	42699	

EMD B23-7 2,250 hp 17 units
TE = 66,925 WT = 267,700
Wheels = 40" Fuel = 3,250
Engine: GE FDL-12 12-cylinder 4-cycle
Min Speed for TE = 10.8 mph
74:18 Gearing 65 mph Max

1st No	2nd No	3rd No	Built	Build#	Notes
MP-4650	UP-150		04/80	42944	
MP-4651	UP-151		04/80	42945	
MP-4652	UP-152		04/80	42946	
MP-4653	UP-153		04/80	42947	Wore MP yellow as MP-4653
MP-4654	UP-154		04/80	42948	
MP-4655	UP-155		04/80	42949	Wore MP yellow as MP-4655
MP-4656	UP-156		04/80	42950	
MP-4657	UP-157		04/80	42951	
MP-4658	UP-158		04/80	42952	
MP-4659	UP-159		04/80	42953	
MP-4660	UP-160		06/80	43021	
MP-4661	UP-161:2		06/80	43022	Wore MP yellow as MP-4661
MP-4662	UP-161:1	UP-162	06/80	43023	
MP-4663	UP-163		06/80	43024	
MP-4664	UP-164		06/80	43025	
MP-4665	UP-165		06/80	43026	
MP-4666	UP-166		06/80	43027	

EMD B23-7 3,000 hp 3 units
TE = 66,925 WT = 267,700
Wheels = 40" Fuel = 3,250
Engine: GE FDL-12 12-cylinder 4-cycle
Min Speed for TE = 10.8 mph
74:18 Gearing 65 mph Max

1st No	2nd No	Built	Build#	Notes
MP-4667	UP-257	06/80	43028	Wore MP yellow as MP-4667
MP-4668	UP-258	06/80	43029	Wore MP yellow as MP-4668
MP-4669	UP-259	06/80	43030	Wore MP yellow as MP-4669

EMD B23-7 2,250 hp 15 units
TE = 66,275 WT = 265,100
Wheels = 40" Fuel = 3,250
Engine: GE FDL-12 12-cylinder 4-cycle
Min Speed for TE = 10.8 mph
74:18 Gearing 65 mph Max
Snow plow both ends

1st No	2nd No	3rd No	Built	Build#	Notes
MP-4670	UP-170		04/81	43533	
MP-4671	UP-171		04/81	43534	
MP-4672	UP-172		04/81	43535	
MP-4673	UP-173		04/81	43536	
MP-4674	UP-174		04/81	43537	
MP-4675	UP-175		04/81	43538	
MP-4676	UP-176		04/81	43539	
MP-4677	UP-177		04/81	43540	
MP-4678	UP-178		04/81	43541	
MP-4679	UP-4679	UP-179	04/81	43542	
MP-4680	UP-180		04/81	43543	
MP-4681	UP-181		05/81	43544	Wore MP yellow as MP-4681
MP-4682	UP-182		05/81	43545	
MP-4683	UP-183		05/81	43546	
MP-4684	UP-184		05/81	43547	

EMD GP50 3,500 hp 10 units
TE = 68,400 WT = 273,600
Wheels = 40" Fuel = 3,600
Engine: EMD 16-645F3 16-cylinder 2-cycle Turbocharged
Min Speed for TE = 10.8 mph
70:17 Gearing 65 mph Max

1st No	2nd No	3rd No	Built	Builder #	Notes
MP-3500:2	UP-50	UP-960	11/80	797322-1	Wore MP yellow as MP-3500
MP-3501:2	UP-961		11/80	797322-2	Wore MP yellow as MP-3501
MP-3502:2	UP-962		11/80	797322-3	Wore MP yellow as MP-3502
MP-3503:2	UP-963		11/80	797322-4	Wore MP yellow as MP-3503
MP-3504:2	UP-964		11/80	797322-5	Wore MP yellow as MP-3504
MP-3505:2	UP-965		11/80	797322-6	Last GP50 painted yellow as MP-3505
MP-3506	UP-966		11/80	797322-7	Wore MP yellow as MP-3506
MP-3507	UP-57	UP-967	11/80	797322-8	Wore MP yellow as MP-3507
MP-3508	UP-968		11/80	797322-9	Wore MP yellow as MP-3508
MP-3509	UP-969		12/80	797322-10	Wore MP yellow as MP-3509

EMD GP50 3,500 hp 20 units
TE = 68,250 WT = 273,000
Wheels = 40" Fuel = 3,600
Engine: EMD 16-645F3 16-cylinder 2-cycle Turbocharged
Min Speed for TE = 10.8 mph
70:17 Gearing 65 mph Max

1st No	2nd No	3rd No	Built	Builder #	Notes
MP-3510	UP-60	UP-970	01/81	807023-1	Wore MP yellow as MP-3510
MP-3511	UP-61	UP-971	01/81	807023-2	Wore MP yellow as MP-3511
MP-3512	UP-972		01/81	807023-3	Wore MP yellow as MP-3512
MP-3513	UP-973		01/81	807023-4	Wore MP yellow as MP-3513
MP-3514	UP-64	UP-974	01/81	807023-5	Wore MP yellow as MP-3514
MP-3515	UP-65	UP-975	01/81	807023-6	Wore MP yellow as MP-3515
MP-3516	UP-66	UP-976	01/81	807023-7	Wore MP yellow as MP-3516
MP-3517	UP-977		01/81	807023-8	Wore MP yellow as MP-3517
MP-3518	UP-978		01/81	807023-9	Wore MP yellow as MP-3518
MP-3519	UP-979		01/81	807023-10	Wore MP yellow as MP-3519
MP-3520	UP-70	UP-980	01/81	807023-11	Wore MP yellow as MP-3520
MP-3521	UP-71	UP-981	01/81	807023-12	Wore MP yellow as MP-3521
MP-3522	UP-982		01/81	807023-13	Wore MP yellow as MP-3522
MP-3523	UP-983		01/81	807023-14	Wore MP yellow as MP-3523

1st No	2nd No	3rd No	Built	Builder #	Notes
MP-3524	UP-74	UP-984	01/81	807023-15	Wore MP yellow as MP-3524
MP-3525	UP-985		01/81	807023-16	Wore MP yellow as MP-3525
MP-3526	UP-76	UP-986	01/81	807058-1	Wore MP yellow as MP-3526
MP-3527	UP-987		01/81	807058-2	Wore MP yellow as MP-3527
MP-3528	UP-78	UP-988	01/81	807058-3	Wore MP yellow as MP-3528
MP-3529	UP-989		01/81	807058-4	Wore MP yellow as MP-3529

GE B30-7A 3,000 hp 55 units
TE = 67,100 WT = 268,400
Wheels = 40" Fuel = 3,250
Engine: GE FDL-12 12-cylinder 4-cycle
Min Speed for TE = 10.8 mph
83:20 Gearing 70 mph Max

1st No	2nd No	3rd No	Built	Build#	Notes
MP-4800	UP-200		11/81	43735	Wore MP yellow as MP-4800
MP-4801:2	UP-201		11/81	43736	Wore MP yellow as MP-4801
MP-4802:2	UP-202		11/81	43737	NLR "block" lettering as UP-202
MP-4803:2	UP-203		11/81	43738	
MP-4804:2	UP-204		11/81	43739	
MP-4805:2	UP-205		11/81	43740	Wore MP yellow as MP-4805
MP-4806:2	UP-206		11/81	43741	Wore MP yellow as MP-4806
MP-4807:2	UP-207		11/81	43742	
MP-4808:2	UP-208		11/81	43743	
MP-4809:2	UP-209		11/81	43744	
MP-4810:2	UP-210		11/81	43745	NLR "block" lettering as UP-210
MP-4811:2	UP-211		11/81	43746	Wore MP yellow as MP-4811
MP-4812:2	UP-212		12/81	43747	Wore MP yellow as MP-4812
MP-4813:2	UP-213		12/81	43748	
MP-4814:2	UP-214		12/81	43749	
MP-4815:2	UP-215		12/81	43750	Wore MP yellow as MP-4815
MP-4816:2	UP-216		12/81	43751	Wore MP yellow as MP-4816
MP-4817:2	UP-217		12/81	43752	NLR "block" lettering as UP-217
MP-4818:2	UP-218		12/81	43753	Wore MP yellow as MP-4818
MP-4819:2	UP-219		12/81	43754	Wore MP yellow as MP-4819
MP-4820:2	UP-220		12/81	43755	
MP-4821:2	UP-221		12/81	43756	
MP-4822:2	UP-222		12/81	43757	
MP-4823:2	UP-223		12/81	43758	Wore MP yellow as MP-4823
MP-4824:2	UP-224		12/81	43759	Wore MP yellow as MP-4824
MP-4825:2	UP-225		12/81	43760	
MP-4826:2	UP-226		12/81	43761	
MP-4827:2	UP-227		12/81	43762	
MP-4828:2	UP-228		12/81	43763	
MP-4829:2	UP-229		12/81	43764	
MP-4830	UP-230		01/82	43765	
MP-4831	UP-231		01/82	43766	Wore MP yellow as MP-4831
MP-4832	UP-232		01/82	43767	
MP-4833	UP-233		01/82	43768	Wore MP yellow as MP-4833
MP-4834	UP-234		01/82	43769	Wore MP yellow as MP-4834
MP-4835	UP-235		01/82	43586	
MP-4836	UP-236		01/82	43587	Wore MP yellow as MP-4836
MP-4837	UP-237		01/82	43588	
MP-4838	UP-238		01/82	43589	
MP-4839	UP-239		01/82	43590	Wore MP yellow as MP-4839
MP-4840	UP-240		01/82	43591	
MP-4841	UP-241		01/82	43592	NLR "block" lettering as UP-241
MP-4842	UP-242		01/82	43593	Last blue B30-7A
MP-4843	UP-243		01/82	43594	
MP-4844	UP-4844	UP-244	01/82	43595	
MP-4845	UP-245		01/82	43596	Wore MP yellow as MP-4845
MP-4846	UP-246		01/82	43597	
MP-4847	UP-247		01/82	43598	
MP-4848	UP-248		01/82	43599	
MP-4849	UP-249		02/82	43674	
MP-4850	UP-250		02/82	43675	Wore MP yellow as MP-4850
MP-4851	UP-251		02/82	43676	Wore MP yellow as MP-4851
MP-4852	UP-252		02/82	43677	Wore MP yellow as MP-4852
MP-4853	UP-253		02/82	43678	
MP-4854	UP-254		02/82	43679	NLR "block" lettering as UP-254

EMD
SD50
GP40
GP40-2

GE
C36-7

The UP announced on January 8, 1980 an agreement in principle to acquire the Missouri Pacific, then an 11,469-mile system compared to UP's 9,420-mile system. The deal was roughly $1 billion. Right on the heels of this announcement, which was an extremely well-kept secret within the industry, was a similar announcement concerning control of the Western Pacific. On April 18, 1980, the stockholders approved the merger plan. The formal merger application was filed on September 12, 1980, and included 4,300 pages of documentation that indicated that the merger of the MoPac, UP and WP would result in a 22,800 mile system with 54,000 employees. Pacific Rail System, Inc. would be formed to control the two major railroads (WP, already 87% owned by UP, would be part of the UP).

In November, 1980, the SP filed suit to block the proposed merger, citing violations of the Pacific Rail-

way Acts of 1862 and 1864 as a primary grievance. That legislation can be put into perspective when it is noted that the legislation in question was signed into law by Abraham Lincoln. SP found itself on the losing end of numerous merger attempts throughout the previous 20 years, including a failed attempt at getting the southern end of the Rock Island and merging with the Western Pacific. They also claimed to be hurt by the UP's and the MoPac's treatment of Midwestern traffic.

By January, 1981 10 railroads had filed motions relative to the proposed merger. It was speculated that the MoPac could retain its separate identity, retaining its locomotives and paint scheme, speculation that obviously didn't pan out.

The scene remained relatively quiet for the next two years, as various phases of the merger hearings were completed. The second phase included testimony from Burlington Northern, Santa Fe, Katy, and Rio Grande. Shipper witnesses were also cross-examined in Denver and Dallas, and the third phase began in September, 1981 after all parties had filed evidence with the ICC in opposition to the merger. Interestingly,

the president of the Public Interests Economists testified that flat denial of the merger would better serve public interests. An economist and witness for the Department of Transportation stated that the benefit of the merger should not override the reductions in competition. Yet another economist testified that the merger would impose costs of between $3 and $11 million on the public annually. Other railroads claimed that they would lose $263 million annually.

By the summer of 1982, things were beginning to look different. The UP/WP/MP merger partners agreed to grant trackage rights to the Rio Grande between Denver and Kansas City as part of the concession package for the merger. This 619-mile package removed what the Justice Department referred to as "the only competitive problem with the merger." All other requests from other railroads were found to be

Below: A pair of SD50's led by 5016 roll another trainload of Wyoming coal into Kansas City, Missouri on September 1, 1985. They are running along the bluff at the south edge of Neff Yard. Two 3,600 horsepower SD50's replaced three 3,000 horsepower SD40-2's on the Wyoming coal trains. *Paul DeLuca*

switchers 1240, 1241, and 1245 were assigned to the MoPac in Texas, while the MoPac's MP15DC's 1389, 1391, and 1392, were assigned to the UP on the west coast.

As the two partners struggled to begin the process of integrating their fleets, a lease agreement between the UP and the MoPac put a number of SD45's on MoPac rails. In mid December, 1983, four UP SD45's (UP-4, 10, 22, and 32) were removed from storage at Yermo, California and leased to the MoPac to help relieve their motive power shortage. In January, 1984, 14 more SD45's came to the MoPac after reconditioning at Salt Lake City, Utah. These included UP-1, 6, 8, 9, 11, 17, 20, 21, 23, 31, 36, 41, 45, and 47. Ownership of at least five of these units (UP-4, 6, 17, 32, and 41) was transferred to the MoPac on March 13, 1986, but like the C&EI GP30's of nearly two decades before,

without justification by the ICC. Rumors began to circulate that the MoPac's 6000-series "SD40-2c's" were headed for the WP after merger approval, and that some of WP's GP40's and GP40-2's were headed for the MoPac proper. These rumors later turned out to be fact.

On September 13, 1982 the ICC announced that its vote approved the merger consolidations. The formal written decision was issued by the ICC on October 20, 1982, and on November 15 the ICC denied all requests to stay the merger.

On December 9 the District of Columbia Court of Appeals refused to stay the merger plans. On December 22, 1982, the Supreme Court denied requests for a stay of the merger and consummated the consolidations at 2:25 pm: The merger was approved. The MoPac would become a subsidiary of the Union Pacific, and the two railroads together would own or lease a total of 3,330 engines. By early May, 1983, the motive power for the two fleets began the process of slowly being integrated and mixed up. UP

Below: Three SD50's are in charge of a train of empties headed north on the ex-MKT on the north side of Parsons, Kansas on May 28, 1988. Their Missouri Pacific lettering has not long to live. *David Fasules*

none were repainted into MoPac colors, another interesting might-have-been.

Eighteen months after the merger took place between the MoPac, the UP, and the WP, the MoPac announced that they would begin painting their fleet into UP's yellow and gray scheme, but employing Missouri Pacific lettering. The official announcement came out on May 31, 1984, but the first unit had actually been

Below: The C36-7 was one of those between-phase models that represents a unique step between two models in a locomotive line. Early C36-7's look entirely like C30-7's, except for the presence of exhaust silencers. After a production hiatus in 1983, C36-7's took on a new appearance, with Dash 8 features including dynamic brake grids and an enlarged equipment blower fan in a high box behind the cab. Late in the production period, the horsepower was boosted from 3,600 to 3,750. Norfolk Southern bought C36-7's with the Dash 8 features, but these were still rated at 3,600 horsepower. Conrail then bought 25 C36-7's, but these returned to the earlier C30-7-style appearance, though rated at 3,750 horsepower. MoPac's order was the last order for C36-7's, and they had both the Dash 8 appearance and the boosted horsepower figure. In many ways they could have been designated as a Dash 8. A pair from the final C36-7 order for GE roll the CHFWZ through Momence, Illinois in March, 1987. *Paul Meyer*

Above: In December, 1983, four UP SD45's were pulled out of the dead line at Yermo, California and reconditioned for lease to the MoPac. One month later an additional 14 SD45's came to work on MoPac rails. Five of these units actually became MoPac units when their ownership was transferred to the MoPac. This included 4, 6, 17, 32, and 41. Two of the lease units, 22 and 20, lead a trio of BN units on a coal train at Neff Yard in Kansas City, Missouri on March 30, 1984. None of the SD45's ever wore any MoPac markings. *Kevin EuDaly*

completed two weeks before, on May 14. The MoPac's painters had already completed a trip to North Platte, Nebraska, where they learned the intricacies of the UP scheme in March, 1984. The last unit that was painted in MoPac blue was SD40-2 MP-3270, which left the paint shop in late March or early April, 1984.

In this same time-frame, the UP decided to try an experimental paint scheme on a MoPac unit. There were no MoPac units handy, so they appropriated a UP SD40, UP-3030, which was

next in line for repainting. The unit was painted solid yellow with a black underframe and trucks. It was lettered MP, but only wore the experimental paint scheme for about two hours. It was then taken right back into the paint shop and painted into standard UP livery. This is without a doubt the shortest-lived MoPac unit.

MoPac's version of the yellow and gray UP scheme included lettering that differed somewhat from the standard UP type. The lettering was much more squared off, and these have been referred to as "North Little Rock" lettered units. The MoPac units also began the demise of the silver trucks on the UP, as MoPac's were painted gray. Additionally, the anti-glare panel on the top of the short hood was painted gray rather than UP's standard green. The UP adopted the gray trucks simultaneously.

When the MoPac announced the plans for painting units yellow and gray on May 31, 1984, they also announced that the MoPac's diesel fleet would be renumbered to eliminate conflicts with UP's roster. A committee was formed to formulate a renumbering plan, and this progressed through the end of 1984 and well into 1985. The final version of the renumbering plan was approved on December 19, 1985, and was referred to as "Revision D."

The railroad soon found the renumbering plan to be confusing to the painters, primarily as a result of MoPac's input into the plan. The MoPac's standard practice was to fill in gaps in locomotive sequences with other units, resulting in each number series being complete with no holes. The UP, on the other hand, left gaps and simply renumbered classes by changing the first digits in the sequence. An initial indication of the problems with the MoPac philosophy showed up as the B23-7's were being renumbered into the 100-series. MP-4636 had been wrecked and retired and its slot in the roster (MP-4636 or UP-136) was "closed" by lowering the number of all higher-numbered B23-7's by one number, thus closing the gap.

When the MP-4662 was renumbered on December 13, 1985, it was given UP-161 as its road number, a reflection of the MoPac philosophy. The UP then decided that this would cause unnecessary confusion for the UP painters, and the unit was "corrected" to UP-162. A similar thing happened when a group of 40 MoPac SD40's were slated to leave the roster due to expired leases (MP-3034-3053 and MP-3070-3089). The remaining units were put in UP's 4100-series, less 40, so MP-3158 became UP-4118. Again these unit's numbers were later "corrected." These corrections also forced the MoPac "SD40-2c's" (MP-6000-6073) to fall in the 3900-series rather than falling in as UP-4222-4295.

These renumberings or "correcting" of numbers affected 12 units. These included three GE units that got their old MoPac numbers after being painted yellow and lettered UP (UP-4616, 4679, and 4844) and the previously mentioned "corrected" UP-161, which was changed to UP-

162. There were eight SD40-2's that were assigned to hump service in Kansas City that had 40 subtracted from their renumbered numbers (UP-4118, 4162-4165, and 4167-4169), and these were later "corrected" to UP-4158, 4202-4205, and 4207-4209.

As merger discussion progressed between the MoPac and the UP, the MoPac hesitated to buy new power. By mid-1984 they were again in need of new road power, but were now in the Union Pacific fold. The final two orders of power for the MoPac - now in yellow and gray - came in equal quantities from EMD and GE, indicating further the gradual swing in GE's favor. The first was an order for 60 SD50's from EMD.

As the horsepower figure crept upward, excessive wheelslip had to be dealt with. The 50-series, pioneered by the 40X models (GP40X and SD40X), incorporated a single axle wheelslip system that had been derived from ASEA licenses, and was the main factor that made the higher horsepower figures attainable without

Above: A pair of SD50's sail through Marche, Arkansas on the Van Buren Subdivision in August, 1985. March lies ten miles north of North Little Rock and 20 miles south of the tunnel at Conway. *Robin Thomas*

excessive wheelslip. This system had been pioneered on five "SD40-2SS's," which were test beds for the "Super Series" electrical system in units with six traction motors. A larger alternator is the only other difference between the "SD40-2SS" and a standard SD40-2. The resultant wheelslip control is found on 50- and 60-series models.

Another change in the SD50 from previous 40-series models was a change in location for the dynamic brakes. Though the dynamic brake

Below: SD50 5008 leads a four unit, 14,400 horsepower lashup of the big EMDs through Fort Worth on March 23, 1986. This would net out at about one horsepower per ton on the average Powder River Basin coal train, a pretty stout figure for the relatively flat MoPac. *Bill Phillips*

Right: The MoPac-izing of ex-Rock Island and Western Pacific GP40's and ex-Western Pacific GP40-2's brought those two models officially to the MoPac roster. There were 29 units that were added to MoPac's all-time list, including GP40 608, on the point of a west-bound manifest at Rock Creek Junction in Kansas City, Missouri on August 29, 1986. *Kevin EuDaly*

location made virtually no difference to the MoPac, who had few engines with dynamic brakes, many roads had problems with dynamic brakes overheating under stressful conditions. The dynamic brake had long been located directly over the prime mover, compounding the heat problem. With the SD40X and 50-series design, the dynamic brake resistors were relocated from up over the prime mover to a location between the central air intake and the cab, which helped reduce overheating problems.

The original SD50's (purchased by the Kansas City Southern, the Norfolk and Western, Chessie System Transportation, and Conrail) were 3,500 horsepower. The MoPac's order in 1984 were the first SD50's that were "uprated" to 3,600 horsepower. These were once dubbed as "SD50+'s" by rail enthusiasts, but there is no external difference between the 3,600 and 3,500 horsepower models.

The MoPac's order of 60 SD50's (MP-5000-5059) came in November and December, 1984, and were the first MoPac units delivered in Union Pacific's yellow and gray. They came lettered "Missouri Pacific." They and the later C36-7's were delivered in the interim period when the Union Pacific had purchased the MoPac but had yet to fully integrate the two companies. It would not be long, however, as the MoPac's headquarters in St. Louis were officially moved to Omaha effective the first day of 1986.

In mid-1985 an order similar to the 1984 order was placed, but this time with GE. GE's competition to the SD50 was the C36-7. The first C36-7 was an Engine Department test unit numbered GE-505, which was built in June, 1978. The first production models went to the Norfolk and Western, and were nearly identical to the C30-7's with the notable exception of the presence of exhaust silencers.

After a production hiatus in 1983, the C36-7's came out in 1984 with GE's new Dash 8 components and features. Dynamic brake grids in a high box over an enlarged equipment blower fan make a significant difference in the appearance of the locomotives. After June, 1985, the C36-7 horsepower rating was boosted to 3,750. Conrail bought 25 boosted units, but they again lacked the Dash 8 appearance, not having the pronounced dynamic brake grid and larger blower openings. The MoPac units had it all - the large raised dynamic brake box, large blower motor grilles, and 3,750 horsepower. They were not, however, microprocessor controlled.

The MoPac's 60 C36-7's (MP-9000-9059) came in yellow and gray like the SD50's, with

"Missouri Pacific" lettering as well. The C36-7's posted a phenomenal availability record early in their career, as high as 96%. Shortly after their delivery the MoPac name followed so many other railroad names into history. Missouri Pacific lettering was discontinued in November, 1985. The SD50's and the C36-7's were quickly and quietly painted or relettered "Union Pacific."

In this same period, one more strange move added a few final units to the MoPac's all-time diesel roster. Twenty two ex-Chicago, Rock Island and Pacific GP40's were repainted in UP colors and were relettered "Missouri Pacific." Some of these were already in UP yellow and gray. These were non-consecutive numbers in the 600-series. Three ex-Western Pacific GP40's were also repainted in "Missouri Pacific" yellow and gray and numbered in the 600-series. These units had been in storage for about four years when traffic demands forced them to be reconditioned and put back in service. They were missing many parts, and returned to service in St. Louis. There was originally a pool of 35 units in this group, but only 25 found their way back onto rails with Missouri Pacific on their flanks.

The first pair relettered were the MP-628 and 662, which "became" MoPac in May, 1984. There were ten units that were not repainted or relettered MoPac, and these were retired in July, 1985 and sold to Precision, officially as MoPac engines. These were as follows: CRI&P-347, 349, 357, 358, 363, 366, 367, 373, 4703, 4710, 4713, 4718, UP-648 (in UP yellow and lettered UP), and CRI&P-4719. There were also four ex-Western Pacific GP40-2's that were repainted in "Missouri Pacific" yellow and gray and renumbered in the 900-series. All subsequently were relettered "Union Pacific."

B23-7 MP-4616 was the first MoPac unit painted yellow with UP lettering, launching the campaign that has eradicated the Missouri Pacific name from locomotive sides.

In early 1986, the UP put the MoPac's first two orders of SD40's in yard service, reclassify-

Opposite page top: SD50's 5005 and 5056 streak south with coal tonnage, passing Oologah, Oklahoma on September 20, 1986. Oologah is the site of a large power plant, but this train is headed further south. A pair of SD50's was standard for coal trains on the line through Coffeyville, Kansas. *Kevin EuDaly*

Opposite page bottom: A trio of SD50's heads east through Allenton, Missouri with a train of empty hoppers from the power plant at West Labadie. The train will go into St. Louis, re-crew, and head for the coalfields of southern Illinois for another trainload of energy in solid form. I-44 is in the background, and the tunnel at Gray Summit is not far behind on April 17, 1987. The MoPac name is on borrowed time. *Terry Chicwak*

ing them as "SD40Y's." The SD40 made a good yard engine for several reasons. UP had first used big road power in yard service when they utilized 15 SD45's as hump power across the UP system. However, the 20-cylinder turbocharged engine tended to get lube oil into the exhaust manifold while in low speed, low demand service. The first time the engine was worked hard, the oil caught fire and the turbocharger exploded due to running overspeed. The SD40's weren't susceptible to this problem, and with almost no electrical work could be placed in this type of service. The "SD40Y's" were also retrofitted with four cab seats for this service.

MoPac dieseldom was over. With the acquisition of the C36-7's, the MoPac was done with their 50-year history of acquiring Rudolph Diesel's invention. In less than a decade, the MoPac fleet would be eradicated, as so many fallen flags have experienced in the past. Other roads fell much faster, and in fact, it took a decade from merger day to paint the last active unit on UP's roster from blue into yellow, and to retire the remaining blue units.

EMD SD50 3,600 hp 60 units
TE = 91,980 WT = 368,000
Wheels = 40" Fuel = 4,500
Engine: EMD 16-645F3B 16-cylinder 2-cycle
Turbocharged
Min Speed for TE = 12.0 mph
70:17 Gearing 70 mph Max
SD50's were delivered in MP yellow

1st No	2nd No	Built	Builder #
MP-5000	UP-5000	11/84	847008-1
MP-5001	UP-5001	11/84	847008-2
MP-5002	UP-5002	11/84	847008-3
MP-5003	UP-5003	11/84	847008-4
MP-5004	UP-5004	11/84	847008-5
MP-5005	UP-5005	11/84	847008-6
MP-5006	UP-5006	11/84	847008-7
MP-5007	UP-5007	11/84	847008-8
MP-5008	UP-5008	11/84	847008-9
MP-5009	UP-5009	11/84	847008-10
MP-5010	UP-5010	11/84	847008-11
MP-5011	UP-5011	11/84	847008-12
MP-5012	UP-5012	11/84	847008-13
MP-5013	UP-5013	11/84	847008-14
MP-5014	UP-5014	11/84	847008-15
MP-5015	UP-5015	11/84	847008-16
MP-5016	UP-5016	11/84	847008-17
MP-5017	UP-5017	11/84	847008-18
MP-5018	UP-5018	11/84	847008-19
MP-5019	UP-5019	11/84	847008-20
MP-5020	UP-5020	11/84	847008-21
MP-5021	UP-5021	11/84	847008-22
MP-5022	UP-5022	11/84	847008-23
MP-5023	UP-5023	11/84	847008-24
MP-5024	UP-5024	11/84	847008-25
MP-5025	UP-5025	11/84	847008-26
MP-5026	UP-5026	11/84	847008-27
MP-5027	UP-5027	12/84	847008-28
MP-5028	UP-5028	12/84	847008-29
MP-5029	UP-5029	12/84	847008-30
MP-5030	UP-5030	12/84	847008-31
MP-5031	UP-5031	12/84	847008-32
MP-5032	UP-5032	12/84	847008-33
MP-5033	UP-5033	12/84	847008-34
MP-5034	UP-5034	12/84	847008-35
MP-5035	UP-5035	12/84	847008-36
MP-5036	UP-5036	12/84	847008-37
MP-5037	UP-5037	12/84	847008-38
MP-5038	UP-5038	12/84	847008-39
MP-5039	UP-5039	12/84	847008-40
MP-5040	UP-5040	12/84	847008-41
MP-5041	UP-5041	12/84	847008-42
MP-5042	UP-5042	12/84	847008-43
MP-5043	UP-5043	12/84	847008-44
MP-5044	UP-5044	12/84	847008-45
MP-5045	UP-5045	12/84	847008-46
MP-5046	UP-5046	12/84	847008-47
MP-5047	UP-5047	12/84	847008-48
MP-5048	UP-5048	12/84	847008-49
MP-5049	UP-5049	12/84	847008-50
MP-5050	UP-5050	12/84	847008-51
MP-5051	UP-5051	12/84	847008-52
MP-5052	UP-5052	12/84	847008-53
MP-5053	UP-5053	12/84	847008-54
MP-5054	UP-5054	12/84	847008-55
MP-5055	UP-5055	12/84	847008-56
MP-5056	UP-5056	12/84	847008-57
MP-5057	UP-5057	12/84	847008-58
MP-5058	UP-5058	12/84	847008-59
MP-5059	UP-5059	12/84	847008-60

GE C36-7 3,750 hp 60 units
TE = 97,750 WT = 391,000
Wheels = 40" Fuel = 4,500
Engine: GE 7FDL-16 16-cylinder 2-cycle
Turbocharged
Min Speed for TE = 10.0 mph
83:20 Gearing 70 mph Max
C36-7s were delivered in MP yellow

1st No	2nd No	Built	Build#
MP-9000:2	UP-9000	9/85	45040
MP-9001:2	UP-9001	9/85	45041
MP-9002:2	UP-9002	9/85	45042
MP-9003:2	UP-9003	9/85	45043
MP-9004:2	UP-9004	9/85	45044
MP-9005:2	UP-9005	9/85	45045
MP-9006:2	UP-9006	9/85	45046
MP-9007:2	UP-9007	9/85	45047
MP-9008:2	UP-9008	9/85	45048
MP-9009:2	UP-9009	9/85	45049
MP-9010:2	UP-9010	9/85	45050
MP-9011:2	UP-9011	9/85	45051
MP-9012:2	UP-9012	9/85	45052
MP-9013	UP-9013	9/85	45053
MP-9014	UP-9014	9/85	45054
MP-9015	UP-9015	10/85	45055
MP-9016:2	UP-9016	10/85	45056
MP-9017:2	UP-9017	10/85	45057
MP-9018:2	UP-9018	10/85	45058
MP-9019:2	UP-9019	10/85	45059
MP-9020:2	UP-9020	10/85	45060
MP-9021:2	UP-9021	10/85	45061
MP-9022	UP-9022	10/85	45062
MP-9023	UP-9023	10/85	45063
MP-9024	UP-9024	10/85	45064
MP-9025	UP-9025	10/85	45065

1st No	2nd No	Built	Build#
MP-9026	UP-9026	10/85	45066
MP-9027	UP-9027	10/85	45067
MP-9028	UP-9028	10/85	45068
MP-9029	UP-9029	10/85	45069
MP-9030	UP-9030	10/85	45070
MP-9031	UP-9031	10/85	45071
MP-9032	UP-9032	10/85	45072
MP-9033	UP-9033	10/85	45073
MP-9034	UP-9034	10/85	45074
MP-9035	UP-9035	10/85	45075
MP-9036	UP-9036	10/85	45076
MP-9037	UP-9037	10/85	45077
MP-9038	UP-9038	10/85	45078
MP-9039	UP-9039	10/85	45079
MP-9040	UP-9040	10/85	45080
MP-9041	UP-9041	10/85	45081
MP-9042	UP-9042	10/85	45082
MP-9043	UP-9043	10/85	45083
MP-9044	UP-9044	10/85	45084
MP-9045	UP-9045	10/85	45085
MP-9046	UP-9046	10/85	45086
MP-9047	UP-9047	10/85	45087
MP-9048	UP-9048	10/85	45088
MP-9049	UP-9049	10/85	45089
MP-9050	UP-9050	10/85	45090
MP-9051	UP-9051	10/85	45091
MP-9052	UP-9052	10/85	45092
MP-9053	UP-9053	10/85	45093
MP-9054	UP-9054	10/85	45094
MP-9055	UP-9055	10/85	45095
MP-9056	UP-9056	11/85	45096
MP-9057	UP-9057	11/85	45097
MP-9058	UP-9058	11/85	45098
MP-9059	UP-9059	11/85	45099

Right: Ex-Rock Island GP40 611 is at West Frankfort, Illinois on January 17, 1986. It is one of 14 ex-300-series Rock units built in 1966. All have been retired from UP's roster. *Mike Wise photo, Kevin EuDaly collection*

MoPac GP40 639 was Rock Island 4708, and was one of eight 4700-series ex-Rock units on MoPac's roster. None are currently active, and the 639 went to the Phoenix Railway, and then to Helm. It is at Council Bluffs, Iowa on December 12, 1988. *Ken Church*

EMD GP40   3,000 hp   14 units
TE = 66,500   WT = 266,000
Wheels = 40"   Fuel = 3,400
Engine: EMD 16-645E3 16-cylinder 2-cycle Turbocharged
Min Speed for TE = 12.0 mph
62:15 Gearing   65 mph Max
MP-626:4 had 61:15 Gearing
As MP units wore only MP yellow

1st No	2nd No	Built	To MP	Build#	Retired	Notes & Dispositions
CRI&P-340	MP-600:2	09/66	06/85	32232	06/91	To NRE
CRI&P-343	MP-603:2	09/66	09/85	32235	10/88	Note 1
CRI&P-344	MP-604:2	09/66	04/85	32236	08/87	Note 2
CRI&P-345	MP-605	09/66	04/85	32237	10/91	To HELM
CRI&P-346	MP-606:2	09/66	11/84	32238	08/87	Note 3
CRI&P-348	MP-608:2	09/66	03/85	32240	10/92	
CRI&P-351	MP-611:2	09/66	08/85	32243	06/91	To NRE
CRI&P-352	MP-612:2	09/66	07/84	32244	08/87	Note 4
CRI&P-355	MP-615:3	09/66	04/85	32247	08/87	Note 5
CRI&P-356	MP-616:3	10/66	04/85	32248	02/90	Note 6
CRI&P-364	MP-622:3	12/66	03/85	32590	10/92	
CRI&P-368	MP-626:4	12/66	12/84	32594	08/87	Note 7
CRI&P-371	MP-628:3	12/66	11/84	32597	08/87	Note 8
CRI&P-372	MP-629:2	12/66	10/84	32598	08/87	Note 9

Note 1: To Wilson Locomotive, Des Moines, IA
Note 2: To MK, rebuilt to Metro North Commuter "GP40FH-2," r# MNCR-4186
Note 3: To MK, rebuilt to New Jersey Transit "GP40FH-2," r# NJT-4140
Note 4: To MK, rebuilt to Metro North Commuter "GP40FH-2," r# MNCR-4185
Note 5: To MK, rebuilt to Metro North Commuter "GP40FH-2," r# MNCR-4187
Note 6: Wrecked by FNM, scrapped
Note 7: To MK, rebuilt to Metro North Commuter "GP40FH-2," r# MNCR-4189
Note 8: To MK, rebuilt to Cotton Belt GP40-2, r# SSW-7274
Note 9: To MK, rebuilt to Metro North Commuter "GP40FH-2," r# MNCR-4188

EMD GP40   3,000 hp   8 units
TE = 66,000   WT = 264,000
Wheels = 40"   Fuel = 3,200
Engine: EMD 16-645E3 16-cylinder 2-cycle Turbocharged
Min Speed for TE = 12.0 mph
62:15 Gearing   65 mph Max
MP-639:2 had 59:18 Gearing
MP-645 had 61:16 Gearing
As MP units wore only MP yellow

1st No	2nd No	Built	To MP	Build#	Retired	Notes & Dispositions
CRI&P-4700	MP-631:3	03/70	11/84	36386		Stored 01/91
CRI&P-4701	MP-632:3	03/70	07/85	36387	03/93	Note 1
CRI&P-4702	MP-633:2	03/70	06/85	36388	10/91	Note 2
CRI&P-4704	MP-635:2	03/70	05/85	36390	10/91	Scrapped
CRI&P-4706	MP-637:3	04/70	05/85	36392	10/88	Note 3
CRI&P-4708	MP-639:2	04/70	09/85	36394	10/91	Note 4
CRI&P-4711	MP-642:2	04/70	06/85	36397	10/91	To NRE
CRI&P-4714	MP-645	04/70	02/85	36400	10/9	Note 5

Note 1: To Missouri & Northern Arkansas, r# MNA-632
Note 2: To Phoenix Railway, to Helm 04/92
Note 3: To VMV, rebuilt and leased 07/89 to UP as UP-856
Note 4: To Phoenix Railway, to Helm 03/92
Note 5: To NRE 05/93, to Missouri & Northern Arkansas, r# MNA-645

EMD GP40   3,000 hp   3 units
TE = 69,250   WT = 277,000
Wheels = 40"   Fuel = 3,600
Engine: EMD 16-645E3 16-cylinder 2-cycle Turbocharged
Min Speed for TE = 12.0 mph
62:15 Gearing   71 mph Max
As MP units wore only MP yellow

1st No	2nd No	3rd No	Built	To MP	Build#	Retired
WP-3501	MP-651	UP-651	05/66	05/85	31662	04/93
WP-3512	MP-662	UP-662	04/67	05/84	33058	04/93
WP-3515	MP-665	UP-665	04/67	05/85	33061	04/93

Right: An era ends. The last MoPac unit is ready for action in February, 1986. It is the final descendent of over 3,000 MoPac diesels, from diminutive Plymouth four-wheelers, covered wagons and geeps, through utilitarian B-B roadswitchers to the high horsepower lady that she is. The last remnants of the great MoPac diesel fleet are now all but extinct. Within a few years the name itself will fade into the ranks of yesteryear. *Kevin EuDaly collection*

EMD GP40-2   3,000 hp   4 units
TE = 69,250   WT = 277,000
Wheels = 40"   Fuel = 3,600
Engine: EMD 16-645E3 16-cylinder 2-cycle Turbocharged
Min Speed for TE = 12.0 mph
62:15 Gearing   71 mph Max
As MP units wore only MP yellow

1st No	2nd No	3rd No	Built	Build#
WP-3545	MP-900:2	UP-3002	07/79	786220-1
WP-3546	MP-901:2	UP-3003	07/79	786220-2
WP-3549	MP-904:2	UP-3006	07/79	786220-5
WP-3552	MP-907:2	UP-907	04/80	786220-8

Below top: The MoPac "acquired" three ex-Western Pacific GP40's after the merger, a result of the MoPac's corporate identity lasting longer then WP's. One of the three, 651 (ex-3501) is at Las Vegas, Nevada on November 30, 1988. *Mark Wayman photo, Randy Keller collection*

Below middle: Four ex-Western Pacific GP40-2's were the last units the MoPac acquired. The 904 is in fresh paint in October, 1985. *Tony Fey*

Right: SD50 5053 leads another SD50 and a C36-7 hard into the curve at Hecla, Kansas on August 17, 1986. They are on a typical assignment, loads for Arkansas Power's White Bluff Generating Station. *Kevin EuDaly*

Below: A four-unit lashup of C36-7's blaze past milepost 33 on the ex-Missouri-Kansas-Texas/BN joint trackage south of Spring Hill, Kansas on May 19, 1986. The four C36-7's have conquered the hill up into Olathe, Kansas, and are now sailing down the hill towards Paola, Kansas, where they can either stay on the ex-MKT, or diverge onto the MoPac to Coffeyville, Kansas. *Lon EuDaly*

Right: A trio of brand new C36-7's is in West Labadie coal train service right after their delivery to the MoPac. They are at Dupo, Illinois on November 16, 1985. The set is consecutively numbered, 9020 followed by 9019 and 9021. They haven't turned many miles yet. *Paul DeLuca*

Below: 9033 and 9051 whisk a hot southbound through Ware, Illinois on March 28, 1987. Eventually, the C36-7 fleet was scattered throughout the system, and could be seen in nearly any type of service where a high horsepower unit was needed. *Kevin EuDaly*

Every major railroad has a fleet of locomotives that are in transition in some way. Time dictates changes within a roster, and often market forces drive even further change. Mergers, acquisitions, and bankruptcy have all played major roles in shaping the railroads of today. All came from the railroads of yesterday. The MoPac is now a railroad of yesterday.

For the MoPac, from Eagles, to buzz-saws, to flying eagle buzz-saws, to yellow and gray, the assimilation into the new owner's system was a somewhat difficult period of transition. There were several major differences in the UP and the MoPac diesel fleets when the two operating departments began to merge their operations, a process that took several years. Within three years of the merger, the new system had accomplished a unit reduction of 618 engines, one of the efficiencies created by the merger. The differences in the fleet included the fact that the MoPac's fleet tended

to be medium horsepower, B-B units without dynamic brakes, while UP's fleet leaned more toward high horsepower C-C's with dynamic brakes on nearly everything.

A complicating factor, and one that caused many MoPac units to stay on the roster longer than they otherwise would have, was that the MoPac fleet was almost entirely made up of units that were not actually owned outright or on an equipment trust, but rather were acquired using leveraged leases which typically ran 15 years. At the end of an equipment trust the railroad owns the locomotive, but at the end of a leveraged lease the unit reverts back to the leasing company, which usually has in place an option for the railroad to then purchase the locomotive. These lease agreements were very restrictive, and tied UP's hands as far as repainting, relettering, and selling the leveraged lease units. For any change, the approval of the lessor had to be obtained.

This only delayed the inevitable. Screaming eagles would soon become only a memory. One unit, GP15-1 MP-1621, became known as the MoPac "Die Hard" unit when an unknown painter sprayed a small red MoPac eagle on the

Victims:

Top: The name plate on the side of KO&G F7 847 is already a relic on March 26, 1964 at Denison, Texas. The unit has already been transferred to the T&P. *Joe McMillan*

Above: The screaming eagle is nearly eradicated by the new look on May 1, 1984 at UP's Armstrong Yard in Kansas City, Kansas. *Kevin EuDaly*

Below: Nearly every merger produces its own set of oddities. Occasionally, the lensman is lucky and perceptive enough to run into circumstances that yield both confusion and interest. Such is the case at Kansas City in

Neff Yard, where a pair of 3294's rest side by side on September 2, 1987. When the roadmaster calls for 3294 to be put on a southbound, which will the hostler move to the train? *J Harlen Wilson*

Right: Long before the image change from blue to yellow was imagined, the MoPac changed images from the attractive blue and gray scheme typically associated with the *Eagles*, to a solid "Jenks" blue scheme with the buzz-saw and white frame stripes. Only two FA's are known to have gotten this scheme, 335 and 382. The pair are at North Little Rock on September 10, 1961. *Louis Marre*

Below: The first visible sign of the impending merger was the sudden presence of inspection trains all over the system. It is believed by many that the UP officials traveled every inch of MoPac mainline and branchline trackage in a thorough attempt to understand exactly what they were buying. The inspection trains ran primarily in 1982, and B30-7A 4831 is in charge of one of them at Lakeview, Arkansas in February, 1982. The presence of one UP car tells of things to come. In a little over a decade, every MoPac unit on the system will be either yellow or gone. *Steve Forrest*

Above: Missouri Pacific GP15-1's in yellow and blue roll through Steger, Illinois in September, 1984. The 1690 is the only road unit known to have received the 16-inch switcher-size lettering. There were 33 GP15-1's that wore the Yellow MoPac scheme. *Paul Meyer*

Left: MoPac B30-7A 4816 blasts around the curve at Kenneth, Kansas on April 6, 1986, leading yellow "SD40-2c" 6059 and blue "SD40-2c" 6065. Twenty one of the 55 B30-7A's were repainted with MoPac lettering, making them one of the classes that experienced a relatively high repaint percentage. *Kevin EuDaly*

Opposite page top: It is most fortunate that there was no period of painting boxes over lettering, which always results in the worst possible appearance. Until the end of the MoPac, the units were either left in MoPac blue, painted yellow with Missouri Pacific lettering, or painted UP. Railroads like the Milwaukee Road were not so fortunate, where black boxes painted over lettering resulted in the last of their once-proud fleet looking hideous. On June 6, 1987, lead GP38-2 2196 is in full UP dress while trailing GP38-2 2096 still wears MoPac blue at Lee's Summit, Missouri. Neither ever wore the yellow MoPac interim scheme. *Kevin EuDaly*

Below: Sparkling fresh yellow paint adorns B30-7A 4819 at Mandeville, Arkansas on January 19, 1985. The B-Boat leads SD40 3021 in the later Jenks blue scheme and an SD40-2 in the earlier turbocharged eagle scheme. *Paul DeLuca*

MoPac in Yellow

There were 275 units that were repainted into the yellow and gray with MoPac style lettering. Additionally, there were 120 units bought new that arrived from the builders in the MoPac yellow and gray, resulting in a grand total of 395 units that wore this scheme. Only one complete class was repainted, the GP50's. The GP50's were repainted incredibly fast, with 21 of the 30 in yellow by December 8, 1984. They were all yellow ten weeks later. The rosters that cover these units include a notation for the units that carried the yellow and gray. All originally wore blue unless indicated otherwise. GP15-1 MP-1690 carried 16-inch switcher lettering rather than the standard road freight size lettering. It is the only known unit with this variation. The MoPac folks nicknamed these "canaries," due to their yellow paint. Here's a complete list:

25 GP40 600, 603, 604, 605, 608, 611, 612, 615, 616, 622, 626, 628, 629, 631, 632, 633, 635, 637, 639, 642, 645, 651, 662, 665
(MP-600-645 were ex-Rock Island and MP-651-665 were ex-Western Pacific, none ever wore MoPac blue)
4 GP40-2 900, 901, 904, 907
(All ex-Western Pacific, none ever wore MoPac blue)
1 SW1200 1153
3 Slug 1407, 1408, 1409
1 SW1500 1518
14 MP15DC 1357, 1362, 1370, 1371, 1372, 1373, 1377, 1379, 1382, 1532, 1540, 1542, 1552, 1553
33 GP15-1 1560, 1567, 1571, 1576, 1577, 1580, 1588, 1590, 1595, 1596, 1600, 1619, 1620, 1621, 1628, 1635, 1642, 1644, 1645, 1650, 1651, 1655, 1689, 1690, 1693, 1694, 1702, 1706, 1708, 1712, 1730, 1739, 1744
1 GP38 2007
37 GP38-2 2071, 2098, 2104, 2113, 2114, 2117, 2118, 2141, 2160, 2161, 2162, 2166, 2170, 2174, 2180, 2187, 2192, 2194, 2198, 2207, 2214, 2219, 2240, 2253, 2262, 2264, 2272, 2287, 2298, 2306, 2307, 2308, 2312, 2313, 2320, 2328, 2330
2 GP35m 2603, 2606
4 U30C 2965, 2967, 2968, 2970
8 SD40 3002, 3007, 3008, 3012, 3026, 3029, 3083, 3086
63 SD40-2 3091, 3097, 3104, 3107, 3109, 3111, 3113, 3115, 3120, 3122, 3123, 3130, 3132, 3136, 3140, 3141, 3144, 3148, 3152, 3159, 3163, 3168, 3171, 3176, 3179, 3186, 3190, 3194, 3195, 3198, 3200, 3204, 3206, 3211, 3212, 3213, 3215, 3226, 3228, 3238, 3239, 3241, 3245, 3246, 3258, 3259, 3265, 3267, 3269, 3270, 3280, 3286, 3289, 3291, 3294, 3297, 3298, 3304, 3306, 3309, 3310, 3311, 3319
30 GP50 3500-3529 (Entire class repainted)
14 B23-7 4604, 4608, 4611, 4619, 4623, 4627, 4644, 4653, 4655, 4661, 4667, 4668, 4669, 4681
21 B30-7A 4800, 4801, 4805, 4806, 4811, 4812, 4815, 4816, 4818, 4819, 4823, 4824, 4831, 4833, 4834, 4836, 4839, 4845, 4850, 4851, 4852
60 SD50 5000-5009 (Entire class delivered in yellow and gray)
14 "SD40-2c" 6002, 6005, 6010, 6019, 6020, 6026, 6033, 6036, 6044, 6045, 6057, 6059, 6068, 6070
60 C36-7 9000-9059 (Entire class delivered in yellow and gray)

The "canaries" were repainted at three shops; Kansas City, Houston, and North Little Rock. Kansas City started things off on May 14, 1984 by repainting SD40-2 MP-3291. The last repaint, GP38-2 MP-2214, was done at North Little Rock on November 21, 1985, encompassing an 18-month MoPac yellow painting period. Kansas City did only 12 units, while Houston did 68, and North Little Rock did the lion's share with 195 repaints. The first North Little Rock unit was "SD40-2c" MP-6002, and the first Houston unit was SW1200 MP-1153. The GP50's went the fastest, and were the only complete class repainted. The last one was repainted yellow when the MP-3505 emerged

from Houston on February 21, 1985, less than a year after the MoPac in yellow had begun.

The entire blue fleet on UP rails is now yellow. The last UP-owned units in blue were repainted into yellow by May, 1994, with the exception of three GP38-2's. All the yellow units lettered Missouri Pacific had already been relettered Union Pacific. A number of blue ex-MoPac units still wander various railroads as part of modern-day lease fleets, such as Helm Leasing. Wisconsin Central also had several ex-MoPac SD40's in blue with WC heralds under the cabs where the small screaming eagles once were. The MoPac name is but a memory left from the days of MoPac's mighty fleet.

Below: MoPac GP38-2 2180 and UP B23-7 162 roll through Ripley, Missouri with the River Subdivision local in March, 1988. The B-Boat has been renumbered into the UP fleet, having left behind its MoPac image. The 2180 would wear its yellow MoPac image for another four years, and then follow the 162 into UP dress. The 162 was the unit accidentally renumbered 161 for a short time. *Mark Hall*

Bottom: SD40-2 3258 is one of 63 non dynamic brake equipped SD40-2's that were repainted in the MoPac yellow. It leads two UP sisters at Cahokia, Illinois on September 12, 1987. *John Carpenter photo, Kevin EuDaly collection*

nose of the yellow unit with MoPac lettering. But the MoPac name would fall. In June, 1988, the UP began a rebuilding of the C36-7 fleet, nearly all of which still carried "Missouri Pacific" lettering. They received engine overhauls, and while in the shop the lettering was painted out and new "Union Pacific" lettering was applied.

By October 6, 1989, there were 133 units still in MoPac blue, and 171 units in yellow with Missouri Pacific lettering. The 133 units included 5 MP15DC's, 26 GP15-1's, 100 GP38-2's, 12 SD40-2's, 3 U23B's, 5 B23-7's, 1 B30-7A, and 1 "SD40-2c." The days of the Missouri Pacific name were numbered. By September 1, 1991, the number had dropped to 121 units, 67 in blue and 54 in yellow. The final GE had lost its Missouri Pacific lettering when B23-7 MP-4611 was renumbered to UP-111 in November, 1991.

By January 1, 1992, the list was down to only 99 units with MoPac lettering, 60 in blue and 39 in yellow. These were the last holdouts from a once monstrous fleet. All were EMDs, and included the following:

3 MP15's: Blue: 1378
               Yellow: 1377, and 1382

26 GP15-1's: Blue: 1618, 1634, 1647, 1658, 1685, 1687, 1691, 1695, 1716, 1722, 1724, 1726, and 1727
               Yellow: 1590, 1595, 1596, 1620, 1650, 1655, 1689, 1690, 1693, 1694, 1730, 1739, and 1744

65 GP38-2's: Blue: 2075, 2076, 2082, 2085, 2089, 2092, 2094, 2103, 2106, 2112, 2119, 2163, 2167, 2171, 2173, 2177, 2181, 2193, 2201, 2205, 2212, 2213, 2217, 2218, 2221, 2233, 2234, 2236, 2241, 2242, 2245, 2246, 2278, 2280, 2290, 2296, 2297, 2302, 2305, 2310, 2315, 2321, 2327, 2329, and 2333
               Yellow: 2113, 2114, 2118, 2141, 2160, 2161, 2162, 2166, 2170, 2180, 2187, 2192, 2207, 2214, 2219, 2307, 2308, 2320, 2328, and 2330

3 SD40-2's: Yellow: 3132, 3270, and 3306
1 SD40-2c: Blue: 6071
1 GP50:   Yellow: 3504

By the end of February, 1993, the blue units were getting hard to find. There were only 29 units left in blue paint, and unfortunately, these were all quite shabby by this date. As sad as it was to see the blue go, it was even sadder to see the last images of the proud fleet to be of units whose paint had fallen into disrepair. The last few MoPac units looked shabby indeed, and the list was down to 49 units, as follows:

16 GP15-1's: Blue: 1685, 1687, 1691, 1716, 1724, 1726, and 1727
               Yellow: 1595, 1596, 1620, 1655, 1689, 1693, 1694, 1730, and 1739

30 GP38-2's: Blue: 2075, 2089, 2092, 2103, 2106, 2163, 2167, 2171, 2181, 2205, 2212, 2218, 2233, 2234, 2242, 2245, 2297, 2302, 2305, 2310, 2327, and 2333
               Yellow: 2161, 2162, 2166, 2170, 2214, 2219, 2307, and 2330

3 SD40-2's: Yellow: 3132, 3270, and 3306

By August, 1993, only GP15-1's, GP38-2's and one SD40-2 were left in Missouri pacific lettering, and only 2 GP15-1's (MP-1685 and 1716) and 13 GP38-2's (MP-2075, 2089, 2092, 2103, 2106, 2163, 2167, 2171, 2181, 2212, 2218, 2242, and 2310) were in blue. In September, 1993, the last SD40-2, yellow MP-3270, became UP-3270, ending the career of six-axle power in the MoPac name, a career that had only begun in March, 1967, two and a half decades before. In October, 1993 the MP-1685 was

repainted, the last blue GP15-1 on the roster. Only GP38-2's remained in blue. By the end of October only nine MoPac units remained: GP15-1 MP-1689 and GP38-2 MP-2214 in yellow, and GP38-2's MP-2075, 2089, 2092, 2103, 2106, 2167, and 2310 in blue.

At the end of January, 1994 only four blue GP38-2's remained, the yellow MoPac units were all relettered into UP. Two of the blue units were scheduled to be purchased by UP after their leases expired (MP-2075 and MP-2106), and the other two were originally scheduled to be returned to the lessor (MP-2092 and MP-2103) in March, 1994. They were still on the railroad in June, 1994, however.

By late June the MP-2092 had become UP-2092, the MP-2075 had interchanged to the KCS on April 19, leaving the system forever, and MP-2106 left UP rails on June 4 when it was interchanged at 18th Street Yard in Kansas City. A few tattered remnants from the MoPac fleet still rolled as part of lease fleets, but by June, 1994 the MoPac name had followed so many others down the final path. The final GP38-2, MP-2103, was stored for a short time in Fort Worth, but by August, 1994 was gone from the roster. When it left, the MoPac's diesel legacy was over. Purchases had begun with EMC SC MP-9000 in July, 1937 and ended with C36-7 MP-9059 in November, 1985. In between, over 3,000 units waved the MoPac flag with eagle's wings in several paint schemes. When the 2103 left, the screaming eagle was silenced, and the final MoPac unit followed its three-thousand-plus siblings into oblivion.

Right: New image B30-7A 4812 leads a trio of B-Boats up Kirkwood Hill at Kirkwood, Missouri on February 17, 1985. Neither of the other two, 4854 and 4809, would wear the MoPac yellow scheme, but would be repainted straight into UP colors and lettering as 200-class locomotives. *Kevin EuDaly*

Opposite page top: By March 10, 1989, lead GP15-1 1697 is looking rather bedraggled, but is already in the minority. The battered unit is rolling the south local LVR57 through Ozark, Arkansas along the Arkansas River on the Van Buren Subdivision. Units that survived the May 14, 1984 through November 21, 1985 yellow MoPac painting phase wore their MoPac blue until they fell to the UP scheme or were retired. *Dan Schroeder*

Opposite page bottom: On October 1, 1984, newly painted GP50 3504 leads an Operation Lifesaver special eastbound at Jefferson City, Missouri. It is trailed by BN GP50 3105, KCS GP40 754, ICG "GP11" 8718, MKT GP39-2 373, and SP "SD40E" 7347. How many of these still wear the same image a decade later? None. *Joe McMillan*

Right: GP50 3529 leads a ballast train near Little Rock in October, 1986. The GP50 class was the only class that was completely repainted in the Missouri Pacific yellow scheme. *Robin Thomas*

Below: The last B30-7A and MoPac GP40 616 ease into Jefferson City with an empty ballast train in May, 1986. The location is just east of the yard, at crossovers named West Drill. MoPac's days are nearing their end. *Dan Schroeder*

Index

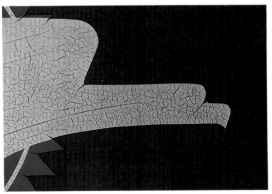

Above: A pair of GP15-1's are silhouetted by the setting sun in November, 1981 in Centennial Yard at Fort Worth, Texas. *Keith Wilhite*

Left: A tattered eagle is all that remains on a sign at the Lee's Summit, Missouri auto facility on June 6, 1987. *Kevin EuDaly*

192